Practice*Plan*

Arthur E. Jongsma, Jr., Series Editor

Helping therapists
help their clients...

Treatment Planners cover all the necessary elements for developing formal treatment plans, including detailed problem definitions, long-term goals, short-term objectives, therapeutic interventions, and DSM-IV diagnoses.

Documentation Sourcebooks provide a comprehensive collection of ready-to-use blank forms, handouts, and questionnaires to help you manage your client reports and streamline the record keeping and treatment process. Features clear, concise explanations of the purpose of each form—including when it should be used and at what point. Includes customizable forms on disk.

The Complete Adult Psychotherapy Treatment Planner, Second Edition
0-471-31924-4 / $44.95

The Child Psychotherapy Treatment Planner, Second Edition
0-471-34764-7 / $44.95

The Adolescent Psychotherapy Treatment Planner, Second Edition
0-471-34766-3 / $44.95

The Chemical Dependence Treatment Planner
0-471-23795-7 / $44.95

The Continuum of Care Treatment Planner
0-471-19568-5 / $44.95

The Couples Psychotherapy Treatment Planner
0-471-24711-1 / $44.95

The Employee Assistance (EAP) Treatment Planner
0-471-24709-X / $44.95

The Pastoral Counseling Treatment Planner
0-471-25416-9 / $44.95

The Older Adult Psychotherapy Treatment Planner
0-471-29574-4 / $44.95

The Behavioral Medicine Treatment Planner
0-471-31923-6 / $44.95

The Group Therapy Treatment Planner
0-471-37449-0 / $44.95

The Family Therapy Treatment Planner
0-471-34768-X / $44.95

The Severe and Persistent Mental Illness Treatment Planner
0-471-35945-9 / $44.95

The Gay and Lesbian Psychotherapy Treatment Planner
0-471-35080-X / $44.95

The Clinical Documentation Sourcebook, Second Edition
0-471-32692-5 / $49.95

The Psychotherapy Documentation Primer
0-471-28990-6 / $45.00

The Couple and Family Clinical Documentation Sourcebook
0-471-25234-4 / $49.95

The Clinical Child Documentation Sourcebook
0-471-29111-0 / $49.95

The Chemical Dependence Treatment Documentation Sourcebook
0-471-31285-1 / $49.95

The Forensic Documentation Sourcebook
0-471-25459-2 / $85.00

The Continuum of Care Clinical Documentation Sourcebook
0-471-34581-4 / $75.00

NEW AND FORTHCOMING

The Traumatic Events Treatment Planner
0-471-39587-0 / $44.95

The Special Education Treatment Planner
0-471-38873-4 / $44.95 p

The Mental Retardation and Developmental Disability Treatment Planner
0-471-38253-1 / $44.95

The Social Work and Human Services Treatment Planner
0-471-37741-4 / $44.95

The Rehabilitation Psychology Treatment Planner
0-471-35178-4 / $44.95

Name_____

Affiliation_____

Address_____

City/State/Zip_____

Phone/Fax_____

E-mail_____

To order, call 1-800-753-0655
(Please refer to promo #1-4019 when ordering.)

Or send this page with payment* to:
John Wiley & Sons, Inc., Attn: J. Knott
605 Third Avenue, New York, NY 10158-0012

❏ Check enclosed   ❏ Visa   ❏ MasterCard   ❏ American Express

Card #_____

Expiration Date_____

Signature_____

*Please add your local sales tax to all orders.

www.wiley.com/practiceplanners

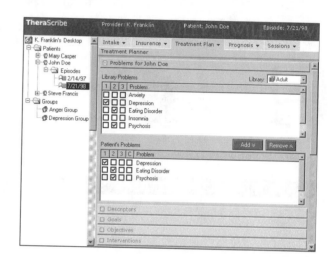

The Adolescent Psychotherapy
Progress Notes Planner

PRACTICE *PLANNERS*® SERIES

Treatment Planners

The Chemical Dependence Treatment Planner
The Continuum of Care Treatment Planner
The Couples Psychotherapy Treatment Planner
The Employee Assistance Treatment Planner
The Pastoral Counseling Treatment Planner
The Older Adult Psychotherapy Treatment Planner
The Complete Adult Psychotherapy Treatment Planner, 2e
The Behavioral Medicine Treatment Planner
The Group Therapy Treatment Planner
The Gay and Lesbian Psychotherapy Treatment Planner
The Child Psychotherapy Treatment Planner, 2e
The Adolescent Psychotherapy Treatment Planner, 2e
The Family Psychotherapy Treatment Planner
The Severe and Persistent Mental Illness Treatment Planner
The Mental Retardation and Developmental Disability Treatment Planner

Progress Notes Planners

The Adolescent Psychotherapy Progress Notes Planner
The Child Psychotherapy Progress Notes Planner
The Adult Psychotherapy Progress Notes Planner

Homework Planners

Chemical Dependence Treatment Homework Planner
Brief Child Therapy Homework Planner
Brief Adolescent Therapy Homework Planner
Brief Therapy Homework Planner
Brief Couples Therapy Homework Planner
Brief Employee Assistance Homework Planner

Documentation Sourcebooks

The Clinical Documentation Sourcebook
The Forensic Documentation Sourcebook
The Psychotherapy Documentation Primer
The Chemical Dependence Treatment Documentation Sourcebook
The Clinical Child Documentation Sourcebook
The Couple and Family Clinical Documentation Sourcebook
The Clinical Documentation Sourcebook, 2e
The Continuum of Care Clinical Documentation Sourcebook

Practice Planners®

Arthur E. Jongsma, Jr., Series Editor

The Adolescent Psychotherapy Progress Notes Planner

Arthur E. Jongsma, Jr.

L. Mark Peterson

William P. McInnis

JOHN WILEY & SONS, INC.

New York • Chichester • Weinheim • Brisbane • Singapore • Toronto

ISBN 0-471-38104-7

Printed in the United States of America.

10 9 8 7 6 5 4 3 2 1

CONTENTS

PREFACE

The Adolescent Progress Notes Planner is the next step in the evolution of the Practice Planner series from John Wiley & Sons. This book is written as a companion to the *Adolescent Psychotherapy Treatment Planner* as it provides a menu of sentences that can be selected for constructing a progress note based on the Behavioral Definitions and Therapeutic Interventions from the Treatment Planner. Parallel progress note planners are currently being written for the *Child Psychotherapy Treatment Planner* and the *Complete Adult Psychotherapy Treatment Planner.*

This work has evolved through several stages before it arrived at its final form for publication. Our hope and desire is that both students and seasoned clinicians will find this resource helpful in writing progress notes that are thoroughly unified with the client's treatment plan. We have tried to provide a range of content covered by the progress note sentences that can document how a patient presented and what interventions were used in the session.

The Practice Planner series has continued to expand, especially in the area of Treatment Planners. There are now 15 Treatment Planners published, with several others in the development stage. The original flagship books of this series, *The Complete Psychotherapy Treatment Planner* and *The Child and Adolescent Psychotherapy Treatment Planner* have both been completely revised into second editions: *The Complete Adult Psychotherapy Treatment Planner,* 2d ed., *The Adolescent Psychotherapy Treatment Planner,* 2d ed., and *The Child Psychotherapy Treatment Planner,* 2d ed. Books for specialized patient populations continue to evolve, such as those for the severe and persistently mentally ill population and the mental retardation/developmentally disabled population. All of these Treatment Planners are available with an optional electronic version that can be easily imported into *TheraScribe 3.0 or 3.5: The Computerized Assistant to Psychotherapy Treatment Planning.* The Practice Planners series also includes several psychotherapy Homework Planners that are coordinated with the Treatment Planners or that can be used independently. Several Documentation Source Books containing useful examples of clinical record-keeping forms and handouts round out the Practice Planner series. Future plans include integrating the Progress Note Planner material into a new version of *TheraScribe* that is currently under development.

We would like to thank Jennifer Byrne for her tireless dedication to this very tedious project. She has transcribed many drafts of this book before it arrived at its final form. Her manuscript preparation skills were invaluable to us.

Since the publication of the original *Complete Psychotherapy Treatment Planner* by John Wiley & Sons in 1995, Kelly Franklin has been the editor and driving force of this project. We appreciate her ongoing encouragement, dedication, and support of the Practice Planner series. Kelly, you're still the best.

Finally, we would like to take this opportunity to thank our families for their encouragement and tolerance, as we all gave many discretionary hours to the writing of this manuscript rather than to relationship building. Thank you Judy, Cherry, and Lynn for your love and encouragement.

ARTHUR E. JONGSMA, JR.
L. MARK PETERSON
WILLIAM P. MCINNIS

INTRODUCTION

INTERFACE WITH TREATMENT PLANNER

Progress notes are not only the primary source for documenting the therapeutic process, but also one of the main factors in determining the client's eligibility for reimbursable treatment. Although the books can be used independently, *The Adolescent Psychotherapy Progress Notes Planner* provides prewritten sentences that are directly coordinated with the symptom descriptions in the Behavioral Definition section and with the Therapeutic Intervention section of *The Adolescent Psychotherapy Treatment Planner,* 2d ed. (John Wiley & Sons, 2000). Used together, you'll find these books to be both a time saver and a guidepost to complete clinical record keeping.

ORGANIZATION OF PROGRESS NOTES PLANNER

Each chapter title is a reflection of the client's potential presenting problem. The first section of the chapter provides a detailed menu of statements that may describe how that presenting problem has manifested itself in behavioral signs and symptoms. The numbers in parentheses within the Client Presentation section correspond to the number of the Behavioral Definition from the Treatment Planner. For example, consider the following three items from the "Academic Underachievement" chapter:

12. Excessive Parental Pressure (9)
   A. The client has viewed his/her parents as placing excessive or unrealistic pressure on him/her to achieve academic success.
   B. The parents acknowledged that they have placed excessive or unrealistic pressure on the client to achieve academic success.
   C. The parents denied placing excessive or unrealistic pressure on the client to achieve; instead they attributed the client's lowered academic performance to his/her lack of motivation and effort.
   D. The client reported that the parents have decreased the amount of pressure that they have placed on him/her to achieve academic success.
   E. The parents have established realistic expectations of the client's level of capabilities.

13. Excessive Criticism (9)
   A. The client described the parents as being overly critical of his/her academic performance.

B. The client expressed feelings of sadness and inadequacy about critical remarks that his/her parents have made in regard to his/her academic performance.

C. The client acknowledged that he/she deliberately refuses to do school assignments when he/she perceives the parents as being overly critical.

D. The parents acknowledged that they have been overly critical of the client's academic performance.

E. The parents have significantly reduced the frequency of their critical remarks about the client's academic performance.

14. Lack of Motivation (9)

A. The client verbalized little motivation to improve his/her academic performance.

B. The client has often complained of being bored or disinterested with his/her schoolwork.

C. The client verbally acknowledged that his/her academic performance will not improve unless he/she shows more interest and puts forth greater effort.

D. The client has shown more interest in his/her schoolwork and has put forth greater effort.

E. The client's renewed interest and motivation has contributed to his/her improved academic performance.

In the preceding example, the numeral 9 in parentheses refers to the related Behavioral Definition from the "Academic Underachievement" chapter in *The Adolescent Psychotherapy Treatment Planner,* which states, "Parents place excessive or unrealistic pressure on client to a degree that it negatively affects client's performance."

The second section of each chapter provides a menu of statements related to the action that was taken within the session to assist the client in making progress. The numbering of the items in the Interventions Implemented section follows exactly the numbering of Therapeutic Intervention items in the corresponding Treatment Planner. For example, consider the following item from the "Academic Underachievement" chapter:

19. Encourage Parental Positive Reinforcement (19)

A. The parents were encouraged to provide frequent positive reinforcement to maintain the client's interest and motivation in completing his/her school/homework assignments.

B. The parents were challenged to look for opportunities to praise the client for being responsible or successful at school instead of focusing on times when the client failed to behave responsibly or achieve success.

C. Explored the contributing factors or underlying dynamics that prevent the parents from offering praise and positive reinforcement on a consistent basis.

In the preceding example, the item number 19 corresponds directly to the same numbered item in the Therapeutic Interventions section from the "Academic Underachievement" chapter of *The Adolescent Psychotherapy Treatment Planner,* which states, "Encourage the parents to give frequent praise and positive reinforcement for the client's effort and accomplishment on academic tasks." Within the Client Presentation and Interventions Implemented sections of each chapter, the statements are arranged to reflect a progression toward resolution of the problem. These are included to be used in later stages of therapy as the client moves forward toward discharge.

Finally, all item lists begin with a few keywords. These words are meant to convey the theme or content of the sentences contained in that listing. The clinician may puruse the list of keywords to find content that matches the client's presentation and the clinician's intervention.

USING *THE ADOLESCENT PROGRESS NOTES PLANNER*

If the user has not used *The Adolescent Psychotherapy Treatment Planner* to initiate treatment, then relevant progress notes can be found by locating the chapter title that reflects the client's presenting problem, scanning the keywords to find the theme that fits the session, and then selecting the sentences that describe first how the client presented for that session and then which interventions were used to assist the client in reaching his/her therapeutic goals and objectives. It is expected that the clinician will modify the prewritten statements contained in this book to fit the exact circumstances of the client's presentation and treatment. Individualization of treatment must be reflected in progress notes that are tailored to the unique client's presentation, strengths, and weaknesses.

In order to maintain complete client records, the following must be entered in the patient's records: progress note statements that may be selected from this book, the date, time, and length of a session, those present during the session, the provider, provider's credentials, and a signature.

All progress notes must be tied to the treatment plan—session notes should elaborate on the problems, symptoms, and interventions contained in the plan. If a session focuses on a topic outside those covered in the treatment plan, providers must update the treatment plan accordingly.

ACADEMIC UNDERACHIEVEMENT

CLIENT PRESENTATION

1. Academic Underachievement (1)*

A. The client's teachers and parents reported a history of academic performance that is below the expected level given the client's measured intelligence or performance on standardized achievement tests.

B. The client verbally admitted that his/her current academic performance is below his/her expected level of functioning.

C. The client has started to assume more responsibility for completing his/her school and homework assignments.

D. The client has taken active steps (e.g., study at routine times, seek outside tutor, consult with teacher before or after class) to improve his/her academic performance.

E. The client's academic performance has improved to his/her level of capability.

2. Incomplete Homework Assignments (2)

A. The client has consistently failed to complete his/her classroom or homework assignments in a timely manner.

B. The client has refused to comply with parents' and teachers' requests to complete classroom or homework assignments.

C. The client expressed a renewed desire to complete his/her classroom and homework assignments on a regular basis.

D. The client has recently completed his/her classroom and homework assignments on a consistent basis.

E. The client's regular completion of classroom and homework assignments has resulted in higher grades.

3. Disorganization (3)

A. Parents and teachers described a history of the client being disorganized in the classroom.

B. The client has often lost or misplaced books, school papers, or important things necessary for tasks or activities at school.

C. The client has started to take steps (e.g., use planner or agenda to record school/homework assignments, consult with teachers before or after school, schedule routine study times) to become more organized at school.

D. The client's increased organization abilities have contributed to his/her improved academic performance.

4. Poor Study Skills (3)

A. The parents and teachers reported that the client has historically displayed poor study skills.

---

* The numbers in parentheses correlate to the number of the Behavioral Definition statement in the companion chapter with same title in *The Adolescent Psychotherapy Treatment Planner* (Jongsma, Peterson, and McInnis) by John Wiley & Sons, 2000.

B. The client acknowledged that his/her lowered academic performance is primarily due to his/her lack of studying.

C. The client has recently spent little time studying.

D. The client reported a recent increase in studying time.

E. The client's increased time spent in studying has been a significant contributing factor to his/her improved academic performance.

5. Procrastination (4)

A. The client has repeatedly procrastinated or postponed doing his/her classroom or homework assignments in favor of engaging in social, leisure, or recreational activities.

B. The client has continued to procrastinate doing his/her classroom or homework assignments.

C. The client agreed to postpone social, leisure, or recreational activities until he/she has completed his/her homework assignments.

D. The client has demonstrated greater self-discipline by first completing homework assignments before engaging in social, leisure, or recreational activities.

E. The client has achieved and maintained a healthy balance between accomplishing academic goals and meeting his/her social and emotional needs.

6. Family History of Academic Problems (5)

A. The client and parents described a family history of academic problems and failures.

B. The client's parents have demonstrated little interest or involvement in the client's schoolwork or activities.

C. The client expressed a desire for his/her parents to show greater interest or involvement in his/her schoolwork or activities.

D. The parents verbalized a willingness to show greater interest and become more involved in the client's schoolwork or activities.

E. The parents have sustained an active interest and involvement in the client's schoolwork and implemented several effective interventions to help the client achieve his/her academic goals.

7. Depression (6)

A. The client's feelings of depression, as manifested by his/her lack of motivation, apathy, and listlessness, have contributed to and resulted from his/her low academic performance.

B. The client appeared visibly depressed when discussing his/her lowered academic performance.

C. The client expressed feelings of happiness and joy about his/her improved academic performance.

D. The client's academic performance has increased since his/her depression has lifted.

8. Low Self-Esteem (6)

A. The client's low self-esteem, feelings of insecurity, and lack of confidence have contributed to and resulted from his/her lowered academic performance.

B. The client displayed a lack of confidence and expressed strong self-doubts about being able to improve his/her academic performance.

C. The client verbally acknowledged his/her tendency to give up easily and withdraw in the classroom when feeling insecure and unsure of himself/herself.

D. The client verbalized positive self-descriptive statements about his/her academic performance.

E. The client has consistently expressed confidence in his/her ability to achieve academic goals.

9. Disruptive/Attention-Seeking Behavior (7)

A. The client has frequently disrupted the classroom with his/her negative attention-seeking behavior instead of focusing on his/her schoolwork.

B. The parents have received reports from school teachers that the client has continued to disrupt the classroom with his/her negative attention-seeking behavior.

C. The client acknowledged that he/she tends to engage in disruptive behavior when he/she begins to feel insecure or become frustrated with his/her schoolwork.

D. The client has started to show greater self-control in the classroom and inhibit the impulse to act out in order to draw attention to himself/herself.

E. The client has demonstrated a significant decrease in his/her disruptive and negative attention-seeking behavior.

10. Low Frustration Tolerance (7)

A. The client has developed a low frustration tolerance as manifested by his/her persistent pattern of giving up easily when encountering difficult or challenging academic tasks.

B. The client's frustration tolerance with his/her schoolwork has remained very low.

C. The client has started to show improved frustration tolerance and has not given up as easily or as often on his/her classroom or homework assignments.

D. The client has demonstrated good frustration tolerance and consistently completed his/her classroom/homework assignments without giving up.

11. Test-Taking Anxiety (8)

A. The client described a history of becoming highly anxious before or during tests.

B. The client's heightened anxiety during tests has interfered with his/her academic performance.

C. The client shared that his/her test-taking anxiety is related to fear of failure and of being met with disapproval or criticism by significant others.

D. The client has begun to take steps (e.g., deep breathing, positive self-statements, challenging irrational thoughts) to reduce his/her anxiety and feel more relaxed during the taking of tests.

E. The client reported a significant decrease in the level of anxiety while taking tests.

12. Excessive Parental Pressure (9)

A. The client has viewed his/her parents as placing excessive or unrealistic pressure on him/her to achieve academic success.

B. The parents acknowledged that they have placed excessive or unrealistic pressure on the client to achieve academic success.

C. The parents denied placing excessive or unrealistic pressure on the client to achieve; instead they attributed the client's lowered academic performance to his/her lack of motivation and effort.

D. The client reported that the parents have decreased the amount of pressure that they have placed on him/her to achieve academic success.

E. The parents have established realistic expectations of the client's level of capabilities.

13. Excessive Criticism (9)

A. The client described the parents as being overly critical of his/her academic performance.

B. The client expressed feelings of sadness and inadequacy about critical remarks that his/her parents have made in regard to his/her academic performance.

C. The client acknowledged that he/she deliberately refuses to do school assignments when he/she perceives the parents as being overly critical.

D. The parents acknowledged that they have been overly critical of the client's academic performance.

E. The parents have significantly reduced the frequency of their critical remarks about the client's academic performance.

14. Lack of Motivation (9)

A. The client verbalized little motivation to improve his/her academic performance.

B. The client has often complained of being bored with or disinterested in his/her schoolwork.

C. The client verbally acknowledged that his/her academic performance will not improve unless he/she shows more interest and puts forth greater effort.

D. The client has shown more interest in his/her schoolwork and has put forth greater effort.

E. The client's renewed interest and motivation has contributed to his/her improved academic performance.

15. Environmental Stress (10)

A. The client's academic performance has markedly declined since experiencing stressors within his/her personal and/or family life.

B. The client's academic performance has decreased since his/her family moved and he/she had to change schools.

C. The client has not been able to invest as much time or energy into his/her schoolwork because of having to deal with environmental stressors.

D. The client has begun to manage his/her stress more effectively so that he/she has more time and energy to devote to schoolwork.

E. The client's academic performance has increased since resolving or finding effective ways to cope with the environmental stressor(s).

16. Loss or Separation (10)

A. The client's academic performance has decreased significantly since experiencing the separation or loss.

B. The client verbalized feelings of sadness, hurt, and disappointment about past separation(s) or loss(es).

C. The client has taken active steps (i.e., socialized regularly with peers, studied with peers, participated in extracurricular activities) to build a positive support network at school to help him/her cope with the past separation(s) or loss(es).

D. The client's academic interest and performance has increased substantially since working through his/her grief issues.

INTERVENTIONS IMPLEMENTED

1. Psychoeducational Testing (1)*

A. The client received a psychoeducational evaluation to rule out the presence of a possible learning disability that may be contributing to his/her academic underachievement.

B. The client was cooperative during the psychoeducational testing and appeared motivated to do his/her best.

C. The client was uncooperative during the psychoeduational testing and did not appear to put forth good effort.

D. The client's resistance during the psychoeducational testing appeared to be due to his/her feelings of insecurity and opposition to possibly receiving special education services.

2. Psychological Testing for ADHD/Emotional Factors (2)

A. The client received a psychological evaluation to help determine whether he/she has ADHD that may be contributing to his/her low academic performance.

B. The client received psychological testing to help determine whether emotional factors are contributing to his/her low academic performance.

C. The client was uncooperative and resistant during the evaluation process.

D. The client approached the psychological testing in an honest, straightforward manner, and was cooperative with the examiner.

3. Obtain Psychosocial History (3)

A. A psychosocial assessment was completed to gather pertinent information about the client's past academic performance, developmental milestones, and family history of educational achievements and failures.

B. The client and parents were cooperative in providing information about the client's early developmental history, school performance, and family background.

C. A review of the client's background revealed a history of developmental delays and low academic performance.

---

* The numbers in parentheses correlate to the number of the Therapeutic Intervention statement in the companion chapter with the same title in *The Adolescent Psychotherapy Treatment Planner* (Jongsma, Peterson, and McInnis) by John Wiley & Sons, 2000.

D. The psychosocial assessment revealed a family history of academic underachievement and failures.

E. The psychosocial assessment revealed a history of strong expectations being placed on family members to achieve academic success.

4. Give Evaluation Feedback (4)

A. The examiner provided feedback on the evaluation results to the client, parents, or school officials and discussed appropriate interventions.

B. The psychoeducational evaluation results revealed the presence of a learning disability and the need for special education services.

C. The psychoeducational evaluation results did not support the presence of a learning disability or the need for special education services.

D. The evaluation results supported the presence of ADHD that may be contributing to the client's lowered academic performance.

E. The evaluation results revealed underlying emotional problems that appear to be contributing to the client's lowered academic performance.

5. Hearing/Vision/Medical Examination Referral (5)

A. The client was referred for a hearing and vision examination to rule out possible hearing or visual problems that may be interfering with his/her school performance.

B. The client was referred for a medical evaluation to rule out possible health problems that may be interfering with his/her school performance.

C. The hearing examination results revealed the presence of hearing problems that are interfering with the client's academic performance.

D. The vision examination revealed the presence of visual problems that are interfering with the client's school performance.

E. The medical examination revealed the presence of health problems that are interfering with the client's school performance.

6. Attend IEPC Meeting (6)

A. The client's IEPC was held with parents, teachers, and school officials to determine the client's eligibility for special education services, to design educational interventions, and to establish educational goals.

B. The recommendation was made at the IEPC that the client receive special education services to address his/her learning problems.

C. At the IEPC meeting, it was determined that the client is not in need of special education services because he/she does not meet the criteria for a learning disability.

D. The IEPC meeting was helpful in identifying specific educational goals.

E. The IEPC meeting was helpful in designing several educational interventions for the client.

7. Consultation about Teaching Intervention Strategies (7)

A. Consulted with client, parents, and school officials about designing effective teaching programs or intervention strategies that build on the client's strengths and compensate for his/her weaknesses.

B. The client, parents, and teachers identified several learning or personality strengths that the client can utilize to improve his/her academic performance.

C. The consultation meeting with client, parents, and school officials identified the client's weaknesses and intervention strategies that he/she can utilize to overcome his/her problems.

8. Refer for Private Tutoring (8)

A. The recommendation was given to the parents to seek private tutoring for the client after school to boost the client's skills in the area of his/her academic weakness.

B. The client and parents were agreeable to seeking private tutoring after school.

C. The client and parents were opposed to the idea of seeking private tutoring.

D. The client and parents reported that the private tutoring has helped to improve the client's academic performance.

E. The client and parents reported that the private tutoring has not led to the desired improvements in the area of the client's academic weakness.

9. Private Learning Center Referral (9)

A. The client was referred to a private learning center for extra tutoring in the areas of academic weakness and assistance in improving his/her study and test-taking skills.

B. The client reported that the extra tutoring and support provided by the private learning center have helped improve his/her performance in the areas of his/her academic weakness.

C. The client reported that his/her performance in the areas of academic weakness has not improved since attending the private learning center.

D. The client reported that his/her study and test-taking skills have improved since attending the private learning center.

E. The client's study skills and test performances have not improved since attending the private learning center.

10. Identify Academic Goals (10)

A. The client and parents identified specific academic goals in today's therapy session.

B. The client's history of academic failure made him/her resistant to formulating goals for successful achievement.

C. The family history of underachievement and academic disinterest has contributed to the client's reluctance to establish academic goals.

11. Teach Study Skills (11)

A. The client was assisted in identifying a list of good locations to study.

B. The client was instructed to remove noise sources and clear away as many distractions as possible when studying.

C. The client was instructed to outline or underline important details when studying or reviewing for tests.

D. The client was encouraged to use a tape recorder to help him/her study for tests and review important facts.

E. The client was instructed to take breaks in studying when he/she becomes distracted and has trouble staying focused.

12. Teach Test-Taking Strategies (12)

A. The client reviewed a list of effective test-taking strategies to improve his/her academic performance.

B. The client was encouraged to review classroom material regularly and study for tests over an extended period of time.

C. The client was instructed to read the instructions twice before responding to questions on a test.

D. The client recognized the need to recheck his/her work to correct any careless mistakes or improve an answer.

13. Utilize Peer Tutor (13)

A. The recommendation was given to parents and teachers that the client be assigned a peer tutor to improve his/her study skills and address areas of academic weakness.

B. The client verbalized a desire and willingness to work with a peer tutor to improve his/her study skills and academic performance.

C. The client expressed opposition to the idea of working with a peer tutor to improve his/her study skills and academic performance.

D. The client reported that the peer tutoring has helped to improve his/her study skills and academic performance.

E. The client reported that the peer tutoring has not helped to improve his/her study skills and academic performance.

14. Self-Monitoring Checklists (14)

A. The client was encouraged to utilize self-monitoring checklists to increase completion of school assignments and improve academic performance.

B. The client reported that the use of the self-monitoring checklists has helped him/her to become more organized and complete school assignments on time.

C. The client has failed to consistently use the self-monitoring checklists and as a result has continued to have trouble completing his/her school/homework assignments.

D. The client's teachers were consulted about the use of self-monitoring checklists in the classroom to help him/her complete school/homework assignments on a regular, consistent basis.

E. Parents and teachers were instructed to utilize a reward system in conjunction with the self-monitoring checklists to increase the client's completion of school/homework assignments and improve his/her academic performance.

15. Use Assignment Planner or Calendar (15)

A. The client was strongly encouraged to use a planner or calendar to record school/homework assignments and plan ahead for long-term assignments.

B. The client's regular use of a planning calendar has helped him/her complete classroom and homework assignments on a regular, consistent basis.

C. The client has failed to use the planning calendar consistently and has continued to struggle to complete school/homework assignments.

D. The client reported that the use of a planning calendar has helped him/her plan ahead for long-term assignments.

E. The client's ADHD symptoms have contributed to his/her failure to use a planner or calendar on a regular basis.

16. "Break It Down into Small Steps" Program (16)

A. The client and parents were instructed to utilize the "Break It Down into Small Steps" program in *The Brief Adolescent Therapy Homework Planner* (Jongsma, Peterson, and McInnis) to help client complete projects or long-term assignments on time.

B. The client and parents were encouraged to utilize the reward system outlined in the "Break It Down into Small Steps" program to reinforce the client for completing each identified step and the final project on time.

C. The client and parents identified a list of rewards and negative consequences for either successfully completing or failing to complete each step of the long-term project.

D. The client reported that the "Break It Down into Small Steps" program has helped to cease his/her pattern of procrastinating or waiting until the last minute to begin working on a large or long-term project.

E. The client has failed to utilize the "Break It Down into Small Steps" program in *The Brief Adolescent Therapy Homework Planner* (Jongsma, Peterson, and McInnis) as recommended and subsequently has failed to complete his/her large or long-term projects on time.

17. Maintain Communication between Home and School (17)

A. The parents and teachers were encouraged to maintain regular communication with each other via phone calls or written notes regarding the client's academic progress.

B. The client's teachers were asked to send home daily or weekly progress notes informing the parents about the client's academic progress.

C. The client was informed of his/her responsibility to bring home daily or weekly progress notes from school, allowing for regular communication between parents and teachers.

D. The parents identified the consequences for the client's failure to bring home a daily or weekly progress note from school.

E. The increased communication between teachers and parents via phone calls or regular progress notes has been a significant contributing factor to the client's improved academic performance.

18. Develop Study and Recreation Schedule (18)

A. The client and parents were assisted in developing a routine schedule to help the client achieve a healthy balance between completing homework assignments and engaging in recreational activities or socializing with peers.

B. The client has followed the agreed-upon schedule and has been able to successfully complete homework assignments and engage in recreational or social activities.

C. The client has failed to consistently complete his/her homework assignments because he/she has not followed the agreed-upon schedule.

19. Encourage Parental Positive Reinforcement (19)

A. The parents were encouraged to provide frequent positive reinforcement to maintain the client's interest and motivation in completing his/her school/homework assignments.

B. The parents were challenged to look for opportunities to praise the client for being responsible or successful at school instead of focusing on times when the client failed to behave responsibly or achieve success.

C. Explored the contributing factors or underlying dynamics that prevent the parents from offering praise and positive reinforcement on a consistent basis.

20. Develop Reward System/Contingency Contract (20)

A. The client and parents identified a list of rewards to reinforce the client's responsible behavior, completion of school assignments, and academic success.

B. A reward system was designed to reinforce the completion of classroom homework assignments.

C. A reward system was designed to reinforce the client for achieving his/her academic goals.

D. The client and parents signed a contingency contract specifying the consequences for the client failing to complete his/her classroom or homework assignments.

E. The client and parents agreed to the terms of the contingency contract for homework completion.

21. Encourage Parental Involvement (21)

A. The parents were strongly encouraged to demonstrate regular interest and involvement in the client's school activities or homework.

B. The parents were encouraged to attend the client's school conferences.

C. The parents were encouraged to attend various school functions to demonstrate interest in the client's school experiences.

D. The parents were encouraged to review the client's planner or calendar on a regular basis to see if the client is keeping up with his/her schoolwork.

E. The parents were given the directive to talk to the client each night about his/her positive school experiences.

22. Teach Stress Coping Strategies (22)

A. The client was taught guided imagery and relaxation techniques to help decrease the level of his/her anxiety and frustration when encountering difficult or challenging school assignments.

B. The client was encouraged to utilize positive self-talk as a means to decrease anxiety and manage frustration when encountering difficult or challenging school assignments.

C. The client was taught cognitive restructuring techniques to decrease his/her anxiety and frustrations associated with schoolwork.

D. The client reported that the use of the positive coping mechanisms (e.g., relaxation techniques, positive self-talk, cognitive restructuring) has helped to decrease his/her level of anxiety and frustration when encountering difficult or challenging school assignments.

E. The client reported experiencing little to no reduction in the level of his/her anxiety or frustration through the use of relaxation techniques, positive self-talk, or cognitive restructuring.

23. Guided Imagery or Relaxation Techniques (23)

A. The client was trained in the use of guided imagery and deep muscle relaxation techniques to help reduce the level of his/her anxiety before or during the taking of tests.

B. The client reported a positive response to the use of guided imagery and deep muscle relaxation techniques to help decrease his/her anxiety before and during the taking of tests.

C. The client appeared uncomfortable during the therapy session when being instructed on the use of guided imagery and deep muscle relaxation techniques.

D. The client was encouraged to continue to practice the use of guided imagery and deep muscle relaxation techniques, even though he/she reports little to no improvement in the reduction of his/her level of anxiety or frustration since the last therapy session.

24. Explore Family/Marital Stress (24)

A. A family therapy session was held to explore the dynamics that may be contributing to the client's lowered academic performance.

B. The family members were asked to list the stressors that have had a negative impact on the family.

C. The family members were asked to identify the things that they would like to change within the family.

D. The parents recognized how their marital problems are creating stress for the client and agreed to seek marital counseling.

E. The parents refused to follow through with the recommendation for marital counseling.

25. Resolve Family Conflicts (25)

A. Today's therapy session focused on the conflicts within the family system that block or inhibit the client's learning.

B. The family members were asked to brainstorm possible solutions to the conflicts that exist within the family and interfere with the client's academic performance.

C. Today's therapy session dealt with the conflict between the parents over how to address the client's lowered academic performance.

D. The parents resolved their differences over how to respond to the client's learning problems and came up with a mutually agreed-upon plan of action.

E. The parents did not resolve their differences between themselves over how to address the client's learning problems.

26. Explore Unrealistic Parental Expectations (26)

A. A family therapy session was held to explore whether the parents have developed unrealistic expectations or are placing excessive pressure on the client to perform.

B. The client and parents discussed and identified more realistic expectations about the client's academic performance.

27. Confront Excessive Pressure (27)

A. The parents were confronted and challenged about placing excessive pressure on the client to achieve academic success.

B. Today's family therapy session explored the reasons that the parent(s) have placed excessive pressure on the client to achieve academic success.

C. The client was seen individually to allow him/her to express thoughts and feelings about excessive pressure placed on him/her by parents.

D. A family therapy session was held to provide the client with an opportunity to express anger, frustration, and hurt about parents placing excessive pressure on him/her.

28. Parents Set Firm Limits for Homework Refusal (28)

A. The parents were strongly encouraged to set firm, consistent limits and to utilize natural, logical consequences for the client's refusal to do his/her homework.

B. The parents identified a list of consequences for the client's refusal to do homework.

C. The parents reported that the client has responded positively to their limits or consequences and has begun to complete his/her homework assignments on a regular, consistent basis.

D. The client has refused to comply with his/her parent's request to complete homework assignments, even though the parents have begun to set firm limits.

29. Challenge Parents Not to Overprotect Client (29)

A. The parents were challenged not to protect the client from the natural consequences of his/her academic performance (e.g., loss of credits, detention, delayed graduation, inability to take driver's training, assume higher cost of car insurance) and instead were encouraged to allow the client to learn from his/her mistakes or failures.

B. The parents reported that they have allowed the client to experience the natural consequences of his/her poor academic performance.

C. The parents have continued to protect the client from the natural consequences of his/her poor academic performance.

D. The parents acknowledged that they have protected the client from experiencing the consequences of his/her academic performance because they don't want him/her to fail or repeat a grade.

30. Teach Avoidance of Unhealthy Power Struggles (30)

A. The parents were instructed to follow through with firm, consistent limits and not become locked into unhealthy power struggles or arguments with the client over his/her homework each night.

B. The client was asked to repeat the rules surrounding his/her homework to demonstrate an understanding of the expectations of him/her.

C. The client and parents were taught effective communication and assertiveness skills to learn how to express feelings in a controlled fashion and to avoid becoming locked into unhealthy arguments over homework.

D. The parents were instructed to read *Negotiating Parent/Adolescent Conflict* (Robin and Foster) to help resolve conflict more effectively with their son/daughter and issues related to schoolwork.

31. Parents Record Responsible Behavior (31)

A. The parents were instructed to observe and record three to five responsible behaviors by the client between therapy sessions that pertain to his/her schoolwork.

B. The parents were encouraged to reinforce the client for engaging in responsible behavior.

C. The client was strongly encouraged to continue to be responsible for completing schoolwork in order to build self-esteem, earn parent's approval, and receive affirmation from others.

D. The parents' recognition and reinforcement of the client's responsible behaviors has helped to ease family tensions and increased the client's willingness to complete schoolwork.

32. Assess Parent's Overprotectiveness (32)

A. A family therapy session was conducted to explore whether a parent's overprotectiveness of the client contributes to his/her academic underachievement.

B. The parents were helped to see how a pattern of overprotectiveness contributes to the client's academic underachievement.

C. The client and parents were helped to recognize the secondary gain that is achieved through a parent's pattern of overindulging the client.

33. Develop Realistic Expectations (33)

A. The parents were helped to develop realistic expectations of the client's learning potential.

B. The client and parents developed realistic academic goals that were in line with the client's learning potential.

34. Consult School Officials to Improve On-Task Behavior (34)

A. The therapist consulted with school officials about ways to improve the client's on-task behavior.

B. The recommendation was made that the client sit toward the front of the class or near positive peer role models to help him/her stay focused and on task.

C. The teachers were encouraged to call on the client often during the class to maintain the client's interest and attention.

D. The teachers were instructed to provide frequent feedback to the client to maintain interest and motivation to complete his/her school assignments.

E. The recommendation was given to teachers to break the client's larger assignments into a series of smaller tasks.

35. Reinforce Successful School Experiences (35)

A. The parents and teachers were encouraged to reinforce the client's successful school experiences.

B. The client was given the homework assignment of making one positive statement about school each day.

C. All positive statements by client about school were noted and reinforced.

36. Identify Rewards to Maintain Motivation (36)

A. The client was asked to develop a list of possible rewards or positive reinforcers that would increase his/her motivation to achieve academic success.

B. The client signed a written contract specifying the positive reinforcers that are contingent on him/her achieving specific academic goals.

37. Resolve Painful Emotions/Core Conflicts (37)

A. An individual therapy session was conducted with the client to help him/her work through and resolve painful emotions, core conflicts, or stressors that have impeded his/her academic performance.

B. The client made productive use of the individual therapy session to express his/her painful emotions surrounding core conflicts or significant stressors.

C. The client was instructed to draw pictures that reflect his/her painful emotions about the core conflicts or significant stressors.

D. The client was instructed to use a journal to record his/her thoughts and feelings about the core conflicts or significant stressors.

E. The empty-chair technique was employed in the therapy session to facilitate the expression of feelings toward a significant other with whom he/she has experienced conflict.

38. Teach Self-Control Strategies (38)

A. The client was taught deep breathing and relaxation techniques to inhibit the impulse to act out or engage in negative attention-seeking behaviors when encountering frustration with his/her schoolwork.

B. The client was encouraged to utilize positive self-talk when encountering frustration with his/her schoolwork instead of acting out or engaging in negative attention-seeking behaviors.

C. The client was taught mediational, self-control strategies (e.g., "stop, look, listen, and think") to inhibit the impulse to act out or engage in negative attention-seeking behaviors when encountering frustration with schoolwork.

39. Confront Self-Disparaging Remarks (39)

A. The client was confronted with his/her self-defeating pattern of making derogatory comments about himself/herself and giving up easily when encountering difficulty with schoolwork.

B. The client was instructed to use positive self-talk when encountering difficult or challenging tasks at school instead of making disparaging remarks about himself/herself and giving up easily.

C. The client was given a directive to verbalize at least one positive self-statement around others at school.

40. Record Positive Statements about School (40)

A. The client was assigned the task of making one positive statement daily about school and either recording the statement in a journal or writing it on a sticky note to place in his/her bedroom or kitchen.

B. The client was compliant with the homework assignment to record at least one positive statement daily about his/her school experiences.

C. The client did not cooperate with the homework assignment to record at least one positive statement daily about his/her school experiences.

D. After reviewing the positive statements about school recorded in the journal, the client was encouraged to engage in similar positive behaviors that would help make school a more rewarding or satisfying experience.

41. Art Therapy Technique (41)

A. The client was instructed to draw a picture in the therapy session reflecting how his/her academic underachievement has affected his/her self-esteem and family relationships.

B. After completing his/her drawing, the client verbalized how his/her academic underachievements or failures have negatively impacted his/her self-esteem and family relationships.

C. The completion of the client's drawing led to a discussion about what steps the client can take to improve his/her academic performance.

42. Past Periods of Academic Success (42)

A. The client explored periods of time when he/she completed schoolwork regularly and achieved academic success.

B. The client was encouraged to use similar strategies or organizational skills that he/she used in the past to achieve academic success.

C. The client shared the realization that involvement in extracurricular or positive peer group activities increased his/her motivation to achieve academic success.

D. The session revealed that the client was more disciplined with his/her study habits when he/she received strong family support and affiliated with positive peer groups.

E. The client recognized that he/she achieved greater academic success in the past when he/she scheduled routine times to complete homework.

43. Past Successful Coping Strategies (43)

A. The client explored other coping strategies that he/she used to solve other problems.

B. The client was encouraged to use similar coping strategies that he/she used successfully in the past to overcome current problems associated with learning.

C. The session revealed that the client overcame past learning problems when he/she sought extra assistance from teachers, parents, or peers.

D. The client recognized that he/she was more successful in completing school assignments in the past when he/she used a planning calender to record homework assignments and long-term projects.

44. Positive Role Models (44)

A. The client was assisted in identifying three to five role models and listed several reasons why he/she thought the role model was successful in achieving goals.

B. The client identified his/her personal goals and was encouraged to begin to take steps to accomplish goals by employing similar strategies that his/her positive role models have used to achieve their goals or success.

C. The client recognized that many of his/her positive role models achieved success, in part, by attending school regularly and achieving academic goals.

45. Identify Resource People within School (45)

A. The client developed a list of resource people within the school to whom he/she can turn for support, assistance, or instruction when encountering difficulty or frustration with learning.

B. After identifying a list of school resource people, the client was given the directive to seek support at least once from one of these individuals before the next therapy session.

C. The client reported that the extra assistance that he/she received from other individuals in the school helped him/her to overcome difficulty and learn new concepts or skills.

46. Place Client in Charge of Task at School (46)

A. The teachers were encouraged to place the client in charge of a task at school to demonstrate confidence in his/her ability to behave responsibly.

B. The client and teachers identified a list of tasks for which the client could assume responsibility at school.

C. The client reported an increase in confidence and motivation to achieve academic success after being placed in charge of a task or responsibility at school.

D. The client failed to follow through in performing the agreed-upon task or responsibility at school.

47. Medication Evaluation Referral (47)

A. The client was referred to a physician for a medication evaluation to help stabilize his/her moods.

B. The client was referred to a physician for a medication evaluation to address his/her symptoms of ADHD.

C. The client and parents agreed to follow through with a medication evaluation by a physician.

D. The client was strongly opposed to being placed on medication to help improve his/her impulse control and/or stabilize moods.

ADOPTION

CLIENT PRESENTATION

1. Questions about Bioparents (1)*

A. The client presented with numerous questions about bioparents that he/she would like immediate answers to.

B. There is an air of expectation and hope to the client's mood and affect regarding learning about bioparents.

C. The client verbalized being very unsure about exploring his/her biological family of origin.

D. Although the client has raised questions about his/her biological parents, there has been no genuine interest in actively seeking answers.

2. Not Feeling a Part of the Family (2)

A. The parents reported that the client has recently expressed that he/she does not feel like he/she fits into the family.

B. The client verbalized feeling different and not like other family members.

C. The client indicated that being adopted makes him/her feel like he/she is not a part of this family.

D. The client reported a change in his/her feeling toward now being a part of the family.

3. Search for Bioparents (3)

A. The client's manner was one of concern, caution, and putting others before self as he/she discussed searching for biological parents.

B. The client expressed concern about upsetting or hurting the adoptive parents if he/she pursues searching for bioparents.

C. Despite approval given by adoptive parents to search for biological parents, the client seemed concerned over what he/she might discover and how that information will affect him/her.

D. The client has worked through his/her concerns regarding searching for bioparents and is now more comfortable with moving ahead.

4. Hopeful/Unrealistic Expectations (3)

A. The client appeared to hold unrealistic expectations regarding the possibilities of contact with birth parents.

B. Since the client has begun to process adoption issues, he/she has adjusted his/her expectations about bioparents to a more realistic level.

5. Shift in Peer Group (4)

A. The parents noted a recent major shift in the client's peer group, dress, and interests.

---

* The numbers in parentheses correlate to the number of the Behavioral Definition statement in the companion chapter with same title in *The Adolescent Psychotherapy Treatment Planner* (Jongsma, Peterson, and McInnis) by John Wiley & Sons, 2000.

B. The parents labeled the new peer group and dress as negative and contrary to the family's standards.

C. The client explained his/her change in dress, peers, and interests as something he/she needed to do to define himself/herself.

D. The client has modified his/her changes in peers and dress as he/she has started to deal with the adoption issue.

6. Excessive Clingy and Helpless Behavior (5)

A. The parents indicated that the client has always been very clingy and has a pattern of helpless behavior.

B. The client expressed that he/she feels most comfortable when he/she is close to parents.

C. The parents reported being frustrated with the client's helpless behavior now that he/she is getting older.

D. The client refused to talk with the therapist without the parents being there and then allowed them do all the talking.

E. There has been a marked decrease in the client's clinginess and helplessness since he/she started working on his/her adoption issues.

7. Testing Limits (6)

A. The parents reported that the client has been acting out dramatically and consistently testing their limit setting.

B. The client indicated he/she has recently been in constant trouble for lying, stealing, or breaking rules.

C. The client has experienced difficulty at school for failing grades, truancy, and verbal abuse of authority figures.

D. The client's extreme testing of limits (i.e., stealing, substance abuse, sexual promiscuity) seemed to be directly connected to his/her issues about being adopted.

E. The client's testing of the limits has decreased as he/she acknowledged and has started to work on his/her adoption issues.

8. Rude/Rebellious (6)

A. The client presented in a rude and rebellious manner.

B. It was clearly stated by the client that he/she doesn't care what others think about him/her.

C. The parents and teachers reported a marked increase in the client's rude and rebellious attitude since he/she entered the teens, and it is beyond what is normal for these years.

D. The client's rebellious attitude and rudeness have begun to settle down since he/she started to openly share his/her feelings and thoughts about being adopted.

9. Adoptive Parents' Fear (7)

A. The adoptive parents verbalized fear related to the client wanting to search for and meet with his/her bioparents.

B. The adoptive parents presented strong, specific justifications regarding the negative impact of the client meeting his/her bioparents.

C. The adoptive parents raised numerous questions about adoptive children meeting their bioparents.

D. The adoptive parents have reached a reasonable level of comfort with the client meeting his/her bioparents.

10. Adoption of Special-Needs Children (8)

A. The parents have recently adopted a special-needs child/sibset.

B. The parents expressed feeling overwhelmed by the demands of the children.

C. The parents asked for support and resources to assist them in coping with the special needs of the adopted child/children.

D. The parents have gradually and slowly adjusted to and become accepting of the special-needs child/children.

11. Frustration with Child Development and Achievement Level (9)

A. The parents expressed frustration with the adopted child's level of achievement and development.

B. The parents expressed unrealistic expectations of where they felt the child should be in terms of his/her development.

C. The parents expressed disappointment about the child's achievement level and how they expected so much more from him/her.

D. The parents have worked to adjust their expectations of the child to more realistic levels.

INTERVENTIONS IMPLEMENTED

1. Establish Trust-Based Relationship (1)*

A. Initial trust level was established with the client through use of unconditional positive regard.

B. Warm acceptance and active listening techniques were utilized to establish the basis for a nurturing relationship.

C. The client has formed a trust-based relationship and has begun to express his/her thoughts and feelings.

D. Despite the use of active listening, warm acceptance, and unconditional positive regard, the client remains resistant to trust and does not share his/her thoughts and feelings.

2. Solicit Family Therapy Participation (2)

A. The family was asked to make a firm commitment to being an active part of the client's psychotherapy treatment in terms of both attendance and participation.

B. The value to the client of having his/her family involved was presented to the family to reinforce their decision to participate in counseling.

C. The family was confronted about their hesitancy to become involved in the client's treatment and on their belief that it was all his/her issue.

---

* The numbers in parentheses correlate to the number of the Therapeutic Intervention statement in the companion chapter with the same title in *The Adolescent Psychotherapy Treatment Planner* (Jongsma, Peterson, and McInnis) by John Wiley & Sons, 2000.

D. The family's commitment to the counseling process is evidenced in their consistent attendance and constructive participation.

3. List Losses Related to Adoption (3)

A. The client was requested to list the losses he/she has experienced in life.

B. The list was processed and connections were made between specific losses and being adopted.

C. The loss of biological parents and a sense of extended family identity were the strongest issues cited by the client.

4. Support Grieving Process (4)

A. The stages of the grieving process were explained to the client to support him/her in understanding and working through the grief process.

B. Identified losses were processed and the client's expressed feelings connected to each were supported with empathic responses.

C. The client has processed the losses surrounding his/her adoption and has become more accepting of his/her current identity within the adoptive family.

D. The client continues to hold onto the hurt, sad, and angry feelings related to being abandoned by bioparents.

5. Read *Common Threads of Teenage Grief* (5)

A. The client was asked to read *Common Threads of Teenage Grief* (Tyson) and select five ideas to process.

B. Key ideas selected about grieving were processed and the client's questions were answered.

6. Identify Feelings of Abandonment/Rejection (6)

A. The client was assisted in identifying and expressing feelings of rejection and abandonment connected with his/her adoption.

B. The client's feelings of abandonment and rejection were recognized and confirmed as normal and to be expected.

C. The client has successfully worked through the feelings of rejection and abandonment and has come to see bioparents as possibly having his/her best interest at heart when they released him/her for adoption.

7. Read *Why Didn't She Keep Me?* (7)

A. The client was asked to read *Why Didn't She Keep Me?* (Burlingham-Brown) to assist him/her in resolving key feelings of rejection, abandonment, and guilt/shame.

B. The client's readings have helped him/her move toward resolving the feelings of rejection, abandonment, and guilt/shame he/she has regarding his/her adoption.

C. The client was assisted and supported in working through the guilt/shame, abandonment, and rejection he/she experienced connected to his/her adoption.

D. The client has successfully worked through the feelings of rejection and abandonment and has come to see bioparents as possibly having his/her best interest at heart when they released him/her for adoption.

8. Read *How It Feels to Be Adopted* (8)

A. The client was asked to read *How It Feels to Be Adopted* (Krementz) and make a list of key concepts gathered from the reading.

B. The feelings the client identifies with from the adoption book were processed.

C. The client has successfully worked through the feelings of rejection and abandonment and has come to see bioparents as possibly having his/her best interest at heart when they released him/her for adoption.

9. Identify Irrational Adoption Beliefs (9)

A. The client was assisted in identifying a list of beliefs that he/she has about adoption.

B. Irrational thoughts and beliefs were separated from client's general belief list and then replaced with new, healthy, rational beliefs.

C. The client reported that the new, reality-based beliefs have helped to reduce his/her feelings of guilt, shame, anger, and sadness.

10. Support Group Referral (10)

A. Options for possible support groups were explored with the family and the client.

B. The parents and the client were given information on the various support groups and asked to make a commitment to attend one.

C. The family questioned their need for support outside of therapy and were noncommittal about even trying one meeting.

D. The client and his/her parents have begun attending a support group and have reported that it has been beneficial to them.

11. "Three Ways to Change Yourself" Exercise (11)

A. The client was asked to complete the "Three Ways to Change Yourself" exercise from *The Brief Adolescent Therapy Homework Planner* (Jongsma, Peterson, and McInnis) to help him/her learn to express needs and desires.

B. The "Three Ways to Change Yourself" exercise was used as a means of assisting the client in developing the skill to express his/her needs and desires.

12. *SEALS & PLUS* Exercise (12)

A. The client was asked to complete a *SEALS & PLUS* (Korb-Khara, Azok, and Leutenberg) exercise directed at assisting him/her in developing self-knowledge, acceptance, and confidence.

B. The client reported that the self-awareness exercise was helpful in building confidence.

C. The client has not followed through on completing the self-awareness exercise.

13. Teach Concept of True/False Self (13)

A. The concept of a true and false self was taught to the client and he/she was directed to read more about this concept in *The Journal of the Adopted Self* (Lifton).

B. The pros and cons of a false or hidden self were explored with the client, and the disadvantages were verbally reinforced.

C. Using the approach of unconditional positive regard, the value of being genuine and real was discussed with the client.

14. "Who Am I?" Exercise (14)

A. The client was asked to keep a daily journal of "Who am I?" and to share his/her entries with the therapist.

B. "Who am I?" journal entries were reviewed, and positive identifications were verbally acknowledged and reinforced.

C. The client's negative journal entries were confronted in a warm, firm, realistic manner.

D. The client's self-descriptive journal entries have become more positive.

15. Expand Knowledge of Family (15)

A. A family genogram that included biofamily was created, along with a list of questions members had regarding adopted and bioparents.

B. The process of raising questions about biological or adopted family was normalized, and fears regarding the child knowing certain information was addressed by asking parents, "Who would you be protecting?"

C. Unanswered questions about family history were explored and assigned to appropriate members for follow-up and reporting back to family.

16. Parents Read Books on Adoption (16)

A. The parents were encouraged to read *The Whole Life Adoption Book* (Schouler) or *Making Sense of Adoption* (Melina) to advance their knowledge and understanding of adopted teens.

B. The parents were taught various aspects of teen development with a special focus on adoptive teens to increase their knowledge and understanding of their teen.

C. The parents rebuffed attempts to be taught more about teens because they felt their knowledge was adequate.

D. The parents' belief that developmental issues are the same for adopted and nonadopted teenagers was confronted and restructured to a more healthy, realistic view.

17. Teach about the Search for Identity (17)

A. The parents were taught specifically about the search for identity that is a primary focus of teenagers and how this issue is even more crucial to adopted teens.

B. Actions that the parents could take to promote the client's independent identity were probed, and several of the actions were chosen to be implemented.

C. The parents had difficulty accepting the importance of a teen developing an independent identity, which they viewed as a sign they were failing as parents.

18. Adoptive Parents Fear Bioparent Search (18)

A. The adoptive parents were asked to discuss their fears and concerns about the adopted teen looking for bioparents and their own openness to meeting the bioparents.

B. Adoptive parents' rights regarding the search were clarified and affirmed and all their questions were answered.

C. The parents were empowered to make a difficult decision regarding the search: either to support, curtail, or postpone it.

D. The parents were not able to tolerate the idea of the client's search and quickly vetoed the process.

E. The adoptive parents have given their support to the adopted client for a search for his/her bioparents.

19. Clarify Parents' Support for Client Searching (19)

A. Support commitments were elicited verbally from the parents in family session along with a commitment from the client to keep the parents up-to-date on all progress.

B. In family session, both the parents and the client agreed in principle to support the search for bioparents and to keep all informed, but would not specifically verbally state it.

C. The parents were not able to tolerate the idea of the client's search and quickly vetoed the process.

20. Clarify Parents' Rejection of Client Searching (20)

A. A family session was conducted that focused on the client's desire to search for bioparents and the parents' position on the issue.

B. Clear statement of approval or disapproval of client's search for bioparent was sought from adoptive parents, along with a rationale for their decision.

C. The client's right to search for his/her own bioparents at the age of 18 was clarified and confirmed with both parents.

D. The client has decided not to pursue a meeting with his/her bioparents.

21. Affirm Parents' Right of Refusal (21)

A. Adoptive parents' decision to deny the search was affirmed and the client's feelings about their decision were processed.

B. The client appears to be accepting parents' decision to deny the search, having worked through his/her feelings of anger, disappointment, and hurt.

C. The parents' right to deny the search was again affirmed, although the client does not accept this and remains very angry.

22. Locate Expert (22)

A. A meeting was arranged between the client and a willing adult who was adopted as a child and who searched for bioparents.

B. The meeting with the adopted adult was very beneficial, providing the client with many useful insights.

23. Prepare Client for Search (23)

A. The client was prepared to begin the search for bioparents by responding to probing questions, by having hopes and fears affirmed, and by addressing all other concerns.

B. A list of questions the client would like answered was developed if the search process resulted in a meeting being scheduled with bioparents.

24. Read *Searching for a Past* (24)

A. The parents and the client were asked to read *Searching for a Past* (Schooler) to advance their knowledge of the process and to answer questions they have concerning it.

B. The parents were given information about the search process, and questions they had were answered.

25. Review or Create Life Book (25)

A. The client's life book was reviewed as a preparatory step toward beginning his/her search.

B. The client was assisted in developing a life book to be shared with new biological relatives and others that he/she will meet in the search process.

26. Contact Adoption Agency (26)

A. The client was directed to contact the agency through which his/her adoption occurred and schedule an appointment with its search specialist.

B. The client scheduled and followed through with his/her first appointment with an adoption agency search specialist.

C. The client has the agency's name and number but remains hesitant to make an appointment.

D. Issues of fear about taking the first step in the bioparent search were processed and resolved, leading to the client calling and scheduling an appointment with the agency.

27. Review Search Information (27)

A. The information gathered from the agency was reviewed and the client's feelings about the information were identified, expressed, and supported.

B. Information gathered as part of the search was processed and feelings of upset and hurt over the information were supported and processed.

28. Process Reaching a Dead End (28)

A. The client was assisted and supported in working through the reality of reaching a dead end regarding contact with bioparents.

B. Dreams regarding contact with bioparents were explored and verbalized to assist the client in resolving the disappointment of reaching a dead end.

29. Reinforce Client/Parent Communication (29)

A. Both the client and the parents were asked individually and in family session to confirm that information regarding the search was being communicated between them as agreed upon.

B. The client's failure to keep the parents informed of the progress of the search was addressed, and a renewed agreement was made as well as a plan for how this information exchange would occur.

30. Decide on Reunion with Bioparents (30)

A. The client was helped in identifying and weighing the pros and cons of pursuing a reunion with bioparents.

B. With the support of the parents and therapist, the client was able to reach a decision to pursue reunion.

C. Despite support from the parents, search worker, and therapist, the client remains ambivalent to the point of not being able to reach a decision to pursue reunion or not.

D. The client has decided not to pursue a meeting with his/her bioparents.

31. Prepare Client for Reunion with Bioparents (31)

A. Preparation for the scheduled reunion with bioparents consisted of helping the client examine his/her expectations to make them realistic as possible and giving the message to let the relationship build slowly.

B. The client's unrealistic expectations regarding the upcoming reunion with bioparents were processed and adjusted to increase likelihood of a successful meeting.

C. The message was seeded with the client to let the new relationship build slowly and naturally.

32. Practice Reunion Meeting (32)

A. The client role-played a bioparent reunion and afterward processed the experience, identifying how this experience decreased his/her anxiety.

B. The client's level of anxiety seemed to dissipate as the role play of a scheduled meeting with the bioparents was processed.

C. The client remains very anxious and threatened by the scheduled meeting with the bioparents, and therefore the meeting was postponed to a later date.

33. Hold Family Meeting with Bioparents (33)

A. A meeting was arranged with the client and the bioparents to facilitate the expression of feelings surrounding this event and to explore with each the next steps they see.

B. The client's meeting with the bioparents was successful and rewarding in that significant information was shared between them and feelings of love and concern were affirmed.

C. The client's meeting with the bioparents was difficult, disappointing, and tense, with little information shared and no support verbalized.

34. Process Contact with Bioparents (34)

A. The client was asked to process his/her reunion experience and verbalize next step(s) he/she foresees happening.

B. The client was very pleased with the first reunion meeting with the bioparents and plans to meet with them in the near future.

C. The client was satisfied with the meeting with the bioparents but does not feel a need to meet with them again.

35. Explore Future Relationship with Bioparents (35)

A. A plan was created with the client that mapped out a possible path for a new relationship with bioparents based on the premise of taking things slowly.

B. The client's desire to push the relationship with bioparents was addressed, with possible negative effects being emphasized.

C. The client has no plan for a further relationship with bioparents beyond this reunion.

36. Update Adoptive Parents on Reunion (36)

A. The parents were given an update on the reunion meeting with bioparents by the client, who also shared the next possible steps for building a relationship with the bioparents.

B. New possible family configurations were presented to adoptive parents and the client to help them in moving in the direction of a new family system.

C. The adoptive parents were affirming and supportive of the client continuing to build a relationship with the bioparents.

D. The adoptive parents were resistive to any further relationship building between the client and his/her bioparents.

ANGER MANAGEMENT

CLIENT PRESENTATION

1. Angry Outbursts (1)*

A. The client has exhibited frequent angry outbursts that are out of proportion to the degree of the precipitating event.

B. The client appeared angry, hostile, and irritable during today's therapy session.

C. The client has recently exhibited several angry outbursts at home and school.

D. The client has started to show greater control of his/her anger and does not react as quickly or intensely when angry or frustrated.

E. The client reported a significant reduction in the frequency and intensity of his/her angry outbursts.

2. Verbally Abusive Language (2)

A. The client has a history of yelling, swearing, or becoming verbally abusive when his/her needs go unmet or when asked to do something that he/she does not want to do.

B. The client began to yell and swear during today's therapy session.

C. The frequency and intensity of the client's screaming, cursing, and use of verbally abusive language has decreased to a mild degree.

D. The client has begun to express his/her feelings of anger in a controlled fashion.

E. The client has consistently demonstrated good control of his/her anger and not yelled or become verbally abusive toward others.

3. Physical Aggression/Violence (3)

A. The client described a history of engaging in acts of physical aggression or violence.

B. The client has recently been physically aggressive or violent.

C. The client has gradually started to develop greater control of his/her anger and has not become involved in as many fights in the recent past.

D. The client has recently exercised good self-control and not engaged in any physically aggressive or violent behaviors.

4. Verbal Threats/Intimidation (4)

A. The client has a history of threatening or intimidating others to meet his/her own needs.

B. The client became verbally threatening during today's therapy session.

C. The client has continued to threaten or intimidate others at home, at school, and in the community.

D. The client reported a mild reduction in the frequency and intensity of his/her verbal threats and acts of intimidation.

E. The client has recently displayed good anger control and reported that he/she has not threatened or intimidated others.

---

* The numbers in parentheses correlate to the number of the Behavioral Definition statement in the companion chapter with same title in *The Adolescent Psychotherapy Treatment Planner* (Jongsma, Peterson, and McInnis) by John Wiley & Sons, 2000.

5. Destructive Behaviors (5)

A. The client described a persistent pattern of becoming destructive or throwing objects when angry or frustrated.

B. The client described incidents in which he/she has been destructive of property.

C. The client has started to control the impulse to destroy or throw objects when angry.

D. The client reported that he/she has not thrown any objects or been destructive of property in the recent past.

6. Blaming/Projecting (6)

A. The client has a history of projecting the blame for his/her angry outbursts or aggressive behaviors onto other people or outside circumstances.

B. The client did not accept responsibility for his/her recent angry outbursts or aggressive behaviors.

C. The client has begun to accept greater responsibility for his/her anger control problems and blames others less often for his/her angry outbursts or aggressive behaviors.

D. The client verbalized an acceptance of responsibility for the poor control of his/her anger or aggressive impulses.

E. The client expressed guilt about his/her anger control problems and apologized to significant others for his/her loss of control of anger.

7. Guarded/Defensive

A. The client appeared guarded and defensive during today's therapy session.

B. The client was difficult to engage in the therapeutic process and was resistant to exploring the factors contributing to his/her problems with anger control.

C. The client's defensiveness has started to decrease and he/she has demonstrated a greater willingness to explore the underlying dynamics contributing to his/her anger control problems.

D. The client was pleasant and cooperative during the therapy session and demonstrated a willingness to discuss the factors contributing to his/her anger control problems.

8. Passive-Aggressive Behavior (7)

A. The parents and teachers described a persistent pattern of the client engaging in passive-aggressive behaviors (e.g., forgetting, pretending not to listen, dawdling, procrastinating).

B. The client verbally acknowledged that he/she often deliberately annoys or frustrates others through his/her passive-aggressive behaviors.

C. The client has started to verbalize his/her anger directly toward others instead of channeling his/her angry or hostile feelings through passive-aggressive behaviors.

D. The client expressed his/her feelings of anger in a direct, controlled, and respectful manner.

E. The client has recently demonstrated a significant reduction in the frequency of his/her passive-aggressive behaviors.

9. Oppositional/Rebellious Behavior (7)

A. The client's anger is frequently channeled into his/her oppositional and rebellious behaviors.

B. The client appeared highly oppositional during today's therapy session and seemed to argue just for the sake of arguing.

C. The client has recently been defiant of the rules and regulations established by authority figures at home, at school, and in the community.

D. The client has exhibited mild improvements in his/her willingness to comply with the rules and regulations at home, at school, and in the community.

E. The client reports that recently he/she has been cooperative and compliant with the rules at home, at school, and in the community.

10. Authority Conflicts (7)

A. The client displayed a negativistic attitude and was highly argumentative during today's therapy session.

B. The client becomes entangled in frequent disputes with authority figures and does not back down easily in an argument.

C. The client often talks back to authority figures in a disrespectful manner when he/she is reprimanded.

D. The client verbally recognized the need to control his/her anger and be more respectful of authority figures.

E. The client reported that he/she has consistently interacted with adult authority figures in a mutually respectful manner.

11. Family Conflict (7)

A. The client repeatedly becomes involved in heated arguments and/or physical fights with his/her parents and siblings.

B. The client expressed strong feelings of anger and resentment toward family members.

C. The client expressed his/her anger in a controlled and respectful manner toward family members.

D. The client has begun to demonstrate good control of his/her anger at home.

12. Poor Peer Relationships (8)

A. The client's anger control problems have been a significant contributing factor to his/her strained interpersonal relationships with peers.

B. The client has often projected the blame for his/her interpersonal problems onto peers and refused to acknowledge how his/her anger control problems contribute to the conflict.

C. The client is beginning to recognize how his/her anger control problems interfere with his/her ability to establish and maintain peer friendships.

D. The client reported that his/her effective anger control has led to improved relations with his/her peers.

13. Lack of Empathy (8)

A. The client displayed little empathy or concern for how his/her angry outbursts or aggressive behaviors impact others.

B. The client has demonstrated a willingness to use intimidation or force to meet his/her needs at the expense of others.

C. The client verbalized an awareness of how his/her rebellious, aggressive, or destructive behaviors negatively affect others.

D. The client verbalized empathy and concern for others in today's therapy session.

E. The client has made progress in consistently demonstrating empathy and sensitivity to the thoughts, feelings, and needs of others.

14. Feelings of Depression and Anxiety (9)

A. The client's anger control problems have often masked a deeper feeling of depression and/or anxiety.

B. The client expressed feelings of depression and anxiety about the struggles to control his/her angry or hostile feelings.

C. The client verbally recognized how he/she often reacts with anger and aggression when he/she begins to feel depressed or anxious.

D. The client expressed feelings of happiness and contentment about his/her ability to control his/her anger more effectively.

E. The client has taken active steps (e.g., expressed feelings of sadness to supportive individuals, faced anxiety-producing situations, socialized with positive peer groups) to reduce his/her feelings of depression and anxiety.

15. Low Self-Esteem (9)

A. The client's angry outbursts and aggressive behaviors have often masked deeper feelings of low self-esteem, insecurity, and inadequacy.

B. The client's persistent anger control problems have resulted in him/her developing a negative self-image and feelings of low self-esteem.

C. The client verbally recognized how his/her angry outbursts and aggressive behaviors are often associated with feelings of inadequacy and insecurity.

D. The client expressed positive self-statements in today's therapy session about his/her improved ability to control his/her anger.

E. The client has taken active steps to improve his/her self-esteem and build a positive self-image.

16. Childhood Abuse (9)

A. The client described a history of physical and verbal abuse that correlates to the onset of his/her anger control problems.

B. The client was resistant to discussing the past incidents of abuse.

C. The client expressed strong feelings of anger, hurt, and sadness about the past abusive episodes.

D. The client is beginning to show improved anger control as he/she works through thoughts and feelings about his/her past abuse.

E. The client has demonstrated a significant reduction in the frequency and severity of his/her angry outbursts and aggressive behaviors since working through many of his/her feelings about the past abuse.

17. Separation/Loss (9)

A. The client reported a history of experiencing significant separations or losses in his/her life that correlate to the onset of his/her anger control problems.

B. The client was guarded and resistant to talking about past separations or losses.

C. The client expressed strong feelings of anger, hurt, and sadness about past separations or losses.

D. The client has started to show improvement in his/her anger control since he/she began exploring his/her thoughts and feelings about past separations or losses.

E. The client has demonstrated a significant reduction in the frequency and severity of his/her angry outbursts or aggressive behavior since working through many of his/her thoughts and feelings surrounding past separations or losses.

INTERVENTIONS IMPLEMENTED

1. Psychological Testing (1)*

A. A psychological evaluation was conducted to determine whether emotional factors or ADHD are contributing to the client's anger control problems.

B. The client approached the psychological testing in an honest, straightforward manner and was cooperative with any requests presented to him/her.

C. The client was uncooperative and resistant to engage during the evaluation process.

D. The client was resistive during the psychological testing and refused to consider the possibility of having ADHD or any serious emotional problems.

2. Psychoeducational Evaluation (2)

A. The client was given a psychoeducational evaluation to rule out the possibility of a learning disability that may be contributing to his/her anger control problems in the school setting.

B. The client was cooperative during the psychoeducational evaluation and appeared motivated to do his/her best.

C. The client was uncooperative during the psychoeducational evaluation and did not appear to put forth good effort.

3. Evaluation Feedback (3)

A. The client, parents, school officials, and/or criminal justice officials were given feedback from the psychological testing.

B. The evaluation findings supported the presence of ADHD, which contributes to the client's anger control problems.

C. The evaluation findings revealed the presence of underlying emotional problems that contribute to the emergence of the client's anger control problems.

D. The findings from the psychoeducational evaluation supported the presence of a learning disability and the need for special education services.

E. The evaluation process did not reveal the presence of a learning disability, emotional problems, or ADHD that might be contributing to the client's anger control problems.

---

* The numbers in parentheses correlate to the number of the Therapeutic Intervention statement in the companion chapter with the same title in *The Adolescent Psychotherapy Treatment Planner* (Jongsma, Peterson, and McInnis) by John Wiley & Sons, 2000.

4. Substance Abuse Evaluation (4)

A. The client was referred for a substance abuse evaluation to assess the extent of his/her drug/alcohol usage and determine the need for treatment.

B. The findings from the substance abuse evaluation revealed the presence of a substance abuse problem and the need for treatment.

C. The findings from the substance abuse evaluation revealed the presence of a substance abuse problem that appears to be contributing to the client's anger control problems.

D. The evaluation findings did not reveal the presence of a substance abuse problem or the need for treatment in this area.

5. Consultation with Criminal Justice Officials (5)

A. Consulted with criminal justice officials about the need for appropriate consequences for the client's destructive or aggressive behaviors.

B. The client has been required to make restitution and/or perform community service for his/her destructive or aggressive behaviors.

C. The client was placed on probation for his/her destructive or aggressive behaviors and instructed to comply with all the rules pertaining to his/her probation.

D. The client was placed in an intensive surveillance treatment program as a consequence of his/her destructive or aggressive behaviors.

6. Placement in Alternative Setting (6)

A. Consulted with parents, school officials, and criminal justice officials about placing the client in an alternative secure setting because of his/her destructive or aggressive behaviors.

B. Recommendation was made that the client be placed in a juvenile detention facility as a consequence of his/her destructive or aggressive behaviors.

C. Recommendation was made that the client be placed in a foster home to help prevent future occurrences of his/her destructive or aggressive behaviors.

D. Recommendation was made that the client be placed in a residential program to provide external structure and supervision for the client.

E. It is recommended that the client be placed in an inpatient or residential substance abuse program to address his/her substance abuse problems.

7. Reinforce Natural Consequences (7)

A. The parents were encouraged and challenged not to protect the client from the natural or legal consequences of his/her destructive or aggressive behaviors.

B. The parents agreed to contact the police or appropriate criminal justice officials if the client engages in any serious destructive or aggressive behaviors in the future.

C. The parents followed through and contacted the police or probation officer after the client engaged in the destructive or aggressive behaviors.

D. The parents failed to contact the police and/or criminal justice officials after the client engaged in some serious destructive or aggressive behaviors.

E. The parents acknowledged that they often failed to follow through with setting limits because of their desire to avoid conflict and tension.

8. Parental Rules and Boundaries (8)

A. Today's family therapy session focused on helping the parents to establish clearly defined rules and appropriate parent-child boundaries to manage the client's angry outbursts and acts of aggression or destruction.

B. The parents were helped to identify appropriate consequences for the client's angry outbursts and acts of aggression or destruction.

C. The parents identified appropriate and reasonable rules and expectations that the client must comply with at home.

D. The parents had difficulty in identifying appropriate consequences for the client's angry outbursts and destructive or aggressive behaviors.

9. Establish Clear Rules (9)

A. A family therapy session was held to discuss the rules and expectations of the client at home and school.

B. Consulted with the client, parents, and teachers to identify rules and expectations in the school setting.

C. The client was asked to repeat the rules to demonstrate an understanding of the rules and expectations of him/her.

D. The client voiced his/her agreement with the rules and expectations at home and school.

E. The client verbally disagreed with the rules and expectations identified by his/her parents and teachers.

10. Build Therapeutic Trust (10)

A. Today's therapy session focused on building the level of trust with the client through consistent eye contact, active listening, unconditional positive regard, and warm acceptance.

B. Listened closely to the client's concerns and reflected his/her feelings.

C. Provided empathy and support for the client's expression of thoughts and feelings during today's therapy session.

D. The client has remained mistrustful and is reluctant to share his/her underlying thoughts and feelings.

E. The client verbally recognized that he/she has difficulty establishing trust because he/she has often felt let down by others in the past.

11. Confront Aggressive Behavior (11)

A. The client was firmly and consistently confronted with how his/her angry outbursts and destructive or aggressive behavior negatively affect himself/herself and others.

B. The client was asked to list the negative consequences of his/her angry outbursts and destructive or aggressive behavior for self and others.

C. Role-reversal techniques were used to help the client realize how his/her angry outbursts and destructive or aggressive behavior negatively impact others.

D. The client was asked to write a letter of apology to the victims of his/her destructive or aggressive behavior.

E. The client was asked to undo some of the consequences of his/her aggressive or destructive behavior by performing altruistic or benevolent acts for others.

12. Teach Acceptance of Responsibility (12)

A. The client was consistently confronted and challenged to cease blaming others for his/her anger control problems and accept greater responsibility for his/her actions.

B. The client was confronted with how his/her pattern of excessively blaming others for his/her anger control problems places a strain on his/her interpersonal relationships.

C. The client was helped to identify more effective ways to resolve conflict and/or meet his/her needs instead of expressing his/her anger through aggressive or destructive behavior.

D. The client was strongly encouraged to apologize to others for his/her aggressive or destructive behavior.

13. Explore Blaming (13)

A. Today's therapy session explored the underlying factors contributing to the client's pattern of blaming others for his/her anger control problems.

B. The client was challenged to accept the consequences of his/her anger control problems instead of blaming others.

C. The client identified how his/her pattern of blaming others is associated with underlying feelings of low self-esteem, inadequacy, and insecurity.

D. The client was assisted in identifying constructive ways to improve his/her self-esteem to help reduce the pattern of blaming others.

E. The parents identified natural, logical consequences that they could use if the client is caught in a lie.

14. Teach Self-Control Strategies (14)

A. The client was taught mediational and self-control strategies (e.g., relaxation, "stop, look, listen, and think") to help express anger through appropriate verbalizations and healthy physical outlets.

B. The client was asked to identify appropriate and inappropriate ways to express or control his/her anger.

C. The client was encouraged to utilize active listening skills to delay the impulse or urge to react with verbal or physical aggression.

D. The client identified healthy physical outlets for his/her strong feelings of anger and aggressive impulses.

15. Relaxation or Guided Imagery (15)

A. The client was trained in the use of progressive relaxation or guided imagery techniques to help calm himself/herself and decrease the intensity of angry feelings.

B. The client reported a positive response to the use of progressive relaxation or guided imagery techniques to help control anger.

C. The client appeared uncomfortable and unable to relax when being instructed in the use of progressive relaxation and guided imagery techniques.

16. Communication and Assertiveness Skills (16)

A. The client was taught effective communication and assertiveness skills to learn how to express his/her feelings in a controlled fashion and meet his/her needs through more constructive actions.

B. Role-playing techniques were used to model effective ways to control anger and identify appropriate ways to meet his/her needs.

C. The client was encouraged to use "I" messages and assertive versus aggressive statements to effectively verbalize his/her needs to others.

D. The client was helped to differentiate between being assertive and overly aggressive.

17. Reward System/Contingency Contract (17)

A. The client and parents identified a list of rewards to be used to reinforce the client for demonstrating good anger control.

B. A reward system was designed to reinforce the client's effective anger control and deter destructive or aggressive behaviors.

C. The client signed a contingency contract specifying the negative consequences for his/her destructive or aggressive behaviors.

D. The client and parents verbally agreed to the terms of the contingency contract.

18. Token Economy (18)

A. A token economy was designed for use in the home to increase the client's positive social behaviors, improve anger control, and deter destructive or aggressive behaviors.

B. The client and parents agreed to the conditions outlined in the token economy program and agreed to follow through with the implementation at home.

C. A token economy was designed and implemented in the classroom to reinforce the client's positive social behaviors, improve anger control, and deter destructive or aggressive behaviors.

D. The token economy has proven to be successful in improving the client's anger control, deterring aggressive or destructive behavior, and increasing the client's social skills.

19. Encourage Parents' Positive Reinforcement (19)

A. The parents were encouraged to provide frequent praise and positive reinforcement for the client's ability to control his/her anger in situations involving conflict or stress.

B. The parents were challenged to look for opportunities to praise the client for controlling his/her anger effectively instead of focusing primarily on his/her behavioral problems.

C. Explored the reasons that the parents have difficulty offering praise and positive reinforcement.

20. Self-Monitoring Checklists (20)

A. The client was encouraged to utilize self-monitoring checklists of anger-provoking situations in the home and at school to help improve his/her anger control.

B. Consulted with the client's teachers about the use of self-monitoring checklists in anger-provoking situations to improve the client's anger control.

C. The parents and school officials were instructed to utilize a reward system in conjunction with the self-monitoring checklists of anger-provoking situations.

21. "Anger Control" Exercise (21)

A. The client and parents were given the "Anger Control" exercise from *The Brief Adolescent Therapy Homework Planner* (Jongsma, Peterson, and McInnis) to reinforce the client for demonstrating good control of his/her anger.

B. The "Anger Control" exercise was utilized to help the client identify the core issues that contribute to his/her angry outbursts and aggressive or destructive behaviors.

C. The parents were encouraged to utilize the Positive Incident Reports in the "Anger Control" exercise to reinforce the client for showing good control of his/her anger.

22. Identify Times of Anger Control (22)

A. The client identified periods of time when he/she demonstrated good anger control and did not lash out as often, either verbally or physically, toward siblings or peers.

B. The client was encouraged to use coping strategies similar to those used successfully in the past to control his/her anger.

C. The client shared the realization that his/her involvement in extracurricular or positive peer group activities helped him/her control anger more effectively.

D. The therapy session revealed that the client exercised greater anger control during periods of time when he/she received strong family support and affiliated with positive peer groups.

23. Assign S.O.S. Help for Emotions (23)

A. The client was instructed to read *S.O.S. Help for Emotions* (Clark) to help him/her manage anger more effectively.

B. The client did not follow through with the assigned reading of *S.O.S. Help for Emotions*.

C. The client identified several helpful strategies that he/she learned from reading *S.O.S. Help for Emotions* to help improve anger control.

24. Explore Family Dynamics (24)

A. A family therapy session was held to explore the dynamics within the family system that have contributed to the emergence of the client's anger control problems.

B. The family members were asked to list the stressors that have contributed to an atmosphere of irritability and aggression.

C. The family members were asked to identify the things that they would like to change within the family.

D. The family's pattern of poor anger management was exposed as a negative modeling influence for the client.

25. Parents Read *Negotiating Parent/Adolescent Conflict* (25)

A. The parents were instructed to read *Negotiating Parent/Adolescent Conflict* (Robin and Foster) to help resolve conflict more effectively and diffuse the intensity of the client's angry feelings.

B. Processed the reading of *Negotiating Parent/Adolescent Conflict* with the parents in today's therapy session.

C. The parents verbalized that the book *Negotiating Parent/Adolescent Conflict* was helpful in identifying constructive ways to resolve conflict and diffuse the intensity of the client's anger.

26. Family-Sculpting Technique (26)

A. The family-sculpting technique was utilized within the session to help gain greater insight into the roles and behaviors of each family member.

B. The client and family members used the family-sculpting technique to identify positive changes they would like to see take place in the family.

C. The family-sculpting technique revealed how the client perceives the parents as being distant and unavailable.

27. Disengaged Parent Involvement (27)

A. The disengaged parent was challenged to spend more time with the client in leisure, school, or work activities.

B. The client verbalized his/her need to spend greater time with the disengaged parent.

C. Today's therapy session explored the factors contributing to the distant relationship between the client and the disengaged parent.

D. The disengaged parent verbalized a commitment to spend increased time with the client.

E. The client and the disengaged parent identified a list of activities that they would both enjoy doing together.

28. Underlying Feelings and Aggressive Behaviors (28)

A. The session was helpful in identifying how the client's underlying, painful emotions are related to an increase in his/her angry outbursts or aggressive behaviors.

B. Role-playing and modeling techniques were used to demonstrate appropriate ways for the client to express his/her underlying, painful emotions.

C. The client was assisted in identifying more appropriate ways to express his/her painful emotions and meet his/her needs instead of reacting impulsively or aggressively with anger.

29. "Surface Behavior/Inner Feelings" (29)

A. The client was given the "Surface Behavior/Inner Feelings" exercise from *The Brief Adolescent Therapy Homework Planner* (Jongsma, Peterson, and McInnis) to help him/her recognize how underlying emotional pain contributes to angry outbursts.

B. The client verbalized that the "Surface Behavior/Inner Feelings" exercise was helpful in identifying the underlying, painful emotions beneath his/her angry outbursts.

30. Family Abuse History (30)

A. The client's family background was explored for a history of physical, sexual, or substance abuse that may contribute to the emergence of his/her anger control problems.

B. The client developed a time line in the therapy session where he/she identified significant historical events, both positive and negative, that have occurred in his/her family.

C. The client was instructed to draw a diagram of the house where the abuse occurred.

D. A diagnostic interview was conducted to assess the extent of the family member's use of drugs and alcohol.

31. Feelings Associated with Neglect or Abuse (31)

A. The client was given the opportunity to express his/her feelings about past neglect, abuse, separation, or abandonment.

B. The client was instructed to draw pictures that reflect his/her feelings about past neglect, abuse, separation, or abandonment.

C. The client was instructed to use a journal to record his/her thoughts and feelings about past neglect, abuse, separation, or abandonment.

D. The empty-chair technique was employed to facilitate expression of feelings surrounding past neglect or abuse.

32. Parents' Abusive Discipline (32)

A. The client's parents were confronted and challenged to cease physically abusive or overly punitive methods of discipline.

B. The parents were asked to identify how physically abusive or overly punitive methods of discipline negatively affect the client and siblings.

C. The parent(s) apologized to the client for abusive behaviors and overly harsh methods of discipline.

D. The parents were taught how aggressive discipline promotes client's aggression and poor anger management.

E. The parents were referred to a parenting class.

33. Protect the Client from Abuse (33)

A. The physical abuse was reported to the appropriate protective services agency.

B. Recommendation was made that the abuse perpetrator be removed from the home and seek treatment.

C. Recommendation was made that the client and siblings be removed from the home to ensure protection from further abuse.

D. The client and family members identified necessary steps to take to minimize the risk of abuse occurring in the future.

E. The nonabusive parent verbalized a commitment to protect the client and siblings from physical abuse in the future.

34. Letter to Absent or Abusive Parent (34)

A. The client was given the homework assignment of writing a letter to the absent or abusive parent to help him/her express and work through feelings of anger, sadness, and helplessness about past abandonment or abuse.

B. In today's therapy session, the client processed the content of his/her letter written to the absent or abusive parent.

C. The client expressed strong feelings of anger, hurt, sadness, and helplessness about the past abandonment or abuse in his/her letter.

D. The client failed to follow through with the homework assignment to write a letter to the absent or abusive parent because of his/her desire to avoid dealing with any painful emotions.

35. Empty-Chair Technique (35)

A. The empty-chair technique was employed to help the client express his/her anger toward the absent or abusive parent.

B. The empty-chair technique was helpful in allowing the client to express feelings of anger, hurt, or sadness toward the absent or abusive parent.

C. The client appeared uncomfortable with the use of the empty-chair technique and had difficulty verbalizing his/her feelings of anger, hurt, or sadness toward the absent or abusive parent.

36. Willingness to Forgive Perpetrator (36)

A. Today's therapy session explored and discussed the client's willingness to forgive the perpetrator for the past emotional or physical abuse.

B. The client expressed a willingness to forgive the perpetrator for the past emotional or physical pain.

C. The client reported that he/she is not willing to attempt to forgive the perpetrator for the past emotional or physical abuse.

D. The client expressed a willingness to meet with the perpetrator of past emotional or physical abuse to receive apology and offer to begin the process of forgiveness.

37. Assign Forgiveness Letter to Target of Anger (37)

A. The client was given the directive to write a letter of forgiveness to the target of his/her anger as a step toward letting go of angry feelings.

B. In today's therapy session, the client processed the letter of forgiveness that was written to the target of his/her anger.

C. The client expressed strong feelings of anger toward the target of his/her anger, but also expressed a willingness to receive an apology and offer to begin the process of forgiveness.

D. The client expressed strong feelings of anger in his/her letter to the target of his/her anger and indicated that he/she was not ready to forgive the other individual.

E. After processing the letter to the target of his/her anger, the client expressed a willingness to meet with the individual to receive an apology and offer to begin the process of forgiveness.

38. List Targets of and Causes for Anger (38)

A. The client was instructed to develop a thorough list of all targets and causes for anger.

B. The client was able to develop a list of individual(s) whom he/she has experienced strong feelings of anger toward in the past.

C. The client was able to identify and list several situations or events that have produced strong feelings of anger.

D. The client had difficulty identifying the targets of and causes for his/her anger.

39. Document Persons/Situations That Evoke Anger (39)

A. The client was instructed to keep a daily journal in which he/she documents persons and situations that evoke strong feelings of anger.

B. The client made productive use of the journal to document persons or situations that evoke strong feelings of anger.

C. The client failed to comply with the homework assignment to use a journal to document persons and situations that evoke strong feelings of anger.

D. After processing the client's feelings of anger that were expressed in the journal, the client was able to identify constructive ways to resolve conflict or overcome his/her problems.

40. Life Experiences That Produce Anger (40)

A. The client was given the homework assignment to list significant life experiences that have produced strong feelings of anger, hurt, or disappointment.

B. The client completed the homework assignment and listed significant life experiences that have produced strong feelings of anger, hurt, or disappointment.

C. The client had difficulty identifying any significant life experiences that have produced his/her strong feelings of anger, hurt, or disappointment.

D. The client verbalized the realization that his/her anger control problems are often linked to important life experiences or stressors.

E. After reviewing the list of significant life experiences that have produced feelings of anger, hurt, or disappointment, the client was helped to see how he/she could grow from these painful experiences.

41. Identify and Express Unmet Needs (41)

A. The client was instructed to list his/her unmet needs.

B. The client was given encouragement to express his/her unmet needs to significant others using assertive "I" messages.

C. The client was able to directly express his/her unmet needs to parents in today's therapy session.

D. Role-playing techniques were utilized to help the client find constructive ways to express his/her unmet needs.

E. Today's therapy session focused on teaching basic problem-solving approaches to help the client identify ways to meet his/her unmet needs.

42. Replace Irrational Thoughts (42)

A. The client was helped to identify how irrational, distorted thoughts have contributed to the emergence of his/her anger control problems.

B. The client was helped to replace his/her irrational thoughts with more adaptive ways of thinking to help control anger.

C. The client reported that he/she has experienced a reduction in the frequency and intensity of his/her angry feelings by being able to replace irrational thoughts with more adaptive ways of thinking.

D. The client has continued to struggle to control anger because of his/her reluctance to give up or let go of irrational beliefs.

43. Positive Self-Descriptive Statements (43)

A. The client was encouraged to make positive self-descriptive statements to improve his/her self-esteem and anger control.

B. The client was given the homework assignment to make at least one positive self-descriptive statement daily around others.

C. The parents were instructed to show interest and enthusiasm when the client makes positive self-statements.

44. Record Positive Self-Descriptive Statements (44)

A. The client was given the homework assignment of recording one positive self-descriptive statement daily in a journal to help improve his/her self-esteem and anger control.

B. The client complied with the homework to record one positive self-descriptive statement daily in a journal.

C. The client failed to comply with the directive to record one positive self-descriptive statement daily in a journal.

D. The client reported that his/her self-esteem and anger control has improved since he/she started to record one positive self-descriptive statement daily in a journal.

45. Participate in Activities or Exercise (45)

A. The client was strongly encouraged to participate in extracurricular activities or engage in regular exercise to provide a healthy outlet for his/her anger and improve self-esteem.

B. The client was assisted in developing a list of extracurricular activities that will provide a healthy outlet for his/her anger and improve self-esteem.

C. The client reported that regular exercise has helped him/her control anger.

46. Anger Management Group Referral (46)

A. The client was referred to an anger management group to improve his/her anger control and interpersonal skills.

B. The client was given the directive to self-disclose at least one time during the group therapy session.

C. The client was encouraged to demonstrate empathy and concern for the thoughts, feelings, and needs of others during the group therapy sessions.

47. Odyssey Islands Game (47)

A. The Odyssey Islands game was employed to establish rapport with the client.

B. The Odyssey Islands game was employed in the therapy session to help the client develop positive social skills and improve his/her self-control.

C. After playing the Odyssey Islands game, the client was able to identify several positive social skills and ways to control his/her anger.

D. The client was given the homework assignment of utilizing self-control strategies on three occasions during the upcoming week that were discussed while playing the Odyssey Islands game.

48. Seek Employment (48)

A. The client was challenged to seek and secure employment in order to obtain money to make restitution for his/her aggressive or destructive acts.

B. The client was challenged to seek and secure employment to assume greater responsibility and gain income to meet his/her needs in an adaptive manner.

C. The client was praised and reinforced for securing employment.

D. The client explored the factors that contributed to his/her reluctance to obtain employment.

49. Need for Control (49)

A. The client verbalized an understanding of how his/her intimidating behaviors or excessive bullying of others are related to his/her need for power or control.

B. The client was assisted in identifying several age-appropriate ways to gain a sense of power and control.

C. The client was given a homework assignment to engage in three responsible or positive social behaviors to build positive self-esteem and provide him/her with a sense of empowerment.

D. The client was given a directive to apologize to the individual(s) whom he/she has intimidated or bullied in the past.

50. Perform Altruistic Acts (50)

A. The client was given the homework assignment of performing three altruistic or benevolent acts to increase his/her empathy and sensitivity to the thoughts, feelings, and needs of others.

B. The recommendation was made that the client perform community service as part of his/her probation to increase empathy and concern for the welfare of others.

C. The client reported an increase in positive feelings toward self and others after showing empathy, kindness, and sensitivity to the needs of others.

D. The client's failure to comply with the homework assignment that he/she perform altruistic or benevolent acts reflects his/her lack of empathy and concern for the welfare of others.

51. Anger-Provoking Situations (51)

A. The client was instructed to draw pictures of three events or situations that commonly evoke feelings of anger.

B. Processed the client's thoughts and feelings reflected in drawings that were related to anger-provoking situations.

C. The client's drawings reflected how he/she often becomes angry when self-esteem is challenged and he/she feels insecure or vulnerable.

D. The client's drawings reflected his/her need for power and control.

52. Art Therapy Techniques (52)

A. The client was instructed to draw an outline of a human body on a large piece of paper or posterboard in the therapy session, then asked to fill in the mural with objects, symbols, or pictures that reflect what he/she feels angry about in his/her life.

B. After filling in a human body outline with pictures that symbolize the objects or sources of anger, the client was able to verbalize his/her feelings of anger in the therapy session and identify more constructive ways to resolve conflict or overcome his/her problems.

53. Music Therapy Techniques (53)

A. The client shared a song in the therapy session that reflected feelings of anger and was then asked to tell of a time when he/she felt angry about a particular issue.

B. The client shared a song in the therapy session that afterward led to a discussion about how the song reflected his/her feelings of anger and what he/she can do to meet his/her needs or overcome problems.

54. Assess Marital Conflicts (54)

A. The marital dyad was assessed for possible conflict and/or triangulation that places the focus on the client's anger control problems and away from marital problems.

B. The parents recognized how their marital problems are creating stress for the client and agreed to pursue marital counseling.

C. The parents refused to follow through with the recommendation to pursue marital counseling.

55. Medication Evaluation Referral (55)

A. The client was referred for a medication evaluation to help stabilize his/her mood and improve anger control.

B. The client and parents agreed to follow through with a medication evaluation by a physician.

C. The client was strongly opposed to being placed on medication to help stabilize his/her mood and improve anger control.

D. The client reported that the medication has helped to stabilize his/her mood and decrease the frequency and intensity of his/her angry outbursts.

E. The client reported that the medication has not helped to stabilize his/her moods or decrease the frequency or intensity of his/her angry outbursts.

ANXIETY

CLIENT PRESENTATION

1. Excessive Worry (1)*

A. The client presented for the session upset and worried about recent events.

B. The client was upset and worried to the point where he/she could not be easily settled down by the therapist.

C. The client was able to work on the core issues that have caused him/her to be upset.

D. The client reported that he/she has been significantly less worried and less preoccupied with anxieties in the recent past.

2. Fearful/Urgent (1)

A. The client revealed a strong sense of urgency and sought any possible reassurance for his/her fears.

B. The urgency surrounding the client's fear is overwhelming.

C. The client's sense of urgency is not diminished by reassurance from the therapist.

D. The sense of urgency that surrounds the client's fears is no longer existent, and he/she no longer presses for reassurance.

3. Panicky/Uncontrollable (1)

A. The client shows that he/she is panicky to the point of being uncontrollable around the source of the anxiety.

B. The parents reported that each intervention they have tried has not been able to calm and settle the client once he/she reaches the point of panic.

C. Efforts by the client, the parents, and the therapist have not been successful in calming him/her after the panic reaches the uncontrollable point.

D. The client was responsive to a calm, reassuring voice and able to work through his/her panic state and process the causes for this specific reaction.

E. The problem of the client's symptoms of panic has been resolved, and there have been no reports of a recurrence of this phenomenon recently.

4. Restless/Tense (2)

A. The client was restless and tense, making it difficult for him/her to sit in session or to complete thoughts or activities.

B. The client is becoming less tense and is now able to respond to questions attentively.

C. The client is more relaxed and able to focus throughout the session, even when addressing issues that cause him/her anxiety.

---

* The numbers in parentheses correlate to the number of the Behavioral Definition statement in the companion chapter with same title in *The Adolescent Psychotherapy Treatment Planner* (Jongsma, Peterson, and McInnis) by John Wiley & Sons, 2000.

5. Autonomic Hyperactivity Symptoms (3)

A. The client presented as being very anxious and experiencing a rapid heartbeat and shortness of breath.

B. The client has been plagued by nausea and diarrhea brought on by his/her anxiety, as all physical reasons have been medically ruled out.

C. The client complained of having a dry mouth and frequently feeling kind of dizzy.

D. The client indicated that he/she has not experienced symptoms of a rapid heartbeat or shortness of breath since he/she started to talk about what makes him/her anxious.

6. Body-Focused/Physical Complaints (3)

A. The client presents with numerous physical complaints and is focused on what is happening to his/her body.

B. Body concerns occupied the entire session, and it was difficult to move the client away from these concerns.

C. The client shared mother's concern for his/her health and how mother takes good care of him/her.

D. The client accepted reassurance regarding physical complaints and moved to talking about other anxieties he/she experiences.

E. The client was diverted from body focus and has begun exploring other concerns.

7. Hypervigilant (4)

A. The client presented in a tense, on-edge manner.

B. The client's level of tension and anxiety was so high that he/she was unable to concentrate on anything and was irritable.

C. The client reported sleep disturbance related to anxious worry.

D. The client's anxiety has diminished and he/she is significantly more relaxed.

8. Specific Fear (Phobia) (5)

A. The client presented as being anxious over the specific stimulus situation to the point of being able to function only on a limited basis.

B. The client reported that the phobic anxiety gradually increased to where it now interferes with his/her daily life and family's life as well.

C. The client indicated that he/she has no idea of why the phobic fear has come to dominate his/her daily existence.

D. The client's daily ability to function has increased steadily as he/she has begun to face the phobic fear.

9. Parental Causes for Anxiety (6)

A. The client complained of being worried and anxious about the constant arguing of his/her parents.

B. The parents reported that they restrict the client's freedom and physical activity to protect him/her from the dangers present today.

C. It was observed that the parents' use of excessive guilt and threats of abandonment caused worry and anxiety in the client.

D. The client indicated that he/she now feels less anxious, as the parents have stopped arguing so often.

E. The parents' relaxing their restrictions and control has reduced the client's level of worry and anxiety.

INTERVENTIONS IMPLEMENTED

1. Establish Trust/Express Anxious Feelings (1)*

A. An initial trust level was established with the client through the use of unconditional positive regard.

B. Warm acceptance and active listening techniques were utilized to establish the basis for a trusting relationship with the client.

C. The client has formed a trust-based relationship and has started to express his/her anxious feelings.

D. Despite the use of active listening, warm acceptance, and unconditional positive regard, the client remains hesitant to trust and share his/her anxious feelings.

2. Talking, Feeling, Doing Game (2)

A. The Talking, Feeling, Doing Game (Creative Therapeutics) was played with the client, who readily responded in detail to all questions.

B. The client played the Talking, Feeling, Doing Game only after some coaxing and then offered only brief responses to some questions.

C. The client eagerly played the Talking, Feeling, Doing Game and was pleased by the therapist's responses. The client would like to play again.

D. Playing the Talking, Feeling, Doing Game has been helpful in getting the client to identify, explore, and express his/her feelings.

3. Teach Understanding of Anxiety (3)

A. The client was ask to read the chapter "Understanding Anxiety" from the *Feeling Good Handbook* (Burns) and list five key ideas from the reading that increased his/her knowledge of anxiety.

B. The client was taught about the many symptoms and sources of anxiety.

4. My Home and Places Game (4)

A. The My Home and Places (Flood) game was played with the client, who participated without resistance.

B. As the client played My Home and Places he/she was able to identify what made him/her anxious.

C. The client played My Home and Places with the therapist under duress and gave only partial and minimal responses.

---

* The numbers in parentheses correlate to the number of the Therapeutic Intervention statement in the companion chapter with the same title in *The Adolescent Psychotherapy Treatment Planner* (Jongsma, Peterson, and McInnis) by John Wiley & Sons, 2000.

5. Recognize/Express Feelings (5)

A. The client was assisted in expanding his/her ability to recognize feelings and then express them in effective, non-self-defeating ways.

B. The client was ask to identify certain feelings and then taught ways he/she could respond to each in a manner that is not self-defeating.

C. The client continues to have difficulty identifying and expressing feelings with any kind of consistent clarity.

D. The client's manner of expressing feelings continues to be self-defeating, as he/she does not implement an adaptive manner of such expression.

6. Explore Messages/Retrain Cognition (6)

A. The client's cognitive messages that cause anxiety were explored and the client was taught their role in the process of creating anxiety.

B. The client was assisted in successfully listing the most frequent, distorted self-talk that precipitates anxiety.

C. The client is having persistent difficulty in identifying and clarifying the distorted cognitive messages that precipitate anxiety.

7. Create New Messages/Expand Coping Skills (7)

A. The client was assisted in identifying and developing positive, realistic cognitive messages to help increase his/her self-confidence.

B. The client was taught specific coping skills to assist him/her in effectively responding to anxious situations.

C. It continues to be very difficult for the client to replace the distorted cognitive messages that precipitate anxiety with positive, realistic messages that would induce calm confidence.

D. The client was asked to continue to work on implementing specific coping skills that would reduce anxiety.

8. *Anxiety and Phobia Workbook* Exercise (8)

A. The client was asked to complete exercises in the *Anxiety and Phobia Workbook* (Bourne) and identify key concepts he/she obtained from each.

B. Key concepts and skills gained by the client from the exercise in the *Anxiety and Phobia Workbook* were stressed and reinforced.

C. The exercises in the *Anxiety and Phobia Workbook* were helpful in teaching the client new coping skills to reduce anxiety.

D. The client has not followed through on completing the exercises in the *Anxiety and Phobia Workbook,* and this assignment was given again.

9. *Ten Days to Self-Esteem* Exercise (9)

A. The client was asked to complete the exercises in the Anxiety section of *Ten Days to Self-Esteem* (Burns) and identify key cognitive skills he/she could implement.

B. Using material from *Ten Days to Self-Esteem,* the client developed cognitive interventions he/she could use to respond to situations that cause anxiety.

C. Role playing and modeling were used to apply the new cognitive interventions developed from *Ten Days to Self-Esteem* to everyday anxiety-producing situations.

D. The client has not followed through with completing the assignment from the *Ten Days to Self-Esteem* book, and this assignment was reissued.

10. "Finding and Losing Your Anxiety" Exercise (10)

A. The client was asked to do the exercise "Finding and Losing Your Anxiety" from *The Brief Adolescent Homework Planner* (Jongsma, Peterson, McInnis) to help him/her locate the source of his/her anxiety.

B. The exercise "Finding and Losing Your Anxiety" helped the client locate the source of his/her anxiety and then he/she was taught ways to help resolve the underlying issues.

C. The client has not followed through on completing the exercise "Finding and Losing Your Anxiety," and this assignment was reissued.

D. The exercise "Finding and Losing Your Anxiety" was reported by the client not to be helpful in identifying causes for anxiety or in learning coping skills.

11. List Past/Present Conflicts (11)

A. The client was asked to make a list of all his/her past and present conflicts to help connect those conflicts with current anxieties.

B. The client processed the list of past and present conflicts with the therapist and was able to make key connections between conflicts and his/her anxiety.

C. The client required assistance in making connections from his/her list of conflicts and the anxiety he/she experiences.

D. The client could identify no past or present conflicts that he/she could connect with current experience of anxiety.

12. Resolve Past/Present Conflicts (12)

A. Cognitive restructuring was utilized in assisting the client to resolve key past and present situations.

B. The client was taught assertiveness techniques to use in resolving past/present conflicts.

C. The client was instructed in various conflict-resolution techniques to apply to resolve key past/present conflicts.

D. The client was gently but firmly confronted on his/her resistance to resolving either past or present conflicts.

13. Behavioral Anxiety Coping Strategies (13)

A. The client was assisted in selecting anxiety coping strategies that he/she felt would be helpful in resolving anxiety.

B. Behavioral rehearsal was used to instruct the client in how to implement behavioral anxiety coping strategies.

C. A contract was developed, agreed upon, and signed by the client to implement the identified behavioral anxiety coping strategies.

D. The client reported that the implementation of the behavioral anxiety coping strategies has been helpful in reducing the experience of anxiety significantly.

14. **Involve Parents in Treatment Process (14)**

A. The parents were encouraged to take part in an experiential family weekend to assist them in facing fears, building trust, and increasing self-confidence.

B. The parents were assisted in locating and scheduling a family experiential weekend.

C. After the family experiential weekend, the family processed the experience and identified the benefits achieved.

D. The family did not follow through on participating in a family experiential weekend.

15. **Connect Anxiety and Wishes (15)**

A. The client participated in an interpretive interview in which he/she expressed his/her suppressed wishes and feelings.

B. The client was assisted in making key connections between his/her anxiety and his/her "unacceptable" wishes or "bad" thoughts.

C. As the client identified and expressed his/her suppressed wishes and censored thoughts, his/her level of anxiety has been reduced.

16. **Teach Positive Imagery/Relaxation (16)**

A. The client was taught deep muscle relaxation, deep breathing, and positive imagery as a means of coping with his/her anxieties.

B. The client practiced positive imagery and relaxation in role-play situations with the therapist.

C. A verbal contract was agreed upon, with the client to use relaxation and positive imagery when anxiety or fear presents itself.

D. The implementation of deep muscle relaxation, deep breathing, and positive imagery as coping skills have been very effective in helping the client reduce his/her level of anxiety.

17. **Stress and Anxiety Game (17)**

A. The Stress and Anxiety Game (Berg) was played with the client to afford him/her the opportunity to practice the anxiety-reduction strategies he/she has learned to date.

B. The client processed the experience of playing The Stress and Anxiety Game, stating that playing made him/her feel more sure and confident to use the coping skills he/she had previously learned.

C. The client was resistant to playing The Stress and Anxiety Game and gained little benefit from this exercise.

18. **Overthinking the Anxiety Situation (18)**

A. The client was encouraged to think for a determined amount of minutes three times each day about the situation that elicits his/her fear or anxiety.

B. A contract was elicited from the client to implement the overthinking coping strategy regularly until the next therapy session.

C. The overthinking exercise has been successfully implemented by the client and has served to reduce the amount of time that the client is preoccupied with anxious thoughts or feelings.

19. **Normal Developmental Anxieties (19)**

A. The parents were taught about the fears and anxieties of various developmental stages.

B. Anxiety and fears were normalized with the parents, and coping strategies were stressed as the way to handle them.

20. **Parents Read Books on Adolescent Development (20)**

A. The parents were asked to read *Between Parent and Teenager* (Ginott) and/or *How to Talk So Kids Will Listen* (Faber and Mazlish) to increase their understanding of adolescents.

B. The assigned reading material was processed with the parents to support what they had learned and to answer any questions that emerged from their reading.

C. The parents were confronted about unrealistic expectations or solutions to adolescent issues.

D. The parents have not followed through with reading the assigned material on adolescent development, and they were encouraged to do so.

21. **Parenting Class Referral (21)**

A. The parents were encouraged to attend a parenting class or support group.

B. The parents gave a commitment to join a parenting class or support group.

C. The parents reported on their experience within a parent support group.

D. The parents were resistive to a referral to a parenting class and refused to commit to attending such a class.

22. **Parents' Response to Client's Fears (22)**

A. The parents were taught effective responses to the client's fears.

B. The parents have learned to identify and eliminate detrimental responses that intensify the client's fears/anxieties.

C. The parents made a verbal commitment to implement new responses to the client's fears/anxieties.

D. The parents reported that they have begun to respond more effectively to the client's fears and that this has resulted in a reduction in the client's level of anxiety.

23. **Underlying Family Conflicts (23)**

A. Family sessions were conducted to look for underlying conflicts that may be present within the family.

B. Family sessions were held and underlying conflicts within the family were identified in specific terms.

C. Attempts were made to hold a family session to look for underlying conflicts, but the family was resistive to the intervention, preferring not to discuss their conflicts.

24. **Resolve Family Conflict (24)**

A. Positive ways of resolving conflicts were identified and examined by the family.

B. In family sessions, the family was able to resolve key family conflicts.

C. Healthy aspects of the family functioning were affirmed, and the family was encouraged to work toward resolving ongoing family conflicts.

D. The resolution of underlying family conflicts has had a very beneficial effect on reducing the client's level of anxiety.

25. Structure Roles within the Family (25)

A. Family sessions were held in which family roles were explored and adjusted to strengthen the parental team and solidify the sibling group.

B. Separate family sessions were held with the parents and siblings in order to emphasize family hierarchy and to define the sibling group as separate from the parents.

C. As clarity has been added to the family roles, the client's level of anxiety has been reduced.

D. The parents were reinforced for reducing their efforts to control the children unnecessarily.

26. Decrease Parental Control (26)

A. Strategic interventions were developed and implemented in family sessions that were aimed at decreasing parental control and increasing children's freedom of choice.

B. Specific situations were identified in which the parents can reduce their control and offer more choice to the children.

27. Mapping Technique (27)

A. Family patterns were mapped in a family session in order to locate points to intervene in the fear.

B. A therapeutic family reaction to the client's anxiety was developed, and the family made a commitment to use this solution whenever the client's anxiety occurs.

C. The brief therapy approach of mapping patterns of anxiety occurrence within the family has been successful in reducing the client's level of anxiety.

28. Resources to Cope with Anxiety (28)

A. Times that the client was free from anxiety were explored to help identify a solution to implement for current fears.

B. The client reported success in applying the anxiety coping technique used in the past.

29. Utilize Teaching Tale (29)

A. A teaching tale related to reducing fear was created and given to the family in a family session.

B. A tape of the tale was given to the family, who agreed to play it two times daily.

C. Utilization of the teaching tale to educate the client about a coping technique has been successful and has resulted in a reduction in the client's level of anxiety.

30. Medication Consultation (30)

A. The value of a medication consultation was discussed with the parents and the client.

B. A medication consultation was scheduled, and the client followed through.

C. The therapist and psychiatrist conferred regarding the recommendation for a medication evaluation.

D. The client and the parents were resistant to the use of medication and have not followed through with the referral to a physician for an evaluation.

31. Monitor Medication Compliance/Effectiveness (31)

A. The issues of medication compliance and effectiveness were addressed with the parents and the client.

B. The client's resistance to taking medication was processed and addressed.

C. Information related to the client's medication compliance and its effectiveness was communicated to his/her psychiatrist.

D. The client's responsible compliance with medications was verbally reinforced.

E. The client reported that the use of the psychotropic medication has been effective in reducing his/her experience of anxiety.

ATTENTION-DEFICIT/HYPERACTIVITY DISORDER

CLIENT PRESENTATION

1. Short Attention Span (1)*

A. The parents and teachers reported that the client displays a short attention span and has difficulty staying focused for extended periods of time.

B. The client had trouble staying focused in today's therapy session and often switched from one topic to another.

C. The client remained focused and was able to discuss pertinent topics for a sufficient length of time.

D. The client's attention span has improved in structured settings where he/she receives supervision and greater individualized attention.

E. The parents and teachers reported that the client has consistently demonstrated good attention and concentration at home and school.

2. Distractibility (2)

A. The parents and teachers reported that the client is easily distracted by extraneous stimuli and his/her own internal thoughts.

B. The client appeared highly distractible during today's therapy session and often had to be redirected to the topic being discussed.

C. The client often has to be redirected to task at home or school because of his/her distractibility.

D. The client appeared less distractible and more focused during today's therapy session.

E. The client appeared less distractible and more focused at home and school.

3. Poor Listening Skills (3)

A. The client has often given others the impression at home and school that he/she is not listening to what is being said.

B. The client did not appear to be listening well to the topics being discussed in today's therapy session.

C. The client listened well during today's therapy session.

D. The client has recently demonstrated improved listening skills at home and school.

4. No Follow-Through on Instructions (4)

A. The parents and teachers reported that the client does not consistently follow through on instructions.

B. The client's repeated failure to follow through on instructions has interfered with his/her ability to complete school assignments, chores, and job responsibilities in a timely manner.

---

* The numbers in parentheses correlate to the number of the Behavioral Definition statement in the companion chapter with same title in *The Adolescent Psychotherapy Treatment Planner* (Jongsma, Peterson, and McInnis) by John Wiley & Sons, 2000.

C. The client has generally been able to follow single or simple instructions, but has had trouble following through on multiple, complex instructions.

D. The client has begun to demonstrate improvement in his/her ability to follow through on instructions.

E. The client has recently followed through on instructions from parents and teachers on a consistent basis.

5. Incomplete Classroom/Homework Assignments (4)

A. The client has consistently failed to complete his/her classroom and homework assignments in a timely manner.

B. The client has often rushed through his/her classroom work and does not fully complete his/her assignments.

C. The client has recently demonstrated mild improvements in his/her ability to complete classroom and homework assignments.

D. The client has consistently completed his/her classroom and homework assignments on a consistent basis.

6. Unfinished Chores (4)

A. The client often failed to comply with parents' requests to complete his/her chores at home.

B. The parents reported that the client often gets sidetracked and does not complete his/her chores.

C. The client has demonstrated mild improvements in his/her ability to finish chores or household responsibilities.

D. The client has been responsible in completing his/her chores on a consistent basis.

7. Poor Organizational Skills (5)

A. The client has displayed poor organizational skills and often loses or misplaces important things necessary for tasks or activities at home and school.

B. The client has a tendency to become more disorganized and impulsive in his/her responding in unstructured settings where there is a great deal of external stimulation.

C. The client has recently taken active steps (e.g., utilizing planner, consulting with teachers about homework, performing homework and chores at routine times) to become more organized at home and school.

D. The client has demonstrated good organizational skills at home and school on a regular basis.

8. Hyperactivity (6)

A. The parents and teachers described the client as being a highly energetic and hyperactive individual.

B. The client presented with a high energy level and had difficulty sitting still for extended periods of time.

C. The client has trouble channeling his/her high energy into constructive or sustained, purposeful activities.

D. The parents and teachers reported a decrease in the client's level of hyperactivity.

E.   The client has consistently channeled his/her energy into constructive and purposeful activities.

9.   Restless Motor Movements (6)

A.   The parents and teachers described the client as being highly restless and fidgety in his/her motor movements.

B.   The client was restless and fidgety in his/her motor movements during today's therapy session.

C.   The client has frequently annoyed or antagonized peers because of his/her trouble keeping hands to himself/herself.

D.   The client exhibited a decrease in the amount of motor activity during today's therapy session.

E.   The client has demonstrated greater control of his/her motor movements on a regular basis.

10.   Impulsivity (7)

A.   The client presents as a highly impulsive individual who seeks immediate gratification of his/her needs and often fails to consider the consequences of his/her actions.

B.   The client has considerable difficulty inhibiting his/her impulses and tends to react to what is going on in his/her immediate environment.

C.   The client has begun to take steps toward improving his/her impulse control and to delay the need for immediate gratification.

D.   The client has recently displayed good impulse control, as evidenced by an improved ability to stop and think about the possible consequences of his/her actions before reacting.

11.   Disruptive/Attention-Seeking Behavior (8)

A.   The parents and teachers described a history of the client frequently disrupting the classroom with his/her silly, immature, and negative attention-seeking behavior.

B.   The client has often disrupted the classroom by blurting out remarks at inappropriate times.

C.   The client has started to exercise greater self-control and recently has not disrupted the classroom as much.

D.   The client has demonstrated a significant reduction in the frequency of his/her disruptive or negative attention-seeking behavior at home and school.

12.   Angry Outbursts/Aggressive Behavior (8)

A.   The client reported a history of losing control of his/her anger and exhibiting frequent angry outbursts or aggressive behaviors.

B.   The client appeared angry and hostile during today's therapy session.

C.   The client reported incidents of becoming easily angered over trivial matters.

D.   The client has begun to take steps to control his/her anger and aggressive impulses.

E.   The client has recently demonstrated good control of his/her anger and has not exhibited any major outbursts or aggressive behavior.

13. Careless/Potentially Dangerous Behavior (9)

A. The client described a history of engaging in careless or potentially dangerous behavior where he/she shows little regard for the welfare or safety of self and others.

B. The client's impulsivity has contributed to his/her propensity for engaging in careless, risky, or dangerous activity.

C. The client verbally recognized a need to stop and think about the possible consequences of his/her actions for self and others before engaging in risky or potentially dangerous behavior.

D. The client has not engaged in any recent careless or potentially dangerous behaviors.

14. Blaming/Projecting (10)

A. The client has often resisted accepting responsibility for the consequences of his/her actions and has frequently projected the blame for his/her poor decisions or problems onto other people or outside circumstances.

B. The client appeared defensive and made excuses or blamed others for his/her poor decisions and behavior.

C. The client has slowly begun to accept greater responsibility for his/her actions and has placed the blame less often for his/her wrongdoing onto other people.

D. The client admitted to his/her wrongdoing and verbalized an acceptance of responsibility for his/her actions.

15. Conflict with Family Members (10)

A. The client reported a history of becoming entangled in numerous arguments or disputes with family members.

B. The client's family relationships are strained due to his/her impulsivity, hyperactivity, and verbally/physically aggressive behavior.

C. The client has recently demonstrated a mild reduction in the frequency of his/her arguments with family members.

D. The client and parents reported significant improvement in family relations due to the client's improved impulse control.

16. Low Self-Esteem (11)

A. The client expressed feelings of low self-esteem and inadequacy as a consequence of his/her poor decisions and impulsive actions.

B. The client's defensiveness and unwillingness to accept responsibility for the consequences of his/her actions have reflected deeper feelings of low self-esteem, inadequacy, and insecurity.

C. The client verbalized an awareness of how his/her feelings of inadequacy contribute to an increase in disruptive and impulsive behavior.

D. The client verbalized positive self-descriptive statements during today's therapy session.

E. The client has taken active steps to improve his/her self-esteem and develop a positive self-image.

17. Poor Social Skills (11)

A. The client historically has had difficulty establishing and maintaining lasting peer friendships because of his/her poor social skills and impulsivity.

B. The client frequently becomes entangled in interpersonal disputes because of his/her failure to pick up on important social cues or interpersonal nuances.

C. The client's interpersonal relationships are strained by his/her intrusive behaviors.

D. The client has begun to take steps (e.g., listen better, compliment others, allow others to go first) to improve his/her social skills.

E. The client has recently demonstrated good social skills and related well to siblings, peers, and adults on a consistent basis.

18. Lack of Empathy/Insensitivity (11)

A. The client has displayed little concern or empathy for the thoughts, feelings, and needs of other people.

B. The client showed little insight or awareness in today's therapy session of how his/her disruptive or impulsive behaviors have negatively affected other people.

C. The client has frequently sought immediate gratification of his/her needs and failed to stop and consider the rights or needs of others.

D. The client verbalized an understanding of how his/her disruptive and impulsive behavior has had a negative impact on others.

E. The client has recently begun to demonstrate empathy and sensitivity to the thoughts, feelings, and needs of other people.

INTERVENTIONS IMPLEMENTED

1. Psychological Testing to Assess ADHD (1)*

A. A psychological evaluation was conducted to determine whether the client has ADHD.

B. The client was uncooperative and resistant during the evaluation process.

C. The client approached the psychological testing in an honest, straightforward manner and was cooperative with the examiner.

2. Psychological Testing for Emotional or Learning Factors (2)

A. The client received a psychological evaluation to help determine whether emotional factors are contributing to his/her impulsive or maladaptive behaviors.

B. The client received a psychoeducational evaluation to rule out the presence of a possible learning disability that may be contributing to his/her problems with attention, distractibility, and impulsivity in the school setting.

C. The client was uncooperative during the psychoeducational evaluation and did not appear to put forth good effort.

D. The client was cooperative during the psychoeducational evaluation and appeared motivated to do his/her best.

---

* The numbers in parentheses correlate to the number of the Therapeutic Intervention statement in the companion chapter with the same title in *The Adolescent Psychotherapy Treatment Planner* (Jongsma, Peterson, and McInnis) by John Wiley & Sons, 2000.

3. Evaluation Feedback (3)

A. The examiner provided feedback on the evaluation results to the client, parents, or school officials and discussed appropriate interventions.

B. The evaluation results supported the diagnosis of ADHD.

C. The evaluation revealed the presence of underlying emotional problems that contribute to the client's problems with inattentiveness, distractibility, and impulsivity.

D. The results of the psychoeducational evaluation supported the presence of a learning disability and the need for special education services.

E. The evaluation process did not reveal the presence of any learning disability, emotional problems, or ADHD that have contributed to the client's problems with attention, distractibility, or impulsivity.

4. Medication Evaluation Referral (4)

A. The client was referred for a medication evaluation to improve his/her attention span, concentration, and impulse control.

B. The client was referred for a medication evaluation to help stabilize his/her moods.

C. The client and parents agreed to follow through with a medication evaluation.

D. The client was strongly opposed to being placed on medication to help improve his/her attention span and impulse control.

5. Medication Compliance and Effectiveness (5)

A. The client reported that the medication has helped to improve his/her attention, concentration, and impulse control without any side effects.

B. The client reported little to no improvement on the medication.

C. The client has not complied with taking his/her medication on a regular basis.

D. The client and parents were encouraged to report the side effects of the medication to the prescribing physician or psychiatrist.

6. Educate Family about ADHD (6)

A. The client's parents and siblings were educated about the symptoms of ADHD.

B. The therapy session helped the client's parents and siblings gain a greater understanding and appreciation of the symptoms of ADHD.

C. The family members were given the opportunity to express their thoughts and feelings about having a child or sibling with ADHD.

7. Implement Organizational System (7)

A. The parents were assisted in developing an organizational system to increase the client's on-task behavior and completion of school assignments, chores, or work responsibilities.

B. The parents were encouraged to communicate regularly with the teachers through the use of notebooks or planning agendas to help the client complete his/her school or homework on a regular, consistent basis.

C. The client and parents were encouraged to use a calendar or chart to help remind the client of when he/she was expected to complete chores or household responsibilities.

D. The client and parents were instructed to ask the teacher for a course syllabus and use a calendar to help plan large or long-term projects by breaking them into smaller steps.

E. The client and parents were encouraged to purchase a notebook with binders to help the client keep track of his/her school or homework assignments.

8. Develop Routine Schedule (8)

A. The client and parents were assisted in developing a routine schedule to increase the completion of school/homework assignments.

B. The client and parents developed a list of chores for the client and identified times and dates when the chores are expected to be completed.

C. A reward system was designed to reinforce the completion of school, household, or work-related responsibilities.

D. The client and parents signed a contingency contract specifying the consequences for his/her success or failure in completing school assignments or household responsibilities.

9. Communication between Home and School (9)

A. The parents and teachers were encouraged to maintain regular communication with each other via phone calls or written notes regarding the client's academic, behavioral, emotional, and social progress.

B. Consulted with the teachers about sending home daily or weekly progress notes informing the parents of the client's academic, behavioral, and social progress.

C. The client was informed of his/her responsibility to bring home daily or weekly progress notes allowing for regular communication between parents and teachers.

D. The parents identified the consequences for the client's failure to bring home the daily or weekly progress notes from school.

10. Teach Effective Study Skills (10)

A. The client was assisted in identifying a list of good locations for studying.

B. The client was instructed to remove noise sources and clear away as many distractions as possible when studying.

C. The client was instructed to outline or underline important details when studying or reviewing for tests.

D. The client was encouraged to use a tape recorder to help him/her study for tests and review important facts.

E. The client was instructed to take breaks in studying when he/she becomes distracted and starts to have trouble staying focused.

11. Consultation with Teachers (11)

A. Consulted with the client's teachers to implement strategies to improve school performance.

B. The client was assigned a seat near the teacher or in a low-distraction work area to help him/her remain on task.

C. The client and teacher agreed to use a prearranged signal to redirect the client to task when his/her attention begins to wander.

D. The client's schedule was modified to allow for breaks between tasks or difficult assignments to help maintain attention and concentration.

E. The teachers were encouraged to obtain and provide frequent feedback to help maintain the client's attention, interest, and motivation.

12. Teach Test-Taking Strategies (12)

A. The client reviewed a list of effective test-taking strategies to improve his/her academic performance.

B. The client was encouraged to review classroom material regularly and study for tests over an extended period of time.

C. The client was instructed to read the directions twice before responding to the questions on a test.

D. The client was taught to recheck his/her work to correct any careless mistakes or to improve an answer.

13. Read *13 Steps to Better Grades* (13)

A. The client was instructed to read *13 Steps to Better Grades* (Silverman) to improve his/her organizational and study skills.

B. After reading *13 Steps to Better Grades,* the client was able to identify several positive study skills that will help him/her remain organized in the classroom.

14. Teach Self-Control Strategies (14)

A. The client was taught mediational and self-control strategies (e.g., relaxation techniques, "stop, look, listen, and think") to help delay the need for immediate gratification and inhibit impulses.

B. The client was encouraged to utilize active listening skills to delay the impulse to act out or react without considering the consequences of his/her actions.

C. The client was asked to identify the benefits of delaying his/her need for immediate gratification in favor of longer-term gains.

D. The client was assisted in developing an action plan to achieve longer-term goals.

15. "Getting It Done" Program (15)

A. The parents and teachers were given the "Getting It Done" program from *The Brief Adolescent Therapy Homework Planner* (Jongsma, Peterson, and McInnis) to help client complete his/her school and homework assignments regularly.

B. The parents and teachers were encouraged to utilize the school contract and reward system outlined in the "Getting It Done" program to reinforce the regular completion of school assignments.

16. Identify Positive Reinforcers (16)

A. The parents identified a list of positive reinforcers or rewards to maintain the client's interest or motivation in completing school assignments or household responsibilities.

B. The parents were encouraged to provide frequent praise and positive reinforcement to maintain the client's interest and motivation in completing his/her school assignments or household responsibilities.

C. The parents were challenged to look for opportunities to praise the client for being responsible, instead of primarily focusing on the times when the client failed to behave in a responsible manner.

17. Parental Rules and Boundaries (17)

A. The family therapy session focused on helping the parents establish clearly defined rules and appropriate parent-child boundaries.

B. The parents were able to identify the rules and expectations that the client is expected to follow at home.

C. The parents were able to identify appropriate consequences for the client's irresponsible or noncompliant behaviors.

D. The parents had difficulty establishing clearly defined rules and identifying appropriate consequences for the client's irresponsible or noncompliant behaviors.

18. Establish Clear Rules (18)

A. Consulted with the client, parents, and teachers to identify the rules and expectations both at home and school.

B. The client was asked to repeat the rules to demonstrate an understanding of the expectations of him/her.

C. The client verbally disagreed with the rules and expectations identified by the parents and school officials.

19. Delay of Gratification (19)

A. The therapy session focused on helping the parents increase the structure in the home to help the client delay his/her needs for immediate gratification in order to achieve longer-term goals.

B. The parents established the rule that the client is unable to engage in social, recreational, or leisure activities until completing his/her chores or homework.

C. The parents identified consequences for the client's failure to complete responsibilities; client verbalized recognition of these consequences.

D. The client and parents designed a schedule of dates and times when the client is expected to complete chores and homework.

20. Reward System/Contingency Contract (20)

A. The client and parents identified a list of rewards to reinforce the desired positive behavior by the client.

B. A reward system was designed to reinforce positive behavior and deter impulsive actions.

C. The client and parents signed a contingency contract specifying the consequences for his/her impulsive behavior.

D. The client and parents verbally agreed to the terms of the contingency contract.

21. Natural Consequences (21)

A. The client and parents developed a list of natural, logical consequences for the client's disruptive and acting-out behavior.

B. The parents were challenged to not protect the client from the natural, logical consequences of his/her disruptive or acting-out behavior.

C. The client agreed to accept the natural, logical consequences of his/her disruptive or acting-out behavior without complaining excessively.

22. Token Economy Design (22)

A. A token economy was designed for use in the home to increase the client's positive social behaviors and deter impulsive, acting-out behavior.

B. The client and parents agreed to the conditions outlined in the token economy, and they agreed to follow through with the implementation at home.

C. A token economy was designed and implemented in the classroom to improve the client's academic performance and reinforce positive social behavior or good impulse control.

23. Parents Read *Negotiating Parent/Adolescent Conflict* (23)

A. The parents were instructed to read *Negotiating Parent/Adolescent Conflict* (Robin and Foster) to help resolve conflict more effectively.

B. The parents verbalized that the book, *Negotiating Parent/Adolescent Conflict,* was helpful in identifying constructive ways to resolve conflict.

24. ADHD Parental Support Group Referral (24)

A. The parents were referred to an ADHD support group to increase their understanding and knowledge of ADHD symptoms.

B. The parents verbalized that their participation in the ADHD support group has increased their understanding and knowledge of ADHD.

C. The parents reported that they have learned new strategies on how to deal with the client's impulsive behavior through attending the ADHD support group.

25. Assigned Reading of *ADHD—A Teenager's Guide* (25)

A. The client was instructed to read *ADHD—A Teenager's Guide* (Crist) to increase his/her knowledge and understanding of ADHD.

B. The client identified several helpful strategies that he/she learned from reading *ADHD—A Teenager's Guide* to help improve attention span, academic performance, social skills, and impulse control.

26. Teach Problem-Solving Skills (26)

A. The client was taught effective problem-solving skills (i.e., identify the problem, brainstorm alternate solutions, select an option, implement a course of action, and evaluate) in the therapy session.

B. The client was encouraged to use effective problem-solving strategies to solve or overcome a problem or stressor that he/she is facing in his/her current life.

C. The client was given a directive to use problem-solving strategies at home or school on at least three occasions before the next therapy session.

27. "Stop, Think, and Act" Assignment (27)

A. The client and parents were given the "Stop, Think, and Act" assignment from *The Brief Adolescent Therapy Homework Planner* (Jongsma, Peterson, and McInnis) to increase client's ability to delay impulses and solve problems more effectively.

B. The client reported that he/she was able to successfully resolve a problem by following the problem-solving steps outlined in the "Stop, Think, and Act" assignment.

28. Communication and Assertiveness Skills (28)

A. The client was taught effective communication and assertiveness skills to learn how to express feelings in a controlled fashion and meet his/her needs through more constructive actions.

B. Role-playing and modeling techniques were used to teach the client effective ways to control emotions and identify appropriate ways to meet needs.

C. The client was encouraged to utilize "I" messages and positive statements to effectively verbalize needs to others.

29. Guided Imagery/Relaxation Technique (29)

A. The client was taught guided imagery and relaxation techniques to help control anger.

B. The client reported a positive response to the use of guided imagery and relaxation techniques to help control anger.

C. The client appeared uncomfortable and unable to relax when being instructed on the use of guided imagery and relaxation techniques.

30. Confront Irresponsible and Acting-Out Behavior (30)

A. The client was firmly and consistently confronted with how his/her irresponsible and acting-out behavior negatively affects himself/herself and others.

B. The client was asked to list the negative consequences of his/her irresponsible and acting-out behavior for both self and others.

C. Role-reversal techniques were used to help the client realize how his/her irresponsible or acting-out behavior negatively impacted others.

31. Teach Acceptance of Responsibility (31)

A. The client was consistently confronted and challenged to cease blaming others for his/her impulsive behavior and accept greater responsibility for his/her actions.

B. The client was asked to list how his/her poor decisions and impulsive actions resulted in negative consequences for himself/herself and others.

C. The client was assisted in identifying more effective ways to resolve conflict and/or meet his/her needs instead of acting out in an impulsive manner.

D. The client was instructed to apologize to others for the negative consequences of his/her impulsive actions.

32. Connect Feelings and Behavior (32)

A. The session was helpful in identifying how the client's underlying negative or painful emotions are related to the increase in his/her impulsive or disruptive behavior.

B. The client verbally recognized how his/her impulsive or disruptive behavior is connected to underlying feelings of sadness, hurt, disappointment, and so forth.

C. Role-playing and modeling techniques were used to teach appropriate ways for the client to express his/her underlying, painful emotions.

D. The client was assisted in listing more appropriate ways to express his/her painful emotions and meet his/her needs instead of impulsively reacting to situations.

33. Identify Trigger Events to Impulsivity (33)

A. The therapy session explored the stressful events or contributing factors that frequently lead to an increase in the client's hyperactivity, impulsivity, and distractibility.

B. The client identified the stressful events or contributing factors that have contributed to an increase in his/her hyperactivity, impulsivity, and distractibility.

C. Role-playing and modeling techniques were used to teach appropriate ways to manage stress or resolve conflict more effectively.

D. The client and parents were assisted in identifying more effective coping strategies that could be used to manage stress or meet important needs instead of responding impulsively to a situation.

34. Periods of Good Impulse Control (34)

A. The client identified periods when he/she demonstrated good impulse control in the past and engaged in significantly fewer impulsive behaviors.

B. The client was encouraged to use coping strategies similar to those used successfully in the past to control his/her impulses.

C. The therapy session revealed that the client exercised greater self-control and was better behaved during periods of time when he/she received strong family support and affiliated with positive peer groups.

35. Parents Reinforce Positive Behaviors (35)

A. The parents were instructed to observe and record three to five positive behaviors by client in between therapy sessions.

B. The parents were encouraged to reinforce the client for engaging in positive behaviors.

C. The client was strongly encouraged to continue to engage in positive behaviors to build self-esteem, gain parents' approval, and receive affirmation from others.

36. Introduce Idea That Positive Change Is Possible (36)

A. The client was introduced to the idea that he/she could make positive changes in the future by asking the question, "What will you be doing in the future when you stop getting into trouble?"

B. The client identified several responsible or positive social behaviors that he/she would like to engage in the future.

C. Guided imagery techniques were used to help client visualize a brighter future.

D. The client identified future goals and developed an action plan needed to achieve goals or desired changes in behavior.

37. Explore Future Stressors or Roadblocks (37)

A. The client explored possible stressors, roadblocks, or hurdles that might cause impulsive and acting-out behavior to increase in future.

B. The client identified successful coping strategies that could be used in the future when facing similar stressful events, roadblocks, or hurdles.

C. Guided imagery techniques were employed to help the client visualize how he/she can solve potential problems or stressors in the future.

D. The client was encouraged to consult and/or enlist the support of family members or significant others when facing problems or stressors in the future.

38. Positive Role Models (38)

A. The client identified three to five role models or heroes and was asked what he/she thought role models would do to overcome problems with impulse control.

B. The client explored reasons for his/her role models' success and was encouraged to take steps to accomplish his/her personal goals by employing similar strategies.

39. Place Client in Charge of Task (39)

A. The client and parents identified a list of tasks that the client could take charge of at home to provide him/her with the opportunity to act responsibly.

B. The parents were given a directive to place client in charge of tasks at home to demonstrate confidence in his/her ability to behave responsibly.

40. One-on-One Time with Parents (40)

A. The client and parents acknowledged that there have been many negative interactions between them in the recent past and recognized the need to spend one-on-one time together to provide an opportunity for positive experiences.

B. The client and parents were instructed to spend 10 to 15 minutes of daily one-on-one time together to increase the frequency of positive interactions and improve the lines of communication.

41. Reinforce Positive Social Behaviors (41)

A. The client was assisted in developing a list of positive social behaviors that will help him/her to establish and maintain meaningful friendships.

B. Role-playing and modeling techniques were used to teach positive social skills that can help the client establish and maintain peer friendships.

C. The parents and teachers were encouraged to reinforce positive social behaviors by the client that will help him/her establish friendships.

42. Encourage Peer Group Activities (42)

A. The client was encouraged to participate in extracurricular or positive peer group activities to provide him/her with the opportunity to utilize newly learned social skills and establish friendships.

B. The client was assisted in developing a list of peer group activities that will provide him/her with the opportunity to establish meaningful friendships.

C. The client agreed that feelings of insecurity and inadequacy have contributed to his/her reluctance to become involved in extracurricular or positive peer group activities.

43. Group Therapy Referral (43)

A. The client was referred for group therapy to improve his/her social skills.

B. The client was given the directive to self-disclose at least one time during the group therapy sessions.

C. The client was encouraged to demonstrate empathy and concern for the thoughts, feelings, and needs of others during the group therapy sessions.

44. Odyssey Islands Game (44)

A. The Odyssey Islands Game was employed in the therapy session to help establish rapport with the client.

B. The Odyssey Islands Game was utilized to improve the client's social and problem-solving skills.

C. After playing the Odyssey Islands Game, the client was able to identify several positive social skills and effective problem-solving strategies.

D. The client was given the homework assignment of implementing three positive social skills that were learned while playing the Odyssey Islands Game.

45. View *Refusal Skills* (45)

A. The client viewed the *Refusal Skills* video in the therapy session to learn effective assertiveness skills and to help him/her resist negative peer influences.

B. After viewing the *Refusal Skills* video, the client was able to identify several effective ways to resist negative peer influences.

C. The client was given a homework assignment to record at least one incident where he/she effectively used the assertiveness skills taught in *Refusal Skills* to successfully resist negative peer influences.

46. Effects of High Energy Level (46)

A. The client was given a homework assignment to identify the positive and negative aspects of his/her high energy level.

B. The client completed his/her homework assignment and identified the positive and negative aspects of his/her high energy level.

C. The client was encouraged to channel his/her energy into healthy physical outlets and positive social activities.

47. Demonstrate Empathy and Kindness (47)

A. The client was given the homework assignment of performing three altruistic or caring acts before the next therapy session to increase his/her empathy and sensitivity to the thoughts, feelings, and needs of others.

B. The client was encouraged to volunteer in a community service organization or fundraising activity to demonstrate empathy and concern for others.

48. Identify Strengths or Interests (48)

A. The client was given a homework assignment to identify 5 to 10 strengths or interests.

B. The client's interests or strengths were reviewed and he/she was encouraged to utilize strengths or interests to establish friendships.

49. Art Therapy Technique (49)

A. The client was instructed to draw a picture reflecting his/her feelings about what it is like to have ADHD.

B. The client was instructed to draw a series of pictures reflecting the positive and negative aspects of ADHD.

C. After completing the drawing on what it is like to have ADHD, the client identified the positive changes he/she would like to make in his/her life.

D. After completing the drawing of what it is like to have ADHD, the client identified constructive ways to channel his/her energy.

50. Self-Monitoring Checklists (50)

A. The client and parents were encouraged to use self-monitoring checklists to improve the client's attention, academic performance, and social skills.

B. Consulted with the client's teachers about the use of self-monitoring checklists in the classroom to improve attention, concentration, and social skills.

C. The parents and teachers were instructed to utilize a reward system in conjunction with the self-monitoring checklist to improve attention, academic performance, and social skills.

51. Utilize Brain-Wave Biofeedback Techniques (51)

A. The client was trained in the use of brain-wave biofeedback techniques to improve his/her attention span, impulse control, and ability to relax.

B. The client responded favorably to the use of brain-wave biofeedback techniques and was able to relax.

C. The client had difficulty relaxing during the use of the brain-wave biofeedback techniques.

52. Transfer Skills to Everyday Life (52)

A. The client was encouraged to transfer the biofeedback training skills of relaxation and focused cognitive functioning to everyday situations.

B. The client reported that the biofeedback techniques have helped improve his/her attention span, impulse control, and ability to relax.

C. The client has not found the biofeedback techniques useful in improving his/her attention span, impulse control, or ability to relax.

53. Use of *Heartbeat Audiotapes* (53)

A. The client was instructed to utilize the *Heartbeat Audiotapes* to improve his/her attention and concentration while studying or learning new material.

B. The client reported that the *Heartbeat Audiotapes* have helped to improve his/her attention while studying.

C. The client reported little to no improvement in his/her ability to concentrate and stay focused through the use of the *Heartbeat Audiotapes*.

AUTISM/PERVASIVE DEVELOPMENTAL DISORDER

CLIENT PRESENTATION

1. Aloof/Unresponsive (1)*
A. The client presented in an aloof, unresponsive manner.
B. The client showed virtually no interest in the counseling process or in even small interactions with the therapist.
C. All attempts to connect with the client were met with no discernable response.
D. The client has begun to respond in small ways to the therapist's interaction attempts.

2. Detached/Uninterested (1)
A. The client presented in a detached manner with no interest in others outside of self.
B. The parents reported a history of pervasive disinterest in other people.
C. The client has started to acknowledge others on a somewhat consistent basis.
D. The client has shown more interest in relating with the therapist in sessions.

3. Social Connectedness (2)
A. The client has little or no interest in social relationships.
B. The parents indicate that the client from an early age has not shown interest in friendships or other social connections.
C. With encouragement, the client has started to interact on a limited basis with a select peer.
D. The client has started to show somewhat more interest in connecting with the therapist, family members, and with selected peers.

4. Nonverbal/Rigid (3)
A. The client's general manner is rigid and nonverbal.
B. The parents indicate the client rarely verbalizes unless he/she is disturbed or upset.
C. The client has started to talk at intervals with the therapist in sessions.
D. Both with the parents and the therapist, the client has begun to verbalize on a regular basis on his/her own initiative.

5. Lack of Social/Emotional Spontaneity (3)
A. The client exhibits virtually no spontaneity, either in mood or behavior.
B. When others show emotions, the client remains unchanged.
C. The client at times has shown glimmers of spontaneity.

---

* The numbers in parentheses correlate to the number of the Behavioral Definition statement in the companion chapter with same title in *The Adolescent Psychotherapy Treatment Planner* (Jongsma, Peterson, and McInnis) by John Wiley & Sons, 2000.

6. Language Deficits (4)

A. The parents reported significant delays in the client's language development.

B. The client has developed only a few words, far below developmental language expectations.

C. The client engages in very limited verbalizations with the therapist during sessions.

D. There has been a slight but significant increase in the client's skill in and use of language with others.

7. Conversation Deficits (5)

A. The parents reported significant delays in the client's language development.

B. The parents reported that the client has never demonstrated conversational skills with family members.

C. The parents reported that the client has given brief responses to their inquiries on occasion.

D. The parents report a slight increase in the client initiating a conversation and consistent single-word responses to their initiatives.

8. Speech and Language Oddities (6)

A. The client presented with a variety of speech oddities such as echolalia and pronominal reversal.

B. Metaphorical language was used as the primary speech pattern throughout the therapy session.

C. The client echoed every sound and word he/she heard while with the therapist.

D. The parents indicated that the client's language oddities have increased and intensified as he/she has grown older.

E. The parents reported that all their attention and the help of professionals to interrupt and advance the client's speech patterns have been frustrating and nonproductive.

F. The speech oddities of the client have decreased as he/she has started to communicate with others in a didactic manner.

9. Inflexible/Repetitive Behavior (7)

A. The behavioral patterns of the client are entirely inflexible and repetitive.

B. The parents report that the client becomes upset if his/her behavioral routine is changed or interrupted.

C. The client has started to decrease his/her repetitive behaviors and seems more open to trying some different activities.

10. Preoccupied/Focused (8)

A. The client appears to be preoccupied nearly all the time and focused on narrowly selected objects or areas of interest.

B. It is nearly impossible to intrude on the client's preoccupation or break his/her focus.

C. The client has started to allow others to interrupt his/her preoccupation and focus.

D. The client is now less focused and preoccupied on any one thing and is open to new outside stimulants.

11. Impaired Intellectual/Cognitive Functioning (9)

A. There appears to be marked impairment in the client's intellectual and cognitive functioning.

B. The parents indicate it is difficult to follow and understand the client's thought process.

C. The client's thinking appears unimpacted by the thinking and feedback of others.

D. The client has begun to show some positive adjustments in his/her cognitive functioning.

12. Intellectual Variability (9)

A. The client showed severe deficits in language-related intellectual abilities but significant advances in other, very focused, areas such as numerical recall.

B. The client's drawing and memory abilities are very superior, whereas language skills are severely limited.

C. The client shows extreme variability in intellectual skills.

13. Resistant to Change (10)

A. The client is resistant to outside stimulation and attempts to engage him/her.

B. The parents and teachers report that the client is very resistant to any changes in his/her daily schedule, routine, or behaviors.

C. The client has started to tolerate small changes in his/her routine without becoming resistant.

D. The client is now trying new things with the therapist without any show of resistance.

14. Angry/Aggressive (10)

A. Anger and aggression dominate the client's mood and manner.

B. Attempts to connect or interact with the client are met with anger and aggression.

C. The client seems to overreact with anger and aggression to minor changes in his/her routine or environment.

D. Gradually, the client has been reacting with less anger and aggression to changes in his/her routine or environment.

15. Flat Affect (11)

A. There is a continual flatness to the client's affect.

B. The parents report that the client only on rare occasions shows more than flat affect.

C. The client has begun to show more affect in interacting with the therapist.

D. The client's range of affect has slowly started to expand.

16. Self-Abuse (12)

A. The client has exhibited a pattern of self-abusive behavior such as head banging and hitting self.

B. The parents report the client becomes self-abusive when he/she is frustrated in any way.

C. The client has decreased the frequency of his/her episodes of self-abuse.

INTERVENTIONS IMPLEMENTED

1. Assess Cognitive/Intellectual Functioning (1)*

A. An intellectual and cognitive assessment was conducted on the client to determine his/her strengths and weaknesses.

B. The client was uncooperative and resistive in the assessment process.

C. With the parents' assistance, the client was moderately cooperative with the assessor.

2. Speech/Language Evaluation Referral (2)

A. The client was referred for a speech and language evaluation.

B. The client was cooperative throughout the entire speech and language evaluation process.

C. Due to client resistance, the speech and language evaluation could not be completed.

D. With urging of the parents and the therapist, the client followed through with the speech and language evaluation with only minimal resistance.

3. Neurological/Neuropsychological Evaluation Referral (3)

A. The client was referred for neuropsychological testing to rule out organic factors.

B. With parent encouragement, the client followed through and completed the neurological evaluation.

C. Neuropsychological testing could not be completed as the client was not cooperative.

D. The parents were helped in seeing the need for neuropsychological testing.

4. Evaluation Feedback (4)

A. The parents were asked to sign appropriate releases of information in order for the therapist to consult with each evaluating specialist.

B. Results of the client's evaluations were obtained from the specialists.

C. The results and recommendations of the evaluations were given and explained to the parents.

D. The parents' questions were encouraged and answered regarding the evaluation results.

E. The parents were encouraged to follow through on all recommendations of each evaluation.

5. Psychiatric Evaluation Referral (5)

A. The client was referred for a psychiatric evaluation.

B. With the parents' assistance, the client followed through with and completed a psychiatric evaluation.

C. A psychiatric evaluation could not be completed as the client was uncooperative and nonverbal.

D. The parents made a verbal commitment to follow through on the recommendations of the psychiatric evaluation.

* The numbers in parentheses correlate to the number of the Therapeutic Intervention statement in the companion chapter with the same title in *The Adolescent Psychotherapy Treatment Planner* (Jongsma, Peterson, and McInnis) by John Wiley & Sons, 2000.

6. Complete an IEPC (6)

A. The parents were asked to request an IEPC for the client to become eligible to receive special education services.

B. IEPC was attended by the parents, teachers, therapist, and other interested professionals.

C. Goals and interventions for the client's educational program were revised by IEPC to enhance the success of the client in the school setting.

7. Design Effective Teaching Program (7)

A. The parents, teachers, and school officials were consulted for their input in designing an effective teaching program for the client.

B. Specific educational/behavioral interventions and assignments were identified that would build on the client's strengths and compensate for his/her weaknesses.

C. The parents and teacher assisted in designing and implementing an effective teaching program with the client.

D. The designed teaching plan was monitored for its effectiveness in building the client's strengths.

8. Explore Need for Alternative Placement (8)

A. The parents, school officials, and mental health professionals were consulted regarding the client's need for an alternative placement outside the home.

B. Placement options were explored with the parents and the client.

C. Measures short of alternative placement that were recommended by mental health professionals were implemented by the parents.

D. An alternative placement was located for the client and a plan for him/her to move into it was developed.

9. Speech/Language Therapy (9)

A. The client was referred to a speech and language pathologist.

B. The parents and the client have followed through on referral and have been regularly attending speech therapy sessions.

C. Client has been cooperative in speech and language therapy, and those skills are improving.

D. Speech therapy has not been effective, as the client remains uncooperative and resistant.

10. Build Trust (10)

A. Frequent attention, unconditional positive regard, and consistent eye contact are used to build a level of trust with the client.

B. An initial level of trust has been established with the client as he/she has increased verbalization with the therapist.

C. Despite use of warm acceptance, frequent attention, and unconditional positive regard, the client remains detached and rarely communicates directly with the therapist.

11. Increase Initiation of Verbalizations (11)

A. Praise and positive reinforcement were frequently used to attempt to increase the client's initiation of verbalization.

B. The use of praise and positive reinforcement have been successful in increasing the client's acknowledgment of and responsiveness to other's verbalizations.

C. Despite frequent praise and positive reinforcement, the client only on rare occasions initiates any verbalizations with others.

12. Facilitate Language Development (12)

A. The speech therapist assisted in designing and implementing a response-shaping program for the client that incorporates positive reinforcement principles.

B. The parents were trained in the response-shaping program and are implementing it with the client in their daily family life.

C. The client has cooperated with the response-shaping program and its positive reinforcement principle, and this has resulted in significant gains in his/her language skills.

D. The client has minimally embraced the response-shaping program, and this has resulted in only small gains in his/her language development.

13. Support Parental Language Development Efforts (13)

A. Encouragement, support, and reinforcement were given to the parents in their efforts to foster the client's language development.

B. Various modeling methods were demonstrated to the parents to aid them in their work in fostering the client's language development.

C. The parents' efforts in fostering language development in the client have produced noticeable gains.

D. Gains in language development were encouraged and reinforced with the client and the parents.

14. Teach Behavior Management Techniques (14)

A. Behavioral management techniques were taught to the parents to assist them in handling the client's difficult behaviors.

B. Plans were developed with the parents for implementing behavioral management techniques in their day-to-day parenting of the client.

C. Role-play and behavioral rehearsal techniques were used with the parents to give them the opportunity to practice new skills.

D. The parents were verbally reinforced for their consistent use of behavioral techniques.

E. Behavioral management techniques were reinforced and evaluated for their effectiveness with the client.

15. Design Token Economy (15)

A. The parents were assisted in designing a token economy and planning how to implement and administrate it.

B. The token economy was monitored for its effectiveness and to make any necessary adjustments.

C. The parents' effective, consistent implementation and administration of the token economy was reinforced with praise and encouragement.

D. The client's embracing of the token economy had produced improvement in his/her social skills, anger management, impulse control, and language development.

E. The client has resisted cooperating with the token economy system.

16. Parental Reward System (16)

A. A reward system was developed to assist the client in improving his/her social skills and anger control.

B. The parents were asked to make a verbal commitment to implementing and administering a reward system.

C. Rewards have had mixed results on improving the client's social skills and anger control.

17. Stop Self-Abuse with Aversive Techniques (17)

A. Aversive therapy techniques were used with the client to decrease self-abusive and self-stimulating behavior.

B. The parents were trained in aversive techniques and encouraged to implement them in their daily parenting.

C. Role play was used with the parents to give them opportunity to practice aversive techniques.

D. Self-abusive behaviors have decreased due to the use of aversive techniques.

18. Stop Self-Abuse with Positive Reinforcement (18)

A. The parents were assisted in developing positive reinforcement interventions to manage self-abusive behaviors.

B. The interventions developed by the parents to terminate client's self-abuse were implemented and monitored for their effectiveness.

C. New interventions of positive reinforcement and response cost have reduced the client's self-abuse behaviors.

D. The parents' effective interventions on self-abusive behavior were affirmed and reinforced.

19. Encourage Structured Family Interaction (19)

A. The family was encouraged to include structured work and playtimes with the client in their daily routine.

B. The parents developed and implemented structured work and playtimes with the client.

C. Structured playtimes and work times have improved the client's social initiation and interest in others.

20. Build Trust and Mutual Dependence (20)

A. A task was assigned to the client and the parents to foster trust and mutual dependence.

B. Parents and the client were able to identify activities they could do at home to build trust and mutual dependence.

C. Level of trust is building between the parents and the client as they continue to follow through on engaging in activities together regularly.

21. Involve Detached Parent (21)

A. Ways to involve the detached parent in interaction with the client were explored with him/her.

B. The detached parent was asked to spend ___ minutes (fill in number) daily with the client in social or physical interaction.

C. Despite efforts to increase his/her involvement, the detached parent has become only slightly more involved.

D. The detached parent was reminded of the importance of his/her involvement in the client's growth and development.

22. Educate Family on Developmental Disabilities (22)

A. The parents and family members were educated on the maturation process in individuals with autism and pervasive development disorders.

B. Challenges in the maturation process for the client were identified and processed with the parents and family members.

C. Unrealistic maturation expectations of parents and family members were confronted and addressed.

D. Realistic hope and encouragement were reinforced with respect to the client's maturation and development.

23. Use Respite Care (23)

A. Options for respite care were given and explained to the parents.

B. Advantages to using respite care were identified, and the parents were encouraged to use this resource regularly.

C. Resistance by the parents to respite care was confronted and resolved.

D. The parents were asked to develop a regular schedule for respite care.

24. Support Group Referral (24)

A. The parents' opinions and feelings about support groups were explored.

B. The parents were referred to and encouraged to attend a support group for families of an individual with a developmental disability.

C. The parents attended an autism/developmental disability support group and indicated they found the experience positive and helpful.

D. Despite encouragement, the parents have continued to be resistive to any involvement in an autism/developmental disability support group.

25. Autism Society of America Referral (25)

A. The parents were directed and encouraged to join the Autism Society of America to expand their knowledge of the disorder and to gain support and encouragement.

B. The parents have received helpful interaction and gained support and encouragement from their contact with the Autism Society of America.

C. The parents remain hesitant and noncommittal in seeking out support services.

26. Encourage Self-Care Skills (26)

A. Various ways to teach and develop self-care skills were processed with the parents.

B. The parents have committed to actively working with the client on a daily basis to teach and develop his/her self-care skills.

C. The parents' work with the client has produced significant gains in the client's hygiene and other self-care skills.

27. Monitor Self-Care Progress (27)

A. The client's progress in developing self-care skills was monitored and frequent feedback was provided to reinforce his/her progress.

B. Positive feedback on the client's achievement in self-care skills was verbally acknowledged by the client.

C. The parents were encouraged to keep working toward and reinforcing the client's progress in the area of self-care skills.

D. The client resistance toward developing self-care skills has decreased and his/her daily hygiene is visibly improving.

28. Refer for Vocational Training (28)

A. The client was referred to a vocational training program to develop basic job skills.

B. The client was cooperative in following through with his/her vocational training interview.

C. The positive aspects of a job training program were explored and reinforced with the client and the parents.

29. Enhance Independent Living Skills (29)

A. The client was referred to a life skills program to acquire skills to live independently.

B. The client has started to attend a life skills program to learn things necessary for independent activities of daily living (IADL).

C. The client has become actively involved in life skills program and is developing skills to live independently.

30. Camp Referral (30)

A. The client was referred to a summer camp to promote independence and to foster social contacts.

B. The client's camp experience was processed and the client's accomplishments in making social contacts were acknowledged and reinforced.

31. Redirect Preoccupation (31)

A. The client's preoccupation with objects and restricted areas of interests were redirected to more productive and socially involved activities.

B. The client's willingness and cooperation in trying new activities was affirmed and positively reinforced.

C. The client has accepted redirection and become actively engaged in several productive activities.

D. The client was reminded and redirected when he/she started again to become preoccupied with objects.

32. Family Review of Vocational Training (32)

A. The family was assisted in arranging interviews with school-based vocational programs.

B. The family followed through with the scheduled interviews.

C. The family processed the possible program for the client and reached a consensus on which program they felt was the best for him/her.

33. Family Acceptance of Client's Limits (33)

A. The parents were assisted in understanding and accepting the client's level of social/emotional age rather than his/her cognitive age.

B. Unrealistic perceptions and expectations regarding the client's level of functioning on the parents' part were confronted and processed.

C. The parents are now verbalizing more realistic expectations in regard to the client's level of functioning.

D. Despite education and processing, the parents continue to hold onto unrealistic expectations of the client in terms of functioning.

34. Address Family Resistance to Client Emancipation (34)

A. The parents were asked to make a list of concerns they have about the client living independently.

B. The parents' list of concerns about the client's emancipation was processed and feelings concerning independence were identified and expressed.

C. The parents have addressed their concerns and are starting to feel comfortable about the client living independently.

D. Concerns about the client's independent living were explored and processed; however, the parents remain fearful and resistant to such a move.

35. Develop Step Plan toward Independence (35)

A. The parents were assisted in developing a step program that will move the client toward living and working independently.

B. As the time approaches for a step program to be implemented that would make the client more independent, the parents have become less anxious about him/her living independently.

36. Implement Step Plan for Independence (36)

A. The parents are being guided and encouraged in implementing the step plan for the client's independent living.

B. The parents' follow-through plan for client's independence was monitored.

C. Encouragement was given to the client and the parents as they moved through the stages in moving toward independent living.

D. Parental resistance to working out the step plan for client independence were confronted and addressed.

37. Assess Independent Living Possibilities (37)

A. The family was assisted in exploring all the possible options of independent living arrangements.

B. Each independent living arrangement was visited and assessed for suitability to the client's needs and level of functioning.

C. The family was assisted in reaching a decision on the choice of independent living arrangements for the client.

BLENDED FAMILY

CLIENT PRESENTATION

1. Angry/Hostile (1)*

A. Anger and hostility have dominated the client's manner since the parents have blended their two families.

B. The client was extremely angry and hostile about having to be a part of the new blended family.

C. The client's level of anger and hostility has started to diminish as he/she has accepted being a part of the new blended family.

D. The client has dropped his/her anger and hostility and has become a cooperative member of the blended family.

2. Frustrated/Tense (1)

A. There was a deep sense of frustration and tension present in the client as he/she talked of the blended family situation.

B. The client reported being frustrated and tense about feeling pushed into a new blended family.

C. The client's level of tension has subsided as he/she is feeling more comfortable with the idea of being a part of a stepfamily.

3. Rejected/Betrayed (1)

A. The client reported feeling betrayed and rejected since his/her parents' remarriage.

B. The client has felt a sense of rejection and mistrust from the new stepparent.

C. The feelings of betrayal and rejection within the client have decreased, and he/she is beginning to form a cordial relationship with stepparent.

4. Resistant toward Stepparent (2)

A. The client presented in a defiant manner toward the stepparent.

B. In a defiant way, the client reported he/she will have no part of the new stepparent.

C. The client threatened to make it difficult for the new stepparent.

D. The client has dropped some of the resistance and seems to be warming a little to the new stepparent.

5. Defiant of Stepparent (2)

A. The client showed a pattern of making alliances and causing conflicts in an attempt to have a degree of control over the new stepparent.

B. The client reported no interest in taking direction or accepting limits from the stepparent.

---

* The numbers in parentheses correlate to the number of the Behavioral Definition statement in the companion chapter with same title in *The Adolescent Psychotherapy Treatment Planner* (Jongsma, Peterson, and McInnis) by John Wiley & Sons, 2000.

C. Gradually, the client has begun to give up his/her rebellion toward the stepparent and to accept some direction from him/her.

6. Stepsibling Conflict (3)

A. The siblings have engaged in ongoing conflict with one another.

B. The two sibling groups stated clearly their dislike and resentment for one another.

C. The parents indicated their frustration with the siblings' apparent attempt to sabotage their efforts to form a new family group.

D. The two sibling groups have stopped their open conflicts and started to tolerate and show basic respect for each other.

7. Defiance of Stepparent (4)

A. The client presented a negativistic, defiant attitude toward the stepparent.

B. The client seemed very closed and extremely resistant to the new stepparent.

C. The limited disclosures by the client reflected strong resistance to joining the new blended family.

D. The client has started to be a little open and a little warmer to the idea of being a member of the new blended family.

8. Threats of Moving to Other Parent's House (5)

A. The parents reported feeling like hostages to siblings' threats to move to the other parents' home whenever the children were crossed or told no.

B. The siblings presented as being ambivalent and manipulative regarding where they would like to live and why.

C. The siblings indicated they have changed their minds several times regarding where they want to reside and are presently still undecided.

D. The siblings have decreased their threats of going to other parents' home and have started to join the new family unit.

9. Ex-Spouse Interference (6)

A. Each spouse reported frequent incidents of interference in their new family by their ex-spouses.

B. Ex-spouse interference has caused ongoing conflict and upheaval in the new family unit.

C. Efforts to keep ex-spouses out of the new family business have been unsuccessful and sabotaged by the siblings.

D. Efforts to keep ex-spouses out of the daily life of the new family have started to be effective and the new family has started to solidify and become connected.

10. Parental Anxiety (7)

A. The client's parents presented with anxiety about the blending of their two families.

B. The parents seemed unsure about how to respond to issues being raised by the new blended family.

C. The parents looked for reassurance and some sense of security about how best to respond to blended family issues.

D. Parental anxiety has decreased as both parties have become more comfortable with working toward forming a new blended family.

11. Lack of Responsibility Definitions (8)

A. The family presented as very chaotic, lacking clear boundaries, rules, and responsibility definitions for members.

B. The parents reported they have struggled in their attempts to establish clear definitions of expectations for responsibility for family members.

C. Siblings indicated that they are not clear about their roles, responsibilities, or expectations in their new family.

D. The family has begun to develop and institute clear areas of responsibility for all members, which has also reduced the chaos and confusion for all.

12. Internal Loyalty Conflicts (9)

A. There seemed to be a great deal of ambivalence and uncertainty within the client about whether to attach himself/herself to the stepparent.

B. The client verbalized loyalty toward the biological, noncustodial parent.

C. The client reported fearing hurting the feelings of the biological, noncustodial parent if an attachment were to be made to the stepparent.

D. Internal conflicts have been resolved, and a sense of loyalty and belonging are beginning to develop between the client and stepparent.

INTERVENTIONS IMPLEMENTED

1. Build Trust and Express Feelings (1)*

A. Warm acceptance and active listening techniques were utilized to establish the basis for a trust relationship with the client.

B. The client seems to have formed a trust-based relationship with the therapist and has started to share his/her feelings.

C. Despite the use of active listening, warm acceptance, and unconditional positive regard, the client and family appear to be hesitant to trust the therapist and share their feelings and conflicts.

2. Address Family and Marital Issues (2)

A. Family sessions were conducted that focused on addressing and facilitating relationship building and joining rituals.

B. Each family member was asked to make a list of his/her recent losses to share with other members in a family session.

C. The parents were educated in the dynamics of stepfamilies and how they work.

D. Conflict negotiation skills were taught to family members and practiced in role-play situations particular to stepfamilies.

---

* The numbers in parentheses correlate to the number of the Therapeutic Intervention statement in the companion chapter with the same title in *The Adolescent Psychotherapy Treatment Planner* (Jongsma, Peterson, and McInnis) by John Wiley & Sons, 2000.

E. Family members have gained information and understanding about stepfamilies, learning to use negotiation skills and building relationships with each other.

3. Cooperative Family Drawing (3)

A. Each family member took part in interpreting and listening to others' interpretations of a drawing that was made through the cooperative effort of all family members.

B. All family members were willing to take part in making the family drawing, but were resistant to interpreting it.

C. The family drawing exercise revealed that the family members have a very difficult time cooperating with each other, as there was resistance to the exercise and bickering within the family during the exercise.

4. List Expectations for New Family (4)

A. Each family member was asked to list his/her expectations for the new family.

B. Each family member's list or expectations regarding the future of the blended family was shared and processed in family session, with common realistic expectations being affirmed and reinforced.

C. Unrealistic expectations of family members were gently confronted and reframed into more realistic and attainable expectations.

5. Remind Family That Instant Love Is a Myth (5)

A. The family was reminded of the myth of "instant love" between new members.

B. Family members' expectations of instant love and connections between blended family members were confronted with the reality that time is necessary for relationships to grow.

C. All the family members have become more realistic regarding the time necessary for meaningful relationships to develop between them.

6. Reinforce Kindness and Respect (6)

A. The family was reminded that new members need not love or like each other but that they need to treat each other with kindness and respect.

B. Family members were confronted when they failed to treat each other with kindness and respect.

C. The parents were taught ways to model respect and kindness for all members and to confront and give consequences for disrespectful interactions.

D. There is a discernable growth of respect and consideration between new family members that is being positively reinforced by the parents.

7. List Losses and Changes (7)

A. Each sibling was asked to make a list of all the losses and changes he/she had experienced in the last year.

B. Each sibling's list of losses was shared with other family members and similarities between each list were identified.

C. Reviewing each sibling's list of losses enhanced the degree of understanding and the feeling of similarity between the siblings.

8. Read *Changing Families* (8)

A. The family was asked to read *Changing Families* (Fassler, Lash, and Ives) to identify and reinforce the recent changes they each have experienced in family life.

B. The family members struggled to identify the losses and changes that they each had experienced even after reading *Changing Families.*

C. The family was reminded that change is an opportunity to grow and thrive, not just survive.

D. After reading *Changing Families,* the family members have a better understanding of the difficult process they have gone through recently in forming the blended family.

9. Play Games to Promote Self-Understanding (9)

A. The family was directed to play either The Ungame (Ungame Company) or the Thinking, Feeling, Doing Game (Gardner) to increase members' awareness of self and their feelings.

B. Expressions of self-awareness and identification of feelings were reinforced in family sessions.

C. The family members were very uncomfortable during the playing of therapeutic games together and most of them had significant difficulty in identifying and expressing feelings.

10. Educate Family Regarding Feelings (10)

A. The family was taught the basic concepts regarding identifying, labeling, and appropriately expressing their feelings.

B. Through the use of role playing and modeling, each family member was assisted in identifying, labeling, and expressing their feelings in family sessions.

C. Family members were prompted when they ignored or skipped over their feelings in dealing with family issues.

11. Practice Identifying and Expressing Feelings (11)

A. Various feelings exercises were used with the family to help expand their ability to identify and express feelings.

B. Positive affirmation was given to family members when they identified and expressed their feelings appropriately.

C. Each family member was confronted and reminded when they were not identifying and expressing their feelings.

12. Read Books on Blended Families (12)

A. The parents and teens were asked to read all or sections of *Stepfamily Realities* (Neuman) and *Stepfamilies Stepping Ahead* (Stepfamily Association of America) to expand their knowledge of stepfamily dynamics.

B. The parents and teens were encouraged to talk with other stepfamilies and to gather knowledge of their experience, past and present.

C. Parents and teens were asked to make a list of questions they had about stepfamilies and to process list with the therapist.

D. Reading books on blended families and talking to other people who have experienced successful blending of families has helped members gather information and develop understanding of the blending process.

13. Stepfamily Association Referral (13)

A. The parents were referred to the Stepfamily Association of America in order to gather information on the process of blending families.

B. Information gathered from the Stepfamily Association of America was processed and incorporated into a more realistic view of the reality of stepfamilies.

C. The reality of stepfamilies not being inferior to regular families, just different, was introduced along with the new information the parents received from Stepfamily Association of America.

D. The parents have not followed through on obtaining further information from the Stepfamily Association of America and were again encouraged to do so.

14. Read *How to Win as a Stepfamily* (14)

A. The parents were asked to read *How to Win as a Stepfamily* (Visher and Visher).

B. Key concepts from the parents' reading of *How to Win as a Stepfamily* were identified and reinforced.

C. Several ideas learned from reading *How to Win as a Stepfamily* were implemented by the parents in their present situations.

D. The parents have not completed the assignment to read the book *How to Win as a Stepfamily* and were encouraged to do so.

15. Build Negotiating Skills (15)

A. The family members were taught essential negotiating skills.

B. Role play was utilized to give family members the opportunity to practice new skills in negotiating conflicts.

C. Family members tried out their new negotiation skills in a family session on a present family conflict.

D. The family struggled to stay with negotiating skills in the family sessions, and they often reverted to arguing and attacking each other.

16. "Negotiating a Peace Treaty" Exercise (16)

A. The siblings were asked to complete and process the "Negotiating a Peace Treaty" exercise from *The Brief Adolescent Therapy Homework Planner* (Jongsma, Peterson, and McInnis).

B. Through the use of the "Negotiating a Peace Treaty" exercise, the clients were assisted in identifying their conflicts and exploring a variety of solutions.

C. The siblings were asked to select, commit to, and implement one of the solutions they identified in the negotiation exercise.

D. The siblings' completion of the negotiation exercise revealed how far apart they are in terms of having any common ground.

17. Use Humor to Decrease Tension (17)

A. Humor was injected into sessions when it was appropriate to decrease tension and to model balance and perspective.

B. Family members were directed to each tell one joke daily to other family members.

C. Positive feedback was given to family members who created appropriate humor during a session.

D. Family members have extreme difficulty being light and humorous toward each other, as tension levels are high and teasing is reacted to angrily.

18. "Cloning the Perfect Sibling" Exercise (18)

A. Siblings were asked to complete the "Cloning the Perfect Sibling" exercise from *The Brief Adolescent Therapy Homework Planner* (Jongsma, Peterson, and McInnis).

B. In processing the cloning exercise, siblings were assisted in identifying and affirming the positive aspects of individual differences.

C. Siblings continued to argue and bicker with each other, complaining about unique traits and characteristics.

19. Normalize Conflict as a Stage (19)

A. A brief solution-focused intervention was utilized with the family to "normalize" conflict as a stage.

B. Family members were assisted in identifying the next stage after conflict and how they might begin to move in that direction.

C. The intervention of normalizing the conflict as a stage has, according to family reports, reduced the frequency of conflicts.

D. The family was unwilling to embrace any reframing or normalizing interventions.

20. Read *Stone Soup* (20)

A. *Stone Soup* (Brown) was read and processed with family.

B. After reading *Stone Soup,* the family members were asked to list all the possible positive things that come about when people cooperate and share.

21. Read *The Sneetches* (21)

A. *The Sneetches* (Dr. Suess) was read and discussed with family.

B. The folly of perceiving people as top dog, low dog and insider, outsider was seeded with family members.

C. Family members were asked to list each way they felt better than or superior to new members.

22. Primary Parenting Role for Biological Parent (22)

A. The parents were educated in the positive aspects of each biological parent taking the main role with their children.

B. The parents were assisted in developing ways to redirect the parenting of the step-children.

C. The parents were asked to refrain from all negative references to ex-spouses.

D. Incidents of a parent making negative references to ex-spouses were confronted and processed.

23. Parenting Group Referral (23)

A. The parents were referred to a parenting group designed for stepparents.
B. The parents were assisted in implementing new concepts that were learned from the parenting group.
C. The parents were confronted on their poor attendance at the stepparenting group.

24. Institute Family Meeting (24)

A. The parents were assisted in developing a process for and scheduling a weekly family meeting.
B. Family meetings were monitored and the parents were assisted in solving conflictual issues.
C. The parents were given positive verbal support and encouragement for their follow-through on implementing weekly family meetings.
D. The parents have not followed through on implementing regularly scheduled meetings, and a commitment for this scheduling was obtained from them.

25. Develop Family Rituals (25)

A. The positive aspects of family rituals were taught to the parents.
B. The parents were asked to develop a list of possible rituals for their new family unit.
C. The parents were assisted in selecting family rituals and developing a plan for their implementation.
D. Family rituals were monitored for their implementation and effectiveness.
E. Verbal affirmation and encouragement were given to the parents for their effort to implement and enforce new family rituals.

26. Select Past Family Rituals (26)

A. Members were asked to make a list of rituals that were followed in their previous family.
B. Rituals from previous families were discussed and key rituals were chosen to implement in the new family.
C. Plans were developed to implement the chosen rituals from previous families.
D. Family members were assisted in establishing the new rituals and making the necessary adjustments to increase their effectiveness.

27. Create Birthday Rituals (27)

A. The family was given the assignment of creating new birthday rituals for the new family.
B. The parents were asked to implement the new birthday rituals at the first opportunity.
C. The value of birthday rituals was reinforced with the parents.
D. A new birthday ritual has been implemented, and the family members have responded very favorably to this recognition of their special status.

28. Teach Patterns of Family Interactions (28)

A. The parents were taught key aspects and patterns of family interaction.

B. Past family interaction patterns were explored and identified, with a special focus on those involving triangulation.

C. The parents were assisted in blocking patterns of triangulation that are occurring within the family.

D. The episodes of triangulation within the family have diminished significantly.

29. Identify Triangulation Interaction with Parents (29)

A. A genogram was developed with the family that identified interaction patterns between members.

B. Triangulation patterns of interaction were identified from the genogram, and plans were developed with the parents to break those patterns.

C. Implementation of plans to break triangulation was monitored and evaluated for effectiveness.

D. The parents were reminded when they were observed creating or using triangulation with the family.

E. The episodes of triangulation within the family have diminished significantly.

30. Marital Therapy Referral (30)

A. The parents were referred to a skills-based marital therapy program.

B. Gains made in marital therapy were affirmed and reinforced with the parents.

C. The parents were asked to identify the gains they achieved in the skills-based therapy program and how they would improve parenting.

31. Identify Individual Parental Needs (31)

A. The parents were assisted in exploring and identifying their individual needs within the relationship and family.

B. The needs of each partner were recognized and affirmed, and plans were developed for meeting these needs on a consistent basis.

C. The parents were confronted when they failed to take care of their individual needs and did not follow through on the plans developed to do this.

D. The importance of meeting individual needs in a relationship was reinforced with the parents.

32. Process Sharing of Affection (32)

A. The ways the parents show affection to each other were explored with them in a conjoint session.

B. The negative aspects of blatant displays of parental physical affection were processed with them.

C. The parents were assisted in developing appropriate ways to show affection to each other when in the presence of their children.

D. Blatant displays of affection between the parents were confronted, reminding them of the negative impact this could have on their children.

33. Draw Family Genogram (33)

A. A genogram was developed with the family that contained all members and how they are connected.

B. From the genogram, the family was asked to identify the ways in which they see themselves being connected.

C. Constructing the family genogram revealed that some family members are virtually unconnected to other family members, and ways to reverse this fact were discussed.

34. Coat-of-Arms Exercise (34)

A. The family was asked to create a coat of arms for their new family by drawing a collage on posterboard.

B. The experience of creating the coat of arms was processed with the family with both old and new identities being acknowledged and reinforced.

C. The parents were asked to display the coat of arms in their new home.

35. Initiatives Camp (35)

A. The family was asked to attend an initiatives weekend to build trust, cooperation, and conflict-resolution skills of each family member.

B. The initiatives experience was processed with the family with each member identifying the positive gains they received from the weekend.

C. The family was assisted in identifying how they could continue to use and expand the gains from the weekend.

36. "Cost-Benefit Analysis" Exercise (36)

A. The family was asked to complete "Cost-Benefit Analysis" (in *Ten Days to Self-Esteem* by Burns) to evaluate a plus-and-minus system of becoming a blended family.

B. The "Cost-Benefit Analysis" exercise was processed, with the positives of joining the family being emphasized.

C. Family members' resistance to working together and accepting one another was confronted using the positive items identified in the "Cost-Benefit Analysis."

37. Plan One-on-One Time (37)

A. The parents were encouraged to build time into their schedules for one-on-one contact with each child and stepchild.

B. The parents were reminded of the importance of taking the time to build parent-child relationships.

38. Emphasize That Relationships Build Slowly (38)

A. Allowing relationships to build slowly was emphasized to the family in family sessions.

B. Ways to build trust in relationships were explored with the parents to help them slowly build relationships with stepchildren.

C. The parents' exhibiting patience in allowing relationships to build was verbally reinforced.

CHEMICAL DEPENDENCE

CLIENT PRESENTATION

1. Substance Use (1)*

A. The client reported using a mood-altering substance frequently throughout a month and regularly using until intoxicated or high.

B. The client indicated that on at least two occasions, he/she was caught high or drunk.

C. The client, friends, family, and others have confronted him/her or expressed concern about his/her substance use.

D. The client has stopped all substance use and now is starting to admit to himself/herself that it was a problem.

2. Caught/Observed High or Intoxicated (2)

A. The parents indicated that they have observed the client visibly intoxicated on numerous occasions in recent months.

B. The school officials have caught the client being high on two occasions in recent months.

C. The client reported that parents and school officials have caught him/her both high and intoxicated on at least two occasions in recent months.

D. The client reported that he/she has not been high or intoxicated in months, and this self-report has been corroborated by authority figures.

3. Peer Group (3)

A. The client described changing his/her peer group to one that was "cooler and more fun."

B. The client reported losing positive friends due to his/her recent issues with the law and other authority figures.

C. The client indicated he/she was upset that the parents and old friends were labeling his/her new friends as "druggies and losers."

D. The client has dropped his/her substance-using friends and reestablished his/her connection with a more positive peer group.

4. Possession of Alcohol/Drug Paraphernalia (4)

A. The client has been caught with drug paraphernalia both at home and at school.

B. The client reported being recently caught by parents with alcohol in his/her bedroom.

C. The client indicated that he/she has disposed of all his/her drug paraphernalia.

D. The client reported that he/she no longer keeps an alcohol stash at home, in his/her car, or at school.

---

* The numbers in parentheses correlate to the number of the Behavioral Definition statement in the companion chapter with same title in *The Adolescent Psychotherapy Treatment Planner* (Jongsma, Peterson, and McInnis) by John Wiley & Sons, 2000.

5. Behavioral Changes (5)

A. The client reported that he/she has been avoiding formerly close friends and keeping a distance from family members.

B. The client indicated that he/she has been sleeping a lot lately and seems to always feel tired.

C. The parents reported that the client has shown a loss of interest in most activities and has had a low energy level.

D. The client reported he/she used to be outgoing and socially active, but now prefers to spend most of his/her time alone because others bother him/her.

E. The parents reported a significant drop in the client's grades in past months.

F. The client has gradually returned to more positive social interaction and academic success since stopping all substance use.

6. Physical Withdrawal Symptoms (6)

A. The client has experienced shaking, nausea, sweating, and headaches when withdrawing from alcohol.

B. The client reported that his/her withdrawal symptoms of sweating, anxiety, and insomnia have gradually subsided and are now very minimal.

C. The client indicated he/she is no longer experiencing withdrawal symptoms and is remaining alcohol free.

7. Continued Substance Use Despite Negative Consequences (7)

A. Despite legal and family problems, the client has continued to use alcohol and illicit drugs.

B. The client reported losing several longtime friendships because he/she liked to party too much, but this has not deterred his/her substance abuse.

C. The client has experienced financial, school, family, and legal problems, all directly related to his/her alcohol and/or drug use, but none of these consequences has stopped him/her from using.

D. The client has started to acknowledge that his/her negative consequences are directly due to his/her substance use.

8. Denial (7)

A. The client reported that he/she has not had any major problems due to his/her use of substances.

B. The client indicated that his/her difficulties at school—skipping classes and falling grades—were due to being bored and denied that they were related to substance use.

C. The client believes the parents and others are not aware of his/her substance use.

D. The client's level of denial has begun to decrease, and he/she has acknowledged more of his/her alcohol/drug use and its effect on his/her life.

9. Mood Swings (8)

A. The client reported rapid, sudden mood swings.

B. The client indicated that others have told him/her they do not know what to expect given how quickly his/her mood can change.

C. The parents reported that the client can suddenly become defensive, angry, and withdrawn.

D. The client's mood swings have been less frequent and less severe since he/she stopped use of all substances.

10. School Issues (9)

A. There has been a reported, unexplainable drop in the client's grades.

B. The client reported skipping school and being tardy and absent on a regular basis.

C. The client has been expelled from school for being high and drunk on several occasions.

D. All school issues have subsided or improved since the client stopped all substance use.

11. Low Self-Esteem (10)

A. The client reported feeling like a total loser and inadequate in most areas.

B. The client indicated he/she rarely looks at or makes eye contact with others when speaking to them.

C. The client described himself/herself in totally negative terms.

D. The client has begun to make eye contact and verbalize positive things about himself/herself.

E. The client has started to connect his/her low self-esteem and his/her substance abuse.

F. The client's self-image has improved as abstinence from substance abuse continues.

12. Negative/Hostile (11)

A. The client presented in a negative, hostile manner.

B. The client's views of life, others, and the world have been very negative and hostile.

C. The client has virtually nothing good to say about anything or anyone.

D. The client has started to have positive, as well as negative, things to say about life, others, and the world.

13. Stealing Alcohol (12)

A. The client has been caught stealing alcohol on several occasions.

B. The parents reported that the client was caught stealing alcohol from them on numerous occasions.

C. The client confessed to stealing alcohol from wherever and whomever he/she could.

14. Legal Conflicts (13)

A. The client has been caught stealing alcohol from stores and friends' parents' homes.

B. The client reported illegal drug and alcohol consumption that dated back to his/her early teens.

C. The client reported that he/she is currently on probation for DUIL and MIP charges.

D. There seemed to be present with the client a consistent disregard for laws, rules, and authority figures.

E. The client's behavior and talk has started to reflect some respect for the law and a willingness to consistently obey laws.

15. Family (14)

A. The client reported a positive history of chemical dependence in the immediate and extended family.

B. The client stated that his/her family has always believed you can't have fun without alcohol.

C. The family indicated that they think all kids go through a phase of experimenting a little with alcohol and drugs.

D. The client and family have become more open and honest about the substance abuse problems within the family.

INTERVENTIONS IMPLEMENTED

1. Chemical Dependence Evaluation (1)*

A. A complete chemical dependence evaluation was conducted with the client.

B. The client followed through and completed the arranged chemical dependence evaluation.

C. The client was cooperative with all areas of the evaluation.

D. The client was uncooperative throughout the evaluation, providing only limited information.

E. The results of the evaluation, which confirmed a chemical dependence problem, were reported and explained to the client.

2. Explore Nature of Substance Use (2)

A. The client's history, nature, and frequency of substance abuse was explored.

B. Attempts to explore the client's history, nature, and frequency of substance abuse was met with resistance and minimization.

C. The client's denial in revealing the nature, history, and frequency of use in particular areas of his/her substance abuse was confronted and further probed.

D. Positive verbal feedback was given to the client for his/her willingness to explore and reveal aspects of his/her substance abuse.

E. The evaluation of the client's substance abuse pattern confirms a chemical dependence problem.

3. Group Therapy Self-Disclosure (3)

A. The client was asked to discuss in group therapy the pattern of his/her substance abuse.

B. The client was encouraged and supported in discussing the pattern of his/her use in group therapy sessions.

C. The client discussed the pattern of his/her substance use with the group and received their feedback in an open manner.

D. The client talked about his/her pattern of substance use in the group but was not open to hearing their feedback.

* The numbers in parentheses correlate to the number of the Therapeutic Intervention statement in the companion chapter with the same title in *The Adolescent Psychotherapy Treatment Planner* (Jongsma, Peterson, and McInnis) by John Wiley & Sons, 2000.

E. The client reported that he/she has not shared much information in the group therapy sessions.

4. Confront Chemical Dependence (4)

A. The client's denial was confronted with the facts of how his/her use has dominated his/her life and the many negative consequences the use has brought.

B. Denial was normalized as a part of the disease and then gently but firmly probed to increase honesty and acceptance.

C. Through the use of respectful confrontation and genuine warmth the client's denial has changed to acceptance of the fact he/she is chemically dependent.

D. In spite of confrontation with the facts and negative consequences of his/her use, the client remains in denial regarding the seriousness of this chemical dependence problem.

5. Complete First-Step Paper (5)

A. The client was asked to write an AA first-step paper and then present it to the therapist or group.

B. The client completed the AA first-step paper, presented it to the therapist/group, and received their feedback.

C. The client was confronted on his/her failure to complete the AA first-step paper.

D. The client marginally completed his/her AA first-step paper after numerous reminders from the therapist.

E. The client's AA first-step paper was completed but still showed significant denial of his/her powerlessness over substance use.

F. The client completed the AA first-step paper, and it shows an open, honest appraisal of the seriousness of his/her substance abuse.

6. Arrange For/Monitor Drug Screens (6)

A. Regular drug screening was arranged for and explained to the client.

B. The client was monitored for his/her compliance with submitting to drug screens as arranged.

C. The client was confronted on his/her failure to submit to the drug screening as arranged.

D. The results of the drug screens, which confirmed that no drugs have been consumed, were given to the client.

E. The drug screen results, indicating recent drug abuse, were presented to the client.

7. Genogram of Chemical Dependence (7)

A. A genogram was developed with the family showing patterns of chemical dependence within the family.

B. Patterns of chemical dependence within the family, as identified in the genogram, were explored further with the family to increase their awareness and to help the client see the repetitive cycle of substance abuse.

C. The family was taught the need to change family patterns that support continued substance abuse.

8. Evaluation Feedback (8)

A. The recommendations of the chemical dependence evaluation, which confirmed a substance abuse problem, were presented to the client and family and compliance was encouraged.

B. Barriers to any recommendation were identified and addressed with the family and the client.

C. Benefits from each recommendation were identified and reinforced to encourage compliance.

D. The client was in denial about the confirmation of a substance-abuse problem and refused to accept the recommendations of the chemical dependence evaluation.

9. Negative Impact of Substance Abuse (9)

A. The client was asked to list all the negative consequences that have resulted from his/her substance abuse.

B. The client's list of the ways substance abuse has had a negative impact was processed, and each negative impact was reinforced with him/her.

C. The client's list of negative impacts of his/her substance abuse was processed, and the shortness of the list was confronted as denial on his/her part.

10. Treatment Program and Support Group (10)

A. Options for treatment programs and support groups were explored with the client and family to identify the most appropriate ones for them.

B. The client and family were assisted in selecting the most appropriate treatment program for the client and support groups for the family.

C. Encouragement was given to the client and family on following through with the selections they made for treatment and support.

11. Construct Sobriety Agreement (11)

A. The family and the client were assisted in developing a sobriety agreement for the client to refrain from all substance use.

B. The client was asked to agree to the contract and to having his/her compliance monitored.

C. The client refused to agree to the sobriety agreement as he/she felt everyone should just trust him/her.

12. Sign Agreement to Terminate Use (12)

A. A contract to terminate all substance use was developed and signed by the client.

B. The client agreed to the specifics of how the contract would be monitored.

C. The client indicted he/she is committed to not using substances but would not sign the contract.

D. The client's refusal to sign the agreement to terminate use was confronted and addressed with him/her.

13. Group Referral (13)

A. The client was assigned and encouraged to attend and participate in group therapy sessions as scheduled.

B. The client's attendance and participation in group therapy was regularly reinforced and monitored.

C. The client was confronted on his/her failure to attend group therapy sessions on a regular basis.

14. Didactic Session Referral (14)

A. The client was assigned to attend a chemical dependence didactic session to increase his/her knowledge of patterns and effects of chemical dependency.

B. Didactic sessions were processed with the client and key points he/she obtained from sessions were reinforced.

15. Attendance at Didactic (15)

A. The client was required to attend all chemical dependence didactic sessions and identify key points to process with the therapist from each.

B. Key points the client identified from each didactic were processed and reinforced with the client.

C. The client was confronted with his/her failure to attend the required chemical dependence didactic and was reminded of the importance of his/her attendance.

16. Read Information on Marijuana (16)

A. The client was asked to read information such as the Ohm pamphlet on marijuana and identify key points from the reading to process.

B. Key points identified by the client from the readings on marijuana were processed, with negative consequences being reinforced.

C. The client refused to read information on marijuana despite the encouragement.

17. Feedback from Significant Others (17)

A. The client was assigned to ask two or three people who were close to him/her to write a letter about how chemical dependence has had a negative impact on the client's life.

B. Letters received from friends about the negative impact of chemical dependence in the client's life were processed to reinforce and identify the negative impact of the chemical dependence.

C. The client was reminded that much of the negative impact is not seen by the user and that this helps to keep the usage going.

18. Assign Good-Bye Letter to Drug of Choice (18)

A. The purpose and possible benefit from a goodbye letter written to the drug of choice was discussed with the client.

B. The client was asked to write a good-bye letter to his/her drug of choice and process completed letter with the therapist.

C. The completed good-bye letter was processed, pointing out key areas where the client was still hanging onto the drug.

D. The client's completed good-bye was processed, and feedback was given to him/her that the effort seemed halfhearted and raised questions about commitment to abstinence.

19. Assess for Depression and Low Self-Esteem (19)

A. The client's level of depression and self-esteem were assessed.

B. The results and recommendations of the assessment were given and explained to the client.

C. The client was given a referral for treatment of his/her mood disorder.

D. The possible connections between the client's depression and low self-esteem and his/her substance use were explored.

E. Because the client showed evidence of depression existing prior to beginning substance abuse, the mood disorder was made a focal point of treatment.

20. Solicit Letters of Recommendation (20)

A. The client was asked to provide the names of three people whom he/she would ask to write positive letters of recommendation for him/her.

B. The client's letters of recommendation were read and processed, with each positive attribute being affirmed and reinforced.

C. The client was confronted with his/her discounting of positive attributes or accomplishments found in the letters of recommendation.

21. Assign Mirror Exercise (21)

A. The client was assigned a mirror exercise to do daily, recording what he/she sees.

B. The mirror exercise and the client's recordings were processed, with each attribute identified by the client being positively affirmed.

C. Issues about the client's self-esteem that were raised by the exercise were addressed and resolved.

22. Experiential Camp Referral (22)

A. A referral was made for the client and his/her family to attend an experiential camp to build members' sense of trust, self-confidence, and connectedness.

B. The experiential weekend experience was processed, and gains were specifically identified and affirmed.

C. Ways to carry forward the gains from the camp experience were explored with the family.

D. The family has not followed through with their commitment to attend an experiential camp.

23. AA Group Referral (23)

A. The different types of AA/NA support meetings were explained to the client.

B. The client was directed to attend a NA or Young People's AA meeting and report on the experience to the therapist.

C. The AA support group experience was processed, with benefits and possible liabilities being identified and affirmed.

D. The client was asked to make a commitment to attend an AA support group on a regular basis.

E. The client has not followed through with the recommendation to attend an AA support group.

24. Meet with AA Member (24)

A. The client was directed to meet with experienced AA/NA members to elicit from them specific things they did that helped them stay sober, after which he/she would process findings with the therapist.

B. Information gathered from the experienced AA/NA members by the client was processed and key ideas were developed for use in the client's own recovery.

C. The client has not followed through with making contact with an AA member.

25. "Welcome to Recovery" Exercise (25)

A. The client was asked to complete the exercise "Welcome to Recovery" from *The Brief Adolescent Therapy Homework Planner* (Jongsma, Peterson, and McInnis) to increase knowledge and familiarity with the terms and process of recovery.

B. The client completed the recovery exercise, and his/her questions regarding the terms and process of recovery were answered.

C. The client failed to complete the recovery exercise and it was reassigned.

26. Read AA *Big Book* (26)

A. The client was asked to read portions of the AA *Big Book* and process key ideas with the therapist.

B. Key ideas selected by the client from his/her reading of AA material were processed and his/her understanding of AA recovery process was expanded.

C. The client was reminded of the importance of reading AA material to understanding, implementing, and working on a recovery program.

D. The client did not read the AA material or the *Big Book*.

27. Find Sponsors and Meet Regularly (27)

A. The client was encouraged to find two sponsors and meet with them regularly.

B. The client has found two sponsors and is beginning to meet regularly with each on a one-on-one basis.

C. The client has not found a sponsor despite encouragement and leads.

D. The client's use of sponsors was monitored and the experience was processed to identify and reinforce the benefits to his/her recovery.

28. Teach "Stop, Think, Listen, and Plan" (28)

A. The basic concepts of "stop, think, listen, and plan before acting" were taught to the client.

B. Role play, modeling, and behavioral rehearsal were used to develop the client's skill and confidence in using the "stop, think, listen, and plan before acting" technique.

C. The client was encouraged to put the "stop, think, listen, and plan before acting" technique to use in day-to-day interactions.

D. The client reported that using the "stop, think, listen, and plan" technique has been helpful in several daily situations.

29. Consequences of "Stop, Think, Listen, and Plan" (29)

A. A review of "stop, think, listen, and plan" techniques was conducted with the client to assess its day-to-day effectiveness.

B. The client reported that using the technique has been helpful in several daily situations.

C. The client was assisted in specifically identifying the day-to-day positive consequences of using the "stop, think, listen, and plan" technique.

D. The client was encouraged to use the impulse control technique more often and more consistently in daily life.

30. Review Consequences of Impulsiveness (30)

A. The client was asked to make a list of all the negative consequences of his/her impulsiveness as it related to substance abuse.

B. The impact of the client's impulsiveness on substance abuse was recognized and reinforced.

C. The client was reminded of the impulsive nature of substance abuse.

31. Connections between Impulsiveness and Consequences (31)

A. The client was assisted in making connections between his/her impulsiveness and past negative consequences.

B. The client was reminded of the connections between impulsiveness and negative consequences.

C. The client was helped to recognize triggers that led to his/her impulsive actions.

32. Dangers of Acting Impulsively (32)

A. The client was assisted in identifying specifically the various dangers of acting impulsively.

B. The client was helped in developing strategies to stop his/her impulsiveness.

C. The client was asked to make a list of negative consequences he/she experienced due to impulsive actions to serve as a reminder.

33. Impulsivity Connected to Substance Abuse (33)

A. The client's impulsive actions that resulted in substance abuse and negative consequences were explored.

B. The client was assisted in making a connection between impulsive actions and substance abuse.

C. Strategies were developed to assist the client in controlling his/her impulsivity.

34. Refer and Monitor Acupuncture Treatment (34)

A. The possible benefits of acupuncture for the client were explored and identified.

B. The client was referred to an acupuncturist for regular treatment.

C. Acupuncture treatment was monitored for client compliance and its overall effectiveness.

D. The client was confronted on his/her inconsistent follow-through with acupuncture treatment.

E. The client reported that the acupuncture treatment has reduced his/her urge to engage in substance abuse.

35. Psychiatric Evaluation Referral (35)

A. The client was referred for a psychiatric evaluation to establish or rule out an underlying psychiatric disorder.

B. The client was cooperative with all aspects of psychiatric evaluation.

C. The purpose of the client having a psychiatric evaluation was explained to him/her and all questions he/she had were answered.

D. The results and recommendations of the evaluation, which confirmed client's mood disorder, were shared.

36. Monitor Medication Regime (36)

A. The client's psychotropic medications were monitored for compliance, possible side effects, and overall effectiveness.

B. The psychotropic medication regime was explained to the client and all of his/her questions concerning the psychotropic medication were answered.

C. The client was asked to report any side effects to the parents or the therapist and to give feedback on the medication's effectiveness.

D. The client was confronted on his/her failure to take the medication as prescribed.

E. The prescribing psychiatrist was consulted regarding the client's compliance with taking the psychotropic medications and the overall effectiveness of the medications on the client's condition.

F. The client has consistently taken the psychotropic medication prescribed and reported an elevation in mood and a reduction in the urge for substance abuse.

37. Friendships with Nonusing Peers (37)

A. The importance of drug-free peer friendships was emphasized with the client.

B. The client was assisted in planning ways to develop friendships with drug-free peers who will support his/her sobriety.

C. The client's fears regarding peer relationships with clean and sober individuals were explored, processed, and resolved.

D. The client was disinterested in exploring the possibility of friendships with drug-free peers.

E. The client has begun to reach out to drug-free peers and establish a social network that will support his/her sobriety.

38. Encourage Extracurricular Activities (38)

A. The positive social advantages of extracurricular activities to the client and his/her sobriety were identified.

B. The client was made aware of social, athletic, and artistic opportunities and was encouraged to join at least one.

C. The client was taught that extracurricular activities with a sober peer group can play a key role in his/her efforts to stay sober.

D. The client was asked to make a commitment to try one extracurricular activity for at least a week.

E. The client has followed through with increasing his/her involvement in extracurricular activities with a positive peer group.

F. The client has not followed through and continues to avoid social activities with a positive peer group.

39. Build Relationship and Assertiveness Skills (39)

A. Role play was used to build the client's relationship and assertiveness skills in a variety of social situations.

B. The client was educated in key components of forming open, honest, and trusting relationships with peers.

C. The client was given guidance and role-play practice in saying no to peers who would encourage him/her to use.

D. The client reported that he/she is interacting more with peers and that he/she has rejected invitations to resume substance abuse.

40. Process Feelings of Rejection (40)

A. The client's feelings of rejection were identified and expressed.

B. The client's feelings of peer rejection and loss were processed.

C. The client was assisted in developing an awareness of the relapse risk involved with unresolved feelings of rejection.

D. The client denied any feelings of rejection that need processing.

41. Cope with Family Triggers (41)

A. Family conflicts that are potential relapse triggers were identified by the client and processed.

B. The client was assisted in developing specific strategies to cope with family dynamics that are relapse triggers.

C. The client was encouraged and supported in his/her implementation of the new coping strategies to cope with family dynamics that are relapse triggers.

D. The specific coping strategies were monitored for client follow-through, needed guidance and encouragement, and overall effectiveness.

E. The client reported that implementation of the coping strategies for family conflict has been successful in reducing his/her impulse to use substance abuse as an escape.

42. Read *It Will Never Happen to Me* (42)

A. The client was asked to read the book *It Will Never Happen to Me* (Black) and process key points with the therapist.

B. The client processed key points from reading the book and identified how he/she has been affected by chemical dependency in his/her family.

C. The client was reminded and encouraged to work at breaking the three rules of chemically dependent families: Don't talk, don't feel, don't trust.

43. Relapse Group Referral (43)

A. The client was directed to attend a lecture series on relapse.

B. The client's knowledge of relapse was explored and expanded.

C. The client has begun attending a relapse group and has demonstrated increased knowledge in this area.

D. The client has not followed through on attending the relapse group as recommended.

44. Relapse Signs/Triggers (44)

A. The client was assisted in developing a list of potential relapse signs and triggers that could lead him/her back to substance abuse.

B. A specific strategy for constructively responding to each of the potential relapse triggers was developed.

C. The client reported that implementation of the coping strategies for the relapse triggers has been successful.

D. The client failed to use a constructive coping strategy when he/she encountered a relapse-triggering situation, and this led to a brief relapse.

45. "Keeping Straight" Exercise (45)

A. The client was assigned the "Keeping Straight" exercise from *The Brief Adolescent Therapy Homework Planner* (Jongsma, Peterson, and McInnis) to help him/her in identifying relapse triggers.

B. The client reported that completing the "Keeping Straight" assignment was beneficial in identifying relapse triggers.

C. The client failed to follow through on completing the "Keeping Straight" exercise.

D. Coping strategies were developed for each of the relapse triggers that were identified through the "Keeping Straight" exercise.

46. Relapse Prevention Plan (46)

A. The client was given the assignment to write out a personalized relapse prevention plan that would include the treatment group and social support systems that would be implemented.

B. The client's relapse prevention plan was processed and he/she was given support for a constructive plan of prevention.

C. The client failed to follow through with the assignment of writing a personalized relapse prevention plan, and this assignment was repeated.

D. The client has reported that he/she has shared his/her personal relapse prevention plan with his/her sponsor and found support for it.

47. Develop Aftercare Plan (47)

A. The client was educated on the essential components of an aftercare program.

B. The client was asked to write an aftercare plan and then process the plan with the therapist and family.

C. The client's written aftercare plan was presented to the therapist and his/her family to inform them of his/her plan and to receive their input and feedback.

D. The family and therapist's input and feedback were incorporated by the client into his/her revised aftercare plan.

E. The client was assisted in implementing his/her aftercare plan, with the importance of follow-through being reinforced.

48. Design and Implement a Daily Schedule (48)

A. The benefits of keeping a daily schedule in maintaining sobriety were identified with the client.

B. The client was assisted in developing and implementing a healthy, daily schedule of meals, sleep, exercise, and school responsibilities.

C. The client's resistance to developing a daily schedule was confronted and addressed in terms of negative consequences.

D. The client was given encouragement and positive affirmation in his/her efforts to stick to the daily schedule.

49. Identify Thinking Errors (49)

A. The client was educated on the distorted thinking process that is involved in chemical dependence.

B. The client was assisted in identifying his/her "thinking errors" and how they play a role in relapse.

C. Plans were developed and implemented by the client to effectively avoid his/her thinking errors.

D. The client reported that he/she has encountered thinking errors, but because of being sensitized to them, they have lost their impact.

50. "Stinking Thinking" Assignment (50)

A. The client was asked to bring up the topic of "stinking thinking" at an AA/NA meeting and in a one-on-one contact with sponsor and then process information gained with the therapist.

B. The client shared the knowledge he/she gathered from AA and his/her sponsor about stinking thinking.

C. The client was reminded of the importance of remembering the key information about stinking thinking to prevent relapse.

51. "The Three Little Pigs" Metaphor (51)

A. The story of "The Three Little Pigs" was read and processed with the client to emphasize the key aspects in relapse: recovery of planning, delayed gratification, and frustration tolerance.

B. The client was helped in identifying the "Big Bad Wolf" that threatens his/her sobriety and in developing coping mechanisms to deal with it.

C. The "Big Bad Wolf" metaphor was consistently reinforced with the client.

52. Support Group Referral (52)

A. The full scope of support groups such as AA or Tough Love was presented to the family and the benefits of involvement were identified.

B. The family was encouraged to attend a support group on a regular basis.

C. The importance of the family's involvement in a recovery program was stressed as being helpful to the client.

D. Family members have followed through with attendance at a support group.

E. There has been no follow-through on the part of family members to attend a support group.

53. Enabling versus Tough Love (53)

A. The family members were educated on the dynamics of enabling and the techniques of tough love.

B. The family was assisted in recognizing and reducing their enabling behaviors.

C. Role play and modeling were used to teach tough love techniques and to give family members opportunities to practice them.

D. Family members were reminded that tough love really reflects care and concern for the client.

E. Family members have decreased their enabling behaviors and become more firm in making the client responsible for his/her behavior.

F. The family members continued to practice enabling behaviors that have been a part of the family dynamic for many years.

54. Education Group Referral (54)

A. The family was asked and encouraged to attend a family education program for chemical dependence.

B. Resistance of family members to attending a family education program was confronted and addressed.

C. The family members have followed through in their attendance at a chemical dependence education group.

D. There has been no follow-through from the family members in attending a chemical dependence education group.

55. Read Chemical Dependence Literature (55)

A. Family members were assigned readings that would increase their knowledge of the disease and recovery.

B. Information that members gained from their reading was processed with them to increase their understanding and to answer any questions.

C. The family members have not followed through on reading the recommended material on chemical dependence.

56. Develop Family Members' Relapse Plans (56)

A. Family members were helped to develop their own plans for action if the client relapses.

B. Members shared their relapse action plans with the client in a family session.

C. Family members were reminded of the importance of following through on implementing their plan if a relapse occurs.

57. Family Enabling Behavior (57)

A. The family was monitored for engaging in enabling behavior and redirected when enabling behaviors occurred.

B. The family was encouraged to resist enabling the client.

C. The family was reminded of the benefits of not enabling the client.

D. Family members have decreased their enabling behaviors and become more firm in making the client responsible for his/her behavior.

E. The family members continued to practice enabling behaviors that have been a part of the family dynamic for many years.

58. Rid House of Substances (58)

A. The parents were assisted in identifying mood-altering substances in their home environment that need to be removed for the client's sobriety benefit.

B. The parents were monitored for their follow-through on keeping the home free of substances that would be a hindrance to the client's recovery.

C. The parents continue to bring alcohol into the home, saying it is for their own use, and they expect the client not to use it.

D. The parents have removed all mood-altering substances from the home to support the client's sobriety.

59. Encourage Tough Love (59)

A. The family was assisted in developing, implementing, and sticking with tough love techniques.

B. The benefits of tough love for the client were identified to keep family members invested in implementing them.

C. The family was encouraged to keep attending their tough love support group.

D. The parents have followed through on implementing tough love techniques, even though it has been difficult for them.

E. The parents have not been consistent on implementing tough love techniques.

60. Eliminate Negative Parenting (60)

A. Parenting techniques were assessed to identify interventions that incite negative responses and reduce esteem in the client.

B. The parents were assisted in identifying and eliminating all interventions that bring out revenge, foster rebellion, or reduce self-esteem in the client.

C. The parents were trained in parenting techniques that are responsive, respectful, reasonable, yet firm.

D. Role play and behavioral rehearsal were used to give the parents opportunities to practice respectful parenting techniques.

E. The parents were monitored and encouraged in their implementation and follow-through of responsive, respectful, reasonable, yet firm parenting techniques.

F. The parents have followed through with implementing more respectful, consistent, reasonable, but firm parenting techniques.

CONDUCT DISORDER/DELINQUENCY

CLIENT PRESENTATION

1. Failure to Comply (1)*

A. The client has demonstrated a persistent failure to comply with the rules or expectations at home, at school, and in the community.

B. The client voiced his/her opposition to the rules at home and school.

C. The client has started to comply with the rules and expectations at home, at school, and in the community.

D. The client verbalized his/her willingness to comply with the rules and expectations at home, at school, and in the community.

E. The client has consistently complied with the rules and expectations at home, at school, and in the community.

2. Aggressive/Destructive Behaviors (2)

A. The client described a series of incidents where he/she became aggressive or destructive when upset or frustrated.

B. The client projected the blame for his/her aggressive/destructive behaviors onto other people.

C. The client has begun to take steps to control his/her hostile/aggressive impulses.

D. The client has recently demonstrated good self-control and not engaged in any aggressive or destructive behaviors.

3. Angry/Hostile (2)

A. The client appeared angry, hostile, and irritable during today's session.

B. The client reported incidents of becoming easily angered over trivial matters.

C. The client has recently exhibited frequent angry outbursts at home and school.

D. The client has recently exhibited mild improvements in his/her anger control.

E. The client has demonstrated good control of his/her anger and has not exhibited any major loss-of-control episodes.

4. Stealing (3)

A. The client has a history of stealing and/or breaking and entering illegally into others' places of residence or businesses.

B. The client has recently engaged in stealing or illegal breaking and entering.

C. The client has not engaged in any stealing or illegal breaking and entering in the recent past.

D. The client has ceased stealing or illegally breaking and entering into places of residence or businesses.

---

* The numbers in parentheses correlate to the number of the Behavioral Definition statement in the companion chapter with same title in *The Adolescent Psychotherapy Treatment Planner* (Jongsma, Peterson, and McInnis) by John Wiley & Sons, 2000.

5. Legal Conflicts (3)

A. The parents reported an extensive history of the client engaging in illegal antisocial behaviors.

B. The client has continued to break laws and has failed to learn from his/her past mistakes or experiences.

C. The client has often minimized the seriousness of his/her offenses against other people or the law.

D. The client verbalized an awareness of how his/her antisocial behavior has produced negative or undesirable consequences for himself/herself and others.

E. The client and parents reported a reduction in the frequency and severity of illegal behaviors.

6. School Behavior Problems (4)

A. A review of the client's history revealed numerous acting-out and rebellious behaviors in the school setting.

B. The client has often disrupted the classroom with his/her silly, immature, or negative attention-seeking behaviors.

C. The client has missed a significant amount of time from school due to truancy.

D. The client has started to exercise greater self-control in the classroom setting.

E. The client has recently demonstrated a significant reduction in the frequency of his/her acting-out or rebellious behaviors at school.

7. Authority Conflicts (5)

A. The client displayed a negativistic attitude and was highly argumentative during today's therapy session.

B. The client has often tested the limits and challenged authority figures at home, at school, and in the community.

C. The client has often talked back to authority figures in a disrespectful manner when reprimanded.

D. The client has recently been more cooperative with authority figures.

E. The client has been cooperative and respectful toward authority figures on a consistent basis.

8. Thrill Seeking (6)

A. The client historically has presented as a highly impulsive individual who seeks immediate gratification of his/her needs and often fails to consider the consequences of his/her actions.

B. The client has engaged in impulsive/thrill-seeking behaviors in order to achieve a sense of excitement and fun.

C. The client has begun to take steps toward improving his/her impulse control and delaying the need for immediate gratification.

D. The client has recently demonstrated good impulse control and has not engaged in any serious acting-out or antisocial behaviors.

E. The client has ceased engaging in acting-out or thrill-seeking behaviors because of his/her improved ability to stop and think about the possible consequences of his/her actions.

9. Substance Abuse (6)

A. The client has engaged in a significant amount of substance abuse.

B. The client's substance abuse has contributed substantially to his/her rebellious and acting-out behavior.

C. The client has continued to abuse drugs and alcohol.

D. The client verbally denied any recent use of drugs or alcohol.

E. The client has ceased his/her substance abuse.

10. Lying/Conning (7)

A. The client described a pattern of lying, conning, and manipulating others to meet his/her needs and avoid facing the consequences of his/her actions.

B. The client appeared to be lying in the therapy session about his/her misbehaviors or irresponsible actions.

C. The client was honest in the therapy session and admitted to his/her wrongdoing or irresponsibility.

D. The parents reported that the client has been more honest and accepting of their decisions at home.

11. Blaming/Projecting (8)

A. The client was unwilling to accept responsibility for his/her poor decisions and behaviors, instead blaming others as the cause for his/her decisions and actions.

B. The client has begun to accept greater responsibility for his/her actions and placed the blame less often for his/her wrongdoings onto other people.

C. The client admitted to his/her wrongdoings and verbalized an acceptance of responsibility for his/her actions.

12. Lack of Insight (8)

A. The client has demonstrated little insight into the factors contributing to his/her behavioral problems.

B. The client has begun to show some insight into the factors contributing to his/her behavior problems.

C. During the therapy session, the client demonstrated insight into the factors that contributed to his/her behavioral problems.

13. Lack of Remorse/Guilt (9)

A. The client expressed little or no remorse for his/her irresponsible, acting-out, or aggressive behaviors.

B. The client expressed remorse for his/her actions, but apparently only because he/she had been caught and suffered the consequences of his/her actions.

C. The client appeared to express genuine remorse or guilt for his/her misbehavior.

14. Lack of Empathy/Insensitivity (10)

A. The client displayed little concern or empathy for the thoughts, feelings, and needs of other people.

B. The client has often demonstrated a willingness to ride roughshod over the rights of others to meet his/her needs.

C. The client verbalized an understanding of how his/her actions negatively impacted others.

D. The client has demonstrated empathy and sensitivity to the thoughts, feelings, and needs of other people.

15. Detached/Guarded (10)

A. The client appeared guarded and defensive during the therapy session.

B. The client was difficult to engage in the therapeutic process and showed little interest in exploring the factors that have contributed to his/her behavioral problems.

C. The client's defensiveness has started to decrease and he/she has demonstrated a greater willingness to explore underlying emotional conflicts.

D. The client was open and talkative about his/her behavioral problems and significant conflicts.

16. Childhood Abuse (10)

A. The client described a history of abuse that correlates to the onset of his/her behavioral problems

B. The client was resistant to discussing past incidents of abuse.

C. The client verbalized feelings of anger, hurt, and sadness about past abusive episodes.

17. Separation/Loss/Abandonment (10)

A. The client reported a history of experiencing significant separations or losses in his/her life.

B. The client was guarded and reticent to talk about past losses or abandonment issues.

C. The client expressed feelings of sadness, hurt, and disappointment about past separations, losses, or abandonment issues.

D. The client vocalized strong feelings of anger about past separations or losses.

18. Work Problems (10)

A. The client has taken little or no initiative in finding or securing employment.

B. The client reported a history of conflict with authority figures in the employment setting.

C. The client has developed strained relationships with coworkers and does not work as part of a team in the job site.

D. The client has recently demonstrated responsibility by actively seeking employment.

E. The client has maintained steady employment.

19. Sexual Promiscuity (11)

A. The client reported a history of having multiple sexual partners where there has been little or no emotional attachment.

B. The client displayed little awareness or concern for the possible consequences (e.g., unwanted pregnancy, contracting sexually transmitted diseases) of his/her irresponsible or promiscuous behavior.

C. The client verbalized an awareness of the negative consequences or potential dangers associated with his/her sexually promiscuous behavior.

D. The client has demonstrated good control over his/her sexual impulses and not engaged in any risky or irresponsible sexual behavior.

INTERVENTIONS IMPLEMENTED

1. Psychological Testing (1)*

A. A psychological evaluation was conducted to determine whether emotional factors or ADHD are contributing to the client's impulsivity and acting-out behaviors.

B. The client was uncooperative and resistant to engage in the evaluation process.

C. The client approached the psychological testing in an honest, straightforward manner and was cooperative with any requests.

2. Psychoeducational Evaluation (2)

A. The client received a psychoeducational evaluation to rule out the presence of a possible learning disability that may be contributing to his/her impulsivity and acting-out behaviors.

B. The client was uncooperative during the psychoeducational evaluation and did not appear to put forth good effort.

C. The client was cooperative during the psychoeducational evaluation and appeared motivated to do his/her best.

3. Evaluation Feedback (3)

A. Feedback from the psychological testing was given to the client, parents, school officials, or criminal justice officials and appropriate interventions were discussed.

B. The evaluation findings supported the presence of ADHD, which contributes to the client's tendency toward impulsive responding.

C. The evaluation findings revealed the presence of underlying emotional problems that have contributed to the emergence of impulsive and acting-out behavior.

D. The findings from the psychoeducational evaluation revealed the presence of a learning disability and the need for special education services.

E. The evaluation process did not reveal the presence of any learning disability, emotional problems, or ADHD that are contributing to the client's impulsive and acting-out behavior.

4. Substance Abuse Evaluation (4)

A. The client was referred for a substance abuse evaluation to assess the extent of his/her drug/alcohol usage and determine the need for treatment.

B. The findings from the substance abuse evaluation revealed the presence of a substance abuse problem and the need for treatment.

C. The evaluation findings did not reveal the presence of a substance abuse problem or the need for treatment in this area.

* The numbers in parentheses correlate to the number of the Therapeutic Intervention statement in the companion chapter with the same title in *The Adolescent Psychotherapy Treatment Planner* (Jongsma, Peterson, and McInnis) by John Wiley & Sons, 2000.

5. Consult with Criminal Justice Officials (5)

A. Consulted with criminal justice officials about the need for appropriate consequences for the client's antisocial behavior.

B. The client was placed on probation for his/her antisocial behaviors and instructed to comply with all the rules pertaining to his/her probation.

C. The client agreed to make restitution and/or perform community service for his/her past antisocial behavior.

D. The client was placed in an intensive surveillance treatment program as a consequence of his/her antisocial behavior.

6. Alternative Placement (6)

A. Consulted with parents, school officials, and criminal justice officials about placing the client in an alternative setting because of his/her antisocial behavior.

B. It is recommended that the client be placed in a juvenile detention facility as a consequence of his/her antisocial behavior.

C. It is recommended that the client be placed in a foster home to help prevent recurrences of antisocial behavior.

D. The recommendation was made that the client be placed in a residential program to provide external structure and supervision for the client.

E. The recommendation was made that the client be placed in an inpatient substance abuse program.

7. Reinforce Legal Consequences (7)

A. The parents were encouraged and challenged not to protect the client from the legal consequences of his/her actions.

B. The parents agreed to contact the police or appropriate criminal justice officials if the client engages in any future antisocial behavior.

C. The parents followed through and contacted the police or probation officer after the client engaged in antisocial behavior.

D. The parents failed to contact the police and/or criminal justice officials after the client engaged in antisocial behavior.

8. Therapeutic Trust (8)

A. An attempt was made to build trust with the client in therapy sessions through consistent eye contact, active listening, unconditional positive regard, and warm acceptance.

B. The client's concerns were listened to closely and his/her feelings were reflected in a nonjudgmental manner.

C. Thoughts and feelings expressed by the client during the therapy session were supported empathetically.

D. The client's mistrustfulness has contributed to his/her reluctance to share underlying thoughts and feelings during the therapy sessions.

9. Connect Feelings and Behavior (9)

A. The session was helpful in identifying underlying painful emotions that contribute to the client's impulsive or reactive behaviors.

B. The client developed insight into how his/her reactive behaviors are connected to underlying feelings of sadness, hurt, and disappointment.

C. Role-playing and modeling techniques were used to demonstrate appropriate ways for the client to express his/her underlying painful emotions.

D. The client was asked to list appropriate ways to express his/her feelings and meet his/her needs instead of impulsively reacting to situations.

10. Confront Antisocial Behavior (10)

A. The client was firmly and consistently confronted with how his/her antisocial behaviors negatively affect himself/herself and others.

B. The client was asked to list the negative consequences of his/her antisocial behavior and negativistic attitude.

C. Role-reversal techniques were used in the therapy session to help the client realize how his/her antisocial behavior negatively impacts others.

D. The client was asked to write a letter of apology to the victim(s) of his/her antisocial behavior.

11. Teach Acceptance of Responsibility (11)

A. The client was consistently confronted and challenged to cease blaming others for his/her misbehavior and accept greater responsibility for his/her actions.

B. The client was asked to list how his/her poor decisions and irresponsible behavior resulted in negative consequences for himself/herself and others.

C. The client identified ways to resolve conflict and/or meet his/her needs that were more effective than acting out or behaving in an irresponsible manner.

D. The client was instructed to verbally acknowledge his/her wrongdoing and apologize to others.

12. Explore Blaming (12)

A. The underlying factors contributing to the client's pattern of blaming others for his/her misbehavior were explored.

B. The client was challenged to accept the consequences of his/her actions instead of arguing and blaming others.

C. The client identified how the pattern of blaming others is associated with underlying feelings of low self-esteem, inadequacy, and insecurity.

D. The client has modeled other family members' patterns of blaming others.

E. The parents identified natural, logical consequences (e.g., grounding, removing privileges, or taking away desired objects) that can be used if client is caught in a lie.

13. Teach Honesty (13)

A. The client was taught the value of honesty as a basis to build trust and mutual respect in all relationships.

B. The client was made aware that a pattern of lying creates distrust and interferes with his/her ability to establish meaningful relationships.

C. The client verbally committed to being more honest to improve his/her relationships with family members and peers.

D. The client agreed to "undo" his/her lies by telling the truth.

14. Teach Self-Control Strategies (14)

A. The client was taught mediational and self-control strategies (e.g., relaxation, "stop, look, listen, and think") to help express anger through appropriate verbalizations and healthy physical outlets.

B. The client was asked to identify appropriate and inappropriate ways to express or control anger.

C. The client was encouraged to utilize active listening skills to delay impulses to react with verbal or physical aggression.

D. The client identified healthy physical outlets for his/her strong feelings of anger and aggressive impulses.

15. Teach Relaxation Techniques (15)

A. The client was taught guided imagery and relaxation techniques to help control anger.

B. The client reported a positive response to the use of guided imagery or relaxation techniques to help control anger.

C. The client appeared uncomfortable and unable to relax during the therapy session when being instructed in the use of guided imagery and relaxation techniques.

16. Self-Monitoring Checklists (16)

A. The client and parents were encouraged to utilize self-monitoring checklists of anger-provoking situations in the home and school to help improve his/her anger and impulse control.

B. Consulted with the client's teachers about the use of self-monitoring checklists of anger-provoking situations to improve the client's anger and impulse control.

C. The parents and school officials were instructed to utilize a reward system in conjunction with the self-monitoring checklists of anger-provoking situations.

D. The use of a journal was recommended to help the client identify factors that trigger strong feelings of anger or contribute to impulsive behaviors.

17. "Anger Control" Exercise (17)

A. The client and parents were given the "Anger Control" exercise from *The Brief Adolescent Therapy Homework Planner* (Jongsma, Peterson, and McInnis) to reinforce client for demonstrating good control of anger.

B. The "Anger Control" exercise was utilized to help the client identify the core issues that contribute to his/her angry outbursts and aggressive behaviors.

18. Teach Communication and Assertiveness (18)

A. The client was taught effective communication and assertiveness skills to learn how to express feelings in a controlled fashion and meet his/her needs through more constructive actions.

B. Role-playing and modeling techniques were used in the therapy session to teach effective ways to control emotions and identify appropriate ways to meet needs.

C. The client was encouraged to utilize "I" messages and positive statements to effectively communicate needs to others.

19. Encourage Delay of Gratification (19)

A. Consulted with the parents on how to increase structure in the home to help the client delay his/her needs for immediate gratification in order to achieve longer-term goals.

B. The parents established a rule that the client would be forbidden to engage in recreational or leisure activities until completing his/her chores or homework.

C. The parents identified consequences for client's failure to complete responsibilities; client verbalized recognition of these consequences.

D. The client and parents designed a schedule of dates and times when client is expected to complete chores and homework.

20. Establish Clear Rules (20)

A. The client was asked to repeat the rules to demonstrate an understanding of the expectations.

B. Consulted with the client, parents, and teachers to identify rules and expectations in the school setting.

C. The client verbally disagreed with the rules and expectations identified by the parents.

21. Establish Parental Rules and Boundaries (21)

A. The family therapy session focused on helping establish clearly defined rules and appropriate parent-child boundaries.

B. The parents were able to identify the rules and expectations that the client is expected to follow at home.

C. The parents were able to identify appropriate consequences for the client's misbehaviors.

D. The parents had difficulty establishing clearly defined rules and identifying appropriate consequences for the client's misbehavior.

22. Reward System/Contingency Contract (22)

A. The client and parents identified a list of rewards to reinforce desired, positive behavior by the client.

B. A reward system was designed to reinforce positive behavior and deter impulsive or aggressive acts.

C. The client signed a contingency contract specifying the consequences for his/her impulsive/acting-out behavior.

23. Prescribe Arguing (23)

A. In an effort to disrupt the client's excessive pattern of challenging and defying authority figures, the therapist prescribed the symptom by directing the client to argue with authority figures at a specific time each day.

B. The client responded favorably to the paradoxical intervention and followed through with the prescribed symptom of arguing for a specific amount of time each day.

24. Parents Read *Negotiating Parent/Adolescent Conflict* (24)

A. The parents were instructed to read *Negotiating Parent/Adolescent Conflict* (Robin and Foster) to help resolve conflict more effectively.

B. Processed the reading of *Negotiating Parent/Adolescent Conflict* with the parents in the therapy session.

C. The parents verbalized that the book was helpful in identifying constructive ways to resolve conflict.

25. Explore Potential Roadblocks (25)

A. The client and parents explored possible stressors, frustrations, or roadblocks that might cause behavioral problems to reappear in the future.

B. The client identified coping strategies that he/she could use in the future to deal with stress or frustration more effectively than acting out.

C. The client was reinforced for times in the past when he/she used positive coping strategies to solve problems and was encouraged to use them again when he/she faces similar problems.

26. Token Economy (26)

A. A token economy was designed for use in the home to increase the client's positive social behaviors and deter impulsive, acting-out behavior.

B. The client and parents agreed to the conditions outlined in the token economy and agreed to follow through with the implementation at home.

C. A token economy was designed and implemented in the classroom to reinforce the client's positive social behavior and good impulse control.

27. Encourage Parental Praise (27)

A. Parents were encouraged to provide frequent praise and positive reinforcement for the client's positive social opportunities and good impulse control.

B. Parents were challenged to look for opportunities to praise the client instead of focusing primarily on behavioral problems.

28. Parents Reinforce Positive Behavior (28)

A. The parents were instructed to observe and record positive behaviors by the client between therapy sessions.

B. The parents were encouraged to reinforce the client for engaging in positive behaviors.

C. The client was strongly encouraged to continue to engage in positive behaviors to build self-esteem, earn parents' approval, and receive affirmation from others.

29. Expose Family Dynamics (29)

A. A family therapy session was held to explore the dynamics within the family system that contribute to the emergence of the client's behavioral problems.

B. The family members were asked to list the stressors that have had a negative impact on the family.

C. The family members were asked to identify the things that they would like to change within the family.

30. Utilize Family Sculpting (30)

A. The family-sculpting technique was utilized within the session to help gain greater insight into the roles and behaviors of each family member.

B. The client and family members were instructed to use the family-sculpting technique to identify positive changes they would like to see happen in the family.

31. Assess Family Problem Solving (31)

A. The client and family members were given a task to solve in order to provide an opportunity to observe the interactions among family members.

B. After successfully solving the problem within the family therapy session, the family was encouraged to use similar strategies at home to solve real-life problems.

32. Increase Disengaged Parent Involvement (32)

A. The disengaged parent attended the therapy session and was challenged to spend more time with the client in leisure, school, or household activities.

B. The client directly verbalized his/her need to spend greater time with the disengaged parent.

C. The factors contributing to the distant relationship between the client and detached parent were explored.

D. The detached parent verbalized a commitment to spend increased time with the client.

33. Expose Family Abuse History (33)

A. The client's family background was explored for a history of physical, sexual, or substance abuse.

B. The client developed a time line in the therapy session that identified significant historical events, both positive and negative, that have occurred in his/her family.

C. The client was instructed to draw a diagram of the house where the abuse occurred.

D. A diagnostic interview was conducted to assess the extent of the family members' use of drugs and alcohol.

34. Confront Parents' Abusive Discipline (34)

A. The client's parents were confronted and challenged to cease physically abusive or overly punitive methods of discipline.

B. The parents were asked to identify how abusive or overly punitive methods of discipline affect the client and siblings.

C. The parent(s) apologized to the client for abusive behaviors and overly harsh methods of discipline.

35. Protect Client from Abuse (35)

A. The abuse was reported to the appropriate agency.

B. A recommendation was made that the perpetrator be removed from the home and seek treatment.

C. A recommendation was made that the client and siblings be removed from the home to ensure protection.

D. The client and family members identified necessary steps to take to minimize the risk of abuse occurring in the future.

E. The nonabusive parent verbalized a commitment to protect client and siblings from physical abuse in the future.

36. Explore Feelings about Neglect or Abuse (36)

A. The client was given the opportunity in session to express his/her feelings about past neglect, abuse, separation, or abandonment.

B. The client was instructed to draw pictures that reflected his/her feelings about neglect, abuse, separation, or abandonment.

C. The client was instructed to use a journal to record his/her thoughts and feelings about past neglect, abuse, separation, or abandonment.

D. The empty-chair technique was employed to facilitate expression of feelings surrounding past neglect or abuse.

37. Probe Abandonment Issues (37)

A. The client shared the extent of contact with the absent or uninvolved parent in the past and discussed possible reasons for the lack of involvement.

B. The client was instructed to write a letter to the absent parent to provide opportunity to express and work through feelings about abandonment or lack of contact.

C. The empty-chair technique was utilized to help the client express feelings toward absent parent.

38. Group Therapy Referral (38)

A. The client was referred for group therapy to improve his/her impulse control, social judgment, and interpersonal skills.

B. The client was given the directive to self-disclose at least one time during group therapy sessions.

C. The client was encouraged to demonstrate empathy and concern for the thoughts, feelings, and needs of others during the group therapy session.

39. View *Refusal Skills* (39)

A. The client viewed the *Refusal Skills* video in the therapy session to learn effective assertiveness skills and help him/her resist negative peer influences.

B. After viewing the *Refusal Skills* video, the client was able to recall several effective ways to resist negative peer influences.

C. The client was given a homework assignment to record at least one incident where he/she effectively used the assertiveness skills that were taught in the *Refusal Skills* video to successfully resist negative peer influences.

40. Reinforce Positive Peer Group Activities (40)

A. The client was strongly encouraged to participate in extracurricular or positive peer group activities to provide a healthy outlet for anger, improve social skills, and increase self-esteem.

B. The client was assisted in developing a list of extracurricular or positive peer group activities that will provide him/her with the opportunity to establish meaningful friendships.

C. The client acknowledged that feelings of insecurity and inadequacy contribute to his/her reluctance to become involved in extracurricular or positive peer group activities.

41. Assign Altruistic Acts (41)

A. The client was given the homework assignment of performing three altruistic or benevolent acts before the next therapy session to increase his/her empathy and sensitivity to the thoughts, feelings, and needs of others.

B. A recommendation was made that the client perform community service as part of probation to increase empathy and concern for the welfare of others.

C. The client's failure to comply with the homework assignment that he/she perform altruistic or benevolent acts reflects his/her lack of empathy and concern for the welfare of others.

42. Art Therapy Techniques (42)

A. The client was instructed to draw a picture reflecting how his/her impulsive, acting-out behaviors affect self-esteem.

B. The client was instructed to draw a picture reflecting how his/her impulsive, acting-out behaviors affect others.

43. Teach Empathy (43)

A. Role-playing and role-reversal techniques were used to increase client's sensitivity to how antisocial behaviors affect others.

B. The client was able to verbally recognize how his/her antisocial behaviors affect others through use of role-playing and role-reversal techniques.

44. "Headed in the Right Direction" (44)

A. The client was given the homework assignment, "Headed in the Right Direction" exercise from *The Brief Adolescent Therapy Homework Planner* to help increase his/her empathy and sensitivity toward the thoughts, feelings, and needs of others.

B. After completing the "Headed in the Right Direction" exercise, the client was able to identify three ways in which he/she could demonstrate caring behavior toward others.

45. Utilize Odyssey Islands Game (45)

A. The Odyssey Islands Game was employed to help establish rapport with the client.

B. The Odyssey Islands Game was employed in therapy session to improve the client's social, moral, and problem-solving skills.

C. After playing the Odyssey Islands Game, the client was able to identify several positive social skills and effective problem-solving strategies.

D. The client was given the homework assignment of implementing three positive social skills that were discussed while playing the Odyssey Islands Game.

46. Read *The Teens' Solution Workbook* (46)

A. The client was instructed to read *The Teens' Solution Workbook* (Shapiro) to improve impulse control and problem-solving skills.

B. Today's therapy session processed what the client learned from the homework assignment in *The Teens' Solution Workbook*.

47. Acknowledge Need for Control (47)

A. The client verbally recognized how his/her intimidating, manipulative, and exploitive behaviors are related to the need for power or control.

B. The client was asked to identify several age-appropriate ways to gain a sense of power and control.

C. The client was given a homework assignment to engage in three responsible or positive social behaviors to build positive self-esteem.

D. The client was given a directive to apologize to individual(s) whom he/she has exploited or manipulated in the past.

48. Identify Positive Role Models (48)

A. The client identified three to five role models and listed several reasons that he/she thought the role model was successful in achieving goals.

B. The client identified his/her personal goals and was encouraged to begin taking steps to accomplish those goals by employing strategies similar to those that role models have used to achieve their goals or success.

49. Identify Times of Good Impulse Control (49)

A. The client explored periods when he/she demonstrated good impulse control in the past and engaged in significantly fewer acting-out behaviors.

B. The client was encouraged to use similar coping mechanisms that he/she used successfully in the past to control impulses.

C. The client shared realization that involvement in extracurricular or positive peer group activities helped him/her to stay out of trouble.

D. The session revealed that the client was better behaved during periods of time when he/she received strong family support and affiliated with positive peer groups.

50. Develop Action Plan for Future (50)

A. Guided imagery techniques were used to help the client visualize a brighter future.

B. The client identified future goals and an action plan needed to achieve goals or desired changes in behavior.

C. Processed the client's answer to the question, "What will you be doing in the future when you're not getting into trouble?"

51. Music Therapy Techniques (51)

A. The client played a song that reflected his/her anger, painful emotions, or unmet needs that lie beneath his/her acting-out behaviors.

B. The client shared a song in the therapy session that afterward led to a discussion of how the song reflected his/her feelings and what he/she can do to meet needs or overcome problems.

52. Perform Household Tasks (52)

A. The client and parents developed a list of responsible behaviors that the client could perform at home.

B. The parents placed the client in charge of tasks at home to demonstrate confidence in his/her ability to act responsibly.

53. Vocational Training Referral (53)

A. The client was referred for a vocational assessment.

B. Recommendation was made that the client receive vocational training to develop basic job skills that will hopefully lead to steady employment.

54. Seek Employment (54)

A. The client was challenged to find employment instead of obtaining money or material goods through illegal activities.

B. The client was praised and reinforced for securing employment.

C. The client explored the factors that contribute to his/her reluctance to obtain employment.

55. Provide Sex Education (55)

A. The client was provided with sex education in an attempt to eliminate his/her pattern of engaging in sexually promiscuous behaviors.

B. The client identified the risks involved with his/her irresponsible or promiscuous sexual behaviors.

56. Explore Reasons for Promiscuous Behavior (56)

A. The client explored the factors contributing to his/her irresponsible or sexually promiscuous behaviors.

B. The client identified more effective ways to meet his/her needs instead of through sexual acting out.

C. Explored and processed the client's irrational thoughts that underlie his/her sexually promiscuous behaviors.

57. Assess Marital Conflicts (57)

A. The therapist assessed the marital dyad for possible conflict and/or triangulation that places the focus on the client's acting-out behaviors and away from marital problems.

B. The parents recognized how their marital problems are creating stress for the client and agreed to seek marital counseling.

C. The parents refused to follow through with a recommendation to pursue marital counseling.

58. Assess Parental Substance Abuse (58)

A. The parents were assessed for possible substance abuse problems.

B. The client's parents agreed to seek substance abuse treatment.

C. The client's parents appeared to be in denial about substance abuse problems and refused to seek treatment.

59. Medication Evaluation Referral (59)

A. The client was referred for a medication evaluation to improve his/her impulse control and stabilize moods.

B. The client and parents agreed to follow through with a medication evaluation.

C. The client was strongly opposed to being placed on medication to help improve his/her impulse control and stabilize moods.

60. Monitor Medication Effects (60)

A. The client's response to the medication was discussed.

B. The client reported that medication has helped to improve impulse control and stabilize moods.

C. The client reports little or no improvement on the medication.

D. The client has not complied with taking his/her medication on a regular basis.

DEPRESSION

CLIENT PRESENTATION

1. Sad, Depressed Moods (1)*

A. Parents and teachers reported that the client has appeared sad and depressed for a significant length of time.

B. The client appeared visibly sad during today's therapy session and reported that he/she feels depressed most of the time.

C. The frequency and intensity of the client's depressed moods are gradually beginning to diminish.

D. The client expressed happiness and joy about recent life events.

E. The client's depression has lifted and his/her moods are much more elevated.

2. Flat, Constricted Affect (1)

A. The parents and teachers reported that the client's affect often appears flat and constricted at home and school.

B. The client's affect appeared flat and constricted, and he/she reports that he/she does not feel any emotion.

C. The client appeared more animated in his/her affective presentation and showed a wider range of emotions.

D. The client has consistently appeared more animated in his/her emotional presentation since the onset of treatment.

3. Preoccupation with Death (2)

A. The parents and teachers reported that the client displays a strong preoccupation with the subject of death.

B. The client displayed a preoccupation with the subject of death during today's therapy session and reported that death is on his/her mind often.

C. The client's preoccupation with the subject of death is gradually beginning to decrease.

D. The client did not talk about the subject of death in today's therapy session.

E. The client's preoccupation with the subject of death has ceased and he/she has demonstrated a renewed interest in life.

4. Suicidal Thoughts/Actions (3)

A. The client reported experiencing suicidal thoughts on a number of occasions.

B. The client made a recent suicide attempt.

C. The client has made suicidal gestures in the past as a cry for help.

D. The client denied that suicidal thoughts or urges are a problem any longer.

---

* The numbers in parentheses correlate to the number of the Behavioral Definition statement in the companion chapter with same title in *The Adolescent Psychotherapy Treatment Planner* (Jongsma, Peterson, and McInnis) by John Wiley & Sons, 2000.

5. Moody Irritability (4)

A. The client has displayed a pervasive irritability at home and school.

B. The client's angry, irritable moods often mask deeper feelings of depression.

C. The client appeared moody and irritable during today's therapy session.

D. The frequency and intensity of the client's irritable moods have started to diminish.

E. The client's moods have stabilized and he/she has demonstrated significantly fewer irritable moods.

6. Isolation from Family and Peers (5)

A. The client has become significantly more isolated and withdrawn from family members and peers since the onset of his/her depression.

B. The client appeared withdrawn in today's therapy session.

C. The client's social isolation has started to diminish and he/she is beginning to interact more often with family members and peers.

D. The client was much more talkative and spontaneous in today's therapy session.

E. The client has become much more outgoing and has interacted with his/her family members and peers on a regular, consistent basis.

7. Academic Performance Decline (6)

A. The client has experienced a decrease in his/her academic performance since the onset of his/her depression.

B. The client appeared visibly depressed when discussing his/her lowered academic performance.

C. The client's academic performance has increased since his/her depression has lifted.

D. The client expressed feelings of happiness and joy about his/her improved academic performance.

8. Lack of Interest (7)

A. The client reported experiencing little interest or enjoyment in activities that used to bring him/her pleasure in the past.

B. The parents and teachers reported that the client has shown little interest or enjoyment in activities at home and school.

C. The client's depression has started to decrease and he/she has shown signs of interest in previously enjoyed activities.

D. The client reported that he/she was recently able to experience joy or happiness in several activities.

E. The client has developed a renewed interest in and zest for life.

9. Lack of Communication about Painful Emotions (8)

A. The client has often suppressed and/or avoided talking about his/her painful emotions or experiences with others.

B. The client avoided talking about any painful emotions or topics during today's therapy session.

C.   The client's avoidance of or refusal to talk about his/her painful emotions or experiences has been a significant contributing factor to his/her depression.

D.   The client has started to talk about his/her painful emotions or experiences.

E.   The client's willingness to talk about his/her painful emotions or experiences has helped to lift his/her depression.

10.   Substance Abuse (9)

A.   The client's substance abuse has masked deeper feelings of depression.

B.   The client acknowledged that he/she has often turned to illegal drugs or alcohol abuse to elevate his/her mood and block out any painful emotions.

C.   The client reported that he/she has experienced an increase in feelings of depression since he/she ceased using drugs or alcohol.

D.   The client's moods have stabilized since he/she ceased abusing drugs and alcohol.

E.   The client reported that he/she is able to enjoy many activities without drugs or alcohol.

11.   Low Energy, Listless, and Apathetic (10)

A.   The client's depression has been manifested, in part, by his/her low energy level, fatigue, listlessness, and apathy.

B.   The client appeared tired, listless, and apathetic during today's therapy session.

C.   The client reported a mild increase recently in his/her level of energy.

D.   The client reported experiencing a return to his/her normal level of energy.

12.   Lack of Eye Contact (11)

A.   The parents and teachers reported that the client displays very little eye contact during his/her social interactions with others.

B.   The client displayed poor eye contact during today's therapy session and acknowledged this to be a common practice.

C.   The client has demonstrated satisfactory eye contact with individuals with whom he/she feels comfortable, but poor eye contact with unfamiliar people.

D.   The client maintained good eye contact during today's therapy session and stated he/she is increasing eye contact with others as well.

E.   The parents and teachers reported that the client consistently maintains good eye contact.

13.   Low Self-Esteem (11)

A.   The client has been troubled by strong feelings of low self-esteem, inadequacy, and insecurity.

B.   The client verbalized negative and disparaging remarks about himself/herself.

C.   The client's low self-esteem, lack of confidence, and feelings of insecurity are significant concomitant aspects of his/her depression.

D.   The client verbalized several positive self-descriptive statements during today's therapy session.

E.   The client has taken active steps to improve his/her self-esteem (e.g., reaching out to others and challenging self with new activities).

14. **Appetite Disturbance (12)**

A. The client reported experiencing a loss of appetite during his/her depressive episodes.

B. The client has lost a significant amount of weight since becoming depressed.

C. The client reports that he/she has often turned to food to feel better during periods of depression.

D. The client reported a significant weight gain since the onset of his/her depression.

E. The client's appetite has returned to a normal level since his/her feelings of depression have decreased.

15. **Sleep Disturbance (13)**

A. The client reported to having difficulty falling asleep and/or experiencing early morning awakenings since he/she became depressed.

B. The client reported sleeping more than usual during his/her bout of depression.

C. The client reported to sleeping well recently.

D. The client's sleep has returned to a normal level.

16. **Poor Concentration and Indecisiveness (14)**

A. The client reported to having difficulty concentrating and making decisions since feeling depressed.

B. The client had trouble concentrating and staying focused during today's therapy session.

C. The client's low self-esteem, lack of confidence, and feelings of insecurity have contributed to his/her difficulty in making decisions.

D. The client reported being able to concentrate and stay focused for longer periods of time now that he/she has ceased feeling depressed.

E. The client's ability to make some constructive decisions has helped to decrease his/her feelings of depression.

17. **Feelings of Hopelessness/Helplessness (15)**

A. The client has developed a pessimistic outlook on the future and is troubled by feelings of hopelessness and helplessness.

B. The client expressed feelings of helplessness and voiced little hope that his/her life will improve in the future.

C. The client expressed confidence about his/her ability to overcome problems or stress and improve his/her life in the future.

D. The client has experienced a renewed sense of hope and feelings of empowerment.

18. **Feelings of Guilt (15)**

A. The client expressed strong feelings of guilt about his/her past actions.

B. The client's strong feelings of irrational guilt are a significant contributing factor to his/her depression and inability to move ahead with life.

C. The client made productive use of today's therapy session by exploring his/her feelings of guilt about past actions.

D. The client denied being troubled by any significant feelings of guilt.

E. The client has successfully worked through and resolved his/her feelings of guilt about his/her past actions.

19. Unresolved Grief Issues (16)

A. The client's unresolved feelings of grief have been a significant contributing factor to his/her episode of depression.

B. The client expressed strong feelings of sadness and grief about past separations or losses.

C. The client was guarded and reluctant to talk about his/her past losses or separations.

D. The client's depression has begun to lift as he/she works through his/her feelings of grief about past losses or separations.

E. The client has experienced a significant increase in the frequency and duration of his/her happy or contented mood since working through the issues of grief.

20. Mood-Related Hallucinations or Delusions (17)

A. The client reported experiencing mood-congruent perceptual and/or cognitive disturbances during his/her major depressive episode.

B. The client expressed delusional thoughts during today's therapy session.

C. The client reported that he/she has recently been troubled by depression-related hallucinations.

D. The client denied experiencing any recent hallucinations or delusional thoughts.

E. The client has not experienced any further hallucinations or delusions since his/her mood has stabilized.

INTERVENTIONS IMPLEMENTED

1. Psychological Testing (1)*

A. The client was referred for a psychological evaluation to assess the depth of his/her depression.

B. The client was uncooperative and resistant during the psychological testing.

C. The client approached the psychological testing in an honest, straightforward manner and was cooperative with any requests presented to him/her.

2. Give Psychological Testing Feedback (2)

A. The client and his/her family members were given feedback on the results of the psychological testing.

B. The results from the psychological testing showed that the client is currently experiencing a mild amount of depression.

C. The results from the psychological testing showed that the client is experiencing a moderate amount of depression.

* The numbers in parentheses correlate to the number of the Therapeutic Intervention statement in the companion chapter with the same title in *The Adolescent Psychotherapy Treatment Planner* (Jongsma, Peterson, and McInnis) by John Wiley & Sons, 2000.

D. The results from the psychological testing showed that the client's level of depression is severe.

E. The results of the psychological testing did not support the presence of a depressive disorder.

3. Explore Self-Defeating Behavior (3)

A. Today's therapy session explored how the client's depression is linked to his/her pattern of engaging in self-defeating behaviors.

B. The client was able to recognize the connection between his/her self-defeating behaviors and his/her periods of depression.

C. The client identified ways to cope with stress or meet his/her needs that would be more effective than engaging in self-defeating behaviors.

D. The client resisted the interpretation that his/her depression is linked to a pattern of self-defeating behaviors.

E. Client-centered therapy approaches were used to help the client realize how his/her pattern of self-defeating behaviors is linked to his/her depression.

4. Interpret Acting-Out Behavior (4)

A. The client's acting-out behaviors were interpreted as a sign of his/her depression.

B. The client has gained insight into how his/her acting-out behaviors are related to underlying feelings of depression.

C. The client was helped to identify ways to meet his/her needs and overcome his/her feelings of depression that would be more effective than engaging in acting-out behaviors.

D. A psychoanalytic approach was utilized to explore how the client's acting-out behaviors are related to deeper feelings of depression.

E. A brief, solution-focused approach was used to help the client identify effective ways to meet his/her needs and overcome feelings of depression.

5. Confront Acting-Out Behavior (5)

A. The client was confronted with how his/her acting-out behaviors serve as a maladaptive coping mechanism to avoid facing the real issues or conflicts.

B. The client responded positively to the confrontation about his/her acting-out behaviors and acknowledged that there are ways to cope with stress and meet his/her needs that are more effective than acting out.

C. The client was resistant to the interpretation that he/she is acting out as a means of avoiding dealing with conflict or emotional pain.

D. The client was strongly encouraged to directly communicate his/her unmet needs to significant others and to terminate the acting-out behavior.

E. The client was taught effective communication and assertiveness skills to help him/her deal with conflict and meet his/her needs.

6. "Surface Behavior/Inner Feelings" (6)

A. The client was given the "Surface Behavior/Inner Feelings" exercise from *The Brief Adolescent Therapy Homework Planner* (Jongsma, Peterson, and McInnis) to show the connection between his/her angry, irritable, acting-out behaviors and feelings of hurt or sadness.

B. The client successfully completed the "Surface Behavior/Inner Feelings" homework and was able to identify how his/her angry, irritable behaviors are connected to underlying feelings of hurt and sadness.

C. The client did not complete the "Surface Behavior/Inner Feelings" homework and was asked to do it again.

D. The client successfully completed the homework assignment and reported that he/she was able to share feelings of hurt and sadness with other trusted individuals.

7. Reinforce Expression of Underlying Feelings (7)

A. The client was reinforced for expressing his/her feelings of anger, hurt, and disappointment.

B. A psychoanalytic therapy approach was utilized to help the client explore his/her underlying feelings of anger, hurt, and disappointment.

C. Client-centered therapy principles were utilized to show that the client's statements or actions reflect underlying feelings of anger, hurt, and disappointment.

D. After identifying his/her feelings of anger, hurt, and disappointment, the client was encouraged to directly verbalize these feelings to family members or other close, trusted individuals.

8. Explore Fear of Loss (8)

A. Today's therapy session explored the client's fears of abandonment by or loss of love from significant others.

B. The client was helped to examine whether his/her fears surrounding abandonment or loss of love from others are realistic or unrealistic.

C. The client was taught cognitive restructuring techniques to help challenge and overcome his/her irrational fears about being abandoned or rejected by significant others.

D. Psychoanalytic therapy approaches were employed to explore the client's underlying fears of abandonment or loss of love from significant others.

9. Identify Missing Aspects of Life (9)

A. The client was asked to identify what is missing from his/her life that contributes to personal unhappiness.

B. The client was able to successfully identify the missing aspects of his/her life that contribute to feelings of unhappiness and depression.

C. A plan was developed with the client to attempt to find ways to satisfy those missing aspects of his/her life.

D. The client was encouraged to utilize his/her strengths and seek out the support of others to help cope with the missing aspects of his/her life.

10. "Unmet Emotional Needs—Identification and Satisfaction" (10)

A. The client was assigned the "Unmet Emotional Needs—Identification and Satisfaction" exercise from *The Brief Adolescent Therapy Homework Planner* (Jongsma, Peterson, and McInnis) to help identify his/her unmet emotional needs and specific ways to meet those needs in the future.

B. The client completed the "Unmet Emotional Needs—Identification and Satisfaction" exercise and was able to identify his/her unmet emotional needs and several effective ways to meet them.

C. The client failed to complete the exercise and was again asked to work on it.

11. Probe Current Life Stressors (11)

A. Today's therapy session probed the aspects of the client's current life situation that are contributing to his/her feelings of sadness.

B. The client made productive use of the therapy session and was able to identify the current life stressors that are contributing to his/her feelings of sadness.

C. Role-playing and modeling techniques were used to help the client identify effective ways to cope with his/her current life stressors.

D. A brief solution-focused approach was utilized to help the client identify effective ways to cope with his/her current life stressors and problems.

E. The client was helped to identify successful strategies that he/she used in the past to overcome similar problems.

12. Explore Emotional Pain from Past (12)

A. Today's therapy session explored the emotional pain from the client's past that contributes to his/her feelings of hopelessness and low self-esteem.

B. The client was given empathy and support in expressing his/her painful emotions about the past experiences that have contributed to current feelings of hopelessness and low self-esteem.

C. The client was encouraged to utilize positive self-talk as a means to offset his/her pattern of negative thinking and overcome feelings of hopelessness.

D. Guided imagery techniques were utilized to help the client visualize a brighter future.

13. Address Family Conflict (13)

A. A family therapy session was held to facilitate a discussion of the conflict that exists in the family.

B. Today's family therapy session was helpful in identifying the core areas of conflict that contribute to the client's depression.

C. The family members were asked to brainstorm possible ways to resolve the conflictual issues affecting the family.

D. The family members were able to agree on solutions to the problem(s) that are contributing to the client's depression.

E. The client and family members were unable to reach an agreement on how to resolve the conflict that is contributing to the client's depression.

14. Expression of Emotional Needs (14)

A. The client was given the opportunity to express his/her emotional needs to family members and significant others.

B. The family members responded with empathy and support to the client's expression of his/her needs.

C. The client and family members were helped to identify ways to meet the client's emotional needs.

D. The client was given a specific task to perform with the family members or significant others to meet his/her emotional needs.

15. Allow Respectful Expression of Feelings (15)

A. The parents were challenged to encourage, support, and tolerate the client's respectful expression of his/her thoughts and feelings.

B. The client and parents were helped to differentiate between respectful and disrespectful ways for the client to express his/her thoughts and feelings.

C. Role-playing and modeling techniques were utilized to identify respectful versus disrespectful ways of expressing thoughts and feelings.

D. The parents were encouraged to ignore mild and occasional verbally aggressive or oppositional behaviors to help the client become more assertive and less depressed.

16. Identify Cognitive Messages of Helplessness (16)

A. The client was helped to identify the negative cognitive messages that reinforce feelings of helplessness and hopelessness.

B. The client was encouraged to utilize positive self-talk as a means to overcome his/her feelings of helplessness and hopelessness.

C. The client was strongly encouraged to challenge his/her irrational thoughts that contribute to his/her feelings of helplessness and hopelessness.

D. The client was given a homework assignment to identify his/her strengths and weaknesses to improve self-esteem and overcome feelings of helplessness and hopelessness.

17. "Bad Thoughts Lead to Depressed Feelings" Exercise (17)

A. The client was given the homework assignment "Bad Thoughts Lead to Depressed Feelings" from *The Brief Adolescent Therapy Homework Planner* (Jongsma, Peterson, and McInnis) to help him/her learn how to replace negative cognitive messages with positive self-talk as a means to overcome depression.

B. The client reported that the homework assignment "Bad Thoughts Lead to Depressed Feelings" helped him/her challenge and cease negative or distorted patterns of thinking that led to feelings of depression in the past.

C. The client did not follow through with completing the homework assignment "Bad Thoughts Lead to Depressed Feelings" and was again asked to work on it.

18. Reinforce Positive Cognitive Messages (18)

A. The client was trained in the use of positive cognitive messages to help increase his/her self-confidence and self-acceptance.

B. The client reported that the use of positive cognitive messages has helped to increase his/her confidence and feelings of acceptance about self.

C. The client reported that he/she attempted to use positive cognitive messages, but still continues to be troubled by feelings of insecurity and a lack of confidence.

D. The client failed to follow through with using positive cognitive messages as a means to increase his/her confidence and feelings of self-acceptance.

19. Assess Potential for Suicide (19)

A. The client acknowledged experiencing suicidal thoughts and/or an urge to harm self and was referred for an evaluation for inpatient hospitalization.

B. The client was admitted into an inpatient psychiatric unit because of his/her risk for suicide or self-harm.

C. The client reported experiencing brief thoughts of suicide, but denied any intent to harm himself/herself; nonetheless, the client's suicide potential will continue to be closely monitored.

D. The suicide assessment revealed that the client is a low risk to harm himself/herself.

20. Reinforce Statements of Hope (20)

A. The client's statements reflecting a will or reason to live were strongly reinforced.

B. The client was asked to develop a list of resource people who he/she can turn to during periods of despair and hopelessness.

C. The support of parent(s) and/or family members was enlisted to help decrease the client's risk for suicide or self-harm.

D. The client was asked to identify 5 to 10 strengths or interests to help reinforce the client's desire or reason to live.

E. The client's past was explored for periods of time when he/she was able to overcome adversity or stress to reinforce the idea that the client can overcome or cope with current stressors.

21. Contract for No Self-Harm (21)

A. The client verbally agreed to contact the therapist, parent(s), or significant others if he/she experiences suicidal thoughts or an urge to harm self in the future.

B. The client signed a contract agreeing to contact the therapist, parent(s), or significant others if he/she contemplates suicide or an urge to harm self in the future.

C. The client was referred for an evaluation for inpatient hospitalization because of his/her refusal to sign a no-self-harm contract or verbally commit to contacting the therapist, parent(s), or significant others if he/she contemplates suicide or experiences an urge to harm self in the future.

D. Signing the no-self-harm contract helped the client realize that there are resource people available that he/she can turn to in times of distress or despair.

22. Participate in Social/Recreational Activities (22)

A. The client was strongly encouraged to participate in social/recreational activities to decrease feelings of depression and enrich the quality of his/her life.

B.   The client was assisted in developing a list of social or recreational activities that will help to enrich the quality of his/her life and provide an opportunity to establish meaningful friendships.

C.   The client reported that his/her recent participation in social or recreational activities has helped to decrease his/her feelings of depression.

D.   The client has not participated in any recent social or recreational activities because of his/her depression and feelings of low self-worth.

23. Assess Need for Medications (23)

A.   The client was assessed for the need for psychotropic medication.

B.   The client was referred for a medication evaluation because he/she continues to experience a significant amount of depressive symptoms.

C.   The client was not referred for a medication evaluation because he/she is not exhibiting any endogenous signs of depression or experiencing any suicidal thoughts.

24. Arrange for Antidepressant Medication (24)

A.   A trial of antidepressant medication is indicated based on the client's reported symptoms.

B.   The client and parents agreed to follow through with a medication evaluation, and arrangements were made for the client to be seen by a physician.

C.   The client was strongly opposed to being placed on medication to help stabilize his/her moods and decrease symptoms of depression.

25. Monitor Medication Effects (25)

A.   The client's response to his/her medication was discussed.

B.   The client reported that the medication has helped to decrease his/her symptoms of depression and stabilize mood.

C.   The client reported little or no improvement since starting to take the medication.

D.   The client has not complied with taking his/her medication on a regular basis.

E.   The client was encouraged to report the side effects of the medication to the prescribing physician or psychiatrist.

F.   Contact will be made with the prescribing physician regarding the lack of effectiveness and the need for an adjustment in the prescription.

26. Encourage Academic Effort (26)

A.   The client was helped to establish academic goals to help lift his/her depression and improve self-esteem.

B.   The client was challenged and encouraged to achieve his/her academic goals to offset feelings of depression and improve self-esteem.

C.   The client and parents were assisted in developing a routine schedule of study times to mobilize the client and help him/her achieve academic success.

D.   A reward system was designed to reinforce the client to achieve his/her academic goals.

E.   The client and parents were encouraged to maintain regular communication with the teachers via phone calls or progress notes to help him/her stay organized and achieve academic goals.

27. Arrange for Tutor (27)

A. The client and parents were encouraged to work with a tutor to improve the client's academic performance.

B. The client and parents agreed to follow up by contacting a tutor through an outside learning center.

C. The client and parents were encouraged to consult with teachers or school officials about using peer tutors to improve his/her academic performance.

D. The client reported that tutoring has helped to improve his/her academic performance.

E. The client reported little or no improvement in his/her academic performance while working with a tutor.

28. Identify Extracurricular Activities (28)

A. The client was strongly encouraged to participate in extracurricular activities at school to help cease his/her pattern of social withdrawal and provide him/her with the opportunity to establish meaningful friendships.

B. The client was assisted in developing a list of extracurricular or peer group activities at school that he/she could participate in to break the pattern of social withdrawal and excessive introspection.

C. The client reported that his/her participation in extracurricular activities at school has helped to decrease his/her feelings of depression.

D. The client has failed to follow through with the recommendation to participate in extracurricular or peer group activities at school.

29. Increase Extracurricular Activity Involvement (29)

A. The client was given the directive to sign up or become involved in extracurricular activities to help decrease his/her depression by socializing with other people.

B. Today's therapy session explored the reasons for the client's resistance to becoming involved in extracurricular activities.

C. The client recognized how his/her feelings of insecurity and inadequacy contribute to his/her reluctance to become involved in extracurricular or peer group activities at school.

D. The client was assisted in developing a list of his/her strengths or interests, and then was encouraged to utilize these while participating in extracurricular activities.

E. A reward system was designed to reinforce the client for regularly participating in extracurricular activities.

30. Monitor Food Consumption (30)

A. The client was instructed to keep a daily log of his/her food consumption.

B. The client was encouraged to eat nutritious, well-balanced meals to cease pattern of weight loss.

C. The client was referred to a nutritionist to receive counseling about his/her diet.

D. Today's therapy session explored the factors contributing to the client's overeating.

E. The client verbally recognized that his/her pattern of overeating is related to unfulfilled dependency needs.

31. Monitor Sleep Patterns (31)

A. Today's therapy session explored the factors that interfere with the client being able to sleep restfully through the night.

B. The client was trained in the use of guided imagery and relaxation techniques to help induce calm before attempting to sleep.

C. The client was asked to track his/her sleep patterns to determine whether he/she should be referred for a medication evaluation.

D. The client was instructed to monitor his/her sleep patterns to help determine whether the medication needs to be changed or the dosage adjusted.

E. The client was administered electromyographic (EMG) biofeedback to reinforce a successful relaxation response to help him/her sleep restfully at night.

32. Encourage Parental Affirmation (32)

A. The parents were strongly encouraged to express warm, positive, affirming statements of love to the client on a regular basis.

B. The parents were directed to make at least three positive, affirmative statements toward the client each day.

C. The parents were challenged to look for opportunities to praise and affirm the client instead of focusing primarily on his/her emotional or behavioral problems.

D. The parents were instructed to observe and record three to five constructive behaviors that the client engaged in to help overcome his/her depression.

E. The client was strongly encouraged to continue to engage in responsible or socially appropriate behaviors to receive his/her parents' approval, affirmation, and expressions of love.

33. Establish Structured Activity Routine (33)

A. The parents were assisted in establishing a routine of positive, structured activities with the client to help mobilize him/her and decrease symptoms of depression.

B. The client and parents were assisted in developing a list of activities that they would enjoy doing together.

C. The client and parents were instructed to spend 15 minutes of daily one-on-one time together in a structured activity to increase the frequency of positive interactions and improve the lines of communication.

34. Identify Pleasurable Activities (34)

A. The client developed a list of pleasurable interests and activities that could be pursued to help lift feelings of depression.

B. The client was strongly encouraged to participate in extracurricular or positive peer group activities to cease social withdrawal and reduce feelings of depression.

C. The client was instructed to engage in at least one potentially pleasurable activity each day.

D. The client explored past interests or activities that provided him/her with a sense of enjoyment and was encouraged to engage in similar activities in the present to help overcome feelings of depression.

E. The client was assisted in identifying three to five role models and was encouraged to engage in pleasurable activities or interests that are similar to his/her role models.

35. Plan to Meet Social/Emotional Needs (35)

A. The client was helped to develop an action plan to meet his/her social and emotional needs.

B. The client explored periods of time in the past when he/she felt less depressed and took active steps to meet his/her social and emotional needs.

C. The client was encouraged to take steps similar to those used successfully in the past to meet his/her social and emotional needs.

D. The client shared the realization that his/her involvement in extracurricular or positive peer group activities in the past helped him/her to meet social and emotional needs.

E. The therapy session revealed how the client felt less depressed in the past when he/she received strong family support and affiliated with positive peer groups.

36. Reinforce Social Interactions (36)

A. Behavior rehearsal and role-playing techniques were used to model positive social skills and appropriate ways to initiate and/or sustain pleasant conversations with friends or family members.

B. A reward system was implemented to reinforce the client for initiating pleasant social interactions with peers and/or family members.

C. The client was given the homework assignment to initiate one pleasant conversation each day.

D. The client was given a homework assignment to initiate three phone calls per week to different individuals.

37. Utilize Art Therapy Techniques (37)

A. Art therapy techniques were used to help the client express his/her depressive feelings.

B. The client's artwork was used as a springboard to help explore the causes of his/her depression or other painful emotions.

C. The use of art therapy helped the client express his/her feelings of depression and identify the causes.

D. The client's artwork provided little insight into the sources of his/her depression.

38. Assess Substance Abuse (38)

A. A diagnostic interview was conducted to determine whether the client is using alcohol or drugs as a means of coping with depressive feelings.

B. The client was referred for a substance abuse evaluation to assess the extent of his/her drug or alcohol use and determine the need for treatment.

C. The client appeared to be cooperative in answering questions about his/her past alcohol or drug usage.

D. The client was resistant to discussing his/her past alcohol or drug usage.

39. Substance Abuse Referral (39)

A. The findings from the substance abuse evaluation revealed the presence of a substance abuse problem, and therefore the client was referred for chemical dependence treatment.

B. The client expressed a willingness to seek treatment for his/her substance abuse problem.

C. The client expressed resistance to receiving substance abuse treatment.

D. The findings from the substance abuse evaluation did not reveal the presence of a substance abuse problem or the need for treatment in this area.

40. Explore Causes for Sexual Promiscuity (40)

A. The client explored the factors contributing to his/her irresponsible or sexually promiscuous behavior.

B. The client shared the realization that he/she often tries to overcome depression and meet his/her dependency needs through sexually promiscuous behavior.

C. The client had difficulty identifying the factors contributing to his/her sexually promiscuous behavior.

D. Today's therapy session explored the client's irrational or unrealistic beliefs that underlie his/her sexually promiscuous behavior.

41. Confront Sexual Acting Out (41)

A. The client was confronted with the potential dangers or risks involved with his/her irresponsible sexual acting-out behavior.

B. The client was provided with sex education in an attempt to eliminate his/her pattern of engaging in irresponsible sexual acting-out behavior.

C. The client identified ways to meet his/her needs and overcome depression that would be more effective than sexual acting out.

D. The client's irrational or unrealistic beliefs about his/her sexual acting out were confronted and replaced with more adaptive ways of thinking.

E. The therapy session was helpful in identifying the core conflicts contributing to the client's irresponsible sexual acting-out behaviors.

42. Assess Unresolved Grief Issues (42)

A. Today's therapy session explored whether unresolved grief and loss issues are contributing to the client's depression.

B. The client was given the opportunity to express his/her feelings about past separations or losses.

C. Art therapy techniques were utilized to help explore whether the client is troubled by unresolved grief and loss issues.

D. Client-centered therapy principles were employed to help the client explore grief and loss issues.

E. Psychoanalytic therapy principles were used to explore how grief issues are related to his/her depression.

43. Treat Grief Issues (43)

A. The client was provided with support in expressing his/her feelings of sadness, hurt, loneliness, and anger surrounding past separations or losses.

B. The client was instructed to write a letter to the deceased or absent person to help him/her express feelings about past separations or losses.

C. The client was instructed to use a journal to record his/her daily thoughts and feelings about past grief issues.

D. The empty-chair technique was employed to facilitate expression of feelings surrounding past separations or losses.

E. The client was instructed to draw pictures reflecting his/her feelings about past losses and how they have impacted his/her life.

DIVORCE REACTION

CLIENT PRESENTATION

1. Reduced Contact with a Parent (1)*

A. The client has had infrequent or no contact with one of his/her parents since the separation or divorce.

B. The client was guarded and reluctant to talk about the infrequent or loss of contact with one of his/her parents.

C. The client expressed feelings of sadness, hurt, and disappointment about the infrequent or loss of contact with one of his/her parents.

D. The client verbalized strong feelings of anger about the limited contact with one of his/her parents.

E. The client has worked through many of his/her emotions surrounding the infrequent or loss of contact with one of his/her parents.

2. Loss of Contact with Positive Support Network (2)

A. The client has experienced a loss of contact with his/her previous support network due to his/her geographic move.

B. The client expressed feelings of sadness about having to move after his/her parents' separation or divorce because it resulted in a loss of contact with his/her previous support network.

C. The client expressed feelings of anger about having to move after his/her parents' separation or divorce.

D. The client has taken active steps to build a positive support network since moving to a new geographic area.

E. The client reported establishing a strong, supportive social network outside of his/her immediate family.

3. Feelings of Guilt/Self-Blame (3)

A. The client expressed feelings of guilt about having acted in some way to cause his/her parents' divorce.

B. The client has continued to hold onto the unreasonable belief that he/she behaved in some manner that either caused his/her parents' divorce or failed to prevent it from occurring.

C. The client has started to work through his/her feelings of guilt about his/her parents' separation or divorce.

D. The parent(s) verbalized that the client is not responsible for the separation or divorce.

E. The client has successfully worked through his/her feelings of guilt and no longer blames himself/herself for the parents' separation or divorce.

* The numbers in parentheses correlate to the number of the Behavioral Definition statement in the companion chapter with same title in *The Adolescent Psychotherapy Treatment Planner* (Jongsma, Peterson, and McInnis) by John Wiley & Sons, 2000.

4. Feelings of Grief and Sadness (4)

A. The client has experienced strong feelings of grief and sadness since his/her parents' separation or divorce.

B. The client was visibly sad when talking about his/her parents' separation or divorce.

C. The client has begun to work through his/her feelings of grief and sadness about the separation or divorce.

D. The client's affect appeared more happy and/or contented in today's therapy session.

E. The client reported a significant reduction recently in the frequency and severity of his/her depressed mood.

5. Low Self-Esteem (4)

A. The client's self-esteem has decreased significantly since his/her parents' separation or divorce.

B. The client verbalized feelings of low self-esteem, inadequacy, and insecurity.

C. The client has begun to take steps to improve his/her self-esteem and develop a positive self-image.

D. The client expressed positive self-descriptive statements during today's therapy session.

E. The client has developed a healthy self-image after working through many of his/her feelings surrounding his/her parents' separation or divorce.

6. Social Withdrawal (4)

A. The client has become significantly more withdrawn and isolated since his/her parents' separation or divorce.

B. The client appeared very quiet and withdrawn during today's therapy session and initiated few conversations.

C. The client has gradually started to socialize more often with his/her peers.

D. The client was more communicative and outgoing during today's therapy session.

7. Anxiety (4)

A. The client reported a significant increase in his/her feelings of anxiety since his/her parents' separation or divorce.

B. The client appeared nervous, anxious, and tense during today's therapy session.

C. The client's feelings of anxiety have gradually started to decrease as he/she works through his/her feelings about the separation or divorce.

D. The client appeared more relaxed and comfortable in today's therapy session.

E. The client reported a significant reduction in the frequency of his/her anxious moods.

8. Intense Emotional Outbursts/Sudden Shifts in Mood (5)

A. The client has exhibited frequent, intense emotional outbursts and sudden shifts in mood since the separation or divorce.

B. The client acknowledged that he/she has difficulty controlling his/her emotions when discussing topics related to the separation or divorce.

C. The client exhibited a wide range of emotions when discussing the separation or divorce.

D. The client's moods have begun to stabilize as he/she works through his/her feelings about the separation or divorce.

9. Neglect, Abuse, or Abandonment (5)

A. The client reported a history of experiencing abuse, neglect, or abandonment in his/her family background.

B. The client was guarded and reluctant to talk about past neglect, abuse, and abandonment.

C. The client expressed feelings of sadness and hurt about the past incidents of neglect, abuse, and abandonment.

D. The client verbalized strong feelings of anger about the past abuse, neglect, and abandonment.

10. Visitation Arrangements (5)

A. The client reported a significant amount of conflict or discord within the family system over the child visitation arrangements.

B. The client expressed dissatisfaction with the current visitation arrangements between himself/herself and the noncustodial parent.

C. The client expressed a desire to spend more time with the noncustodial parent.

D. The client verbalized his/her preference for socializing with peers instead of visiting with the noncustodial parent.

E. The parents have established and maintained consistent, yet flexible, visitation arrangements that have met the client's social and emotional needs.

11. Oppositional, Acting-Out, and Aggressive Behaviors (6)

A. The client has exhibited a significant increase in the frequency and severity of his/her oppositional, acting-out, and aggressive behaviors since his/her parents' separation or divorce.

B. The client appeared angry and irritable when discussing the separation or divorce.

C. The frequency of the client's oppositional, acting-out, and aggressive behaviors has gradually started to diminish.

D. The client has recently demonstrated good self-control and has not engaged in a significant amount of oppositional, acting-out, or aggressive behaviors.

E. The client has successfully worked through many of his/her feelings surrounding the separation or divorce and has demonstrated a significant reduction in the frequency and severity of his/her oppositional, acting-out, and aggressive behaviors.

12. Lack of Consistency by Parents (6)

A. The parent(s) have not set firm, consistent limits for the client's irresponsible or acting-out behaviors since the separation or divorce.

B. The parent(s) acknowledged that their lack of consistency has contributed to an increase in the client's acting-out and irresponsible behaviors.

C. The parent(s) acknowledged that their feelings of guilt about the separation or divorce have contributed to their lack of consistency.

D. The parent(s) have started to take steps to increase the structure in the home and to be more consistent in setting limits for the client's irresponsible or acting-out behaviors.

E. The parent(s) reported that the increase in consistency and structure has led to a decrease in the frequency of the client's irresponsible and acting-out behaviors.

13. Overindulgence by Parents (6)

A. The parent(s) have exhibited a pattern of being overindulgent in meeting the client's desires since the separation or divorce.

B. The parent(s) acknowledged that their feelings of guilt about the separation or divorce have contributed to their pattern of overindulgence.

C. The noncustodial parent acknowledged that he/she is overindulgent with the client on visits to avoid any possible conflict or stress.

D. The parent(s) have begun to establish reasonable limits on the fulfillment of the client's wishes.

14. Parents Critical of Each Other (6)

A. The client reported that his/her parent(s) often make hostile, critical remarks about one another in his/her presence.

B. The client expressed feelings of anger, sadness, and frustration about one parent's pattern of making unnecessary, hostile, or overly critical remarks about the other parent.

C. The client verbalized his/her request for the parents to cease making unnecessary, hostile, or overly critical remarks about each other in his/her presence.

D. The parent(s) acknowledged that their hostile or critical remarks about the other parent are upsetting to the client and his/her siblings.

E. The client reported that his/her parent(s) have ceased making hostile or overly critical remarks about the other parent in his/her presence.

15. Decline in School Performance (7)

A. The client's school performance has decreased markedly since his/her parents' separation or divorce.

B. The client verbalized that he/she has experienced a loss of interest or motivation to achieve academic success since the separation or divorce.

C. The client has experienced a renewed interest in his/her schoolwork and has begun to take steps to improve his/her academic performance.

D. The client reported completing his/her school or homework assignments on a regular basis.

16. Substance Abuse (8)

A. The client has engaged in a significant amount of substance abuse since his/her parents' separation or divorce.

B. The client acknowledged that he/she has often turned to alcohol or drug abuse to block out the emotional pain related to his/her parents' separation or divorce.

C. The client verbalized an awareness of the negative consequences or potential dangers associated with his/her substance abuse.

D. Instead of turning to drug or alcohol abuse, the client has started to develop more adaptive coping mechanisms to help him/her deal with the stress and emotional pain surrounding the separation or divorce.

E. The client stated that he/she has terminated his/her substance abuse.

17. Sexually Promiscuous Behavior (9)

A. The client described a pattern of engaging in sexually promiscuous or seductive behavior since his/her parents' separation or divorce.

B. The client acknowledged that he/she has engaged in sexually promiscuous or seductive behavior to compensate for the loss of security or support within the family system.

C. The client verbalized an awareness of the negative consequences and potential dangers associated with his/her sexually promiscuous behavior.

D. The client has demonstrated good control over his/her sexual impulses and has not engaged in any risky or irresponsible sexual behavior.

18. Pseudomaturity (10)

A. The client has responded to his/her parents' separation or divorce by displaying an air of pseudomaturity.

B. The client presented with a facade of pseudomaturity and coolly denied being troubled by any painful emotions about his/her parents' separation or divorce.

C. The client has responded to the separation or divorce by often assuming parental roles or responsibilities.

D. The client verbalized an awareness of how his/her willingness to take on many parental roles or responsibilities has prevented him/her from meeting his/her own emotional or social needs.

E. The client has achieved a healthy balance between fulfilling his/her school or household responsibilities and meeting his/her social and emotional needs.

19. Psychosomatic Ailments (11)

A. The client has demonstrated a significant increase in psychosomatic complaints since his/her parents' separation or divorce.

B. The client complained of not feeling well when the issue of his/her parents' separation or divorce was being discussed.

C. The client was resistant to the interpretation that his/her psychosomatic complaints are related to his/her underlying painful emotions about the separation or divorce.

D. The client verbalized an understanding of the connection between his/her psychosomatic complaints and anticipated separations, stress, or frustration related to the parents' marital conflict.

E. The client has demonstrated a significant reduction in the frequency of his/her psychosomatic complaints.

INTERVENTIONS IMPLEMENTED

1. Build Therapeutic Trust (1)*

A. The objective of today's therapy session was to establish trust with the client so that he/she can begin to express and work through his/her feelings related to the parents' separation or divorce.

B. Attempts were made to build the level of trust with the client through consistent eye contact, active listening, unconditional positive regard, and warm acceptance.

C. The therapy session was helpful in building a level of trust with the client.

D. The therapy session was not successful in establishing trust with the client, as he/she remained guarded in sharing his/her feelings about the separation or divorce.

2. Explore and Encourage Expression of Feelings (2)

A. Today's therapy session explored the client's feelings associated with his/her parents' separation or divorce.

B. The client was given encouragement and support in expressing and clarifying his/her feelings associated with the separation or divorce.

C. Client-centered therapy principles were utilized to assist the client in expressing his/her thoughts and feelings about the parents' separation or divorce.

D. The client made productive use of today's therapy session and expressed a variety of emotions related to his/her parents' separation or divorce.

E. The client remained guarded in sharing his/her feelings regarding the separation or divorce, despite receiving encouragement and support.

3. Develop a Time Line (3)

A. The client developed a time line on which he/she recorded significant developments that have positively or negatively impacted his/her family life, both before and after the separation or divorce.

B. The use of the time line was helpful in allowing the client to express his/her thoughts and feelings about the impact of the separation or divorce on his/her life.

C. The use of the time line exercise was not helpful in facilitating a discussion about the impact of the parents' separation or divorce on the client's life.

D. The client was able to identify a number of positive and negative changes that have occurred within the family system since the parents' separation or divorce.

E. The client used the time line to express his/her ambivalent feelings about the divorce and the subsequent changes within the family system.

4. Utilize the Empty-Chair Technique (4)

A. The empty-chair technique was used to help the client express the mixed emotions that he/she feels toward both parents about the separation or divorce.

B. The empty-chair technique was helpful in allowing the client to identify and express the emotions that he/she feels toward both parents about the separation or divorce.

---

* The numbers in parentheses correlate to the number of the Therapeutic Intervention statement in the companion chapter with the same title in *The Adolescent Psychotherapy Treatment Planner* (Jongsma, Peterson, and McInnis) by John Wiley & Sons, 2000.

C. The client appeared uncomfortable with the use of the empty-chair technique and was reluctant to share the emotions that he/she feels toward both parents about the separation or divorce.

D. The empty-chair technique was useful in allowing the client to express his/her thoughts and feelings about the custodial and noncustodial parent.

5. Keep a Journal (5)

A. The client was instructed to keep a journal in which he/she records experiences or situations that evoke strong emotions pertaining to the separation or divorce.

B. The client shared entries from his/her journal that reflected his/her thoughts and feelings about the separation or divorce.

C. The use of the journal has proven to be helpful in allowing the client to express and work through his/her feelings about the separation or divorce.

D. The client has failed to keep a journal reflecting his/her thoughts and feelings about the separation or divorce.

6. Develop a List of Questions (6)

A. The client was assisted in developing a list of questions about the parents' separation or divorce.

B. The client first identified the questions that he/she has about the separation or divorce and then explored possible answers for each question.

C. The client carefully considered whether he/she wanted to ask the parent(s) specific questions about the separation or divorce.

D. The client was encouraged to ask each parent specific questions about the separation or divorce to help him/her gain a greater understanding of the factors contributing to the separation or divorce.

E. The client decided not to ask specific questions to each parent about the separation or divorce because of the possible negative responses that he/she might receive.

7. Family Therapy to Facilitate Expression of Feelings (7)

A. A family therapy session was held to allow the client and his/her siblings to express feelings and ask questions about the separation or divorce in the presence of the parents.

B. The custodial parent was supportive in allowing the client and siblings to express their feelings and ask questions about the separation or divorce.

C. The noncustodial parent was supportive in allowing the client and siblings to express their feelings and ask questions about the separation or divorce.

D. The custodial parent became defensive when the client and siblings began expressing their feelings and asking questions about the separation or divorce.

E. The noncustodial parent became defensive when the client and siblings began expressing their feelings and asking questions about the separation or divorce.

8. Provide Opportunities at Home to Express Feelings (8)

A. The parent(s) were encouraged to provide opportunities at home to allow the client and siblings to express their feelings and ask questions about the separation or divorce and subsequent changes in the family system.

B. The parent(s) were encouraged to hold family meetings at home to allow the client and siblings an opportunity to express their feelings and ask questions about the separation or divorce and subsequent changes in the family system.

C. The family members were helped to identify healthy and unhealthy ways to express their feelings about the separation or divorce and subsequent changes in the family system.

D. The parent(s) were encouraged to explore the client's feelings about the separation or divorce and subsequent changes in the family system when he/she becomes more withdrawn or demonstrates an increase in emotional outbursts.

E. The client and siblings were asked to identify the specific, positive changes that they would like to see happen in the family.

9. Assess Factors Contributing to Guilt (9)

A. Today's therapy session explored and identified the factors contributing to the client's feelings of guilt and self-blame about the parents' separation or divorce.

B. The client expressed feelings of guilt about how his/her acting-out or rebellious behaviors may have contributed to his/her parents' separation or divorce.

C. Today's therapy session did not reveal any specific events that have contributed to the client's feelings of guilt and self-blame about the parents' separation/divorce.

D. The client denied being troubled by any strong feelings of guilt about his/her parents' separation or divorce.

10. Teach That Client's Behaviors Did Not Cause Divorce (10)

A. The client was helped to understand that his/her negative behaviors did not cause his/her parents' divorce to occur.

B. The client was gently confronted with the fact that he/she does not have the power or control to bring his/her parents back together.

C. The client has continued to hold onto feelings of guilt about how his/her negative behaviors caused his/her parents' divorce, despite efforts to reassure him/her that he/she is not responsible.

D. The client was helped to realize how his/her negative behaviors will not bring the parents back together.

11. Affirm Client as Not Being Responsible for Separation/Divorce (11)

A. The custodial parent strongly affirmed that the client and siblings were not responsible for the separation or divorce.

B. The noncustodial parent strongly affirmed that the client and siblings were not responsible for the separation or divorce.

C. The parent(s) verbalized responsibility for the separation or divorce.

D. The client and siblings responded positively to the parents' affirmation that they are not responsible for the separation or divorce.

E. The client has continued to be troubled by feelings of guilt about his/her parents' divorce despite the parents' statements that he/she is not responsible.

12. Confront Blaming by Parents (12)

A. The custodial parent was challenged and confronted about making statements that place the blame or responsibility for the separation or divorce on the client or siblings.

B. The noncustodial parent was challenged and confronted about making statements that place the blame or responsibility for the separation or divorce on the client or siblings.

C. The custodial parent verbalized a commitment to cease making statements that place the blame or responsibility for the separation or divorce onto the client or siblings.

D. The noncustodial parent verbalized a commitment to cease making statements that place the blame or responsibility for the separation or divorce onto the client or siblings.

E. The parent(s) have continued to make statements that place the blame or responsibility for the separation or divorce onto the client or siblings despite challenges to cease making such remarks.

13. List Positive and Negative Aspects of Divorce (13)

A. The client was given a homework assignment to list both the positive and negative aspects of his/her parents' divorce.

B. The client was reassured of the normalcy of feeling a variety of emotions while processing both the positive and negative aspects of his/her parents' divorce.

C. The client expressed his/her emotions about the negative aspects of his/her parents' divorce but was unable to identify any positive aspects.

D. The client's failure to complete the homework assignment of listing both the positive or negative aspects of his/her parents' divorce appeared to be due to his/her desire to avoid dealing with any painful emotions.

14. Reinforce Healthy Coping with Divorce (14)

A. The therapy session focused on empowering the client's ability to cope with his/her parents' divorce.

B. The client was asked to identify a list of behaviors or signs that would indicate he/she has made a healthy adjustment to the parents' divorce.

C. The client was reinforced for the positive steps that he/she has taken to adjust to his/her parents' divorce.

D. The client remains pessimistic and resistant to the idea that he/she can make a healthy adjustment to the divorce.

15. Provide Support for Expression of Painful Emotions (15)

A. The client was given support to express his/her feelings of sadness, depression, and anxiety about the divorce.

B. The client was encouraged to record his/her thoughts and feelings in a daily journal as a way to clarify and express painful emotions.

C. The client has remained resistant to expressing any painful emotions about his/her parents' divorce despite receiving support and encouragement.

16. Encourage Parents to Spend Time with Client (16)

A. The parent(s) were given the directive to spend 10 to 15 minutes of one-on-one time with the client and siblings on a regular or daily basis.

B. The client reported that the one-on-one time spent with the parent(s) has helped to decrease his/her feelings of depression.

C. The client and parents reported that the one-on-one time spent together has helped to improve his/her anger control.

D. The client and parents reported that they have spent little time together because of their busy schedules.

E. The client and parents were strongly challenged to spend time together in order to help the client adjust to his/her parents' divorce.

17. Assist Transition from One Parent's Home to Another (17)

A. The client was asked to identify a list of activities that he/she could engage in to make a successful transition from one parent's home to another without exhibiting excessive emotional distress, fighting, or arguing.

B. The client reported that he/she has made a smoother transition from one parent's home to another by engaging in relaxing or enjoyable activities.

C. The client has continued to make a difficult transition from one parent's home to another after visits, but has failed to follow through with the recommendation to engage in relaxing or enjoyable activities.

18. Connect Painful Emotions to Angry Outbursts (18)

A. The session was helpful in identifying how the client's underlying, painful emotions about his/her parents' divorce are related to an increase in the frequency of his/her angry outbursts or aggressive behaviors.

B. The client verbalized an understanding of how his/her aggressive behaviors are connected to underlying feelings of sadness, hurt, or disappointment about his/her parents' divorce.

C. Role-playing and modeling techniques were used to demonstrate appropriate ways for the client to express his/her underlying painful emotions.

D. The client was asked to list ways to express his/her painful emotions about the divorce that would be more appropriate than reacting impulsively with anger or aggression.

19. Teach Appropriate versus Inappropriate Anger Expressions (19)

A. The client was helped to identify appropriate and inappropriate ways to express or control his/her anger about the parents' separation, divorce, or changes in family.

B. The client was taught mediational and self-control strategies (e.g., relaxation, "stop, look, listen, and think") to help express anger through appropriate verbalizations and healthy physical outlets.

C. The client was encouraged to utilize active listening skills to delay the impulse or urge to react with anger or physical aggression when upset about his/her parents' separation, divorce, or changes in family.

D. The client identified healthy physical outlets for his/her strong feelings of anger and aggressive impulses.

20. Teach Relaxation or Guided Imagery Techniques (20)

A. The client was taught relaxation and guided imagery techniques to help control his/her anger.

B. The client reported a positive response to the use of relaxation or guided imagery techniques to help control anger.

C. The client has failed to consistently use the relaxation or guided imagery techniques and, as a result, has continued to display anger control problems.

21. Reinforce Parents in Setting Consistent Limits (21)

A. The parent(s) were strongly encouraged to set firm, consistent limits for the client's acting-out, oppositional, or aggressive behaviors and not to allow guilt feelings about the divorce to interfere with the need to impose consequences for such behaviors.

B. The parent(s) acknowledged their failure to follow through with firm, consistent limits for the client's acting-out, oppositional, or aggressive behaviors because of guilt feelings about the divorce.

C. The parent(s) reported that they have begun to set firm, consistent limits and have not allowed their guilt feelings to interfere with the need to impose consequences.

D. The parent(s) reported that the client has demonstrated improvements in his/her behavior since they began to set firm, consistent limits for his/her acting-out, oppositional, or aggressive behaviors.

22. Encourage Parents to Establish Clear Rules (22)

A. The parent(s) were helped to establish clearly defined rules and boundaries for the client.

B. The client and parents were helped to identify natural, logical consequences for the client's acting-out, oppositional, or aggressive behaviors.

C. The client was asked to repeat the rules to demonstrate an understanding of the expectations of him/her.

D. The client verbally disagreed with the rules and expectations identified by the parent(s).

23. Develop Reward System for Anger Control (23)

A. The client and parents identified a list of rewards to reinforce the client for demonstrating good anger control.

B. A reward system was designed to reinforce the client for demonstrating good anger control.

C. The client and parents signed a contingency contract specifying the consequences for his/her acting-out, oppositional, or aggressive behaviors.

D. The client and parents verbally agreed to the terms of the contingency contract.

24. Assist Parents in Developing Homework Routine (24)

A. The parent(s) were assisted in establishing a new routine to help the client complete his/her school or homework assignments.

B. The client and parent(s) were helped to develop a routine schedule of times to increase the completion of homework assignments.

C. The parents were strongly encouraged to maintain regular communication with the teachers or school officials via phone calls or written notes regarding the client's academic progress.

D. Consulted with the teachers about sending home daily or weekly progress notes informing the parents of how well the client has been doing at completing his/her school or homework assignments.

25. Develop Reward System to Improve Academic Performance (25)

A. The client and parents identified a list of rewards to reinforce the client for completing his/her school or homework assignments on a regular basis.

B. A reward system was designed to reinforce the client for completing his/her school or homework assignment.

C. The client and parents signed a contingency contract specifying the consequences for his/her failure to complete school or homework assignments.

D. The client and parents verbally agreed to the terms of the reward system and/or contingency contract.

26. Explore Relationship of Physical Complaints to Emotional Conflicts (26)

A. Today's therapy session focused on the relationship between the client's somatic complaints and underlying emotional conflicts associated with the parents' divorce.

B. Today's therapy session attempted to refocus the discussion away from the client's physical complaints and onto the underlying emotional conflicts and the expression of feelings associated with the parents' divorce.

C. Today's therapy session explored the secondary gain that is achieved by the client's somatic complaints.

D. The client verbally acknowledged that his/her somatic physical complaints are associated with the stress and conflict surrounding his/her parents' divorce.

E. The client verbalized an understanding of how his/her somatic complaints are related to unfulfilled dependency needs.

27. Clarify Roles and Responsibilities of Family Members (27)

A. A family therapy session was held to discuss the roles and division of responsibilities of all family members.

B. Today's therapy session was helpful in identifying the rules, roles, and responsibilities of all family members.

C. The family members disagreed about the roles and division of household responsibilities.

D. A reward system was designed to reinforce the client and siblings for completing their household responsibilities.

E. A contingency contract was established to identify the consequences for family members' failure to complete their household responsibilities.

28. Assignment of Responsibilities by Noncustodial Parent (28)

A. The noncustodial parent was given the directive to assign chore(s) to the client and siblings during their visits.

B. The noncustodial parent was encouraged to schedule times for the client and siblings to complete their homework.

C. The noncustodial parent acknowledged that he/she is reluctant to assign chores or require the children to complete homework because of the desire to avoid upsetting the client or siblings or creating potential conflict.

D. The noncustodial parent was helped to develop a reward system to reinforce the client and siblings for completing chores and homework during visits.

E. The noncustodial parent was helped to identify consequences for the failure of his/her children to complete chores or homework.

29. Encourage Limit Setting by Noncustodial Parent (29)

A. The noncustodial parent was strongly encouraged to set firm, consistent limits for the client's misbehavior and to refrain from overindulging the client's desires during visits.

B. The noncustodial parent was helped to identify logical, natural consequences for the client's misbehavior.

C. The noncustodial parent verbally acknowledged how his/her pattern of overindulgence contributes to the client's immaturity and resistance to take on responsibilities.

D. The noncustodial parent acknowledged his/her reluctance to set limits for the client's misbehavior because of his/her feelings of guilt and desire to avoid conflict during visits.

E. The noncustodial parent reported that the frequency of the client's misbehavior has decreased since he/she began setting firm, consistent limits on the client's acting out.

30. Teach Enmeshed Parent(s) to Set Limits (30)

A. The enmeshed or overly protective parent was helped to see how his/her failure to set limits reinforces the client's immature or irresponsible behavior.

B. The enmeshed or overly protective parent was helped to identify natural, logical consequences for the client's immature or irresponsible behavior.

C. The parent(s) were encouraged to offer frequent praise and positive reinforcement for the client's responsible behavior.

D. A reward system was designed to reinforce the client for behaving in a responsible manner.

31. Identify Age-Appropriate Ways to Meet Needs (31)

A. The client and parent(s) identified age-appropriate ways for the client to meet his/her needs for affiliation, acceptance, and approval.

B. The client was given the homework assignment to engage in a specific, age-appropriate behavior three to five times before the next therapy session.

C. Role-playing and modeling techniques were utilized to demonstrate age-appropriate ways to gain affiliation, acceptance, and approval from others.

D. The client was taught effective communication skills to help meet his/her needs for affiliation, acceptance, and approval.

32. Challenge Parent(s) to Assume Parental Role (32)

A. The parent(s) were challenged to assert their appropriate authority and take active steps to prevent the overly responsible child from assuming too many parental or household responsibilities.

B. The parent(s) were helped to identify ways to assert appropriate parental authority.

C. The parent acknowledged that he/she has often turned to the older child for help in performing many of the household responsibilities since the separation.

D. The parent reported that he/she has taken positive steps to decrease the amount of responsibilities expected of the overly responsible or parental child in the family.

E. The parent reported that the overly responsible or parental child has resisted giving up some of his/her parental or household responsibilities.

33. Parents Encourage Client's Social Activities (33)

A. The parents were instructed to schedule or allow time for the overly responsible client to engage in positive peer group or extracurricular activities.

B. The overly responsible client identified a list of interests or extracurricular activities that he/she likes to engage in with peers.

C. The overly responsible client was given a homework assignment to engage in three to five positive peer group or extracurricular activities before the next therapy session.

34. Urge Parents to Stop Criticizing Ex-Spouse (34)

A. The parent was challenged and confronted about making hostile or overly critical remarks about the other parent in the presence of the client and siblings.

B. The client's parent(s) verbally recognized how hostile or overly critical remarks about the other parent are upsetting to the client and siblings.

35. Teach Parents to Avoid Placing Client in Middle (35)

A. The parent(s) were challenged to cease the pattern of placing the client in the middle role by soliciting information about the other parent or sending messages through the client to the other parent about adult matters.

B. The parent(s) verbalized an awareness of how placing the client in the middle role is upsetting to him/her.

36. Confront Playing One Parent against the Other (36)

A. The client was challenged and confronted about playing one parent against the other to meet his/her needs, obtain material goods, or avoid responsibility.

B. Today's therapy session explored the reasons for the client's attempt to play one parent against the other.

C. The parent(s) were encouraged to deal directly with the client and set limits on his/her manipulative behaviors.

D. The client was helped to identify ways to meet his/her needs or obtain material goods that are more constructive than manipulating the parent(s).

E. The client acknowledged how his/her pattern of playing one parent against the other is aimed at trying to bring the parents back together.

37. Facilitate Expression of Feelings about Disruption in Life (37)

A. The client was given the opportunity to express his/her feelings about the family move and change in schools.

B. The client was asked to list the positive and negative aspects of having to move and change schools.

C. The client expressed his/her feelings about the infrequent contact or abandonment by the noncustodial parent.

D. The client made productive use of today's therapy session to express feelings of anger, hurt, sadness, and disappointment about the infrequent contact or abandonment by the noncustodial parent.

E. The client was given the opportunity to express his/her feelings about the past abuse within the family.

38. Encourage Noncustodial Parent to Maintain Visitation (38)

A. The noncustodial parent was challenged and encouraged to maintain regular visitation and involvement in the client's life.

B. The client asserted his/her wish in today's family therapy session for the noncustodial parent to maintain regular visitation and involvement in his/her life.

C. Today's therapy session explored the factors contributing to the noncustodial parent's failure to maintain regular visitation and involvement in the client's life.

D. The noncustodial parent verbally recognized that the lack of regular visitation has exacerbated the client's adjustment problems to the divorce.

E. The family therapy session focused on developing a regular visitation schedule between the noncustodial parent and the client.

39. Assign Disengaged Parent to Increase Time with Client (39)

A. The disengaged parent was given a directive to spend more quality time with the client and siblings.

B. The disengaged parent was given a homework assignment of performing a specific task with the client.

C. The client and disengaged parent developed a list of tasks or activities that they would like to do together.

D. The client reported that the increased time spent with the previously disengaged parent has helped the two of them establish a closer relationship.

E. The client reported that his/her relationship with the disengaged parent remains distant because the two have spent little time together.

40. Assign Letter to Uninvolved or Absent Parent (40)

A. The client was given a homework assignment to first write a letter to the uninvolved or absent parent, then bring it back to the next therapy session to process his/her thoughts and feelings.

B. The client's letter to the uninvolved or absent parent reflected feelings of sadness and hurt, as well as a desire for a closer relationship.

C. The client expressed strong feelings of hurt and anger in his/her letter to the uninvolved or absent parent.

D. The client discussed whether he/she wanted to send the letter to the uninvolved parent or preferred to express his/her emotions directly in a face-to-face meeting.

E. The client's failure to write a letter to the uninvolved or absent parent reflected his/her desire to avoid dealing with any painful emotions surrounding the lack of contact.

41. Utilize Guided Imagery to Visualize Better Future (41)

A. Guided imagery techniques were utilized to help the client visualize how his/her life will be better in the future when he/she resolves feelings of grief.

B. Through the use of guided imagery, the client was able to visualize what he/she sees himself/herself doing in the future to help cope with the parents' divorce and move on with his/her life.

C. The client was able to successfully identify a task or activity that he/she could perform in the future to show that he/she has moved on with his/her life.

D. The client was encouraged to engage in activities or tasks that will help him/her cope with divorce and move on with his/her life.

E. The client appeared uncomfortable during the guided imagery and was unable to visualize a brighter future.

42. Introduce Idea of Brighter Future (42)

A. The idea was introduced that the client could cope with his/her parents' divorce by asking the question, "What will you be doing in the future that shows you are happy and have moved on with your life?"

B. The client's response to the question "What will you be doing in the future that shows you are happy and have moved on with your life?" was processed.

C. The client responded positively to the question about finding happiness in the future by identifying his/her strengths or resources that he/she can utilize to overcome adjustment problems.

D. The client identified several strengths or resources that he/she could use to overcome adjustment problems related to the parents' divorce.

43. Identify Positive Role Models (43)

A. The client identified three to five positive role models who had to overcome adversity or stress to achieve their goals.

B. The client was encouraged to use coping strategies similar to those used successfully by positive role models to help him/her manage the stress surrounding the parents' divorce.

C. The client understood that many of his/her positive role models overcame adversity by setting goals and taking active steps toward achieving them.

44. Utilize Art Therapy Techniques (44)

A. The client was instructed to draw pictures reflecting his/her feelings about the parents' divorce, family move, or change in schools.

B. The client's drawings reflected his/her feelings of anger, sadness, and hurt about the parents' divorce.

C. The client's drawings reflected feelings of anger, sadness, and loneliness about the family move and/or change in school.

D. After completing his/her drawings, the client was able to verbalize his/her feelings about the parents' divorce, family move, or change in schools.

45. Utilize Music Therapy Techniques (45)

A. The client shared a song that reflected his/her feelings about the parents' separation/divorce.

B. The client shared a song that afterward led to a discussion of how the song reflects his/her feelings about the parents' separation/divorce and what he/she can do to cope with the changes in his/her life.

46. Read *S.O.S. Help for Emotions* (46)

A. The client was instructed to read *S.O.S. Help for Emotions* (Clark) to help him/her learn effective ways to manage or control his/her negative emotions connected to parent's divorce.

B. Processed the reading of *S.O.S. Help for Emotions.*

C. The client identified several helpful strategies that he/she learned from reading *S.O.S. Help for Emotions* to help manage negative emotions surrounding the parents' divorce.

47. Encourage Participation in Positive Peer Group Activities (47)

A. The client was strongly encouraged to participate in school, extracurricular, or positive peer group activities to offset the loss of time spent with his/her parents.

B. The client developed a list of school, extracurricular, or positive peer group activities that will help him/her cope with the parents' divorce and establish meaningful friendships.

C. The client reported that the participation in school, extracurricular, or positive peer group activities has helped him/her cope with the parents' divorce and feel less depressed or lonely.

D. The client has continued to struggle to cope with his/her parents' divorce, but as of yet has not taken many steps to become involved in school, extracurricular, or positive peer group activities.

48. "Unmet Emotional Needs—Identification and Satisfaction" Exercise (48)

A. The client was assigned the "Unmet Emotional Needs—Identification and Satisfaction" exercise from *The Brief Adolescent Therapy Homework Planner* (Jongsma, Peterson, and McInnis) to help him/her identify unmet needs and the steps that he/she can take to meet those needs.

B. The client completed the "Unmet Emotional Needs—Identification and Satisfaction" exercise and reported that he/she has begun to take steps to meet his/her unmet needs.

C. The client failed to complete the homework assignment and was asked to work on it again before the next therapy session.

49. Group Therapy Referral (49)

A. The client was referred for group therapy to help him/her share and work through his/her feelings about the divorce with other adolescents who are going through a similar experience.

B. The client was given the directive to self-disclose at least once during the group therapy session about his/her parents' divorce.

C. The client's involvement in group therapy has helped him/her realize that he/she is not alone in going through the divorce process.

D. The client's active participation in group therapy sessions has helped him/her share and work through many of his/her emotions pertaining to the parents' divorce.

E. The client has not made productive use of the group therapy sessions and has been reluctant to share his/her feelings about the divorce.

50. Identify Supportive Adults (50)

A. The client was assisted in developing a list of supportive adults outside of the family to whom he/she can turn for support and guidance in coping with the divorce.

B. The client was given the homework assignment to seek guidance and support from at least one adult outside of the family before the next therapy session.

C. The client reported that he/she has talked with other significant adults outside of the family who have been helpful in offering support and guidance.

D. The client has taken active steps to develop a network of significant adults outside of the family system to whom he/she can turn for guidance and support when needed.

E. The client has failed to follow through with the recommendation to make contact with significant adults outside of the family because of his/her mistrust and expectation of experiencing further disappointment.

51. Provide Sex Education (51)

A. The client was provided with sex education in an attempt to eliminate his/her pattern of engaging in sexually promiscuous behavior.

B. The client identified the risks involved with his/her sexually promiscuous or seductive behavior.

C. The client responded favorably to the sex education provided by asking several pertinent questions and openly sharing his/her past sexual experiences.

D. The client displayed an attitude of cool indifference when discussing the potential risks involved with his/her sexually promiscuous or seductive behavior.

52. Explore Reasons for Sexually Promiscuous Behaviors (52)

A. The client's sexual history was gathered to help gain insight into the factors contributing to the emergence of his/her sexually promiscuous behavior.

B. The client's irrational beliefs about his/her sexually promiscuous behavior were challenged.

C. Psychoanalytic therapy approaches were used to explore the etiology of the client's sexually promiscuous behavior.

D. Client-centered therapy approaches were employed to help the client discover ways to meet his/her unmet needs that are more effective than sexually promiscuous behaviors.

E. A brief solution-focused therapy approach was utilized to help the client identify ways to cope with stress that are more effective than sexually promiscuous behaviors.

53. Arrange for Substance Abuse Evaluation/Treatment (53)

A. The client was referred for a substance abuse evaluation to help determine whether he/she has developed a substance abuse problem in response to his/her parents' divorce.

B. The findings from the substance abuse evaluation revealed the presence of a substance abuse problem and the need for treatment.

C. The chemical dependence evaluation did not reveal the presence of a substance abuse problem or the need for treatment in this area.

D. The client acknowledged the existence of a substance abuse problem and agreed to follow through with treatment.

E. The client denied the existence of a substance abuse problem and voiced his/her objection to seeking treatment in this area.

54. Explore Emotional Pain Related to Substance Abuse (54)

A. Today's therapy session explored the underlying feelings of depression, insecurity, and rejection that have contributed to the client's escape into substance abuse.

B. A psychoanalytic therapy approach was utilized to explore the etiology of the client's escape into substance abuse.

C. Client-centered therapy approaches were employed to help the client discover how his/her escape into substance abuse has arisen out of underlying feelings of depression, insecurity, and rejection.

D. A brief solution-focused therapy approach was used to help the client identify ways to cope with feelings of depression, insecurity, and rejection that are more effective than through escaping into substance abuse.

E. The client identified a list of resource people to whom he/she can turn for support when feeling the urge to drink or use drugs.

55. Develop Agreement to Refrain from Using Substances (55)

A. An agreement was constructed and signed by the client to refrain from using substances.

B. The client was encouraged to post the signed agreement to refrain from using substances in his/her room or on the refrigerator as a reminder.

C. The client agreed to follow through with substance abuse treatment if he/she fails to refrain from using substances.

D. The client refused to sign an agreement that he/she would refrain from using drugs or alcohol.

56. Psychological Evaluation (56)

A. The client received a psychological evaluation to help rule out the presence of either an affective or an anxiety disorder.

B. The findings from the psychological evaluation revealed that the client has developed an affective disorder in response to his/her parents' divorce.

C. The findings from the psychological evaluation revealed that the client has developed an anxiety disorder in response to his/her parents' divorce.

D. The findings from the psychological evaluation did not reveal the presence of an affective disorder.

E. The findings from the psychological evaluation did not reveal the presence of an anxiety disorder.

57. Medication Evaluation Referral (57)

A. The client was referred for a medication evaluation to help stabilize his/her mood and improve anger control.

B. The client and parents agreed to follow through with the medication evaluation.

C. The client was strongly opposed to being placed on medication to help stabilize his/her mood or improve anger control.

58. Monitor Effects of Medication (58)

A. The client's response to the medication was discussed.

B. The client reported that the medication has helped to stabilize his/her mood and improve anger control.

C. The client reported little or no improvement in his/her mood or anger control since being placed on the medication.

D. The client reported that he/she has consistently taken the medication as prescribed.

E. The client has failed to comply with taking the medication as prescribed.

EATING DISORDER

CLIENT PRESENTATION

1. Binge Eating (1)*

A. The client described a recurrent pattern of binge eating during times of stress or emotional upset.

B. The client reported experiencing recent episodes of binge eating.

C. The client has not experienced any recent episodes of binge eating.

D. The client has terminated his/her pattern of binge eating.

2. Self-Induced Vomiting (1)

A. The client reported a recurrent pattern of purging to either lose weight or prevent a weight gain.

B. The client reported that he/she has continued to induce vomiting.

C. The client verbally recognized that he/she tends to induce vomiting more often during times of stress or emotional conflict.

D. The client denied any recent episodes of purging.

E. The client has terminated his/her pattern of purging.

3. Use of Laxatives (1)

A. The client reported a history of using laxatives to lose weight or prevent a weight gain.

B. The client reported that he/she has recently used laxatives.

C. The client acknowledged that he/she tends to use laxatives more often during times of stress or emotional conflict.

D. The client denied any recent use of laxatives.

E. The client has discontinued his/her pattern of using laxatives to either lose weight or prevent a weight gain.

4. Extreme Weight Loss (2)

A. The client has lost an extreme amount of weight during the recent past.

B. The client appeared to be in denial and displayed little concern or anxiety about his/her significant weight loss.

C. The client recognized that his/her weight loss is significant and expressed a desire to regain weight.

D. The client has slowly begun to gain weight.

E. The client's weight has returned to the previous normal level.

---

* The numbers in parentheses correlate to the number of the Behavioral Definition statement in the companion chapter with same title in *The Adolescent Psychotherapy Treatment Planner* (Jongsma, Peterson, and McInnis) by John Wiley & Sons, 2000.

5. Current Weight (2)

A. The client weighed ____ lbs. at the beginning of treatment.
B. The client has lost ____ lbs. since the last therapy session.
C. The client has gained ____ lbs. since the last therapy session.
D. The client currently weighs ____ lbs.
E. The client weighed ____ lbs. at the end of treatment.

6. Low Food Intake/Loss of Appetite (2)

A. The client's food intake in recent weeks/months has decreased drastically.
B. The client reported that he/she continues to have very little appetite.
C. The client's food intake has continued to be very low.
D. The client reported that his/her appetite is slowly returning to the previous normal level.
E. The client's food intake has returned to the previous normal level.

7. Excessive Strenuous Exercise (2)

A. The client described a history of engaging in very strenuous physical activity or exercise to either lose weight or prevent a weight gain.
B. The client has continued to engage in very strenuous physical activity or exercise.
C. The client has gradually started to decrease the intensity and length of his/her exercise workouts.
D. The client stated that he/she has stopped engaging in any overly strenuous physical exercise.
E. The client has achieved a healthy balance between eating nutritious meals and getting the proper amount of exercise.

8. Preoccupation with Body Image (3)

A. The client displays a strong preoccupation with his/her body image.
B. The client spoke at length in today's therapy session about his/her body image.
C. The client expressed much dissatisfaction with his/her body image.
D. The client's preoccupation with his/her body image has begun to decrease, and he/she is more willing to discuss his/her painful emotions or conflictual issues.
E. The client expressed satisfaction with his/her body image.

9. Unrealistic Assessment of Body (3)

A. The client has developed an unrealistic assessment of his/her body image and perceives self as being overweight.
B. The client has remained in denial about his/her body image and does not see himself/herself as being too thin or emaciated.
C. The client recognized that he/she is too thin or emaciated and needs to regain weight.
D. The client has developed a realistic assessment of his/her body image.

10. Depression and Anxiety (3)

A. The client's eating disorder emerged around the time he/she became significantly depressed or anxious.

B. The client appeared visibly sad and anxious when discussing the issues related to his/her eating disorder.

C. The client expressed feelings of sadness and anxiety about his/her body image.

D. The client's symptoms of depression and anxiety have started to decrease as he/she gains control of his/her eating disorder behavior.

E. The client reported no longer feeling depressed or anxious, and his/her weight has returned to the previous normal level.

11. Independence/Emancipation Conflict (3)

A. The client's struggles and conflict over his/her quest for independence have contributed to the emergence of his/her eating disorder.

B. The client's anger and frustration about his/her parents' rigidity and resistance to "letting go" has been channeled into his/her power struggle with the parents over food intake.

C. The client acknowledged that he/she has resisted his/her parents' attempts at control by refusing to eat and/or bingeing and purging.

D. The client has begun to assert his/her thoughts and feelings about the desire for greater independence, and this has contributed to a decrease in the eating disorder behavior.

E. The client's ability to resolve the issues related to his/her quest for independence or emancipation with the parents has helped to eliminate his/her eating disorder behaviors.

12. Irrational/Distorted Thoughts (4)

A. The client has developed a number of irrational thoughts about his/her food intake or body image that have contributed to the emergence of the eating disorder.

B. The client verbalized an irrational fear of becoming overweight.

C. The client has acknowledged that his/her fear of becoming overweight is irrational.

D. The client has begun to challenge his/her irrational or distorted thoughts about being too fat.

E. The client has consistently replaced negative thoughts about his/her body image with more positive, reality-based messages.

13. Low Self-Esteem (4)

A. The client's feelings of low self-esteem, inadequacy, and insecurity have been a significant contributing factor to his/her eating disorder.

B. The client's eating disorder behavior has generally emerged during periods when he/she feels insecure, inadequate, or inferior to others.

C. The client verbalized several self-derogatory remarks.

D. The client has begun to take steps to improve his/her self-esteem, and this has helped him/her manage or control the eating disorder behavior.

E. The client verbalized several positive self-descriptive statements about the progress he/she is making in therapy.

14. Perfectionism/Fear of Failure (4)

A. The client's drive for perfection and fear of failure have been significant contributing factors to his/her eating disorder behaviors.

B. The client verbalized his/her fear of failure.

C. The client acknowledged that his/her perfectionistic tendencies contribute to irrational or distorted thoughts about his/her body image or food intake.

D. The client verbalized an acceptance of his/her shortcomings or failures.

E. The client has developed a healthy acceptance of his/her shortcomings and normal failures.

15. Fluid and Electrolyte Imbalance (5)

A. The results from the medical examination revealed a serious fluid and electrolyte imbalance due to the client's eating disorder.

B. The client's fluid and electrolyte levels have gradually started to return to a healthy level.

C. The client's fluid and electrolyte levels have returned to a normal, healthy level.

16. Threat to Life (6)

A. The client's weight has dropped to a dangerously low level that threatens his/her life.

B. The client has been in denial about the threat to his/her life due to inadequate nutrition, fluid and electrolyte imbalance, and a general weakening of bodily systems.

C. The client verbally recognized the dangers imposed on his/her life by his/her eating disorder behavior.

D. The client has begun to eat nutritious foods and gain weight, thus decreasing the risk to his/her health or life.

E. The client's medical condition has stabilized since he/she began eating nutritious meals on a regular basis.

17. Avoidance of Nutritious Foods (6)

A. The client described a persistent pattern of bingeing on nonnutritious foods during times of stress.

B. The client has continued to consume many nonnutritious foods or unhealthy meals.

C. The client has started to eat more nutritious, well-balanced meals.

D. The client has been eating healthy, well-balanced meals on a regular, consistent basis.

INTERVENTIONS IMPLEMENTED

1. Gather Eating Disorder History (1)*

A. Today's therapy session explored the frequency and chronicity of the client's eating disorder behavior.

---

* The numbers in parentheses correlate to the number of the Therapeutic Intervention statement in the companion chapter with the same title in *The Adolescent Psychotherapy Treatment Planner* (Jongsma, Peterson, and McInnis) by John Wiley & Sons, 2000.

B. A complete history of the client's eating disorder behavior was taken in today's therapy session.

C. Today's therapy session explored periods of time when the client lost a significant amount of weight.

D. The frequency and chronicity of the client's bingeing and purging episodes were explored.

E. Today's therapy session explored periods of time when the client used laxatives inappropriately to either lose weight or prevent a weight gain.

2. Assess Client's Attitude (2)

A. The client's attitude about his/her eating disorder behavior was assessed to determine whether he/she perceives self as having a serious problem.

B. The assessment of the client's attitude showed that the client perceives his/her eating disorder behavior as being harmful and detrimental to his/her health.

C. The assessment of the client's attitude showed that the client remains in denial about the seriousness of his/her eating disorder behaviors.

3. Confront Denial (3)

A. The client's minimization and denial of the seriousness of the eating disorder was confronted.

B. Today's therapy session was helpful in breaking through the client's denial surrounding the seriousness of his/her eating disorder.

C. Today's therapy session was not helpful in breaking through the client's denial and minimization regarding the seriousness of his/her eating disorder.

D. The family members' denial and minimization of the seriousness of the client's eating disorder was challenged.

4. Physical Examination Referral (4)

A. The client was referred for a thorough physical examination to assess the effects that the eating disorder has had on the client's health.

B. The client followed through by receiving a thorough physical examination.

C. The client is opposed to receiving a thorough physical examination to assess the effects of his/her eating disorder.

D. The findings from the physical examination revealed that the client's eating disorder has had a detrimental effect on his/her health.

E. The findings from the physical examination do not reveal any serious health problems.

5. Dental Examination Referral (5)

A. The client was referred for a complete dental examination.

B. The client followed through by obtaining a complete dental examination.

C. The client has refused to follow through with a dental examination.

D. The findings from the dental examination revealed that the client's eating disorder has negatively affected his/her dental condition.

E. The findings from the dental examination did not reveal the presence of any serious dental problems.

6. Hospitalization Referral (6)

A. The recommendation was made that the client be hospitalized in a medical facility because of his/her severe weight loss and seriously compromised health status.

B. The client was admitted into a medical hospital because of his/her severe weight loss and serious health problems.

C. Medical hospitalization was not deemed necessary at this time, although the client's weight and food intake will continue to be closely monitored in the future.

7. Establish Minimum Daily Caloric Intake (7)

A. The client's minimum daily caloric intake was established.

B. Consulted with the client's physician and/or nutritionist about establishing a minimum daily caloric intake.

C. The client verbally agreed to consume enough food to meet the minimum daily caloric intake.

8. Develop Meal Planning (8)

A. The client was assisted in developing a healthy and well-balanced meal plan.

B. The client verbally committed to following through with the meal plan.

C. The client was confronted about not following through with the devised meal plan.

D. The client's resistance to following through with the meal plan was explored.

9. Monitor Weight (9)

A. The client was given realistic feedback about his/her body thinness.

B. Recommendation was made that the client's weight be closely monitored by his/her physician during regular physical examinations.

C. The client verbally agreed to a weigh-in before each therapy session.

10. Reinforce Weight Gain (10)

A. The client was given much praise and positive reinforcement for his/her recent weight gain.

B. The client was reinforced for assuming personal responsibility in consuming a normal amount of food.

C. The client was affirmed for following the agreed-upon meal plan and for gaining weight.

11. Monitor Purging, Hoarding, Exercise, and Laxative Usage (11)

A. The therapy sessions have continued to closely monitor the frequency of the client's self-induced vomiting.

B. The therapy sessions have continued to closely monitor the client's pattern of hoarding food.

C. The client's exercise level has continued to be closely monitored.

D. The client's inappropriate use of laxatives has continued to be closely monitored.

E. The client was instructed to keep a journal detailing the frequency of the self-induced vomiting, food hoarding, exercise level, and laxative usage.

12. Reduce Purging (12)

A. The client was helped to establish weekly goals to gradually reduce the frequency of his/her purging.

B. A reward system was designed to reinforce the client for gradually reducing the frequency of his/her purging.

C. The client was counseled about accepting the full feeling that accompanies normal eating.

D. The client was taught alternate coping strategies to help him/her resist the urge to purge after eating a normal amount of food.

E. The client was encouraged to call a friend or talk to significant others when he/she feels the urge to purge after eating a normal amount of food.

13. Keep Food Journal (13)

A. The client was instructed to keep a journal detailing his/her daily food intake and allowing space to record thoughts and feelings about food consumption.

B. The client followed through by keeping a journal detailing his/her thoughts, feelings, and daily food intake.

C. The client failed to follow through with the journal detailing his/her food intake, thoughts, and feelings, but was challenged to begin keeping one.

D. The client's resistance to keeping a journal was explored in today's therapy session.

14. Review Journal Data (14)

A. A review of the client's journal revealed some specific distorted thoughts that the client has developed regarding his/her food intake and body weight.

B. A review of the client's journal revealed that he/she has developed a distorted view of himself/herself as being too fat.

C. A review of the client's journal revealed that the client continues to be in denial about being too thin or emaciated.

D. After reviewing the journal, the client was taught to replace his/her distorted thoughts with more realistic, positive self-talk.

E. A review of the client's journal revealed that the client's eating disorder behaviors are closely tied to his/her emotional pain or conflicts.

15. "Reality: Food Intake, Weight, Thoughts, and Feelings" (15)

A. The client was given the homework assignment "Reality: Food Intake, Weight, Thoughts, and Feelings" from *The Brief Adolescent Therapy Homework Planner* (Jongsma, Peterson, and McInnis) to help him/her identify his/her distorted thoughts about eating.

B. The client was given the assignment "Reality: Food Intake, Weight, Thoughts, and Feelings" to help break through his/her denial regarding actual food intake, weight gain, and body size.

C. The client completed the journal from the "Reality: Food Intake, Weight, Thoughts, and Feelings" homework assignment and found it useful in identifying the distorted thoughts associated with his/her eating patterns.

D. The client completed the journal from the "Reality: Food Intake, Weight, Thoughts, and Feelings" homework assignment, and found it useful in breaking through his/her denial regarding actual food intake, weight gain, and body size.

E. The client failed to complete the homework assignment and was again asked to do it.

16. Identify Negative Cognitions (16)

A. The client was helped to identify the negative cognitive messages that he/she uses to avoid consuming a normal amount of food.

B. The client was helped to identify how his/her belief of becoming overweight after consuming a normal amount of food is irrational.

17. Establish Realistic Cognitions (17)

A. The client was trained to establish realistic cognitive messages regarding his/her food intake and body size.

B. The client was given a homework assignment to record in a journal one positive statement each day about himself/herself or his/her body size.

C. The client reported that the use of the realistic cognitive messages has helped him/her resist being influenced by distorted thoughts or negative cognitive messages.

18. "Fears Beneath the Eating Disorder" (18)

A. The client was given the homework assignment, "Fears Beneath the Eating Disorder," from *The Brief Adolescent Therapy Homework Planner* (Jongsma, Peterson, and McInnis) to help identify the irrational fears that contribute to his/her eating disorder behaviors.

B. The client completed the homework assignment, "Fears Beneath the Eating Disorder," and found it helpful in identifying his/her specific irrational fears.

C. The client reported that the homework assignment, "Fears Beneath the Eating Disorder," helped him/her identify ways to overcome his/her irrational fears.

D. The client failed to complete homework assignment and was asked to do it again.

19. Emphasize Responsibility for Eating (19)

A. In today's therapy session, emphasis was placed on the client being responsible for all decisions regarding his/her eating and unhealthy means of weight control.

B. The client acknowledged that he/she is responsible for any decisions regarding his/her eating patterns and means of controlling weight.

C. The client rejected the notion that he/she is responsible for any decision regarding food intake and instead expressed feelings of being out of control.

20. Identify Thoughts That Trigger Hoarding (20)

A. The client was helped to identify the distorted thoughts that trigger his/her hoarding behavior.

B. The client was helped to replace the distorted thoughts that trigger hoarding behavior with more realistic, positive self-talk.

C. The client reported that the use of realistic, positive self-talk has helped him/her to cease hoarding.

21. Limit Exercise (21)

A. The client signed a contract to limit his/her exercise to 20 minutes per day or less.

B. The client reported that he/she followed through with the terms of the contract and limited his/her exercise to 20 minutes per day or less.

C. The client failed to comply with the terms of the contract and continued to exercise more than 20 minutes per day.

D. The client was instructed to cease exercising because of his/her severe weight loss.

22. Set Realistic Weight Goals (22)

A. The client was helped to establish realistic goals regarding his/her weight gain.

B. The client was helped to identify a list of adaptive behaviors that will help him/her achieve realistic goals pertaining to his/her weight gain.

23. Support Group Referral (23)

A. The client was referred to a support group with other individuals who have an eating disorder.

B. The client was given the directive to self-disclose at least once in the eating disorder support group.

C. The client reported that his/her participation in the support group has helped to identify the underlying core emotional issues that have contributed to the emergence of his/her eating disorder.

24. Confront Unrealistic Body Image (24)

A. The client's unrealistic assessment of his/her body image was confronted.

B. The client was given the homework assignment to make one positive self-statement each day while standing in front of a mirror.

C. The client was instructed to shop for clothes that flatter his/her personal appearance or provide a more realistic appraisal of his/her body image.

25. Confront Perfectionism (25)

A. The client was confronted about placing unrealistic expectations on self to achieve a perfect body image.

B. The client was helped to realize how his/her perfectionistic tendencies regarding body image contribute to feelings of depression, anxiety, inadequacy, and inferiority.

C. Today's therapy session focused on helping the client achieve a reasonable acceptance of his/her body flaws.

26. Probe Emotional Struggles (26)

A. Today's therapy session explored the client's underlying emotional struggles that may be camouflaged by the existing eating disorder.

B. Today's therapy session was helpful in identifying the underlying emotional struggles or pain that contributed to the emergence of the client's eating disorder.

C. The client was resistant to exploring the possible underlying emotional struggles or conflicts that may have contributed to the emergence of his/her eating disorder.

D. Role-playing and modeling techniques were utilized to teach the client how to express his/her painful emotions to significant others.

E. After identifying his/her underlying feelings of anger, hurt, sadness, and disappointment, the client was encouraged to directly verbalize these feelings to his/her family members or significant others.

27. Explore Passive-Aggressive Patterns (27)

A. Today's therapy session explored how the client uses food as a passive-aggressive means to rebel against authority figures.

B. The client was taught effective assertiveness and communication skills to help him/her express and identify his/her thoughts, feelings, and needs directly to authority figures instead of using food to exert control in a passive-aggressive manner.

C. Today's therapy session explored the client's underlying feelings of anger that he/she harbors toward significant authority figures in his/her life.

28. Explore Issues of Control (28)

A. Today's therapy session explored how the client's avoidance of food is related to his/her fear of losing control of eating or weight.

B. Today's therapy session helped the client identify effective coping strategies that he/she can use to overcome or manage the fear of losing control of eating or weight.

29. Family Therapy to Discuss Control (29)

A. A family therapy session was held to provide the client with the opportunity to express his/her genuine thoughts and feelings directly toward his/her family members.

B. A family therapy session was held to allow for an open discussion of the control conflicts that exist within the family.

C. A family therapy session was conducted to identify more age-appropriate boundaries within the family system.

D. The family therapy session was helpful in resolving the core conflicts that are related to the issue of control.

E. The parents were challenged to begin to let go and loosen their control to allow the client the opportunity to make age-appropriate decisions for himself/herself.

30. Explore Fear of Sexual Development (30)

A. Processed the client's fear regarding his/her sexual development and impulses.

B. The relationship between the client's eating disorder and sexual development was explored.

C. Explored whether the client's eating disorder is in any way related to a past sexual trauma or victimization.

31. Process Fear of Sexual Impulses (31)

A. Today's therapy session focused on the client's fears about losing control of his/her sexual impulses.

B. Today's therapy session identified how the client's fear of losing control of his/her sexual impulses contributed to him/her being overly thin.

C. Today's therapy session identified how the client's fears or anxieties about his/her sexual impulses are related to significant weight gain or lack of motivation to lose weight.

32. Teach Acceptance of Sexual Feelings (32)

A. The client was counseled about normal sexual thoughts, feelings, and desires.

B. The client was given support and acceptance when expressing his/her normal sexual thoughts, feelings, and desires.

C. The client was challenged to cease feeling guilty or ashamed about his/her normal sexual thoughts, feelings, and desires.

D. The client was helped to differentiate between appropriate and inappropriate sexual thoughts, feelings, and behaviors.

33. Process Fear of Failure (33)

A. Today's therapy session processed the client's strong fear of failure and how he/she often strives to be perfect to avoid failure and establish a sense of control over his/her life.

B. Today's therapy session explored how the client's fear of failure and striving for perfection are related to his/her body image and attitude about food or dieting.

C. The client acknowledged that his/her perfectionistic strivings and strong need for control contribute to his/her eating disorder behaviors.

D. A psychoanalytic approach was utilized to explore the etiology of the client's excessive fear of failure and need to achieve perfection.

34. Reinforce Positive Qualities (34)

A. The client's positive qualities and successes were identified and reinforced to help improve his/her self-esteem and decrease the fear of failure.

B. The client was given a homework assignment to list his/her positive qualities and past successes.

C. The client was given a homework assignment to record at least one positive self-descriptive statement daily to help improve his/her self-esteem.

D. The client was given the homework assignment to make at least one positive self-descriptive statement daily around others.

E. The parents were strongly encouraged to reinforce the client's positive qualities and any successes that he/she achieves.

35. Normalize Failure (35)

A. The client was helped to see how failure is a common experience for all and is a necessary part of learning and growing.

B. The client explored periods of time when he/she was able to learn or grow from failure experiences.

C. The client was helped to identify positive coping strategies that he/she could use to undo or manage failure experiences.

D. The client identified a list of resource people to whom he/she can turn for support in the face of failure or adversity.

36. Explore Fear of Independence (36)

A. Today's therapy session focused on the client's fear of independence and emancipation from his/her parents.

B. The client was helped to identify healthy and unhealthy ways to move toward greater independence and emancipation from his/her parents.

C. Today's therapy session revealed how the client's low self-esteem and fear of failure contributed to his/her fear of independence and emancipation.

D. The client was helped to realize that his/her movement toward independence and emancipation can occur gradually and in incremental steps.

E. Guided imagery was utilized to help the client visualize what steps he/she needs to take in order to achieve future goals.

37. Family Therapy to Discuss Emancipation (37)

A. A family therapy session was held to discuss the issues of separation, dependency, and emancipation.

B. A family therapy session was held to explore the dynamics within the family system that contribute to the client's excessive dependency and fear of separation.

C. The parents were encouraged to begin letting go and allowing the client a normal degree of independence.

D. The client was encouraged to engage in independent activities outside of the home and/or away from parents.

E. Today's therapy session revealed how the overly enmeshed or controlling parents reinforce the client's excessive dependency and impede his/her quest for greater independence.

38. Teach Assertiveness (38)

A. The client was referred to an assertiveness training class to help him/her become more assertive in the expression of his/her thoughts, feelings, and needs.

B. The client was taught effective assertiveness skills to help communicate his/her thoughts, feelings, and needs more openly and directly.

C. Role-playing and modeling techniques were used to teach the client effective assertiveness skills.

39. Reinforce Assertive Behaviors (39)

A. The client was reinforced for effectively asserting his/her thoughts and feelings within the session.

B. The client was reinforced for the occasions between therapy sessions when he/she effectively asserted himself/herself around others.

C. The parents were helped to differentiate between times when it is appropriate to allow the client to be assertive (even mildly oppositional) and times when it is appropriate to set limits for moderate-to-strong oppositional behaviors.

40. Identify Self-Worth Building Blocks (40)

A. The client was helped to identify ways to develop a sense of self-worth apart from his/her body image.

B. Today's therapy session reviewed the client's talents and successes to help him/her develop a basic sense of self-worth apart from his/her body image.

C. Today's therapy session affirmed the client's importance to others to help increase his/her feelings of self-worth.

D. The client's intrinsic spiritual value was reinforced to help increase his/her feelings of self-esteem and self-worth.

41. Read *Body Traps* or *Afraid to Eat* (41)

A. The client was instructed to read *Body Traps* (Rodin) and/or *Afraid to Eat* (Berg) to help him/her gain greater knowledge about his/her eating disorder behaviors.

B. The main themes of the book *Body Traps* were processed in today's therapy session.

C. The main themes of the book *Afraid to Eat* were processed in today's therapy session.

D. After processing the main themes of the book *Body Traps,* the client was helped to realize how he/she obsesses over his/her body image.

E. After processing the main themes of the book *Afraid to Eat,* the client was helped to realize how he/she obsesses over his/her body image.

42. View *Bradshaw on Eating Disorders* (42)

A. The client was instructed to view the videotape *Bradshaw on Eating Disorders.*

B. The key ideas from *Bradshaw on Eating Disorders* were processed in today's therapy session.

C. The client reported that *Bradshaw on Eating Disorders* helped him/her realize some of the dynamics contributing to his/her eating disorder.

43. Explore Unexpressed Feelings (43)

A. The client was taught how his/her eating disorder may be connected to unexpressed thoughts and feelings.

B. A client-centered approach was utilized to help the client realize how his/her eating disorder is related to unexpressed thoughts and feelings.

C. A psychoanalytic approach of interpretation was used to explore suppressed thoughts and feelings that may be connected to the client's eating disorder.

D. Today's therapy session explored the client's hesitancy to express his/her underlying thoughts and feelings to significant others.

E. The client was strongly encouraged to express his/her underlying thoughts and feelings directly to family members and/or significant others.

44. Examine Bingeing and Purging Impact on Family (44)

A. Today's therapy session examined how the client's bingeing and purging impacts other members of the household.

B. The client was encouraged to be considerate and empathic to the other family members' thoughts, feelings, and needs.

C. The client's family members were given the opportunity to express their thoughts and feelings about the client's bingeing and purging.

D. The client verbally recognized the need to be considerate of other family members' thoughts and feelings before bingeing or hoarding food.

45. Implement Behavioral Contract (45)

A. The client and parents agreed to a behavioral contract where the client will receive a consequence for bingeing on other family members' food.

B. The client and parents agreed to a behavioral contract where the client will receive a consequence if he/she is caught hoarding food.

C. The client and parents signed a contract where the client will receive a specific consequence if he/she fails to clean up after purging.

D. A family therapy session was held to discuss specific consequences that the client would receive for bingeing, hoarding food, or failing to clean up after purging.

E. The client and parents were unable to agree on specific consequences for the client's bingeing on other family members' food, failing to clean up after purging, or hoarding food.

46. Teach Parents Not to Take Responsibility (46)

A. The parents were counseled about how to detach themselves from taking responsibility for the client's eating behavior without becoming hostile or indifferent.

B. Today's therapy session explored the reasons for the parents' unwillingness to let go of their control over the client's eating.

C. The client reported that the parents have successfully detached themselves from taking responsibility for the client's eating while also remaining supportive.

D. The client reported that the parents have detached themselves from taking responsibility for his/her eating behavior, but they have treated him/her in a hostile or indifferent manner.

E. The client and parents were instructed to spend quality time with one another without any discussion about food.

47. Assign Cleanup of Bingeing/Purging (47)

A. The client made a verbal commitment to clean up after himself/herself subsequent to bingeing and/or purging.

B. The client has followed through with his/her agreement to clean up after himself/herself subsequent to bingeing and/or purging.

C. The parents reported that the client has failed to follow through with his/her commitment to clean up after himself/herself subsequent to bingeing and/or purging.

48. Read *Surviving an Eating Disorder* (48)

A. The client's parents and friends were encouraged to read *Surviving an Eating Disorder* (Seigel, Brisman, and Weinshel) to help learn more about eating disorders.

B. Processed the key concepts from *Surviving an Eating Disorder* in today's therapy session.

49. Set Regular Mealtimes (49)

A. The client was helped to understand the relationship between bingeing and lack of regular mealtimes or total deprivation from specific foods.

B. The client was encouraged to chart his/her food intake for the week to help him/her understand the relationship between bingeing and lack of regular mealtimes or total deprivation from specific foods.

C. The client verbalized his/her commitment to eat regular meals while not totally depriving himself/herself of specific foods.

50. Set Weight Goals (50)

A. The client was helped to establish healthy weight goals using the Body Mass Index.
B. The client was helped to establish healthy weight goals using the Metropolitan Height and Weight Tables.

51. Dietician Referral (51)

A. The client was referred to a dietician to receive counseling and education about healthy eating and proper nutrition.
B. The client followed through with the recommendation to consult with a dietician.
C. The client has failed to follow through with the recommendation to consult with a dietician.
D. The consultation with the dietician helped the client realize the importance of eating healthy, regular meals.
E. The dietician developed a dietary plan for the client, who has thus far followed the plan.
F. The client has failed to follow through with the dietary plan outlined by the dietician, but in today's therapy session was encouraged to follow the plan.

52. Read *Overcoming Binge Eating* (52)

A. The client was encouraged to read books such as *Overcoming Binge Eating* (Fairburn) to help increase his/her awareness of the components of eating disorders.
B. Processed the key concepts from *Overcoming Binge Eating* in today's therapy session.
C. The client reported that the book helped increase his/her insight into the factors contributing to his/her bingeing and purging.

GRIEF/LOSS UNRESOLVED

CLIENT PRESENTATION

1. Parent Death Reaction (1)*

A. The client presented as visibly upset and distressed over the recent loss of his/her parent.

B. Teachers, friends, and others have reported that the client is exhibiting various grief reactions such as anger, depression, and emotional lability around the recent loss of his/her parent.

C. The client indicated he/she cannot think of anything but the death of his/her parent.

D. The client frequently expressed that he/she still cannot accept that this parental death really happened.

E. The client revealed that the feeling of being so alone and hopeless has been overwhelming for him/her since the parent's death.

F. The client has started to talk about the loss of his/her parent and has begun to accept consolation, support, and encouragement from others.

2. Termination of Parental Rights (2)

A. The client presented as sad and withdrawn after recently being told his/her parents' rights are being terminated.

B. The client indicated that he/she refuses to believe that he/she will not see parents again.

C. Foster parents reported that the client is continually angry and upset since receiving the news that his/her parents' rights have been terminated.

D. The client has made progress in coming to terms with his/her parents' loss of their rights and has started to look forward to a new home and family.

3. Parental Incarceration Grief (3)

A. The client expressed feeling a big hole in his/her life since his/her parent went to prison.

B. The client reported being angry most of the time since his/her parent was incarcerated.

C. The client indicated he/she has felt sad and embarrassed about parent's imprisonment and has socially withdrawn from activities to avoid feeling more uncomfortable.

D. The client has begun to accept and adjust to parent's imprisonment and return to his/her normal level of functioning.

4. Grief Due to Geographic Move (4)

A. The client presented as depressed and focused on the loss of previous home and friends that have been left behind because of the move.

---

* The numbers in parentheses correlate to the number of the Behavioral Definition statement in the companion chapter with same title in *The Adolescent Psychotherapy Treatment Planner* (Jongsma, Peterson, and McInnis) by John Wiley & Sons, 2000.

B. The client reported feeling angry and upset all the time now at parents for their decision to move him/her away from his/her neighborhood and friends.

C. The parents indicated that the client is always sad and refuses to leave home except to go to school.

D. The client has started to accept the family's new location and is beginning to make new friends and involve himself/herself in other activities.

5. Parent Emotional Abandonment (5)

A. The client verbalized feeling abandoned emotionally since losing nearly all contact with his/her parent.

B. The client reported he/she has been cut off from nearly all contact with his/her other parent.

C. The client indicated he/she is devastated by the loss of nearly all meaningful contact with his/her parent.

D. The client has begun to openly grieve the emotional abandonment he/she has experienced from his/her parent.

6. Emotionally Upset (6)

A. The client presented in an upset, tearful, and distraught manner.

B. The client related he/she is having a difficult time coming to terms with the recent loss he/she has experienced.

C. The client is gradually making progress in coming to terms and accepting his/her loss, and he/she reports crying less and not being as upset as before.

D. It appears the client is stuck in his/her grieving process and is finding it difficult to move beyond being upset and distraught.

7. Social Withdrawal (7)

A. The client presents as very withdrawn and nonverbal around his/her past loss(es).

B. "I find it impossible to talk about," is one of the few verbalizations coming from the client.

C. The client, with encouragement and support, has slowly moved from his/her withdrawn state and started to talk about the loss.

8. Angry/Tense (8)

A. Anger and tension dominate the client's affect, mood, and manner.

B. The client reports frequent verbal temper outbursts toward others, breaking things, and incidents of road rage following the loss.

C. Anger is freely vented toward God, doctors, and others who "had a hand" in the loss.

D. There is a decrease in the client's anger as he/she acknowledges and explains that now he/she is feeling more hurt and sadness about the loss.

9. Guilty/Responsible (9)

A. The overall mood and manner of the client reflects a deep sense of guilt and responsibility for the recent loss.

B. The client reported those things that make him/her feel guilty and responsible for the loss.

C. The client is moving toward letting go of his/her guilt and accepting that he/she is not responsible for the loss.

D. To maintain control, the client appears to be stuck in his/her guilt and either unwilling or unable to move beyond this point in the process of grieving.

10. Avoidance of Loss (10)

A. The client presented with a high level of denial and strong resistance to acknowledging and accepting his/her loss.

B. The client's family system has a definite pattern of denial and nonacceptance of losses.

C. The client states, "I don't believe this really happened; I won't accept this," and he/she did not attend any part of the funeral process.

D. Cracks are starting to show in the client's denial, and he/she is now believing the loss is real.

E. The client's denial has broken and he/she is now being overwhelmed with feelings of anger, hurt, and sadness.

INTERVENTIONS IMPLEMENTED

1. Establish Trust/Express Feelings (1)*

A. Initial trust level was established with the client through the use of unconditional positive regard.

B. Warm acceptance and active listening techniques were utilized to establish the basis for a nurturing relationship with the client.

C. The client has formed a trust-based relationship with therapist and has started to express his/her feelings about the recent loss.

D. Despite the use of active listening, warm acceptance, and unconditional positive regard, the client remains hesitant to trust and begin sharing his/her feelings connected to the recent loss.

2. Identify/Express Feelings about Loss (2)

A. The client was ask to write a letter to the lost loved one describing his/her feelings, desires, and wishes connected to that person.

B. The client read the letter that he/she had written to the lost loved one with appropriate affect and expression of feelings.

C. The client read the letter to the lost loved one with flat affect and showed no outward emotions in his/her voice or facial expression.

3. Tell Story of Loss (3)

A. The client was asked to tell the story of his/her loss using photographs of the loved one.

---

* The numbers in parentheses correlate to the number of the Therapeutic Intervention statement in the companion chapter with the same title in *The Adolescent Psychotherapy Treatment Planner* (Jongsma, Peterson, and McInnis) by John Wiley & Sons, 2000.

B. The client told the story of his/her loss with appropriate affect.

C. The client received affirmation and validation for the feelings he/she expressed in telling the story of the loss.

D. The client told the story of the loss with little or no affect.

4. *Mother Loss Workbook* Exercise (4)

A. The client was assigned an exercise from the *Mother Loss Workbook* (Hambrook) to help facilitate his/her working through the grief process.

B. The completed *Mother Loss Workbook* exercise was processed while supporting the affirming feelings and thoughts that were brought out by the exercise.

C. The *Mother Loss Workbook* assignment was not completed by the client.

5. "Create a Memory Album" Exercise (5)

A. The client was asked to complete the "Create a Memory Album" exercise from *The Brief Adolescent Therapy Homework Planner* (Jongsma, Peterson, and McInnis) to facilitate expression and sharing of grief.

B. The completed "Create a Memory Album" was reviewed, and important memories were identified and reinforced.

C. The client has not worked on the "Create a Memory Album" and was encouraged to give effort to this assignment soon.

6. Read Books on Grief (6)

A. Selections from *Common Thread of Teenage Grief* (Tyson) were read and discussed with the client, expanding his/her knowledge of what the grief process is like.

B. The client was ask to read *Straight Talk About Death* (Grollman) and identify five key ideas to discuss in subsequent sessions.

C. The client's reading of books on the topic of grief has been helpful in expanding the client's knowledge base and promoting self-understanding.

D. The client has not followed through with the assignment to read material on the topic of grief, perhaps because of his/her tendency to avoid this painful topic.

7. Teach Stages of Grieving Process (7)

A. The parents were educated on the stages and process of grief and had their questions answered so they can better understand this process.

B. It was emphasized with the family that grief is not a one-time event ("Just get over it") but an ongoing process.

C. All of the family members seem to have a better understanding of the grief process and, as a result, seem more capable of showing empathy and support toward one another.

D. Some family members are resistant to any new information about grief and are in denial about the power of its impact on people's lives.

8. Express Thoughts and Feelings about Loss (8)

A. The UnGame was played with the client to assist him/her in starting to identify and express thoughts and feelings.

B. A checklist of things people think and feel pertaining to loss was reviewed with the client, who was then asked to select items from the list that he/she is currently thinking or feeling.

C. The client denied experiencing any of the thoughts or feelings on the list of grief-related phenomenon.

9. Teach Feelings Identification/Clarification (9)

A. *The Five Faces Techniques* (Jewett) was used to help the client move beyond his/her emotional block and become able to identify and express his/her feelings.

B. The client's ability to recognize feelings and express them has grown and been helpful in clarifying his/her many conflicting emotions connected to the grieving process.

C. The client continues to be blocked in his/her ability to identify and express grief-related feelings.

10. Explore Grief (10)

A. The Goodbye Game and the Good Mourning Game were played with client to help him/her explore the process of grief.

B. The client received positive verbal reinforcement for disclosing his/her thoughts and feelings connected to his/her loss.

C. The client was resistive to using the therapeutic games as a springboard for expressing his/her thoughts and feelings related to the grief experience.

11. View Films Dealing with Grief (11)

A. The client was asked to view one or more of the following films: *Terms of Endearment, Ordinary People,* or *My Girl,* observing how key individuals in each film grieve or avoid grieving.

B. Grief-related films that the client viewed were processed to identify examples of healthy grieving and examples of those who were avoiding the process or stuck at an early stage.

C. Using the *Five Stages of Grief* (Kubler-Ross), the client was assisted in identifying the various stages of grief of key people in the films.

D. Although the client did view the films related to the grief theme, he/she continues to distance himself/herself from the struggle with grief personally.

E. The client has not followed through with the assignment to view the films and compare his/her experience to that of the films' characters.

12. Support Group Referral (12)

A. The client was referred to and encouraged to attend a grief support group for adolescents.

B. The client's experience in attending a grief support group was processed and his/her continued attendance was supported and encouraged.

C. The client was resistive to a referral to a support group and has continued to refuse to attend such a group.

D. The client was once again encouraged to attend a grief support group even though he/she has been resistive to this idea in the past.

13. List Ways Grief Was Avoided (13)

A. The client was asked to list all the ways he/she has avoided the pain of grieving.

B. The client's list of his/her grief avoidance tactics was used with the client to help make connections between how the avoidance in each instance has had a negative impact on him/her.

C. The client was given the message that he/she is strong enough to work through the grief if he/she will only trust self and those supporting him/her.

14. Explore Use of Substances (14)

A. The client's use of substances, past and present, was explored, including the use of mood-altering prescriptions.

B. The client was reminded of the negative long-term impact that substance use can have on the grieving process.

C. The client denied that he/she has been using any mood-altering substances.

D. The client admitted to the use of mood-altering substances and acknowledged that this use is related to a desire to escape from the pain of grieving.

15. Contract Abstinence from Substance Use (15)

A. The client contracted to abstain from all substance use.

B. Compliance with the contract to abstain from substance use will be monitored by checking with the client and parents and, if necessary, by drug screens.

C. The client was confronted with the reality of the consequences (e.g., substance abuse evaluation, residential treatment) if he/she is unable to keep the contract to abstain from substance use.

D. The client refused to agree to abstain from substance abuse and a referral was made to a more intense chemical dependence treatment program.

16. Assign Grief Journal (16)

A. The client was ask to keep a daily grief journal to record his/her thoughts and feelings associated with the loss.

B. The client's grief journal was reviewed, and significant disclosures of thoughts and feelings were supported and reinforced.

C. The client's grief journal was reviewed, but it revealed that the client continues to distance himself/herself from struggling with the pain of grieving.

D. The client has not followed through with recording his/her thoughts and feelings related to grief in a journal.

17. Identify Questions about Loss (17)

A. The client was ask to develop a list of any and all questions he/she has that in any way pertain to causes for the loss.

B. The client was assisted in finding resources who could possibly help him/her find the answers to questions about the causes for the loss.

C. The client continues to be preoccupied with the causes of the death of the loved one and whether he/she has any responsibility for that death.

D. The client's questions about the death of the loved one seemed to have been sufficiently resolved, resulting in a loss of guilt and confusion.

18. Read *Lifetimes* (18)

A. To help the client understand death more fully, the *Lifetimes* (Mellanie and Ingpen) book was read with him/her.

B. The client's questions that arose from reading *Lifetimes* were answered and supported.

C. The client's lack of questions was gently but firmly confronted as being an avoidance of grieving.

19. Connect Client with Experienced Griever (19)

A. The client was assisted in identifying a peer or adult he/she knows who has successfully worked through the grieving process and might be willing to talk with him/her about the experience.

B. The client was guided in developing a list of questions he/she would like to have answered by the experienced person.

C. The client was encouraged to set a date to talk with the experienced griever, either at a time outside of a session or within a conjoint session in the future.

D. The client has followed through with talking with the experienced griever, and this positive experience was processed within today's session.

20. Conjoint Session with Experienced Peer Griever (20)

A. A conjoint session was held in which the client met with a peer who had experienced and worked through a loss. The client asked him/her a list of questions concerning death, loss, and grieving.

B. The experience of the peer survivor of loss was processed with the client, emphasizing how the survivor had worked through each stage of the grief process.

C. The client's talk with the experienced peer griever has been reassuring and supportive to the client.

21. Interview Clergy/Adult (21)

A. The client was asked to interview a clergyperson and another adult who has experienced a loss to learn about their experiences and how each has worked through it.

B. The client's interviews with the clergyperson and other adult were reviewed, with key elements of the experience being identified and the message of "You will make it, too" being reinforced.

C. The client failed to follow through with interviewing either a clergyperson or another experienced adult griever and the assignment was given again.

22. List Positive Things about Deceased (22)

A. The client was asked to list all the positive things about the deceased and how he/she plans to remember each.

B. The list was processed with the client, and each positive thing/memory was affirmed and the importance of remembering each was emphasized.

C. The client enjoyed the experience of listing positive memories about the deceased significant other.

D. The client was overwhelmed with emotion when talking about positive memories about the deceased significant other.

E. The client can now recall positive things about the deceased significant other without becoming overwhelmed with sadness.

23. Talk about Pictures and Other Mementos (23)

A. The client was asked to bring pictures and mementos of the deceased significant other to the therapy session.

B. The client followed through in bringing pictures and mementos of the deceased, and he/she talked about the memories attached to each in an open, free manner and without much probing.

C. The client had to be encouraged and prodded to talk about the pictures and mementos he/she brought as requested.

D. The client's grief appears to be lifting somewhat as he/she talks about positive memories attached to the deceased significant other.

24. Explore Thoughts of Guilt and Blame (24)

A. The client's thoughts and feelings of guilt and blame for the loss were explored.

B. The client's irrational thoughts and feelings were identified and replaced with more realistic ones.

C. The client's irrational thoughts and feelings regarding guilt and self-blame are no longer present.

25. Help Lift Self-Imposed Curse (25)

A. The client's belief in a self-imposed curse that makes him/her responsible for the death of the significant other was explored.

B. The client was encouraged to ask the person who indicated that the death of the significant other was the client's fault to retract the statement.

C. A role-play phone conversation was done between the client and the deceased in which he/she had the opportunity to apologize for his/her behavior that "caused" the loss.

D. The client's unrealistic beliefs around the curse that caused the death of the significant other were confronted.

E. The client no longer believes that he/she was responsible for the death of the significant other through some curse phenomenon.

26. Implement Absolution Rituals (26)

A. An absolution ritual was created for the client to assist him/her in resolving guilt and loss.

B. The client was asked for a commitment to implement and follow through with the ritual as created.

C. The ritual was monitored for its effectiveness and adjusted as required.

D. The absolution ritual seems to have been effective in reducing the client's feelings of guilt or blame for the loss.

27. Encourage and Support Appropriate Anger (27)

A. The client was encouraged and reminded in sessions to look angry when feeling angry, act angry, and then to put his/her anger into words.

B. The client's fear of looking and expressing anger was explored with him/her.

C. The client was supported and given positive verbal feedback when he/she acted angry and expressed it.

D. The client was confronted when he/she appeared to be feeling angry but acted otherwise.

E. The client's feelings of anger toward God, self, and others has diminished as he/she was able to express it freely.

28. Prepare for an Apology/Asking Forgiveness (28)

A. The client was asked to write either a letter of apology or one asking for forgiveness from the deceased.

B. Role play was used with the client to practice asking for forgiveness or apologizing to the deceased.

C. Letters and role-play exercises have been successful in reducing the client's feelings of guilt.

29. Assign Good-Bye Letter (29)

A. The client was ask to write a letter of good-bye to the deceased and was given a form to utilize from the "Grief Letter" chapter in *The Brief Adolescent Therapy Homework Planner* (Jongsma, Peterson, and McInnis).

B. The client was asked to make arrangements to visit the loved one's grave site with a friend or relative and to say good-bye to the deceased while at the grave.

C. The experience of saying good-bye was processed with the client and evaluated in terms of where he/she was in the process of finally letting go.

D. The experience of saying good-bye has helped the client take a positive step in the grief process and achieve more closure to his/her feelings.

30. List Grief Resolution Indicators (30)

A. The client was assisted in developing a list of behavioral and emotional indications that would signify that the loss is becoming resolved.

B. The developed list of grief-resolution indicators was used to support the fact that the client has made significant progress in accepting the loss.

C. Because many of the grief-resolution indicators are not present in the patient's life or experience, it is clear that the patient has yet to attain acceptance of the loss and move on with his/her life.

31. Teach Parents Supportive Methods (31)

A. The parents were taught various specific ways to support and encourage the client in successfully working through the grief process.

B. The parents' efforts to show love, consolation, and provide comfort were affirmed and reinforced.

C. The parents have been resistant to increase their behaviors that show comfort, consolation, and support for the client's grief.

D. The client has responded favorably to the parents' showing more support and empathy for his/her grief.

32. Assign Parents to Read Grief Books (32)

A. The client's parents were asked to read *Learning to Say Good-Bye* (LeShan) to give them knowledge of the grieving process.

B. Accurate information that the parents gathered from their reading on the subject of grief was reinforced and any questions they had were answered.

C. The parents' unrealistic expectations about the grieving process were confronted and redirected into more healthy or appropriate expectations.

33. Refer Parents to Grief Group (33)

A. The client's parents were referred and encouraged to attend a grief/loss support group.

B. The client's parents were open to the suggestion of attending a support group and have committed themselves to attending the next meeting.

C. The client's parents were resistant to the idea of attending a grief/loss support group and refused to follow through with this referral.

34. Family Session to Express Grief (34)

A. A family session was conducted in which each family member was encouraged to talk about his/her experience related to the loss.

B. Family members who found it impossible to talk about their grief feelings were reminded of the importance of doing so if they were going to work through the loss.

C. Family members were encouraged to talk more about the loss at appropriate times outside of sessions.

D. The client felt reassured and understood by virtue of other family members sharing their feelings of grief connected to the loss.

35. The Good Mourning Game (35)

A. The Good Mourning Game was played by family members in family sessions to encourage sharing their individual grieving processes.

B. The family was encouraged to set aside times to play the Good Mourning Game at home between sessions.

C. The experience of playing the game was processed with the family, and each member identified what he/she learned about other members' grief processes.

36. Encourage Involvement in Grieving Rituals (36)

A. The parents were encouraged to allow the client to be a part of all of the grieving rituals he/she requests to participate in.

B. The parents were directed to be sensitive, supportive, and comforting to the client during the grieving rituals he/she attends.

C. The various grieving rituals were explained to the client, and he/she was given the choice of which ones to attend.

D. The client's attendance at the funeral and other grieving rituals was beneficial in sharing grief with others and in saying good-bye to the deceased.

37. Develop New Grieving Rituals (37)

A. The family was assisted in developing new grieving rituals that could help the client heal from the loss.

B. The family was asked to make a commitment to implement these rituals in a timely manner.

C. The new grieving rituals instituted by the family have provided the client with support in the expression of his/her feelings about the loss.

38. Educate Family about Anniversary Dates (38)

A. The parents and the client were taught about the effect of anniversary dates and typical feelings associated with these dates.

B. Strategies for effectively dealing with anniversary dates were explored with the client and family.

C. The parents' tendency to assume "Things will be okay after this" was confronted and the reality of a grief reaction to anniversary dates was reinforced.

39. Prepare Parents to Say Good-Bye (39)

A. The parents were prepared to say good-bye in a healthy, affirming way to their children over whom they have lost custody.

B. The parents' plan to just leave their children without having a final visit to say good-bye was confronted and processed.

C. The parents have made adequate preparations for saying good-bye to their children and have agreed to a final visit to do so.

40. Facilitate Good-Bye Session (40)

A. A good-bye session was facilitated with the parents who were losing custody of their children so the parents could give an appropriate message of permission to each child to move on.

B. The parents were given affirmation and positive verbal feedback on their following through in saying good-bye to children in a positive, healthy way.

C. The good-bye session was a conflictual one in that the parents left the child feeling guilty for the parents' grief and sadness.

D. The parents have written a letter of good-bye and affirmation to their children over whom they have lost custody.

41. "Create a Memory Album" Exercise (41)

A. The client was assisted in making a life book that reflected his/her past, present, and future by following the exercise "Create a Memory Album" from *The Brief Adolescent Therapy Homework Planner* (Jongsma, Peterson, and McInnis).

B. A completed memory album was kept by the client and one was given to his/her current parents.

C. The client's parents affirmed the client's previous life experiences and accepted the memory album with interest.

D. The parents seemed anxious and resistive to the client talking about his/her previous life experiences outside of the family.

LOW SELF-ESTEEM

CLIENT PRESENTATION

1. Self-Disparaging Remarks (1)*

A. The client's deep sense of inferiority was reflected in frequent self-disparaging remarks about his/her appearance, worth, and abilities.

B. The lack of any eye contact on the client's part and negative remarks about self are evidence of how little the client thinks of himself/herself.

C. The client reported feeling inferior to others and generally believes that he/she is a loser.

D. The client has stopped making self-critical remarks and even has begun to acknowledge some positive traits and successes.

2. Childhood Abuse/Neglect (1)

A. The client reported incidents of physical and emotional abuse that gave him/her the strong message of being worthless, unloved, and rejected.

B. The client provided numerous examples that the parents frequently said negative things about him/her (e.g., "You can't do anything right," "If you could only be like your sister").

C. The client described his/her parents as being good people whom he/she loves, but who have always been too busy to do things with him/her or attend school events he/she was a part of.

D. The client has started to make some connection between how he/she was treated by the parents as a child and how negatively he/she feels about himself/herself now.

3. Accepting Compliments (2)

A. The client acknowledged his/her problem in believing others when they say nice or complimentary things.

B. The parents reported that the client discounts any praise from them or others.

C. The client reported never hearing compliments from parents, so now he/she is unsure how to respond to accolades from anyone.

D. The client has now begun to accept compliments at face value, feeling uncomfortable but good when these instances occur.

4. Refusal to Try New Experiences (3)

A. The client's pervasive failure expectation was reflected in his/her refusal to try new experiences.

B. The client reported being frustrated with his/her pattern of never trying any new experiences.

---

* The numbers in parentheses correlate to the number of the Behavioral Definition statement in the companion chapter with same title in *The Adolescent Psychotherapy Treatment Planner* (Jongsma, Peterson, and McInnis) by John Wiley & Sons, 2000.

C. The client listed many experiences in which he/she experienced failure, but his/her perception was often slanted and distorted.

D. The client expressed that failure is his/her greatest fear.

E. The client has begun to take a few risks and try new experiences with encouragement and support.

5. Avoidant/Quiet (4)

A. The client presented in a quiet, avoidant manner.

B. The client reported that he/she avoids more than brief contact with others and usually has little to say in social situations.

C. The parents reported that the client has always been shy with adults and peers.

D. The client has gradually started to withdraw less and is feeling less tense around others.

6. Cautious/Fearful (4)

A. The client presented with a frightened affect and a very cautious manner.

B. From the earliest times the client can remember, others have always scared him/her and he/she always has been cautious not to upset anyone.

C. The client indicated he/she is cautious and fearful of doing something wrong in social situations.

D. The client has started to be less cautious and now takes some carefully chosen social risks.

7. Pleasing/Friendly (5)

A. The client presented in a friendly, outgoing manner and seems eager to please others.

B. Everything was carefully checked out by the client to make sure what he/she is doing or saying is right or acceptable to others.

C. Past actions done to please others have gotten the client in trouble or left him/her feeling taken advantage of.

D. A noticeable decrease in the client's pleasing behaviors was observed, and he/she is now starting to offer his/her thoughts and opinions more assertively.

8. Inability to Accept/Recognize Positive Traits (6)

A. The client denied having any talents or positive attributes that others would admire.

B. The client struggled to identify any positive traits or talents about himself/herself.

C. The client rejected all the identified positive traits pointed out to him/her by others.

D. The client was able to recognize and accept positive things about himself/herself.

9. Insecure/Anxious (7)

A. There was visible insecurity and anxiousness to the client's affect and manner.

B. The client described several instances in which he/she did not say or do anything in front of peers because of fear of ridicule and rejection.

C. The client reported feeling anxious and insecure at home and in all social/peer situations, believing that others may not like him/her.

D. As the session progressed, the client became less anxious and able to open up to the therapist.

E. The client reported feeling more self-confident when in the presence of peers.

10. Self-Defeating Behavior (8)

A. The client has often engaged in self-defeating behavior (e.g., drinking and sexual activity) to gain the acceptance of his/her peers.

B. The client identified that he/she found it easier to feel accepted by peers when he/she was using substances.

C. The client indicated that he/she has done various "bad acts" to gain the attention and acceptance of peers.

D. The client has dropped most of his/her self-defeating behavior and has begun to work on accepting himself/herself.

11. Difficulty Saying No (9)

A. The client indicated he/she rarely says no to others out of fear of not being liked.

B. The client reported believing he/she will not be liked unless he/she says yes.

C. The client identified the paralyzing fear he/she experiences when saying no to others.

D. The client has worked on starting to say no to others to be more true to his/her real beliefs, values, feelings, or thoughts.

INTERVENTIONS IMPLEMENTED

1. Confront/Reframe Self-Disparaging Remarks (1)*

A. The client's self-disparaging comments were confronted with the strong message that these comments were not an accurate reflection of reality.

B. The client's self-disparaging comments were realistically reframed and given to the client to replace the negative comments.

C. The client reported that he/she is more aware of his/her tendency to make self-disparaging remarks and has been more successful at reducing the frequency of this behavior.

2. Explore How Negative Feelings Are Acted Out (2)

A. Client was asked to construct a list of ways he/she sees himself/herself expressing or acting out negative feelings about himself/herself.

B. Client's self-awareness was increased by exploring how he/she expresses or acts out negative feelings about self and how he/she could stop this habit.

C. It was consistently pointed out to the client in a warm, respectful manner whenever he/she was projecting a negative self-image.

---

* The numbers in parentheses correlate to the number of the Therapeutic Intervention statement in the companion chapter with the same title in *The Adolescent Psychotherapy Treatment Planner* (Jongsma, Peterson, and McInnis) by John Wiley & Sons, 2000.

3. Group Therapy Referral (3)

A. The client was referred to group therapy that is focused on building self-esteem.

B. Progress reports reflected that the client is actively taking part in group therapy and is slowly building some self-confidence.

C. The client's fear of social interaction was given as a reason for his/her refusal to attend group therapy.

4. Read *Reviving Ophelia* (4)

A. The client was asked to read selected sections from *Reviving Ophelia* (Pipher) and discuss key points gathered from it.

B. The client has read selected sections from *Reviving Ophelia* and reported an increased awareness of the dynamics of low self-esteem.

5. Read *Why I'm Not Afraid to Tell You Who I Am* (5)

A. The client was asked to read *Why I'm Not Afraid to Tell You Who I Am* (Powell) to increase his/her comfort with self-disclosure.

B. The client's hesitancy and fear about self-disclosure were explored and barriers removed.

C. The client has demonstrated increased self-disclosure within therapy sessions and in daily life.

6. Record Positive Aspects of Self (6)

A. The client was asked to identify one positive thing about himself/herself daily and record it in a journal.

B. The client's journal was reviewed, and positive traits or accomplishments were identified, affirmed, and supported.

C. The client reported that he/she is feeling more positive about self and is more aware of his/her positive traits.

7. Develop Positive Self-Talk (7)

A. Positive self-talk techniques were taught to the client to assist in boosting his/her confidence and self-image.

B. Role play was used to practice positive self-talk techniques.

C. A commitment was elicited from the client to employ positive self-talk on a daily basis.

D. The positive self-talk technique has been effective in increasing the client's self-esteem.

8. Identify Parents' Critical Interactions (8)

A. In family sessions, critical interaction patterns were identified within the family and redirected to supportive, affirming interaction patterns.

B. Videotape of family session was used to illustrate critical family interaction patterns.

C. Negative parenting methods were discussed with the parents and new, affirming methods were recommended.

D. The parents have become more aware of their disparaging parenting methods and reported implementation of more affirming child guidance techniques.

9. Reinforce Positive Statements (9)

A. The client's statements of self-confidence and positive things about self were verbally affirmed and supported.

B. The frequency of the client's positive self-descriptive statements has increased.

10. Develop Affirmations List (10)

A. The client was assisted in developing a list of positive affirmations for himself/herself.

B. A commitment was elicited from the client to read the affirmation list three times each day.

C. The client reported that the regular reading of the self-affirmation list was beneficial in building self-esteem.

11. Assign Mirror Exercise (11)

A. The client was asked to examine self in a mirror for two minutes daily and record his/her responses in order to expand his/her acceptance of his/her physical traits.

B. Positive physical traits that were identified from the mirror exercise were reinforced, and negative ones were downplayed or normalized.

C. The client's predominance of negative responses was discussed and confronted as unrealistic and exaggerated.

12. Assign Self-Esteem Exercise (12)

A. The client was asked to complete "Self-Esteem—What Is It—How Do I Get It" from *Ten Days to Self-Esteem* (Burns) to provide a road map for attaining self-esteem.

B. Completed self-esteem exercises were processed and discussed, with key points and issues of esteem being emphasized.

C. The client has implemented self-esteem-building thoughts that were learned from the book *Ten Days to Self-Esteem*.

13. Play Therapeutic Games (13)

A. The UnGame (UnGame Company) and the Thinking, Feeling, Doing Game (Creative Therapeutics) were played with the client to give opportunities for self-disclosure.

B. Opportunities for identifying feelings during games were seized to affirm the client's self-disclosure.

C. The client has become more adept at identifying and expressing his/her emotions.

14. Educate about Feelings Identification (14)

A. Education was provided for the client on identifying, labeling, and expressing feelings.

B. The client was given a list of feelings, then given various scenarios and asked to identify what the individual in the scenario might be feeling.

C. The client was asked to keep a daily feelings journal.

D. The client has become more adept at identifying and expressing his/her emotions.

15. Encourage Eye Contact (15)

A. The client's lack of eye contact was discussed with the client.

B. An agreement was obtained from the client to have regular eye contact with the therapist during sessions.

C. The client was confronted by the therapist when he/she was avoiding or failing to make eye contact.

D. The client reported an increase in the frequency of making eye contact with others outside of therapy sessions.

16. Broaden Eye Contact Experience (16)

A. The client was asked to make a commitment to increase eye contact with parents, teachers, and others.

B. The client's experience of making eye contact with all adults was processed, and feelings specific to this experience were identified.

C. The client reported an increase in the frequency of making eye contact with others outside of therapy sessions.

17. Read *Feed Your Head* (17)

A. The client was asked to read *Feed Your Head: Some Excellent Stuff on Being Yourself* (Hipp) to help him/her understand the concept of how to be himself/herself.

B. Risks of being yourself were discussed with the client and ways to start to do this were explored.

C. The client reported positive experiences recently in expressing honestly his/her own thoughts and feelings.

18. Life-Changing Exercise (18)

A. The client was asked to do either "Three Wishes Game" or "Three Ways to Change Yourself" from *The Brief Adolescent Therapy Homework Planner* (Jongsma, Peterson, and McInnis) to help him/her identify desired life changes.

B. The completed life-changing exercise was processed and a plan of implementation for key desired life changes was developed.

C. The client was asked to make a commitment to implement and follow through on the program.

D. The client reported success at beginning to implement the changes in self that he/she has desired for a long time.

19. Utilize Solution-Focused Approach (19)

A. A brief, solution-focused intervention called "Externalizing the Problem" was implemented with the client's approval and commitment to follow through.

B. The client's externalizing of the low-self-esteem problem was monitored for follow through and effectiveness, and necessary adjustments were made.

C. The client was confronted on his/her lack of consistency in following through on the intervention.

20. Identify Emotional Needs (20)

A. The client was taught basic concepts of how to identify and verbalize his/her emotional needs.

B. Ways to meet more of the client's emotional needs were explored.

21. Encourage Sharing Emotional Needs (21)

A. A family session was conducted in which parents and the client exchanged and identified their emotional needs.

B. The client and family were educated in ways to be sensitive to each other's needs and to ask for their own emotional needs to be met.

22. Explore Incidents of Abuse (22)

A. Possible incidents of physical, sexual, and emotional abuse were explored with the client.

B. The client was assisted in exploring how being a victim of abuse has affected his/her feelings about self.

C. The client's denial and resistiveness were explored and resolved so the client could connect past abuse with present negative feelings about self.

23. Identify Distorted Beliefs (23)

A. The client was asked to list his/her beliefs about self and the world.

B. The client's distorted, negative beliefs about self and the world were reframed.

24. Develop Positive Messages (24)

A. The client was helped to identify and develop more positive, realistic messages about self and the world.

B. New positive, realistic life messages were implemented by the client and used on a daily basis.

C. The client was confronted whenever he/she failed to make positive, realistic statements about self or life events.

D. The client reported that he/she has developed a more positive outlook about self and the world.

25. Identify Esteem-Building Tasks (25)

A. The client was helped to identify daily tasks that, when performed, would increase his/her sense of responsibility and esteem.

B. The client's follow-through on daily tasks was monitored for consistency.

C. The client was given positive verbal feedback for his/her follow-through on self-care responsibilities.

D. The client reported feeling better about himself/herself as he/she has become more active in performing daily responsibilities.

26. Teach Acceptance of Compliments (26)

A. Neurolinguistic and reframing techniques were used to alter the client's self-messages to enable him/her to receive and accept compliments.

B. Role-play techniques were utilized to give the client opportunities to practice accepting compliments.

C. The client reported a positive experience in accepting compliments from others recently.

27. Assign Letters of Reference (27)

A. The client was asked to provide the names of three nonrelatives from whom letters of reference could be obtained.

B. Letters of reference obtained by the client were read with him/her and compliments were identified and affirmed.

C. The client was asked to write a thank-you note to each person who wrote a reference letter, confirming each positive characteristic that was identified in the reference letter.

28. Assign Parents to Read *Full Esteem Ahead!* (28)

A. The parents were given the book *Full Esteem Ahead!* (Loomans and Loomans) to read first and then asked to select two or three self-esteem-building ideas they would like to implement with the client.

B. The self-esteem-building ideas chosen by the parents were processed and a plan for implementation was made.

C. The parents were reminded of the importance of consistent follow-through if the interventions are to be successful.

D. The parents have successfully implemented self-esteem-building ideas from *Full Esteem Ahead!* and the client has reported appreciating their efforts.

29. Assign Increased Peer Group Activities (29)

A. The parents were presented with various options (scouting, sports, music, etc.) that could help boost the client's self-esteem and asked to encourage him/her to get involved in at least one of them.

B. The role of extracurricular activities in building the client's self-esteem was explored, with positive aspects being identified.

C. The parents have followed through with enrolling the client in more peer group activities.

30. Explore Parental Expectations (30)

A. Expectations that the parents hold for the client were explored and then affirmed where appropriate and adjusted when they were unrealistic.

B. The parents were educated to understand age-appropriate and realistic developmental expectations for the client given his/her abilities.

C. The parents were challenged in a respectful way when their expectations of the client seemed unrealistically high or age-inappropriate.

D. The parents have adjusted their expectations to a more realistic level given the client's developmental stage.

31. Teach Parents Three R's Discipline Technique (31)

A. The three R's discipline technique was taught to the parents, and they were encouraged then to read *Raising Self-Reliant Children in a Self-Indulgent World* (Glenn and Nelson).

B. The parents were assisted in implementing discipline that is respectful, reasonable, and related (three R's) to the misbehavior and coached to offer support, guidance, and encouragement as they followed through.

C. The parents have successfully implemented discipline that is respectful, reasonable, and related to the client's behavior.

32. Positive Parenting Class Referral (32)

A. The parents were asked to attend a parenting class that focuses on the issues of positive parenting.

B. The experiences of positive parenting classes were processed along with key gains received.

33. Teach Anxiety-Coping (33)

A. The client was taught "Pretending to Know How" (Thesis) and "The Therapist on the Inside" (Grigoryev)—techniques for facing new and uncomfortable situations.

B. The anxiety-coping techniques were rehearsed using two different situations that the client might face, and the client was asked to commit to using these techniques.

C. The experience of using "Pretending to Know How" and "The Therapist on the Inside" was processed and the client was asked to try these techniques on two additional situations/problems.

D. The client has successfully faced challenging situations using the new coping skills and has reported that his/her confidence is growing.

34. Read *How to Say No and Keep Your Friends* (34)

A. The client was requested to read *How to Say No and Keep Your Friends* (Scott) to encourage assertiveness.

B. The client was taught that saying no can boost your self-esteem.

C. Role play was utilized for the client to practice saying no to friends in a variety of social situations.

D. The power of saying no was consistently reinforced with the client.

E. The client reported that he/she has said no to others' requests and that he/she felt justified and affirmed.

35. Teach Assertiveness and Social Skills (35)

A. The client was asked to list situations in which he/she has had social difficulties or finds it hard to be assertive.

B. Difficult social situations that the client identified were role-played with him/her to teach assertiveness.

C. Behavioral rehearsal was utilized with the client to prepare him/her for facing the identified difficult social situations.

36. Camp Referral (36)

A. It was recommended to the parents that they schedule an alternative camp weekend experience for the client to build trust and self-confidence.

B. The weekend alternative camp experience was processed with the client, and gains in trust and self-confidence were identified, affirmed, and reinforced.

37. Encourage Parents to Praise Accomplishments (37)

A. The parents were assisted in identifying opportunities they could seize to praise, reinforce, and recognize positive things done by the client.

B. The parents were reminded of the importance of praise, reinforcement, and recognition in building the client's self-esteem.

C. Missed opportunities for praise, reinforcement, or recognition with the client were pointed out to the parents in family session.

D. Both the client and his/her parents report that the frequency of parental praise and recognition for the client's accomplishments has increased.

MANIA/HYPOMANIA

CLIENT PRESENTATION

1. Overly Friendly Social Style (1)*

A. The client becomes overly friendly or gregarious in his/her social interactions with others during his/her manic or hypomanic episodes.

B. The client appeared loud, boisterous, and overly friendly.

C. The client appeared more relaxed, calm, and subdued.

D. The client reported that he/she is more relaxed, calm, and subdued in his/her recent social interactions.

2. Poor Social Judgment (1)

A. The client frequently becomes entangled in interpersonal disputes during his/her manic or hypomanic episodes because of his/her failure to pick up on important social cues or interpersonal nuances.

B. The client has frequently disclosed personal information too readily and makes others feel uncomfortable by demanding that they do the same.

C. The stabilization of the client's mood and reduction in energy level has resulted in improved social relationships and fewer interpersonal conflicts with others.

D. The client has established appropriate boundaries regarding his/her social relationships and has self-disclosed personal information to only his/her close friends.

3. Elated/Euphoric Mood (1)

A. The client's mood often appears extremely euphoric or elated during his/her manic or hypomanic episodes.

B. The client's mood appeared elated, euphoric, and overly enthusiastic.

C. The client's mood has started to stabilize without the extreme amount of euphoria or elation.

D. The client's mood has stabilized and returned to a normal level without the extreme highs or lows.

4. Inflated Sense of Self-Esteem (2)

A. The client has frequently displayed an inflated sense of self-worth and grandiosity during his/her manic or hypomanic episodes.

B. The client expressed grandiose thoughts and made exaggerated claims about his/her abilities during today's therapy session.

C. The client verbalized delusions of grandeur and announced extravagant, unrealistic plans to achieve success.

---

* The numbers in parentheses correlate to the number of the Behavioral Definition statement in the companion chapter with same title in *The Adolescent Psychotherapy Treatment Planner* (Jongsma, Peterson, and McInnis) by John Wiley & Sons, 2000.

D. The client has gradually started to decrease the frequency of his/her grandiose statements and is slowly beginning to develop a more realistic picture of his/her capabilities.

E. The client no longer makes grandiose statements and has developed a healthy, realistic understanding of his/her capabilities.

5. Flight of Ideas/Racing Thoughts (3)

A. The client has experienced a flight of ideas or racing thoughts during the manic or hypomanic episodes.

B. The client experienced racing thoughts and a flight of ideas during today's therapy session.

C. The client was able to communicate his/her thoughts in a logical and organized manner.

D. The client reported recently experiencing a significant decrease in his/her flighty or racing thoughts.

6. Pressured Speech (4)

A. The client's speech was pressured and he/she spoke very rapidly during today's therapy session.

B. The client exhibited a mild decrease in his/her rate of speech during today's therapy session.

C. The client's rate of speech has returned to a normal level.

7. High Energy and Restlessness (5)

A. The client displayed a very high energy level during his/her manic or hypomanic episodes.

B. The client presented with a high energy level and appeared agitated in his/her motor movements.

C. The client appeared calmer and displayed less energy and a mild degree of motor activity.

D. The client was able to sit still without showing an excessive amount of motor activity.

E. The client has recently demonstrated a significant decrease in his/her level of energy and restlessness.

8. Impulsivity (6)

A. The client sought immediate gratification of his/her needs and often failed to stop and consider the consequences of his/her actions during the manic or hypomanic phases.

B. The client has demonstrated good impulse control in the recent past as demonstrated by an improved ability to stop and think about the possible negative consequences of his/her actions.

C. The client has shown an improved ability to delay his/her impulses to receive instant gratification of his/her needs in favor of achieving longer-term goals.

D. The client has consistently demonstrated good impulse control.

9. Erratic Shifts in Mood/Behavior (6)

A. The client has a pattern of exhibiting erratic and unpredictable shifts in his/her mood and behavior during the manic or hypomanic episodes.

B. The client's mood during the manic or hypomanic phases can change quickly from elation and euphoria to dejection, hostility, or extreme irritability.

C. The client's emotions changed quickly and suddenly during today's therapy session.

D. The client's mood and emotional controls have begun to stabilize.

E. The client has recently demonstrated good emotional control, and his/her mood has stabilized significantly since the last therapy session.

10. Reduced Need for Sleep (7)

A. The client has experienced a reduced need for sleep during his/her manic or hypomanic episodes.

B. The client reported feeling little or no need for sleep during his/her most recent manic or hypomanic episodes.

C. The client has continued to stay up at night until early morning without feeling a need to sleep more.

D. The client has started to return to a normal amount of sleep.

E. The client reported that he/she is now sleeping a normal amount on a consistent nightly basis.

11. Feelings of Low Self-Esteem (7)

A. The client's grandiose statements and exaggerated claims about self mask deeper feelings of low self-esteem, inadequacy, and insecurity.

B. The client expressed feelings of shame and embarrassment about his/her decisions and actions during the most recent manic or hypomanic episode.

C. The client verbalized an awareness of how threats to his/her self-esteem often coincide with the onset of the manic or hypomanic episodes.

D. The client has taken active steps to improve his/her self-esteem and develop a positive self-image since his/her mood has stabilized.

E. The client verbalized several positive self-descriptive statements during today's therapy session.

12. Depression (7)

A. The client's manic or hypomanic episodes are frequently followed by periods of depression.

B. The client expressed fear and apprehension about his/her current manic or hypomanic episode being followed by a period of depression.

C. The client's elated or euphoric mood has subsided, and he/she is now exhibiting signs of depression.

D. The client's symptoms of depression have subsided and his/her moods are beginning to return to the previous, normal level.

13. Family History of Affective Disorder (8)

A. The client and parents reported an extensive history of affective disorders in the family.

B. The client and parents are not aware of any other family member having a serious affective disorder.

C. The parent(s) reported experiencing episodes of a major affective disorder in the past.

14. Rejection/Failure Experiences (8)

A. The client described a history of experiencing a significant amount of rejection or failure.

B. The client began to express grandiose statements and make exaggerated claims about self soon after discussing significant rejection or failure experiences.

C. The client was reluctant to talk about past rejection or failure experiences.

D. The client was open and talkative about past rejection or failure experiences.

E. The client expressed genuine feelings of sadness, hurt, and disappointment about past rejection or failure experiences.

15. Separation and Loss (8)

A. The client reported a history of experiencing significant separations or losses in his/her life.

B. The client's most recent manic or hypomanic episode was precipitated by a significant separation or loss.

C. The client was guarded and reticent to talk about past separations or losses.

D. The client was open and talkative about past significant separations or losses.

E. The client expressed genuine feelings of sadness, hurt, and disappointment about past separations or losses.

16. Angry Outbursts/Aggressive Behaviors (9)

A. The client has a history of losing control of his/her temper and exhibiting frequent angry outbursts or aggressive behavior during the manic or hypomanic episodes.

B. The client appeared angry, irritable, and agitated.

C. The client reported incidents of becoming easily angered over minor or trivial matters.

D. The client has started to control his/her anger and aggressive impulses in a more effective manner.

E. The client has consistently demonstrated good control of his/her anger and has not exhibited any major outbursts or aggressive behaviors.

17. Short Attention Span and Distractible (10)

A. The parents and teachers reported that the client displays a very short attention span and has difficulty staying focused for any significant length of time during the manic or hypomanic episodes.

B. The client appeared very distractible during today's therapy session and often had to be directed back to the topic of discussion.

C. The client appeared more focused and less distractible during today's therapy session.

D. The parents and teachers reported that the client has consistently demonstrated good attention and concentration at home and school.

18. Failure to Complete Tasks (11)

A. The client frequently switches from one uncompleted activity to another during his/her manic or hypomanic episodes.

B. The client has trouble completing tasks and channeling his/her energy into constructive or sustained, purposeful activities because of his/her high energy level, impulsivity, lack of discipline, and racing thoughts.

C. The client has recently exercised greater self-control and discipline, as evidenced by his/her ability to follow through and complete tasks or projects.

D. The client has been able to complete tasks or projects on a regular, consistent basis.

19. Self-Defeating or Dangerous Behavior (12)

A. The client described a history of engaging in self-defeating, risky, or potentially dangerous behavior during his/her manic or hypomanic episodes.

B. The client's impulsivity and restlessness has contributed to his/her propensity for engaging in self-defeating, risky, or potentially dangerous behavior.

C. The client gained insight into the need to stop and think about the possible consequences of his/her actions for self and others before engaging in self-defeating, risky, or potentially dangerous behaviors.

D. The client has not recently engaged in any self-defeating, risky, or potentially dangerous behaviors.

20. Outlandish Dress/Grooming (13)

A. The client has often dressed or groomed himself/herself in an outlandish manner during the manic/hypomanic phases.

B. The client came to the therapy session dressed and groomed in an unusual and outlandish manner.

C. The client was appropriately groomed and attired.

D. The client has consistently dressed and groomed himself/herself in an appropriate manner since his/her moods have stabilized.

INTERVENTIONS IMPLEMENTED

1. Assess Manic/Hypomanic Episode (1)*

A. A diagnostic interview was conducted to assess whether the client is experiencing symptoms of a manic or hypomanic episode.

B. The client's mood, impulse control, anger control, social judgment, frustration tolerance, rate of speech, thought processes, and self-esteem were all assessed in today's diagnostic interview.

C. The client was pleasant and cooperative during today's diagnostic interview.

D. The client was agitated and resistant during today's diagnostic interview.

2. Assess Need for Medication (2)

A. A diagnostic interview was conducted to assess whether the client has a bipolar disorder and needs to be referred for a medication evaluation.

---

* The numbers in parentheses correlate to the number of the Therapeutic Intervention statement in the companion chapter with the same title in *The Adolescent Psychotherapy Treatment Planner* (Jongsma, Peterson, and McInnis) by John Wiley & Sons, 2000.

B. The client's history was explored to determine whether he/she has ever been prescribed any medication for a bipolar disorder.

C. The client's thoughts and feelings about taking medication to stabilize his/her mood were processed.

3. Psychological Testing (3)

A. A psychological evaluation was conducted to determine whether the client is experiencing symptoms of bipolar disorder.

B. The client was uncooperative and difficult to engage during the psychological testing.

C. The client approached the psychological testing in an honest, straightforward manner and was cooperative with any request directed toward him/her.

D. The psychological testing results supported the diagnosis of a bipolar disorder.

E. The psychological testing results did not support the diagnosis of a bipolar disorder.

4. Obtain Psychosocial History (4)

A. A complete psychosocial history was gathered from the parents to assess for patterns of mania and the extent of bipolar illness in the client's extended family.

B. A review of the client's background revealed several episodes of mania or hypomania.

C. The psychosocial history information gathered during today's therapy session was helpful in that it revealed a strong history of bipolar illnesses in the client's family.

D. The psychosocial history information did not reveal the presence of any bipolar illnesses in the client's extended family.

5. Psychiatric Examination Referral (5)

A. The client was referred for a psychiatric evaluation to help determine the need for medication to stabilize his/her mood.

B. The client and parents agreed to follow through with a psychiatric examination to determine the need for medication.

C. The client's resistance to taking medication was explored and worked through in today's therapy session.

D. The client was strongly opposed to being placed on medication to help stabilize his/her mood.

6. Assess Medication Compliance and Effectiveness (6)

A. The client reported that taking the medication regularly has helped to decrease his/her energy level and stabilize moods without any side effects.

B. The client reported little or no improvement since taking the psychotropic medication.

C. The client has not complied with taking his/her medication on a regular basis.

D. The client and parents were encouraged to report the effectiveness and side effects of the medication to the psychiatrist.

7. Develop Trust Relationship (7)

A. A level of trust was built with the client through consistent eye contact, active listening, unconditional positive regard, and warm acceptance.

B. The client was given support by listening closely to his/her concerns and reflecting his/her feelings.

8. Explore Fears of Abandonment (8)

A. The client's background was explored for a history of abandonment or rejection experiences that may have coincided with the triggering of his/her manic/hypomanic episodes.

B. The client expressed his/her fear about how future manic/hypomanic episodes may lead to rejection or abandonment by significant others.

C. The parents expressed their love and pledged their continued support to help alleviate the client's fear about being abandoned or rejected because of his/her manic/hypomanic episodes.

9. Probe Real or Perceived Losses (9)

A. The client's family background was explored for a history of significant losses or separations that may have coincided with the onset of his/her manic/hypomanic episodes.

B. The client was given the opportunity to express his/her thoughts and feelings about real or perceived losses in the past.

C. The empty-chair technique was employed to facilitate expression of feelings surrounding past losses or separations.

D. The client was instructed to draw pictures that reflect his/her feelings about past separations or losses.

10. Identify Impact of Impulsivity (10)

A. The client identified his/her goals of improving impulse control and increasing sensitivity to how his/her impulsive behaviors impact others.

B. The client verbalized a commitment to contact his/her psychiatrist or therapist if he/she demonstrates a significant increase in impulsive behaviors.

C. The client was assisted in listing the negative consequences of his/her impulsive actions or socially inappropriate actions.

D. The client was firmly and consistently confronted with how his/her impulsive or inappropriate behavior negatively impacts himself/herself and others.

E. Role-reversal techniques were used to help the client realize how his/her impulsive behavior negatively impacts others.

11. Teach Techniques to Resolve Past Losses (11)

A. The client was instructed to use a journal to help him/her express and work through feelings surrounding past losses.

B. The client was assigned a "letting go" exercise (e.g., writing a letter) to help him/her resolve past losses and move ahead in his/her life.

C. The client was assisted in developing an action plan to help him/her cope with past losses and move forward in his/her life.

D. The client was strongly encouraged to participate in positive peer group activities to provide him/her with the opportunity to establish meaningful friendships and replace or cope with past losses.

E. The client was assisted in developing a list of positive peer group activities that will provide him/her the opportunity to establish meaningful friendships.

12. Differentiate Actual and Exaggerated Losses (12)

A. The client was helped to differentiate between real and imagined, actual and exaggerated losses.

B. The client was gently challenged and confronted about his/her fear of abandonment and loss that is based on irrational and faulty thinking.

C. The client was helped to replace irrational thoughts about imagined or exaggerated losses with reality-based thoughts.

D. Client-centered approaches were utilized to help the client work through his/her feelings about real, actual losses.

13. Explore Low Self-Esteem Causes (13)

A. The client's family background was explored for a past history of separation, loss, abandonment, or rejection experiences that may have contributed to his/her feelings of low self-esteem.

B. The client developed a time line where he/she identified significant historical events, both positive and negative, that have occurred in his/her family and have impacted his/her self-esteem.

C. Today's therapy session revealed how the client's feelings of low self-esteem and fear of abandonment are related to significant separations, losses, and abandonment in the past.

14. Family Therapy to Explore Parental Rejection (14)

A. A family therapy session was held to explore how the onset of the client's manic/hypomanic episodes is related to parental rejection or emotional abandonment.

B. The client was given the opportunity to express his/her thoughts and feelings about past rejection or emotional abandonment.

C. The client verbalized his/her need to spend greater quality time with parent(s) and receive more frequent praise or positive reinforcement.

D. The disengaged parent(s) were challenged to spend more time with the client in leisure, school, or household activities and increase positive reinforcement.

E. The disengaged parent(s) verbalized a commitment to spend increased time with the client.

15. Confront Grandiosity and Demanding Behaviors (15)

A. The client's grandiose thinking and demanding behaviors were gently confronted.

B. The client's grandiose thoughts and demanding behaviors were firmly confronted.

C. The client was helped to realize how his/her grandiose thoughts are related to underlying feelings of low self-esteem, insecurity, and inadequacy.

D. The client was confronted with how his/her demanding behaviors negatively impact his/her relationship with others.

E. Role-playing techniques were utilized to help the client learn more constructive ways to meet his/her needs instead of placing excessive demands on others.

16. Identify Stressors That Precipitate Mania (16)

A. The client's background was explored for significant stressors that have precipitated manic/hypomanic episodes.

B. The client was helped to identify how past manic/hypomanic episodes were related to past failure experiences at school and/or threats to self-esteem.

C. The client was helped to realize how the onset of past manic/hypomanic episodes were related to previous rejection experiences by peers or friends.

D. The client identified how the onset of past manic/hypomanic episodes was related to trauma within the family system.

E. The client developed a time line in the therapy session where he/she identified significant historical events that have occurred near the onset of his/her depressive or manic phases.

17. Encourage Parental Limit Setting and Reinforcing (17)

A. The parents attended today's therapy session and were strongly encouraged to set firm, consistent limits for the client's angry outbursts or rebellious behaviors.

B. The parents were helped to identify appropriate consequences for the client's angry outbursts or rebellious behaviors.

C. The parents were strongly encouraged to reinforce the client's prosocial behaviors.

D. A reward system was designed to reinforce positive social behaviors and deter his/her aggressive or rebellious behaviors.

E. The parents were instructed to observe and record three to five positive behaviors by the client in between therapy sessions.

18. "Clear Rules, Positive Reinforcement, Appropriate Consequences" Exercise (18)

A. The parents were given the homework assignment "Clear Rules, Positive Reinforcement, Appropriate Consequences" in *The Brief Adolescent Therapy Homework Planner* (Jongsma, Peterson, and McInnis) to help them establish clearly defined rules and expectations for the client.

B. The parents reported that the homework assignment "Clear Rules, Positive Reinforcement, Appropriate Consequences" helped them establish clear rules and identify appropriate consequences for the client's impulsive behaviors.

C. The parents reported that the homework assignment helped them identify natural consequences and follow through with limits in a calm, controlled, and respectful manner.

D. The parents reported that they completed the homework assignment but that the client has continued to test the limits and defy the rules.

E. The parents failed to complete the homework assignment and were asked to do it again.

19. List Impulsive Behavior Consequences (19)

A. The client was asked to list the negative consequences of his/her impulsive behavior.

B. Role-reversal techniques were used in the therapy session to help the client realize how his/her impulsive behavior negatively impacts himself/herself and others.

C. The client was encouraged to apologize to individuals who have been negatively impacted by his/her impulsive behavior.

D. The client was taught mediational and self-control strategies (e.g., relaxation techniques, "stop, look, listen, and think") to help delay the need for immediate gratification and inhibit impulses.

20. "Action Minus Thought Equals Painful Consequences" Exercise (20)

A. The client was given the homework assignment "Action Minus Thought Equals Painful Consequences" in *The Brief Adolescent Therapy Homework Planner* (Jongsma, Peterson, and McInnis) to help him/her understand how impulsive behaviors have negative consequences for both self and others.

B. The client was given the homework assignment "Action Minus Thought Equals Painful Consequences" to help the client identify more reasonable, alternative replacement behavior for his/her impulsive behavior.

C. The client reported that the homework assignment helped him/her stop and think about the possible consequences of his/her actions before impulsively embarking on a course of action.

D. The client completed the homework assignment but has continued to act out in an impulsive manner.

E. The client failed to complete the homework assignment and was again assigned to do it.

21. Confront Thoughtless Impulsivity (21)

A. The client was repeatedly confronted with the consequences of his/her thoughtless, impulsive behavior.

B. The parents were strongly encouraged to set firm, consistent limits for the client's impulsive actions.

C. The client was asked to identify the benefits of delaying his/her need for immediate gratification in favor of longer-term gains.

D. The client was encouraged to use mediational and self-control strategies (e.g., relaxation techniques, "stop, look, listen, and think") to help deter his/her impulsive behaviors during manic/hypomanic episodes.

22. Teach Sensitivity through Role Playing (22)

A. Role-playing and role-reversal techniques were used to help increase the client's sensitivity to how his/her impulsive behaviors negatively affect others.

B. Through the use of role-playing and role-reversal techniques, the client gained insight into how his/her impulsive actions or inappropriate social behavior negatively impacts others.

C. The client had much difficulty staying focused on any one topic in today's session, so the role-playing and role-reversal techniques were not helpful in identifying how his/her impulsive actions affect others.

23. Provide Structure to Behavior Plans/Conversations (23)

A. The client appeared very flighty and frequently had to be directed back to the essential focus of the conversation.

B. The therapy session focused on helping the parents increase the structure in the home to help deter the client's impulsivity and help him/her stay focused when performing daily tasks or routines.

C. The client and parents designed a schedule of dates and times when the client is expected to perform certain tasks or responsibilities.

D. The parents were encouraged to use effective communication techniques (e.g., maintain good eye contact, request positive behaviors, give one instruction at a time) and clear away as many distractions as possible when talking with the client during his/her manic or hypomanic episodes.

24. Reinforce Slower Speech and Deliberate Thought (24)

A. The client was consistently encouraged to speak more slowly and in a calmer voice.

B. The client was verbally reinforced for speaking more slowly and expressing his/her thoughts in a rational and coherent manner.

C. Client-centered approaches were utilized to help the client stay focused and express his/her thoughts and feelings in a rational, deliberate manner.

D. The client was taught effective communication skills to help slow his/her rate of speech and communicate thoughts and feelings in a constructive manner.

E. The client was often stopped and asked to utilize deep breathing techniques to help slow down his/her rate of speech and communicate thoughts in a more deliberate manner.

25. Reinforce Appropriate Dress and Grooming (25)

A. The client was reinforced for being neatly groomed and appropriately dressed.

B. The client was encouraged to dress more appropriately and improve personal hygiene to enhance his/her chances of establishing meaningful friendships.

C. The client was gently confronted with how his/her outlandish dress and poor grooming interfere with his/her ability to establish friendships.

26. Interpret Underlying Fear and Insecurity (26)

A. The client was helped to recognize how his/her braggadocio and denial of dependency is related to underlying fear and feelings of dependency.

B. The client verbally recognized how his/her angry outbursts and hostile behaviors are related to underlying fear and insecurity.

C. The client was encouraged to express his/her fears and insecurities more directly to significant others instead of reacting with excessive bragging, boasting, or hostility.

D. The client was helped to identify how his/her braggadocio and excessive boasting are related to the need for acceptance and approval from others.

E. The client was helped to identify more appropriate ways to meet his/her dependency needs.

27. Identify Balance between Dependency and Independence (27)

A. A family therapy session was held to help the client achieve a balance between meeting his/her dependency needs and striving to become more independent.

B. The client and parents were helped to identify specific dates and times when the client could talk one-on-one with the parents or engage in leisure or social activities with them.

C. The client and parents were helped to establish clear-cut rules pertaining to the client's quest for greater independence.

D. The client and parents identified appropriate ways for him/her to achieve greater independence.

E. The client was given a homework assignment to engage in three to five responsible and independent behaviors before the next therapy session.

28. Identify Strengths and Interests (28)

A. The client was helped to identify a list of his/her strengths and interests.

B. The client was encouraged to share his/her interests with peers to improve self-esteem and provide opportunities to establish peer friendships.

C. The client reported that his/her self-esteem has increased by sharing his/her interests with others.

D. The client has continued to have difficulty sharing his/her interests with others because of deep-seated feelings of insecurity.

29. "I Am a Good Person" Exercise (29)

A. The client was assigned the "I Am a Good Person" exercise from *The Brief Adolescent Therapy Homework Planner* (Jongsma, Peterson, and McInnis) to help increase his/her self-esteem by identifying his/her positive character and personality traits.

B. The client successfully completed the exercise and identified several positive character and personality traits.

C. The client did not follow through with completing the exercise and was again asked to work on it.

30. Encourage Sharing Deeper Feelings (30)

A. The client was encouraged to share his/her feelings at a deeper level to facilitate openness, intimacy, and greater trust in his/her relationships.

B. The client was helped to identify a list of close, trusted individuals with whom he/she could share his/her more intimate thoughts and feelings.

C. The client was challenged to share his/her more intimate thoughts and feelings with others to counteract his/her pattern of superficiality and fear of intimacy.

D. The client expressed that his/her willingness to share deeper emotions has helped him/her to establish closer, more intimate relationships.

E. The client's interpersonal relationships have remained at a superficial level because of his/her fear of rejection if he/she shares deeper thoughts and emotions.

31. Identify Negative Cognitive Messages (31)

A. The client was helped to identify the negative cognitive messages that feed his/her fear of rejection and failure.

B. The client explored whether his/her fears of rejection and/or failure are rational or irrational.

C. The client was helped to realize how his/her frequent derogatory remarks about self impede his/her chances of establishing friendships.

32. Identify Positive, Realistic Thoughts (32)

A. The client was helped to identify positive, realistic thoughts that can replace his/her negative self-talk that reinforces low self-esteem and a fear of failure or rejection.

B. The client was encouraged and challenged to replace his/her negative self-talk with positive self-talk.

C. The client's consistent practice of replacing negative self-talk with positive messages has helped to increase his/her self-esteem and confidence.

D. The client was challenged to verbalize positive self-talk when initiating conversations or social contacts to help overcome his/her fear of rejection.

E. The client acknowledged that he/she has not replaced negative self-talk with positive self-talk and, as a result, has continued to be troubled by feelings of low self-esteem.

33. Establish Consequences for Acting-Out Behavior (33)

A. Today's family therapy session focused on helping the parents to establish clearly defined rules and identifying consequences for the client's manipulative or acting-out behavior.

B. The parents were assisted in writing down rules and expectations that the client is expected to follow at home and were encouraged to make sure they will be consistently implemented.

C. The parents were able to identify appropriate consequences for the client's manipulative and acting-out behavior.

D. The parents had difficulty establishing clearly defined rules and identifying appropriate consequences for the client's manipulative or acting-out behavior.

E. The client was asked to repeat the rules to demonstrate an understanding of the expectations of him/her.

34. Reinforce Parental Limit Setting and Expressions of Love (34)

A. The parents were reinforced for setting reasonable limits on the client's impulsive, manipulative, or acting-out behavior.

B. The parents were challenged to follow through in setting reasonable limits for the client's behavior to demonstrate their love and commitment to the client.

C. The parents were encouraged to verbalize their unconditional love and commitment to the client to help reduce his/her feelings of insecurity and fear of rejection.

D. The parents' verbalized commitment to love the client unconditionally has helped him/her feel more secure and less afraid of rejection.

MEDICAL CONDITION

CLIENT PRESENTATION

1. Diagnosis of a Chronic, Non-Life-Threatening Illness (1)*

A. The client recently received a diagnosis of a chronic, non-life-threatening illness that will have a significant impact on his/her life.

B. The client presented as upset and worried after he/she received confirmation of having a chronic, non-life-threatening medical condition.

C. The client was overwhelmed after he/she received the diagnosis of a chronic illness and the life changes it will require.

D. The client has started to accept his/her medical condition and has begun to make the required life changes.

2. Lifestyle Changes (1)

A. The client reported numerous lifestyle changes that need to be made in order to stabilize his/her medical condition.

B. The client is struggling with letting go of certain things in his/her lifestyle that will assist in treating the medical condition.

C. The client refused to consider making certain life changes that were recommended as part of his/her treatment.

D. Outside pressure from the family has moved the client to make the recommended life changes to improve his/her long-term physical health.

3. Diagnosis of an Acute, Life-Threatening Illness (2)

A. The client presented as very upset after he/she received a diagnosis of having an acute, life-threatening illness.

B. The client reported feeling an overwhelming sadness about having been diagnosed with an acute, life-threatening illness.

C. The client indicated that he/she has not told any of his/her friends about the diagnosis and its seriousness.

D. The client has begun to share his/her diagnosis and what it means with others close to him/her.

4. Diagnosis of a Terminal Illness (3)

A. The client reported with hesitation and difficulty his/her diagnosis of terminal illness.

B. The client failed to disclose his/her diagnosis of a terminal illness until he/she was asked.

C. The client indicated that he/she finds it impossible to talk about his/her diagnosis of terminal illness.

D. The client has begun to openly acknowledge his/her diagnosis and its terminal nature.

* The numbers in parentheses correlate to the number of the Behavioral Definition statement in the companion chapter with same title in *The Adolescent Psychotherapy Treatment Planner* (Jongsma, Peterson, and McInnis) by John Wiley & Sons, 2000.

5. Anxious/Sensitive (4)

A. The client presented with anxious feelings related to his/her serious medical condition.

B. The client reported that a discussion of anything related to his/her medical condition makes him/her feel anxious.

C. The client has developed some peace of mind about his/her serious medical condition.

6. Sad/Quiet (4)

A. The client presented in a sad, quiet manner.

B. The client found it very difficult to talk about his/her medical condition.

C. The client reported feeling overwhelming sadness about the loss of his/her health when the condition was diagnosed.

D. The client's sadness has decreased, and he/she has been willing to talk more openly about the medical diagnosis and prognosis.

7. Social Withdrawal (4)

A. Recently, the client has dropped most of his/her friends.

B. The client reported that he/she has been spending all of his/her spare time alone.

C. The client appeared to be avoiding family and friends since learning of his/her medical condition.

D. Due to his/her particular medical condition, the client has seen no reason to interact or have relationships with others.

E. As the client has accepted his/her medical condition, he/she has begun to reconnect with others and has received their support.

8. Depression (4)

A. The client's mood has been depressed since his/her medical condition was confirmed.

B. The client presented in a depressed manner with low energy and little interest in life's activities.

C. As the client's depression has lifted, he/she has started to have more energy and sees some hope in living with his/her medical condition.

9. Suicidal Ideation (5)

A. The client presented in a negative, despondent manner.

B. The client reported feeling very hopeless and helpless regarding the future due to his/her medical condition.

C. Suicidal thoughts and feelings seemed to dominate the client at the present time.

D. The client revealed a plan and a backup plan to take his/her own life.

E. The client has gradually started to feel more hopeful and less despondent about his/her medical condition.

10. Denial (6)

A. The client presented as though there were nothing wrong with him/her despite evidence to the contrary.

B. The client reported that he/she did not agree with the seriousness of the condition diagnosed by the physicians.

C. The client seemed to vacillate between accepting and denying the diagnosed medical condition.

D. The client refused to disclose or acknowledge having any medical condition.

E. The client's denial has started to lessen and he/she is beginning to talk about his/her condition in a realistic manner.

11. Resistive to Treatment (7)

A. The client presented in a resistive manner.

B. The client reported that he/she is not open to treatment of any kind for his/her medical condition.

C. The client's resistiveness to accepting treatment for his/her medical condition has had a negative effect on his/her general health.

D. The client has refused to cooperate fully with the recommended medical treatments.

E. The client has become more cooperative with medical treatment procedures.

INTERVENTIONS IMPLEMENTED

1. Gather History of Medical Condition (1)*

A. A history of the client's medical condition that included symptoms, treatment, and prognosis was gathered.

B. During the history-gathering process, the client was assisted in connecting feelings to aspects and stages of his/her medical condition.

C. A sketchy, vague history of the client's medical condition was gathered due to his/her unwillingness to provide specific information.

2. Obtain Additional Medical History (2)

A. Informed consent was obtained from the client so family and physician could be contacted for further information on his/her medical condition.

B. Additional information regarding the client's diagnosis, treatment, and prognosis was gathered from his/her physician.

C. Various family members contributed additional information when contacted about the client's medical condition and its progression.

D. The client refused to give consent to have either his/her physician or family members contacted about his/her medical condition.

3. Identify Feelings regarding Medical Condition (3)

A. The client was assisted in identifying and verbalizing feelings connected to his/her medical condition.

---

* The numbers in parentheses correlate to the number of the Therapeutic Intervention statement in the companion chapter with the same title in *The Adolescent Psychotherapy Treatment Planner* (Jongsma, Peterson, and McInnis) by John Wiley & Sons, 2000.

B. The client was encouraged to recognize and express feelings related to the medical condition on a daily basis.

C. Instances of the client recognizing, identifying, and expressing his/her feelings were affirmed and reinforced verbally.

D. The client was not open with his/her feelings regarding the current medical condition.

4. Explore Family's Feelings regarding Medical Condition (4)

A. Feelings associated with a family member's medical condition were explored and normalized for the family.

B. Family sessions were conducted to help members clarify and share feelings they have experienced about the client's medical condition.

C. Family members were reminded that having a safe place to express feelings about the client's condition was helpful and healthy for all involved.

D. Strong feelings of helplessness and fear about the client's medical condition deteriorating in the future were expressed.

E. The client's siblings expressed feelings of anger and jealousy regarding the attention focused on the client's medical condition.

5. List Limitations Caused by Medical Condition (5)

A. The client was asked to list all changes, losses, and limitations that have resulted from his/her medical condition.

B. The client was assisted in making a list of his/her losses, changes, and limitations that resulted from the medical condition due to his/her difficulty connecting the two things.

C. The changes in the client's life brought on by the medical condition caused feelings of depression, frustration, and hopelessness.

6. Teach Stages of Grief (6)

A. The client was educated on the stages and process of grief.

B. The client was asked to identify the stages of the grief process he/she has experienced.

7. Assign Books on Grief (7)

A. The client was encouraged to expand his/her knowledge of the grieving process by reading recommended books on the subject of grief.

B. The client has followed through with reading some of the recommended material on grief and has developed a deeper understanding of his/her own grief feelings.

C. The client has not followed through with reading the recommended material on grief.

8. Assign a Grief Journal (8)

A. The benefits of keeping a grief journal were explained, identified, and reinforced to the client.

B. The client was asked to commit to keeping a daily grief journal to share in therapy sessions.

C. Daily grief journal material that the client recorded was shared in sessions, and entries were processed.

D. The client has not recorded his/her feelings on a daily basis and was reminded of his/her commitment to keep a grief journal.

9. Assign Daily Mourning Time (9)

A. The client was educated in the value of mourning a loss.

B. Ways for the client to daily mourn loss were explored, and several were selected and developed for implementation.

C. The client was asked to commit to implementing his/her mourning ritual for a specific amount of time daily and then getting on with other daily activities.

D. The daily mourning ritual has been followed by the client and it has been effective in focusing grief feelings and increasing productivity during other times of the day.

E. The client has failed to follow through on implementing the daily mourning ritual and has avoided the grieving process.

F. Instead of limiting the intense grieving to specific times of the day, the client continues to be preoccupied with grief throughout the day.

10. List Positive Life Aspects (10)

A. The client was assisted in listing all the positive aspects still present in his/her life.

B. The client was challenged to focus on the positive aspects of life that he/she identified rather than the losses associated with the medical condition.

C. Gentle confrontation was used when the client focused on his/her losses rather than positive life aspects.

D. The client's focus on positive life aspects within sessions was reinforced.

11. Identify Spiritual Support Resources (11)

A. The client was assisted in identifying sources of spiritual support that could help him/her now.

B. The client was encouraged to actively utilize his/her identified spiritual resources and support on a daily basis.

C. The client has denied any interest in spiritual resources.

D. The client's spiritual faith is deep and a significant source of strength and peace during this time of pain and stress.

12. Confront Denial of Need for Treatment (12)

A. Gentle confrontation was used with the client regarding his/her denial of the seriousness of his/her condition and of the need for compliance with recommended treatment.

B. Denial was normalized as part of the adjustment process, and barriers to acceptance of the need for treatment on the client's part were explored and addressed.

C. Despite gentle confrontation, the client continues to deny the seriousness of his/her condition and refuses to follow through with the recommended treatment.

D. The client's denial regarding the reality of the medical condition and the need for treatment has dissipated, resulting in consistent follow-through with medical recommendations.

13. Reinforce Acceptance of Condition (13)

A. The positive aspects of acceptance over denial of the medical condition were reinforced with the client.

B. The client's statements indicating acceptance of the condition were affirmed and reinforced.

C. Ambivalent statements by the client about medical condition and its treatment were reframed to more positive ones and reinforced.

D. The client's denial regarding the reality of the medical condition and the need for treatment has dissipated, resulting in consistent follow-through with medical recommendations.

14. Encourage Expression of Fears regarding Health (14)

A. The client was asked to express his/her fears about failing health, death, and dying.

B. The fear of death and dying expressed by the client were explored and processed.

C. The concept of facing your fears was presented to and processed with the client.

D. The client was open in expressing his/her fears regarding death and dying and seems to have resolved these fears, resulting in peace of mind.

15. Normalize Anxious Feelings (15)

A. The client was assisted and supported in identifying and expressing feelings of anxiety connected to his/her medical condition.

B. The anxious and sad feelings identified by the client were affirmed and normalized.

C. The client was reminded of the value and benefit to his/her health and recovery of identifying and expressing feelings.

16. Assess/Treat Depression and Anxiety (16)

A. The client was assessed for level of depression and anxiety, and treatment was recommended.

B. It was determined that the client's level of depression was significant enough to merit focused treatment.

C. The client's anxiety was explored and appropriate interventions were implemented to assist the client in coping with these feelings.

D. The client was assisted in recognizing his/her depression and in beginning to express the feelings associated with it.

17. Support Group Referral (17)

A. The client was educated on the various types of support groups available in the community.

B. The client was referred to a support group of others living with the same medical condition.

C. The benefits of the support group experience were identified and reinforced with the client.

D. The client's experience with attending the support group was processed, and continued attendance was encouraged.

E.   The client has failed to follow the recommendation to attend a support group.

18.   Family Support Group Referral (18)

A.   The purpose and benefits of attending a support group were identified and reinforced with the family.

B.   Support group options were provided for the family.

C.   The family was referred to a community support group associated with the client's medical condition.

D.   The initial support group experience was processed with family, and continued attendance was encouraged and reinforced.

E.   The family has not followed through with attending the recommended support group.

19.   Monitor/Reinforce Treatment Compliance (19)

A.   The client's compliance with the recommended medical treatment regimen was monitored.

B.   The client's failure to comply with medical treatment recommendations was confronted and addressed.

C.   Positive affirmation and encouragement were given to the client for his/her consistent follow-through on all aspects of the medical treatment regimen.

D.   Despite gentle confrontation and encouragement, the client still fails to comply with the medical treatment recommendation for his/her medical condition.

20.   Explore Factors Interfering with Compliance (20)

A.   Misconceptions, fears, and situational factors were explored with the client for their possible interference with medical treatment compliance.

B.   The client's misconceptions, fears, and other situational factors were resolved to improve his/her follow-through with recommended medical treatment.

C.   Since making the connection between his/her fears and misconceptions and avoiding medical treatment, the client has started to cooperate fully and responsibly with his/her medical treatment.

D.   The client's resistance to compliance with the medical treatment regimen continues to be a problem.

21.   Confront Defenses That Block Medical Compliance (21)

A.   All the client's defense mechanisms that block compliance with the medical regimen were confronted.

B.   As defense mechanisms of manipulation and denial have been confronted, the client's compliance with the medical regimen has increased.

C.   The client's defense mechanisms continue to block consistent compliance with the medical treatment regimen.

22.   List Pleasurable Activities (22)

A.   The client was asked to list all the activities that he/she has enjoyed doing.

B.   The client's list of activities was examined for the ones that can still be enjoyed alone and with others.

C. The client was encouraged to again start involving himself/herself in these pleasurable activities on a regular basis.

D. In spite of encouragement, the client continues to resist engagement in pleasurable activities that he/she is capable of participating in.

23. Reinforce Pleasurable Activities (23)

A. The client was asked to make a verbal commitment to increase his/her activity level in pleasurable social and physical activities.

B. The client's involvement in activities was affirmed and reinforced.

C. The client's failure to keep his/her commitment to increase his/her activity level was gently confronted.

D. The client avoided the requested commitment by saying he/she would give it a try and that's the best he/she could do.

E. In spite of encouragement, the client continues to resist engagement in pleasurable activities that he/she is capable of participating in.

24. Teach Relaxation Techniques (24)

A. Deep muscle relaxation, deep breathing, and positive imagery techniques were taught to the client to enhance the ability to relax.

B. Behavioral rehearsal was utilized to give the client opportunity to practice each relaxation skill.

C. The client was reminded of the benefits of deep muscle relaxation, deep breathing, and positive imagery and encouraged to use each on a regular basis.

D. The client has implemented the relaxation techniques and reports a reduction in stress and anxiety.

E. The client has failed to follow through with implementation of relaxation techniques.

25. Utilize Biofeedback (25)

A. EMG biofeedback was utilized with the client to monitor, increase, and reinforce his/her depth of relaxation.

B. The use of biofeedback with the client has improved his/her overall depth of relaxation.

26. Develop Physical Exercise Routine (26)

A. The client was assisted in developing a plan for a daily physical exercise routine within the limits of his/her medical condition.

B. The benefits of daily physical exercise were identified and reinforced.

C. The physical exercise plan was implemented by the client along with a commitment to follow the plan on a daily basis.

D. The client's follow-through with daily exercise was monitored and reinforced.

E. The client has not followed through with implementing any regular pattern of physical exercise.

27. Identify Distorted, Negative Thoughts (27)

A. The client was assisted in identifying his/her cognitive distortions that contribute to a negative attitude and hopeless feeling regarding medical condition.

B. The connection between cognitive distortions and feelings of helplessness and negativity surrounding the medical condition were established and made clear to the client.

C. The client was resistive to identifying and in denial of engaging in cognitive distortion.

28. Teach Positive, Realistic Self-Talk (28)

A. The client was helped to generate a list of positive, realistic self-talk to replace the cognitive distortions and catastrophizing that accompanies his/her medical condition.

B. The techniques of positive self-talk were taught to the client.

C. Role-play situations about the client's medical condition were utilized so that the client could practice using positive self-talk.

D. The benefits of using positive self-talk reported by the client were reinforced.

29. Teach Healing Imagery (29)

A. Positive, healing imagery techniques were taught to the client.

B. The client practiced using healing imagery techniques in the session.

C. Plans for implementing positive imagery techniques were developed with the client.

D. The client was asked to make a commitment to use positive imagery techniques as planned.

E. The client reported consistent daily use of the positive, healing imagery technique and has developed a positive mental attitude regarding the improvement in his/her medical condition.

30. Provide Accurate Medical Information (30)

A. The client was asked to develop a list of all questions he/she has concerning any aspect of his/her medical condition and treatment.

B. The client was given clear, accurate information in terms that were understandable on the causes, treatment, and prognosis for medical condition.

C. The client's questions were answered in ways he/she could understand.

D. After the use of role play and modeling to teach assertiveness, the client was encouraged to raise questions about his/her medical condition and treatment with his/her physician.

31. Provide Information Resource Referral (31)

A. The parents and the client were given resource materials on the medical condition and Internet sites where further information is available.

B. Parents' and the client's questions that resulted from reading the resource material were answered and processed.

C. The client and parents quest for information on the client's medical condition was encouraged and reinforced.

32. Assess Parents' Resources for Support (32)

A. The parents' sources of emotional support were probed and assessed.

B. The parents were asked to identify their sources of emotional support.

33. Encourage Parents' Acceptance of Support (33)

A. The parents were assisted in identifying community resources for support.

B. Barriers to accepting support were explored with the parents and addressed.

C. The parents' need for support was identified and reinforced.

D. The parents have accepted their need for support and have followed through in making contact with potential resources for support.

34. Draw Out Parents' Fears (34)

A. The parents were encouraged to express their underlying fears about the client's possible death.

B. Empathy, affirmation, and normalization were used in responding to the fearful feelings that the parents verbalized.

C. The parents were given the reassurance of God's presence as the giver and supporter of life.

35. Explore Marital Conflict (35)

A. How the parents were dealing with the stress of the client's illness was explored with each individually.

B. The issue of increased conflicts between the parents due to the client's medical condition was addressed.

C. Specific ways that each parent could be supportive and accepting of the other were identified.

36. Reinforce Members' Spirit of Tolerance (36)

A. In family sessions, a spirit of tolerance for individually different responses to stress was facilitated and encouraged between members.

B. Members were reminded of each person's individual differences regarding internal resources and response styles in face of threat.

C. Tolerance was modeled to family members in sessions through active listening and warm acceptance of their feelings and thoughts.

37. Promote the Power of Family's Involvement (37)

A. The family was educated in the potential healing power of members' involvement in all aspects of the client's care and recovery.

B. Assistance was provided to the family to help them make their care and home environment as warm, positive, kind, and supportive for the client as possible.

C. The family was provided with ongoing encouragement and reinforcement in providing warm, positive, supportive care to the client.

MENTAL RETARDATION

CLIENT PRESENTATION

1. Subaverage Intellectual Functioning (1)*

A. The client has developed significant intellectual or cognitive deficits.

B. The results from the past intelligence testing revealed that the client's overall level of intellectual functioning lies in the Mild Mental Retardation range.

C. The results from the past intelligence testing revealed that the client's overall level of intelligence lies in the Moderate Mental Retardation range.

D. The results from the past intelligence testing revealed that the client's overall level of intelligence lies in the Severe Mental Retardation range.

E. The results from the past intelligence testing revealed that the client's overall level of intelligence lies in the Borderline range of functioning.

2. Impaired Academic Functioning (2)

A. The client has performed significantly below his/her expected grade and age levels in all academic areas.

B. The client's academic performance has been commensurate with his/her overall level of intelligence.

C. The client has performed academically below his/her expected grade and age levels, even when considering the results from the past intellectual testing.

D. Academically, the client has performed above his/her expected levels based on the results from the past intelligence testing.

3. Speech/Language Delays (2)

A. The results from the past speech/language evaluation demonstrated that the client has developed significant speech/language deficits.

B. The client's vocabulary and expressive language abilities are quite limited.

C. The client often has difficulty understanding what is being said to him/her because of his/her low receptive language skills.

D. The client displayed noticeable speech articulation problems during today's therapy session.

4. Poor Communication Skills (2)

A. The client has much difficulty communicating his/her thoughts and feelings in an effective manner because of his/her speech/language delays.

B. The client had much difficulty expressing his/her thoughts and feelings in today's therapy session.

C. The client had difficulty comprehending what was being discussed in today's therapy session because of his/her low receptive language abilities.

---

* The numbers in parentheses correlate to the number of the Behavioral Definition statement in the companion chapter with same title in *The Adolescent Psychotherapy Treatment Planner* (Jongsma, Peterson, and McInnis) by John Wiley & Sons, 2000.

D. The client was able to communicate his/her thoughts and feelings in a simplistic but straightforward and effective manner in today's therapy session.

E. The client has demonstrated improvements in his/her ability to identify and express his/her basic thoughts and feelings.

5. Inadequate Self-Care (2)

A. The parents or caregivers reported that the client's self-care skills are very low.

B. The client has required a great deal of supervision when performing household chores or tasks at school.

C. The client has recently started to perform simple chores at home.

D. The client has recently performed his/her household chores or school responsibilities on a fairly consistent basis with prompting from caregivers.

6. Poor Personal Hygiene (2)

A. The parents or caregivers reported that the client's personal hygiene is often poor.

B. The client appeared unkempt during today's therapy session.

C. The client has a great deal of difficulty dressing himself/herself independently even when clothes have been preselected for him/her.

D. The client appeared neatly groomed and attired during today's therapy session.

E. The client has recently been dressing himself/herself independently.

7. Difficulty Following Instructions (3)

A. The client historically has had much difficulty comprehending and following instructions at home and school.

B. The parents and teachers reported that the client is capable of comprehending and following simple instructions, but has trouble following through with multiple or complex instructions.

C. The teachers reported that the client is best able to follow instructions when they are presented in simple terms and are given one at a time.

D. The parents and teachers reported that the client has shown improvement in following simple instructions on a consistent basis.

8. Short Attention Span (3)

A. The client has developed a short attention span and has difficulty staying focused for extended periods of time.

B. The client is easily distracted by extraneous stimuli and his/her own internal thoughts.

C. The client had trouble staying focused and often switched from one topic to another.

D. The client remained focused and was able to discuss important topics for a satisfactory length of time.

E. The client's attention span has improved in structured, low-distraction settings where he/she receives supervision and greater individualized attention.

9. Memory Impairment (4)

A. The results from past intellectual and cognitive assessments have shown that the client has developed significant short- and long-term memory impairments.

B. The client has often had difficulty retaining or recalling what was said to him/her because of his/her short-term memory deficit.

C. The client has had difficulty recalling significant past events because of his/her long-term memory deficit.

D. The client demonstrated improvements in his/her everyday functioning by following a structured daily routine.

10. Concrete Thinking (5)

A. The client has much difficulty understanding psychological concepts because of his/her intellectual limitations and poor abstract reasoning abilities.

B. The client presented as very concrete in his/her thinking during today's therapy session.

C. The client's concrete thinking and poor abstract reasoning abilities have interfered with his/her problem-solving abilities.

D. The client demonstrated an understanding of basic psychological terms or concepts during today's therapy session.

E. The parents report that the client has demonstrated improvement in his/her ability to resolve or manage everyday, routine problems by following specific, concrete steps that are outlined for him/her.

11. Poor Social Skills (6)

A. The client has developed poor social skills and frequently engaged in immature or socially inappropriate behavior.

B. The client has often failed to pick up on important social cues or interpersonal nuances that are necessary to build and sustain meaningful relationships.

C. The client has started to develop the ability to differentiate between appropriate and inappropriate social behaviors.

D. The client displayed good social skills during today's therapy session.

12. Lack of Insight (7)

A. The client historically has shown very poor insight into the factors contributing to his/her emotional, behavioral, or interpersonal problems.

B. The client demonstrated a lack of insight into the factors contributing to his/her adjustment problems.

C. The client verbalized an awareness of the basic factors contributing to his/her adjustment problems, but had difficulty understanding the more complex factors.

13. Failure to Learn from Experience (7)

A. The client displayed a marked inability to learn from previous experiences or past mistakes because of his/her intellectual limitations.

B. The parents or caregivers reported that the client repeatedly makes many of the same mistakes without appearing to learn from his/her experience.

C. Parents or caregivers reported that the client has started to show mild improvement in his/her ability to learn from past experiences or mistakes.

D. The client does not repeat as many mistakes when he/she is placed in a highly structured setting with an established routine.

14. Low Self-Esteem (8)

A. The client's intellectual limitations and learning problems have been a significant contributing factor to his/her feelings of low self-esteem, inadequacy, and insecurity.

B. The client's low self-esteem has contributed to his/her hesitancy to try new tasks or apply himself/herself at school.

C. The client verbalized self-derogatory remarks when discussing his/her intellectual limitations or learning problems.

D. The client verbalized positive self-descriptive statements during today's therapy session.

E. The client has developed a healthy acceptance of his/her intellectual and cognitive limitations, as evidenced by his/her ability to consistently verbalize feelings of self-worth.

15. Depression (8)

A. The client's intellectual deficits and academic struggles have contributed substantially to his/her feelings of depression.

B. The client appeared visibly sad when discussing his/her learning problems.

C. The client's feelings of depression have begun to decrease as he/she works toward gaining a greater acceptance of his/her intellectual limitations.

D. The client expressed feelings of happiness about his/her recent accomplishments at home and school.

E. The client's feelings of depression have decreased substantially.

16. Parents' Unrealistic Expectations (8)

A. The parents appeared to be in denial about the client's intellectual limitations.

B. The parents have developed unrealistic expectations of the client and have placed excessive pressure on him/her to function at a level that he/she is not capable of achieving.

C. The parents acknowledged that they have placed unrealistic expectations on the client to perform on a level that he/she is not capable of achieving.

D. The parents have started to adjust their demands on the client and are placing more realistic expectations on him/her.

E. The parents have gained an acceptance of the client's intellectual capabilities and have placed appropriate expectations on his/her functioning.

17. Parents' Overprotectiveness (8)

A. The parents have demonstrated a persistent pattern of overprotectiveness that interferes with the client's intellectual, emotional, and social development.

B. The parents became defensive when discussing how their overprotectiveness interferes with the client's growth and development.

C. The parents acknowledged that their overprotectiveness or infantilization of the client has interfered with his/her intellectual, emotional, and social development.

D. The parents have started to verbalize their expectations that the client assume household responsibilities and take care of his/her personal hygiene.

E. The parents' overprotectiveness has greatly diminished, and they have placed realistic expectations on the client.

18. Acting-Out Behaviors (9)

A. The client has demonstrated a persistent pattern of acting out when he/she becomes frustrated or upset because of his/her intellectual limitations or learning problems.

B. The client began to act in a silly and immature manner in today's therapy session when discussing his/her intellectual limitations or learning problems.

C. The client was helped to realize how he/she frequently begins to act out or engage in disruptive behavior when frustrated or upset about not being able to perform a task.

D. The client has started to seek help when frustrated about not being able to perform a task instead of acting out or engaging in disruptive behavior.

E. The client has demonstrated a significant reduction in the frequency of his/her acting-out or disruptive behavior.

INTERVENTIONS IMPLEMENTED

1. Conduct Intellectual and Cognitive Assessment (1)*

A. A comprehensive intellectual and cognitive assessment was conducted to determine the presence of mental retardation and help gain greater insight into the client's learning strengths and weaknesses.

B. The findings from the current intellectual and cognitive assessment revealed the presence of Mild Mental Retardation.

C. The findings from the current intellectual and cognitive assessment revealed the presence of Moderate Mental Retardation.

D. The findings from the current intellectual and cognitive assessment revealed the presence of Severe Mental Retardation.

E. The findings from the current intellectual and cognitive assessment demonstrated that the client is currently functioning in the Borderline range of intellectual abilities.

2. Conduct Psychological Testing for Emotional/ADHD Factors (2)

A. The client received a psychological evaluation to assess whether emotional factors or ADHD are interfering with his/her intellectual functioning.

B. The findings from the psychological testing supported the presence of ADHD, which is interfering with the client's intellectual and academic functioning.

C. The findings from the psychological testing revealed the presence of serious emotional problems that are interfering with the client's intellectual and academic functioning.

D. The findings from the evaluation did not support the presence of ADHD that could be interfering with the client's intellectual and academic functioning.

E. The findings from the psychological testing did not reveal any serious emotional problems that could be interfering with the client's intellectual and academic functioning.

---

* The numbers in parentheses correlate to the number of the Therapeutic Intervention statement in the companion chapter with the same title in *The Adolescent Psychotherapy Treatment Planner* (Jongsma, Peterson, and McInnis) by John Wiley & Sons, 2000.

3. Refer for Neurological Examination/Neuropyschological Testing (3)

A. The client was referred for a neurological examination and neuropsychological testing to rule out possible organic factors that may be contributing to the client's intellectual or cognitive deficits.

B. The findings from the neuropsychological evaluation revealed organic factors that may be contributing to the client's intellectual or cognitive deficits.

C. The findings from the neuropsychological evaluation did not reveal any organic factors that may be contributing to the client's intellectual or cognitive deficits.

4. Provide Evaluation Feedback (4)

A. The client, parents, and school officials were given feedback from the intellectual and psychological testing.

B. The staff from the client's residential program were given feedback from the intellectual and psychological testing.

C. The client, parents, and school officials were given feedback from the neuropsychological testing.

D. The staff from the client's residential program were given feedback from the neuropsychological testing.

5. Refer for Physical/Occupational Therapy (5)

A. The client was referred to physical and occupational therapists to assess for the presence of perceptual or sensory-motor deficits and determine the need for ongoing physical and/or occupational therapy.

B. The evaluation revealed significant perceptual or sensory-motor deficits and the need for ongoing physical and/or occupational therapy.

C. The evaluation did not reveal any significant perceptual or sensory-motor deficits or the need for ongoing physical and/or occupational therapy.

6. Refer for Speech/Language Evaluation (6)

A. The client was referred for a comprehensive speech/language evaluation to assess possible deficits in this area and to determine the need for speech/language therapy.

B. The comprehensive speech/language evaluation revealed a communication impairment and supported the need for speech/language therapy.

C. The comprehensive speech/language evaluation did not reveal a communication impairment or the need for ongoing speech/language therapy.

7. Attend Individualized Educational Planning Committee (IEPC) (7)

A. An Individualized Educational Planning Committee meeting was held to determine the client's eligibility for special education services, to design educational interventions, and to establish goals.

B. The decision was made at the IEPC meeting that the client is eligible to receive special education services because of his/her intellectual or academic deficits.

C. The decision was made at the IEPC meeting that the client is not eligible to receive special education services.

D. Consulted with the client's parents, teachers, and other appropriate professionals about designing educational interventions to help the client achieve his/her academic goals.

E. The client's academic goals were identified at the IEPC meeting.

8. Design Effective Teaching Programs (8)

A. Consulted with the client, his/her parents, teachers, and other appropriate school officials about designing effective teaching programs or interventions that build on the client's strengths and compensate for his/her weaknesses.

B. The client's learning strengths and weaknesses were identified in the consultation meeting with the client, parents, teachers, and other appropriate school officials.

C. Consulted with the client, his/her parents, teachers, and other appropriate school officials about the ways to maximize the client's learning strengths.

D. Consulted with the client, his/her parents, teachers, and other appropriate school officials about ways to compensate for the client's learning weaknesses.

9. Consult about Placement Outside the Home (9)

A. Consulted with the client's parents, school officials, or mental health professionals about the need for placement in a foster home, group home, or residential program.

B. After consulting with the client's parents, school officials, or mental health professionals, the recommendation was made that the client should be placed in a foster home.

C. The recommendation was made that the client be placed in a group home or residential program to address his/her intellectual, academic, social, and emotional needs.

D. Placement of the client in a foster home, group home, or residential program was not recommended during the consultation meeting with parents, school officials, and mental health professionals.

10. Sheltered Workshop Referral (10)

A. The client was referred to a sheltered workshop or educational rehabilitation center to help him/her develop basic job skills.

B. The client and parents were supportive of the referral to a sheltered workshop or educational rehabilitation center to develop the client's basic job skills.

C. The client and parents were opposed to the idea of referring him/her to a sheltered workshop or educational rehabilitation center to develop basic job skills.

D. The client's attendance at the sheltered workshop or educational rehabilitation center has helped him/her to develop basic job skills.

E. The client has shown little or no progress in developing basic job skills while attending the sheltered workshop or educational rehabilitation center.

11. Encourage Communication between Home and School (11)

A. The parents, teachers, and school officials were encouraged to maintain regular communication with each other via phone calls or written notes regarding the client's academic, behavioral, emotional, and social progress.

B. Consulted with the teachers and school officials about sending home daily or weekly progress notes informing the parents of the client's academic, behavioral, emotional, and social progress.

C. The client was informed of his/her responsibility to bring home daily or weekly progress notes that allow for regular communication between parents and teachers.

D. The parents identified the consequences for the client's failure to bring home the daily or weekly progress notes from school.

12. Design Token Economy (12)

A. A token economy was designed for use in the classroom to improve the client's academic performance, impulse control, and social skills.

B. A token economy was designed for use in the residential program to improve the client's academic performance, impulse control, and social skills.

C. The client, parents, and teachers agreed to the conditions outlined in the token economy and pledged to follow through with the implementation of the program.

D. The conditions of the token economy were explained to the client in terms that he/she could understand.

13. Praise Positive Behavior (13)

A. The parents were encouraged to provide frequent praise and positive reinforcement for the client's positive social behaviors and academic successes.

B. The parents praised the client's positive social behaviors and academic performance during today's therapy session.

C. The parents were assisted in identifying opportunities to praise the client's positive social behaviors and academic successes.

D. The client was strongly encouraged to engage in positive social behaviors and work hard to achieve academic goals to receive the parents' approval and affirmation.

14. Design Reward System/Contingency Contract (14)

A. The client and parents were assisted in identifying a list of rewards to reinforce the client's adaptive or positive social behaviors.

B. A reward system was designed to reinforce the client's adaptive or positive social behaviors.

C. A contingency contract was designed to specify the negative consequences for the client's maladaptive or inappropriate social behaviors and the rewards for specified positive behaviors.

D. The conditions of the contingency contract were explained to the client in terms he/she could understand.

E. The client and parents verbally agreed to the terms of the reward system and/or contingency contract.

15. Educate Parents about Mental Retardation (15)

A. The client's parents were educated about the symptoms of mental retardation.

B. The therapy session helped the client's parents gain a greater understanding of the symptoms and characteristics of mental retardation.

C. The parents were given the opportunity to express their thoughts and feelings about raising a child with mental retardation.

D. The parents were given support in verbalizing their feelings of sadness, hurt, anger, or disappointment about having a child with mental retardation.

16. Confront Parents' Denial of Client's Intellectual Deficits (16)

A. A family therapy session was held to assess the parents' denial surrounding the client's intellectual deficits.

B. The parents' denial about the client's intellectual deficits was confronted and challenged so that they will begin to cooperate with the recommendations regarding placement and educational interventions.

C. The therapy session was helpful in working through the parents' denial surrounding the client's intellectual deficits, and they agreed to follow through with recommendations regarding placement and educational interventions.

D. The parents have remained in denial about the client's intellectual deficits and are opposed to following through with the recommendations regarding placement and educational interventions.

17. Assess Excessive Parental Pressure (17)

A. A family therapy session was held to assess whether the parents are placing excessive pressure on the client to function at a level that he/she is not capable of achieving.

B. The parents were asked to verbalize their expectations of the client's level of capabilities.

18. Confront Excessive Parental Pressure (18)

A. The parents were confronted and challenged about placing excessive pressure on the client to function at a level that he/she is not capable of achieving.

B. The parents acknowledged that they have placed unrealistic expectations and/or excessive pressure on the client to function at a level that he/she is not capable of achieving.

C. The parents agreed to cease placing excessive pressure on the client to perform at unrealistic levels.

D. The parents expressed resistance to the idea that they are placing excessive pressure on the client to function at unrealistic levels.

19. Assign Family Kinetic Drawing (19)

A. The client was asked to produce a family kinetic drawing to assess how he/she perceives his/her role in the family.

B. The client's family kinetic drawing was helpful in providing insight into how he/she perceives his/her role in the family.

C. The client's family kinetic drawing did not provide any insight into how he/she perceives his/her role in the family.

D. The evidence from the family kinetic drawing indicated that the client perceives himself/herself as being ostracized and isolated within the family.

E. The evidence from the family kinetic drawing indicated that the client experiences a sense of belonging and acceptance in his/her family.

20. Assess Parental Overprotectiveness (20)

A. The parent-child interactions were observed in today's therapy session to assess whether the parent's overprotectiveness or infantilization of the client interferes with his/her intellectual, emotional, or social development.

B. The client and parents were given a task to perform in today's therapy session to assess whether the parents are overprotective of the client.

C. The parents acknowledged that their pattern of overprotectiveness has interfered with the client's intellectual, emotional, and social development.

D. The therapy session was helpful in identifying various ways that the parents are overprotective of the client and/or interfere with his/her intellectual, emotional, and social development.

E. The parents became defensive in today's therapy session when discussing their pattern of overprotectiveness.

21. Help Parents Develop Realistic Expectations (21)

A. Today's therapy session focused on helping the parents or caregivers develop realistic expectations of the client's intellectual capabilities and level of adaptive functioning.

B. The parents or caregivers were assisted in identifying a number of tasks that the client is capable of performing.

C. The therapy session helped the parents or caregivers identify several tasks that the client is not able to perform because of his/her intellectual capabilities and level of adaptive functioning.

D. The parents or caregivers were instructed to provide supervision initially on tasks that they are not sure that the client is capable of performing.

E. The parents or caregivers have developed a good understanding of the client's intellectual capabilities and level of adaptive functioning.

22. Include Client in Family Outings (22)

A. The parents and family members were strongly encouraged to include the client in outings or activities on a regular basis.

B. A family therapy session was held to explore the family members' resistance or objections to including the client in some outings or activities.

C. The parents and family members pledged to include the client in regular family outings or activities.

D. The client and family members were assisted in identifying a list of outings or activities that they would enjoy doing together.

E. The parents and family members were confronted about their failure to include the client in many outings or activities.

23. Assign Observation of Positive Behavior (23)

A. The parents and family members were instructed to observe and record positive behavior by the client between therapy sessions.

B. The parents were encouraged to praise and reinforce the client for engaging in the positive behavior.

C. The client was praised in today's therapy session for his/her positive behavior.

D. The client was strongly encouraged to continue to engage in the positive behavior to help improve his/her self-esteem, gain parents' approval, and receive affirmation from others.

24. Assign Household Chores (24)

A. The client and family members developed a list of tasks or chores that the client is capable of performing at home.

B. The client was assigned a task to perform within the family to provide him/her with a sense of responsibility or belonging.

C. The client was given praise in today's therapy session for the successful completion of his/her assigned task or chore.

D. The client attempted to perform the assigned task or chore, but encountered difficulty when performing it.

E. The client failed to follow through with completing the assigned chore or task.

25. Routine Task Assignment (25)

A. The client was placed in charged of a routine or basic task at home to increase his/her self-esteem and increase feelings of self-worth in the family.

B. A reward system was designed to reinforce the client for following through and completing his/her routine or basic task at home.

C. The client was placed in charge of another routine or basic task (appropriate to his/her level of adaptive functioning) after showing he/she could be responsible in performing the earlier assigned task.

D. Today's therapy session explored the reasons the client did not follow through and complete the routine or basic task that was assigned to him/her.

26. "You Belong Here" Exercise (26)

A. The client and parents were assigned the "You Belong Here" exercise from *The Brief Adolescent Therapy Homework Planner* (Jongsma, Peterson, and McInnis) to promote feelings of acceptance and a sense of belonging in the family system, school setting, or community.

B. The client and parents were given the "You Belong Here" exercise to increase the client's responsibilities or involvement in activities at home, at school, or in the community.

C. The "You Belong Here" exercise was assigned to help the parents develop a greater awareness of the client's intellectual capabilities and level of adaptive functioning.

D. The client and parents successfully completed the exercise, and the client was encouraged to continue to engage in the responsible behaviors or social activities to further increase feelings of self-worth.

E. The client and parents failed to follow through and complete the exercise and were challenged to do it again.

27. School/Residential Job Assignment (27)

A. Consulted with school officials about assigning a job to help build the client's self-esteem and provide him/her with a sense of responsibility.

B. Consulted with the staff at the residential program about assigning a job to help build the client's self-esteem and provide him/her with a sense of responsibility.

C. The client was given much praise in today's therapy session for being responsible in performing his/her job at school.

D. The client was given much praise in today's therapy session for being responsible in performing his/her job at the residential program.

E. Today's therapy session explored the reasons for the client's failure to comply with performing his/her job at school or the residential program.

28. Identify Components of Goal Accomplishment (28)

A. Today's therapy session identified periods of time when the client achieved success or accomplished a goal.

B. Today's therapy session was helpful in identifying the positive steps that the client took to successfully accomplish goals in the past.

C. The client was strongly encouraged to take steps similar to those he/she successfully took in the past to accomplish present goals.

D. The therapy session revealed that the client achieved past success during periods of time when he/she received strong family support.

29. Teach Parents Behavior Management (29)

A. The parents were taught effective behavior management techniques to help decrease the frequency and severity of the client's temper outbursts, acting-out, and aggressive behaviors.

B. The parents were trained in the use of time-out to manage the client's temper outbursts and aggressive behaviors.

C. The parents were instructed to remove privileges if the client engages in specific acting-out or aggressive behaviors.

D. The parents were challenged to follow through consistently with limits when the client displays temper outbursts, aggression, or acting-out behaviors.

E. The parents reported improvements in the client's behavior since they began consistently using time-outs and removal of privileges to deal with the client's temper outbursts, acting-out, and aggressive behaviors.

30. Teach Parents Use of Natural Consequences (30)

A. The parents were instructed to utilize natural, logical consequences for the client's inappropriate social or maladaptive behaviors.

B. The parents were helped to identify natural, logical consequences for a variety of socially inappropriate or maladaptive behaviors.

C. The parents reported improvement in the client's behavior since they began using natural, logical consequences.

D. The therapy session revealed that the parents have not been consistent in following through or using natural, logical consequences to deal with the client's socially inappropriate or maladaptive behavior.

31. Establish Allowance/Finance Management (31)

A. The parents were assisted in establishing an allowance plan to increase the client's responsibilities at home and to help him/her learn simple money management skills.

B. The client and parents established a budget whereby a certain percentage of the client's allowance money goes for both savings and spending.

C. The parents were encouraged to consult with school teachers about teaching the client basic money management skills.

D. The parents reported that the allowance plan has been successful in increasing the client's responsibilities around the home and teaching him/her simple money management skills.

E. The parents reported that, unfortunately, the allowance plan has not motivated the client to perform his/her household chores or responsibilities on a consistent basis.

32. "Activities of Daily Living" Program (32)

A. The parents were directed to use the reward system in the "Activities of Daily Living" program from *The Brief Adolescent Therapy Homework Planner* (Jongsma, Peterson, and McInnis) to improve the client's personal hygiene and self-care skills.

B. The parents were strongly encouraged to praise and reinforce the client for improvements in his/her personal hygiene and self-care skills.

C. The parents reported that the "Activities of Daily Living" program has helped to improve the client's personal hygiene and self-care skills.

D. The parents reported that the client has demonstrated little improvement in his/her personal hygiene and self-care skills since utilizing the "Activities of Daily Living" program.

33. Teach Mediational/Self-Control Strategies (33)

A. The client was taught basic mediational and self-control strategies to help delay his/her need for immediate gratification and to inhibit impulses.

B. The parents were encouraged to establish a routine schedule for the client so that he/she postpones recreational or leisure activities until after completing his/her homework or household responsibilities.

C. The client was encouraged to utilize active listening skills and talk with significant others before making quick, hasty decisions about important matters or acting out without considering the consequences of his/her actions.

D. The client was helped to develop an action plan that outlined specific, concrete steps that he/she could take to achieve his/her identified long-term goals.

E. The client was helped to see the benefits of delaying his/her immediate need for gratification to achieve a longer-term goal.

34. Teach Guided Imagery/Relaxation (34)

A. The client was trained in the use of guided imagery or deep muscle relaxation techniques to help calm himself/herself and improve anger control.

B. The client and parents reported that the use of guided imagery and deep muscle relaxation techniques has helped to calm the client and control anger more effectively.

C. The client and parents reported little or no improvement with the use of guided imagery and deep muscle relaxation techniques to help calm the client and control anger.

D. The client failed to utilize the guided imagery and deep muscle relaxation techniques to help him/her control anger.

35. Reinforce Social Behaviors (35)

A. The client was educated about a variety of positive social behaviors.

B. A reward system was developed to reinforce specific, positive social behaviors.

C. The parents were strongly encouraged to look for opportunities to praise and reinforce any emerging positive social behaviors.

D. The client's positive social behaviors were praised during today's therapy session.

E. The client was given a homework assignment to practice a newly learned positive social skill at least three to five times before the next therapy session.

36. Role-Play and Model Social Skills (36)

A. Role-play and modeling techniques were used to teach the client positive social behaviors.

B. The client was able to identify several positive social skills after engaging in the role-play exercises.

C. After role-playing in the therapy session, the client expressed a willingness to practice a newly learned social skill in his/her everyday life situations.

D. The client and parents reported that he/she followed through with practicing the positive social skill that was taught through role playing and modeling.

E. The client did not follow through with practicing the newly acquired social skill that was modeled in the previous therapy session.

37. Encourage Participation in Special Olympics (37)

A. The client was encouraged to participate in the Special Olympics to help build his/her self-esteem.

B. The client and parents followed through with the recommendation to enroll the client in the Special Olympics.

C. The client expressed happiness about his/her participation and experiences in the Special Olympics.

D. The client and parents failed to follow through with the recommendation to participate in the Special Olympics.

38. Teach Communication Skills (38)

A. The client was taught basic communication skills to improve his/her ability to express thoughts, feelings, and needs more clearly.

B. Role-playing, modeling, and behavior rehearsal techniques were used to teach the client effective ways to express his/her thoughts, feelings, and needs.

C. The client was taught the importance of listening well and maintaining good eye contact when communicating his/her thoughts and feelings with others.

D. The client was taught to utilize "I" messages to communicate his/her thoughts, feelings, and needs more clearly.

39. Educate Client about Emotions (39)

A. The client was helped to identify and label different emotions in today's therapy session.

B. Client-centered therapy principles were used to help the client identify and express his/her emotions.

C. The parents were encouraged to reflect the client's feelings at home to help him/her express feelings more effectively.

D. The client has demonstrated improvements in his/her ability to identify and express basic emotions since the onset of therapy.

E. The client has continued to have difficulty identifying and labeling his/her basic emotions.

40. Utilize Art Therapy (40)

A. The client was instructed in today's therapy session to draw faces of basic emotions and then share various times when he/she experienced the different emotions.

B. The art therapy technique helped the client to identify and express different emotions.

C. An art therapy technique was employed, but the client had difficulty sharing times when he/she experienced the different emotions in the past.

41. Help Client Accept Intellectual Limits (41)

A. The client was helped to gain greater understanding and acceptance of the limitations surrounding his/her intellectual deficits and adaptive functioning.

B. A client-centered therapy approach was employed to reflect the client's feelings and move toward a greater acceptance of the limitations surrounding his/her intellectual deficits and adaptive functioning.

C. The client was helped to identify his/her unique strengths or interests as well as his/her individual weaknesses.

D. The client's self-worth was affirmed to help him/her come to a greater acceptance of the limitations surrounding his/her intellectual deficits and adaptive functioning.

42. Explore for Depression and Insecurity (42)

A. Today's therapy session explored the underlying feelings of depression, anxiety, and insecurity related to the client's intellectual limitations.

B. The client was provided with support and unconditional positive regard as he/she worked through feelings of depression, anxiety, and insecurity related to his/her cognitive or intellectual limitations.

C. The client was strongly encouraged to utilize his/her unique strengths and engage in activities of interest to help cope with or offset feelings of depression, anxiety, and insecurity related to cognitive or intellectual limitations.

D. The parents provided support and affirmed the client's self-worth.

43. Identify Times to Ask for Help (43)

A. The client was assisted in identifying appropriate and inappropriate times to ask for help.

B. The client was helped to identify several basic or uncomplicated tasks that he/she can perform independently of others.

C. The parents were encouraged to allow the client to independently perform simple or basic tasks that required him/her to follow only one or two simple instructions at a time.

D. The client was encouraged to seek assistance from others on tasks that require him/her to follow multiple or detailed instructions.

E. The parents were instructed to provide supervision and frequent feedback to the client when he/she performs tasks of moderate or greater difficulty.

44. Identify Supportive People (44)

A. The client was helped to identify a list of resource people to whom he/she can turn for support, help, and supervision.

B. The client was recently able to successfully turn to a resource person to help him/her face a stressor or overcome a problem that occurred since the last therapy session.

C. The client has often failed to turn to resource people for support when he/she encounters stress or problems.

D. The client has developed a network of resource people to whom he/she can turn for support, help, and supervision.

45. Express Loss Fears through Art (45)

A. Art therapy techniques were utilized to help the client identify and verbalize his/her feelings related to issues of loss, separation, or abandonment by parental figures or key staff members in residential programs.

B. The client was instructed to draw a picture reflecting his/her feelings about past losses, separations, or abandonment.

C. The client's artwork reflected feelings of sadness about past losses or separations.

D. The client's artwork did not provide any insight into his/her feelings about past losses, separations, or abandonment.

46. Provide Sex Education (46)

A. Sex education was provided to help the client identify appropriate and inappropriate sexual urges and behaviors.

B. The client was assisted in listing several appropriate and inappropriate sexual urges and behaviors.

C. The client had difficulty differentiating between appropriate and inappropriate sexual urges and behaviors.

47. Medication Evaluation Referral (47)

A. The client was referred for a medication evaluation to improve his/her impulse control and stabilize moods.

B. The client and parents agreed to follow through with a medication evaluation by a physician.

C. The client and parents have failed to follow through with seeking a medication evaluation to help improve the client's impulse control and stabilize his/her mood.

D. The client has been taking his/her psychotropic medication as prescribed.

E. The client has not complied with taking his/her psychotropic medication on a regular basis.

OPPOSITIONAL DEFIANT DISORDER

CLIENT PRESENTATION

1. Negativistic/Hostile (1)*

A. The client presented in a negative, hostile manner.

B. The client was negative regarding all matters great or small and hostile to all the therapist's responses.

C. The client expressed hostile defiance toward his/her parents.

D. The client has noticeably reduced his/her level of hostility and defiance toward most adults.

2. Acts As If Adults Are the Enemy (2)

A. The client voiced that he/she has seen parents and other adults who have authority as the enemy.

B. The client verbalized a "me versus them" attitude when referring to his/her interactions with most adults, especially those in authority.

C. The client has begun to see some adults, teachers, and even parents as possible allies as he/she has decreased his/her hostile attitude.

3. Argumentative (3)

A. The client's total mood was argumentative regarding even the most insignificant points.

B. There was an edgy, argumentive manner present in the client.

C. There was a marked decrease in the client taking issue with or arguing most points.

D. The client has reached a point where he/she is able to accept direction without arguing.

4. Unreasonable/Defiant (4)

A. The client presented with a strong sense of defiance toward rules or requests.

B. The client viewed all expectations of him/her as unreasonable and defied them.

C. The client has gradually become more reasonable and less defiant on small issues.

5. Annoyed/Irritating (5)

A. The client's mood was one of being annoyed with anyone who crosses him/her.

B. Being annoyed with everyone was the predominant mood of the client, who exhibits irritation with those who come in contact with him/her.

C. Overall, the client presented in a manner of being less annoyed with others and being somewhat tolerant of them.

D. The client is slowly coming to the point where he/she does not try to annoy others.

---

* The numbers in parentheses correlate to the number of the Behavioral Definition statement in the companion chapter with same title in *The Adolescent Psychotherapy Treatment Planner* (Jongsma, Peterson, and McInnis) by John Wiley & Sons, 2000.

6. Blaming (6)

A. The client displayed an attitude of blaming others for his/her problems.

B. The client refused to take any responsibility for recent decisions and misbehavior, instead projecting it onto the parents and other authority figures.

C. The client carried the air that "I am not responsible or to blame for anything; it's all them."

D. Gradually, the client has started to take some responsibility for his/her decisions and behavior.

E. The client's general mood and manner reflect a noticeable decrease in blaming others for things that happen to him/her.

7. Lying (6)

A. The client continued to lie and to avoid responsibility for his/her actions/decisions without any sign of shame or guilt.

B. The client appeared to be lying regarding how things were going for him/her.

C. There has been a noticeable marked decrease in the client's lying and he/she is beginning to take some responsibility for his/her behavior.

8. Angry/Resentful (7)

A. The client presented in an angry, resentful, and generally uncooperative manner.

B. Anger predominated the client's mood, which was vented freely because "that's what I'm paying for."

C. The client's overall manner was sullen and quiet, which covered a strong mood of anger and resentfulness.

D. The client's general mood and presentation reflected a noticeable decrease in anger and resentfulness.

9. Vindictive/Spiteful (8)

A. The client's mood was vindictive and spiteful toward all whom he/she perceived as "against me."

B. There was a vindictive, spiteful edge toward all key figures in his/her daily life.

C. The client listed and vented acts of vengeance and spite he/she would to do to others.

D. The client has reduced his/her level of vindictiveness and spite toward others and has, at times, showed a little kindness in his/her speech.

10. Significant Impairments in Key Areas of Life (9)

A. The client reported impairments in his/her social, academic, and occupational functioning.

B. The client indicated that, according to most people, he/she was not doing well socially and academically, but it did not concern him/her.

C. The client's social and academic functioning have improved as he/she has taken responsibility for his/her actions and been less defiant.

INTERVENTIONS IMPLEMENTED (1)

1. Build Trust (1)*

A. Initial level of trust was established with the client through use of unconditional positive regard.

B. Warm acceptance and active listening techniques were utilized to establish the basis for a trusting relationship.

C. The client seems to have formed a trust-based relationship and has started to share his/her feelings about conflictual relationships.

D. The client seems to have formed an initial trusting relationship and has started to disclose his/her thoughts and feelings.

2. Identify Oppositional Patterns (2)

A. The client's behavior patterns were explored to establish how he/she responds to rules and authority.

B. The client was willing and able to identify his/her oppositional patterns but did not perceive them as his/her problem.

C. The client's oppositional patterns were reviewed and pointed out with specific behavioral examples from his/her history.

3. Assign "The Little Crab" (3)

A. The story of "The Little Crab" from *Stories for the Third Ear* (Wallas) was read and processed with the client and family.

B. "The Little Crab" metaphor was established with the family as a reference for change/growth.

4. Conduct Family Sessions to Promote Respect/Cooperation (4)

A. Family sessions were held in which the key issues of mutual respect, cooperation, and conflict resolution were addressed and possible solutions were explored.

B. The family decided upon solutions to implement to change past patterns of unsuccessful conflict resolution, disrespect, and uncooperativeness.

C. The family therapy sessions have been successful at reducing the level of tension between family members and increasing respect and cooperation.

5. Explore Negative, Hostile Feelings (5)

A. An open, accepting, and understanding approach was utilized to encourage the client to express his/her negative, hostile feelings.

B. The causes for the client's angry and oppositional feelings were explored, and he/she identified the perception that parents were unfair, overly controlling, and inclined to favor other siblings.

C. Negative and hostile feelings were normalized with the client to remove any barriers to verbalizing these feelings.

D. The client was taught about feelings, with special focus on the negative, hostile ones.

* The numbers in parentheses correlate to the number of the Therapeutic Intervention statement in the companion chapter with the same title in *The Adolescent Psychotherapy Treatment Planner* (Jongsma, Peterson, and McInnis) by John Wiley & Sons, 2000.

6. Provide Paradoxical Interpretation (6)

A. Negative, hostile, and defiant behaviors were processed and probed with the client.

B. The client was given paradoxical interpretations for his/her negative, hostile, and defiant behaviors.

C. Each identified negative, hostile, and defiant behavior was reframed for the client.

7. Teach Value of Respectfulness (7)

A. The client was worked with to establish a framework for treating others in a respectful manner.

B. The client was asked to list negative consequences of treating others with disrespect.

C. The client was taught the principle of reciprocity in relationships and asked to treat everyone with respect for the next week while observing respect received in return.

D. Role play was utilized to assist the client in practicing reciprocity principles in relating to others.

8. "If I Could Run My Family" Exercise (8)

A. The client was asked to complete the "If I Could Run My Family" exercise from *The Brief Adolescent Therapy Homework Planner* (Jongsma, Peterson, and McInnis), to explore the pros and cons of controlling the family.

B. The client was asked to identify the cons of being in control of the family, and each identified point was reinforced by the therapist.

9. "Switching from Defense to Offense" Exercise (9)

A. The parents were asked to complete the "Switching from Defense to Offense" exercise from *The Brief Adolescent Therapy Homework Planner* (Jongsma, Peterson, and McInnis) to help explore and establish new ways of intervening with the client.

B. New methods identified by the parents in the switching-strategies exercise were refined and plans for implementation made.

C. Role play was utilized with the parents to increase their confidence and to work out any bugs in the new intervention techniques.

D. The parents are responding positively to their switch of parenting strategies from defensive to offensive, and the client's oppositional behaviors have diminished.

10. Teach Respectful Expression of Feelings (10)

A. The client was taught how to recognize and express his/her needs and feelings in a constructive, respectful way.

B. The client was asked to practice expressing his/her needs and feelings to the therapist in a constructive, respectful way.

C. The client was reminded of how his/her disrespectful manner of expressing feelings and wants had a negative impact on self and others.

D. The client and parents reported that the client is expressing his/her feelings and opinions in a more respectful manner.

11. Play Therapeutic Game (11)

A. The Thinking, Feeling, Doing Game (Gardner) was played with the client, during which he/she had numerous opportunities to express his/her feelings appropriately.

B. Playing The Thinking, Feeling, Doing Game with the client has given him/her the opportunity to experiment with recognizing and expressing feelings.

C. The client has become more free to express his/her feelings in a respectful manner.

12. Connect Feelings and Defiance (12)

A. The client's feelings associated with defiance were probed, and connections between feelings and behaviors were established.

B. The client was asked to list any connections he/she saw between his/her feelings and his/her defiant behaviors.

C. The client's feelings of hurt or anger were explored as motivators of the defiant, rebellious behavior.

D. As the client expressed his/her feelings of hurt and frustration more openly, the oppositional and defiant behavior has diminished in intensity.

13. Utilize Dominoes Demonstration (13)

A. Utilize a Domino Rally with the client to draw a visual representation of how feelings lead to behavioral events.

B. The client was taught the connection between feelings and behavioral events, and then his/her history and the domino effect were used to illustrate and reinforce the point.

14. "Filing a Complaint" Exercise (14)

A. The client was asked to complete the "Filing a Complaint" exercise from *The Brief Adolescent Therapy Homework Planner* (Jongsma, Peterson, and McInnis) to assist him/her in reframing complaints to requests.

B. The client was asked to identify the pros and cons of complaints versus requests, focusing on which is more respectful.

C. The client's past pattern of disrespectful interactions were reviewed and negative results were reinforced.

D. The client reported several instances of switching from making complaints to making requests of others around him/her and also noted the positive results from this change.

15. Videotape Destructive Interaction Patterns (15)

A. Videotaping was utilized in family sessions to help identify destructive patterns of interaction within the family.

B. The family was assisted in identifying destructive interaction patterns from viewing the video of a session and helped to develop new, respectful interactions through role play, role rehearsal, and modeling.

C. The family members reported an increase in respectful interaction between them and an increase in sensitivity to the pattern of disrespectful interaction that has been so prevalent in the past.

16. List Angry Feelings and Causes (16)

A. The client was asked to list all those with whom he/she feels angry, complete with reasons for the anger.

B. The client was taught the negative effects of being too angry and how it can lead to behavioral problems.

C. The client was confronted when the reasons for his/her anger were unrealistic or self-serving.

D. The causes for the client's anger were more fully explored, and steps were taken to resolve these angry feelings.

E. The client is beginning to resolve his/her angry feelings, and this is reflected in more pleasant, cooperative behavior.

17. Promote Respecting Rules (17)

A. Checker rules were established by the client and the therapist, then games were played and the client confronted when he/she was violating or attempting to change the agreed-upon rules.

B. The importance of rules was reinforced, with the client pointing out the chaos that would be present without them and the negative feelings that result when people break or bend rules.

18. Institute Positive Consequences (18)

A. The client's parents and teachers were worked with to develop positive consequences to administer when the client exhibits negative behavior.

B. The implementation of positive consequences has helped to reduce the client's oppositional behavior.

19. Develop Contingent Excommunication (19)

A. The parents were assisted in clarifying acceptable and unacceptable behavioral standards for the client and instructed how to directly communicate them to him/her.

B. A system of "banishment" from the family was established with the parents as a significant consequence for unacceptable behavior.

C. The issue of not consistently following through with the temporary contingent banishment was addressed with the parents, with emphasis on the client's past behavioral patterns of manipulation and utilization of "divide and conquer" methods.

20. Model Effective Child Interaction (20)

A. Healthy, respectful teen interaction techniques were modeled by the therapist for the parents in family sessions.

B. Videotape of family sessions was reviewed with the parents to examine the positive points of the therapist's teen interaction techniques.

C. The parents' unhealthy interaction patterns with the client were identified, and they practiced replacing them with the healthy interaction techniques modeled by the therapist in family sessions.

D. The parents and the client reported that their interaction at home was more pleasant, respectful, and productive.

21. Reduce, Simplify Parental Interactions (21)

A. The negative aspects of parental oververbalization were reviewed with the parents, with special emphasis on the amount of power they lose by doing so.

B. The parents were asked to list the client's nondestructive negative behaviors that they felt could be ignored, and then they were asked to start doing so.

C. The parents have become more aware of their tendency to try to reason too much with the client and have reduced their oververbalizations.

22. Monitor Parents' Techniques (22)

A. The parents' use of new parenting techniques and interventions was monitored to encourage consistent use and to address any difficulties that were being experienced.

B. The parents were observed in the waiting area and in family sessions effectively employing the new parenting techniques that they had learned.

C. The parents were asked to describe how new techniques and interventions were going, and any lack of follow-through was addressed.

D. The parents report being pleased with the new techniques they are utilizing in their interactions with the client.

23. Develop Time-Out Procedure (23)

A. The parents were asked to list behaviors that are acceptable for the client and those that are unacceptable and will result in a time-out being implemented.

B. Behavioral limitations were given to the client in a family session and explained briefly by the parents, complete with time-out consequences.

C. These behavioral parameters and components of the time-out consequence were developed with the parents.

D. The parents reported that the implementation of the time-out consequence has been successful in reducing the targeted negative behaviors.

24. Develop Behavior Modification Plan (24)

A. The parents were assisted in developing a behavior modification plan, which included rewards for positive behavior and fines for negative behavior.

B. The parents' resistance to giving rewards for positive behavior was worked through so that a behavior modification program could be developed and implemented.

25. Implement Behavior Modification Plan (25)

A. The parents were given positive feedback on their follow-through in implementing and maintaining the behavior modification program for the client.

B. The parents were confronted on their inconsistent follow-through in administering the behavior modification plan they developed.

C. The parents were given support and encouragement in their efforts to implement and follow through on the behavior management/time-out program in the face of the client's strong resistance.

D. The parents report that the behavior modification plan is working smoothly and that the client is responding favorably to the increase in targeted positive behavior.

26. Expose Parental Conflict (26)

A. In family sessions, conflict between the parents was uncovered, and the parents made a commitment to work conjointly on resolving the conflict.

B. The parents were confronted in family sessions about the conflicts present between them and shown the role it plays in the client's oppositional behavior.

C. The parents worked in conjoint sessions to resolve the underlying conflicts in their marriage.

27. Utilize Family System Approach (27)

A. A family system approach was utilized to identify family strengths and to use strengths to address areas of family dysfunction.

B. After normalizing dysfunction as a part of all families, the family was able to identify specific dysfunctions in their family and began to address them.

28. Teach Barkley Method (28)

A. The parents were asked to view Barkley videos or read *Your Defiant Child* (Barkley and Benton) to gain an understanding of the Barkley approach.

B. The parents were asked to make a commitment to pursue this approach or not.

C. The family was assessed for having the strength and commitment to implement and follow through with the Barkley method.

29. Implement Barkley Method (29)

A. Details of the Barkley method were discussed with the parents before implementation.

B. The parents were assisted in developing a plan for implementing the Barkley method.

C. The parents reported favorable changes in the client's behavior since using Barkley method.

D. The parents were confronted on their inconsistent use of the Barkley method.

30. Sculpt Family (30)

A. A family sculpture was created to depict the family as they are, followed by another sculpture as they would like to be.

B. The family was cooperative in sculpting themselves as they are, but were unable to sculpt themselves in terms of how they would like to be.

31. Assess Interaction Patterns (31)

A. In family sessions, family interaction patterns were analyzed to locate points for a possible intervention.

B. The analysis of interaction patterns was utilized to determine which intervention could be most appropriate for this family.

C. The experiential/strategic/structural intervention was implemented and embraced in the family, with a commitment to follow through with what was prescribed.

32. Explore Out-of-Home Placement (32)

A. Out-of-home placement options for the client were presented and explored with the parents.

B. The parents reached the decision to pursue out-of-home placement for the client.

C. The parents were confronted about their unrealistic expectations of keeping the teen in their home.

33. Present Legal Emancipation Option (33)

A. The parents were directed to seek legal counsel to explore the option of emancipating the client.

B. Information gathered from their attorney was processed and the parents reached the decision to emancipate the client.

C. The family was asked to identify how postponing this emancipation decision would affect the parents and other siblings.

34. Support Decision to Emancipate Client

A. Past client behaviors and the parents' ineffective interventions were reviewed as a means of supporting the parents' decision to emancipate the client.

B. Feelings of guilt, loss, abandonment, and failure were processed in the wake of parents' emancipation decision.

PEER/SIBLING CONFLICT

CLIENT PRESENTATION

1. Angry/Tense (1)*

A. The client described a pattern of frequent, intense conflict with peers and siblings.

B. The client appeared angry at everything and everybody and was not willing to be very cooperative in the counseling process.

C. The client denied responsibility for the frequent, overt verbal and physical fighting with both peers and siblings.

D. The level of anger and fighting between the client and siblings has decreased as they have actively worked with the therapist in session.

2. Competitive/Energetic (1)

A. There is an energetic and highly competitive nature to the client.

B. The client described himself/herself as someone who loves a challenge and any type of competition.

C. The client's dialogue contains consistent references to numero uno, winners/losers, top dog, low dog in describing his/her relationship with peers and siblings.

D. The client reports he/she has always competed seriously in everything.

E. The amount of competition between the siblings has started to decrease, and they are getting along better and more cooperatively.

3. Projecting/Blaming (2)

A. The client displayed a propensity for blaming others for his/her problems.

B. The client refused to take any responsibility for the ongoing verbal and physical conflicts he/she has with peers and siblings.

C. All problems or conflicts were viewed by the client as the responsibility of others, not his/hers.

D. Slowly, the client has started to take responsibility for some of the conflicts in which he/she is involved.

4. Parents' Unfairness/Favoritism (3)

A. The client reported that the parents always treat his/her siblings more favorably than they do him/her.

B. The client cited incidences of his/her perception of parents' unfairness toward him/her.

C. The parents acknowledged that they find the other siblings easier to like than the client.

D. The client's complaints about unfairness and favoritism have started to decrease, and the parents are beginning to be seen in a more favorable light.

---

* The numbers in parentheses correlate to the number of the Behavioral Definition statement in the companion chapter with same title in *The Adolescent Psychotherapy Treatment Planner* (Jongsma, Peterson, and McInnis) by John Wiley & Sons, 2000.

5. Defiant/Vengeful (4)

A. The client presented in a vengeful, defiant manner.

B. The client reported a long list of people who have wronged or slighted him/her in some way and how he/she has gotten back at them.

C. The client's level of bullying has caused him/her to be constantly at odds with peers and siblings.

D. The client has gradually let go of some of his/her intimidation and vengeance and has started to have less conflict with peers and siblings.

6. Isolated/Intense (5)

A. The client presented as a lonely, isolated individual.

B. The client reported a history of aggressive relationships with peers, which he/she resolved by staying to himself/herself.

C. The client stated that he/she cannot get along with either peers or siblings without trouble, so he/she chooses to stay to himself/herself.

D. Since taking part in the counseling process, the client has gradually started to relate at least superficially with others.

7. Impulsive/Intimidating (6)

A. The client showed a pattern of impulsiveness and intimidation within the session by not considering the consequences of his/her actions and by challenging the therapist.

B. The client described a pattern of relating with peers and siblings in an impulsive, intimidating manner.

C. The client reported a history of impulsive, intimidating actions toward peers that have caused him/her repeated social problems.

D. The client has gradually accepted that he/she is intimidating and that this has been the reason for his/her conflicts with peers and siblings.

8. Aggressive/Mean (7)

A. The client seems to have an aggressive, mean manner of relating to others.

B. The client indicated he/she has been involved in encounters that resulted in physical injuries to others.

C. No remorse appeared evident on the client's part for the painful way he/she treats others.

D. All responsibility for his/her aggressive, mean acts are blamed on others or given great justification.

9. Insensitivity (7)

A. The client did not appear to be bothered by the ongoing conflicts he/she has with peers and siblings.

B. The hurtful impact on others of client's verbally hostile, aggressive behavior does not appear to have an effect on the client.

C. The client has started to understand the effect of his/her conflictual behaviors on others and his/her need to be more sensitive to them.

10. Fails to Respond to Praise/Encouragement (8)

A. Efforts to praise or encourage the client were rebuffed and negated.

B. The client indicated that he/she does not believe people when they say nice or encouraging things.

C. The client reported that he/she views praise as a way for people to try to "buy you off."

D. The client has started to respond to and affirm the praise and encouragement he/she receives from others.

11. Parents' Hostility (9)

A. The client described instances from his/her childhood in which severe and abusive punishment resulted whenever he/she was blamed for negative behavior.

B. The client described how parents always unfavorably compared him/her with peers and siblings, which led to feelings of anger, inadequacy, and resentment.

C. The parents' style of relating to the client was rude and hostile.

D. The parents' home environment appears to be highly competitive, where one sibling is often pitted against the other to outdo him/her in a given area and thus win parent's praise.

E. The client has begun to understand how his/her attitude and behavior toward others are connected to parents' treatment of him/her in childhood.

F. The parents have begun to treat the client in a more respectful and less hostile manner.

INTERVENTIONS IMPLEMENTED

1. Build Trust (1)*

A. Initial trust level was established with the client through the use of unconditional positive regard.

B. Warm acceptance and active listening techniques were utilized to establish the basis for a trust relationship with the client.

C. The client seems to have formed a trust relationship with the therapist and has started to share his/her feelings about conflictual relationships.

D. Despite the use of active listening, warm acceptance, and unconditional positive regard, the client appears to be hesitant to trust and to share his/her feelings and conflicts.

2. Explore Relationships and Assess Denial (2)

A. The client's perception of how he/she relates to siblings and peers was explored.

B. The client's degree of denial was found to be high regarding conflict and acceptance of responsibility for any part in it.

C. The client was open in acknowledging the high degree of conflict between the siblings and accepted responsibility for his/her part in the conflict.

---

* The numbers in parentheses correlate to the number of the Therapeutic Intervention statement in the companion chapter with the same title in *The Adolescent Psychotherapy Treatment Planner* (Jongsma, Peterson, and McInnis) by John Wiley & Sons, 2000.

3. Teach Social Learning Techniques (3)

A. The parents and teachers were asked to identify all nonaggressive, cooperative, and peaceful behaviors of the client that they could praise and positively reinforce.

B. Role-play and modeling techniques were used to show the parents and teachers how to ignore the client's nonharmful aggressive behaviors and how to praise prosocial behaviors.

4. Play Anger Control Game (4)

A. The Anger Control game (Berg) was played with the client to expose him/her to new ways of handling aggressive feelings.

B. The client was asked to make a commitment to handle aggressive feelings by trying one of the new ways learned through playing the Anger Control game.

C. The client has reported that he/she has successfully implemented new anger control techniques.

D. The client reported that he/she continues to have problems managing anger.

5. Play Helping, Sharing, and Caring Game (5)

A. The Helping, Sharing, and Caring Game (Gardner) was played with the client to expose him/her to feelings of respect for self and others.

B. The client was assisted in identifying how people feel when they show respect to and receive respect from others.

C. The client was reminded of how others feel when they are treated in a rude, disrespectful manner.

D. The client has consistently shown more respect for the feelings of others.

6. Play Social Conflict Game (6)

A. The Social Conflict Game (Berg) was played with the client to introduce prosocial behavioral skills.

B. The client was asked to list all the negative consequences that have resulted from his/her antisocial behaviors.

C. The client was reminded of the emotional and physical pain his/her actions have caused others.

D. The client was assisted in identifying two positive consequences of showing respect and concern for others.

7. "Negotiating a Peace Treaty" Exercise (7)

A. The client and the parents were asked to complete the "Negotiating a Peace Treaty" exercise from *The Brief Adolescent Therapy Homework Planner* (Jongsma, Peterson, and McInnis) to introduce the concept of negotiation.

B. The parents were asked to start negotiating key areas of conflict with the client.

C. Role-play sessions involving negotiation were used with the client and the parents to build their negotiating skills.

D. The positive aspects of negotiation versus winning and losing were identified and reinforced with the client.

8. **Teach Understanding of Feelings (8)**

A. The client was taught to identify basic feelings using a feelings chart.

B. Aggressive actions were focused on to assist the client in identifying how others might feel when they were the object of such actions.

C. The idea of how the client would like to be treated by others was explored, along with what he/she would need to do to make this possible.

9. **Group Therapy Referral (9)**

A. The client was referred to a peer therapy group to expand his/her social sensitivity and behavioral flexibility.

B. The client accepted the referral to group therapy and has been attending regularly.

C. The client reported that the group therapy experience has taught him/her to be more sensitive to the feelings of others.

D. The client has been resistive to group therapy and has not attended on a regular basis.

10. **Play Thinking, Feeling, Doing Game (10)**

A. The Thinking, Feeling, Doing Game (Gardner) was played with the client to build and reinforce his/her awareness of self and others.

B. After playing the Thinking, Feeling, Doing Game, the client began sharing more about himself/herself and showing some sensitivity to others.

11. **Behavioral Group Referral (11)**

A. The client was asked to attend a behavioral contracting group that works to develop positive peer interactions.

B. Client's group goals for positive peer interaction were set and reviewed each week.

C. The client reported positive verbal feedback from peers on his/her interaction goals.

D. The client's positive gains in peer interaction were verbally reinforced and rewarded.

12. **Encourage Involvement in Cooperative Activities (12)**

A. The benefits of involving the client in cooperative activities were discussed with the parents.

B. Options for cooperative activities were presented to the parents and they were asked to make a commitment to get the client involved.

C. The client was assisted in identifying positive gains he/she could make through participating in cooperative activities such as sports, music, scouts.

D. The client's involvement in cooperative activities with peers has increased significantly since the parents have encouraged this activity.

13. **Camp Referral (13)**

A. The client was referred to a summer camp that focuses on building self-esteem and positive peer relationships.

B. The client was helped to identify a list of specific things he/she could do at camp to increase his/her self-esteem.

C. Gains in self esteem and in peer relationships reported by the client as having been gained through the camp experience were affirmed and reinforced.

D. The client and his/her parents have not followed through on enrolling the client in a summer camp experience focused on building self-esteem and peer cooperation.

14. "Joseph, His Amazing Technicolor Coat and More" Exercise (14)

A. The client was asked to complete the "Joseph, His Amazing Technicolor Coat and More" exercise from *The Brief Adolescent Therapy Homework Planner* (Jongsma, Peterson, and McInnis).

B. In processing the favoritism homework assignment, the client was assisted in identifying the negative as well as the positive aspects of being the parent's favorite child.

C. In processing the favoritism homework assignment, the client was reminded of the reality that even though nearly all parents love their children, they may still have favorites.

15. Promote Acceptance of Praise and Encouragement (15)

A. The client was assisted in identifying how he/she responds to praise and encouragement from others.

B. The client's barriers to being open to positive feedback were identified.

C. New ways to respond positively to praise and encouragement were taught to the client.

D. Role play, modeling, and behavioral rehearsal were used to provide the client the opportunity to practice new, accepting responses to praise and encouragement.

16. Teach Parents to Praise (16)

A. The parents were asked to list all the possible ways they might give verbal affection and appropriate praise to the client.

B. The parents' resistance to giving affection and praise to the client for expected behavior was addressed and resolved.

C. The parents were asked to choose three ways to give verbal affection and appropriate praise and to implement each with the client when appropriate.

D. Affirmation and reinforcement was given to the parents for their reported use of verbal affection and praise with the client.

17. Reduce Parental Aggression, Rejection, and Quarreling (17)

A. Parental patterns of aggression and rejection were identified in family sessions.

B. The parents were assisted in removing acts of aggression and messages of rejection from their parenting.

C. Various methods were modeled for the parents to respond to the client in a warm, firm, yet caring way.

D. Parent messages of rejection were blocked and confronted in family sessions.

18. Read *Between Parent and Child* (18)

A. The parents were asked to read the chapters "Jealousy" and "Children Who Need Professional Help" in *Between Parent and Child* (Ginott).

B. The parents were assisted in identifying and changing key areas of their family structure to decrease the level of rivalry.

C. The parents were reminded that the level of rivalry within their family system is destructive as they continue to work toward the level of normal family interaction.

19. Read *Siblings Without Rivalry* (19)

A. The book *Siblings Without Rivalry* (Faber and Mazish) was assigned to the parents to read and process with the therapist.

B. Based on their reading of *Siblings Without Rivalry,* the parents identified two new ways to reduce rivalry and began implementing them in their family.

C. The parents reported positive results from the new methods that they have implemented to decrease the level of rivalry in the family.

D. The parents gave numerous excuses for their inconsistent use of new parenting methods and for the mixed results they experienced.

20. Explore Rejection Experiences (20)

A. The client's rejection experiences with family and friends were probed.

B. The client expressed numerous causes for his/her anger, which were based on rejection by family and friends.

C. The client denied any rejection experiences as being the basis for his/her anger.

21. Reframe Rivalry as Stage (21)

A. Rivalry within the family was reframed as a normal stage and something they will successfully resolve.

B. Reframing of the family's rivalry experiences as normal seems to have relieved concern over this issue and even reduced the rivalry experience itself.

22. Identify Past Success at Decreasing Rivalry (22)

A. Times without sibling conflict problems were identified with the family and probed.

B. A solution was developed for the issue of rivalry by analyzing times identified by the family as rivalry-free.

C. Encouragement was given to the family to keep implementing the solution from successful experiences.

D. The family struggled to implement the solutions from the past because they were unclear on the directions and timing.

23. Parenting Class Referral (23)

A. The parents were referred to and encouraged to attend a support group.

B. The parents reported attending a support group and receiving helpful feedback and encouragement.

C. The parents offered several reasons for not yet attending a support group.

24. Develop Behavior Modification Plan (24)

A. A behavior modification plan targeting cooperative sibling interaction was developed by the parents and the therapist for the client.

B. The parents were taught how to effectively implement and sustain a behavior modification program focused on reinforcing positive sibling interaction.

C. Parents' administration of the behavior modification plan was monitored and encouragement given to the parents to continue their work.

D. The parents were confronted when they failed to immediately reinforce positive interactions by client.

E. The behavior modification plan to reinforce positive sibling interaction has been successful in increasing such behaviors and reducing the sibling conflicts.

25. Evaluate Behavior Modification Contract (25)

A. The effectiveness of the behavior modification plan was reviewed with the client, and the parents were given positive feedback for implementing the contract.

B. Aspects of the behavior modification contract that focused on reinforcing positive sibling interaction were modified with the client and the parents because expectations were set unrealistically high.

C. The parents and the client were confronted on their lack of follow-through on the behavior modification contract, and resistance issues were addressed and resolved.

26. Teach Use of Positive Consequences (26)

A. The parents were taught to use positive consequences when the client's behavior is unacceptable or disrespectful.

B. The parents were assisted in constructing a list of possible positive consequences to use when the client exhibits unacceptable behavior, along with a plan for implementation of them.

C. The parents reported a reduction in the client's arguments with siblings due to the parents using positive consequences, and they were encouraged to continue their use.

D. The parents indicated they found it difficult to use positive consequences and slipped back into using natural consequences, which were easier.

27. Read Fable Regarding Rivalry (27)

A. "Raising Cain" and "Cinderella" from *Friedman's Fables* (Friedman) were read and processed in family session.

B. The reading and processing of the fables normalized the issue of sibling rivalry and helped family members identify their role in promoting it.

C. Each family member was asked to identify one thing they could do to decrease the rivalry within the family.

28. Confront Disrespect and Teach Conflict-Resolution Skills (28)

A. Family members' disrespectful interactions were highlighted and confronted in family session.

B. Conflict-resolution skills were taught to the parents and siblings.

C. Role plays, behavioral rehearsal, and modeling were utilized to teach the family effective conflict-resolution skills and to give them each opportunities to practice these new skills.

D. The family has struggled to implement conflict-resolution techniques, as they give up easily and fall back to old patterns of arguing and verbal abuse.

29. Identify Environmental Changes (29)

A. The parents were assisted in identifying specific things they could do in their physical environment to reduce conflicts between siblings.

B. The parents implemented the plan to move siblings into two separate bedrooms and to stop leaving the older child in charge of the younger.

C. Physical changes made by the parents in the home environment were monitored for their effectiveness, and the parents were given support and encouragement for their actions.

30. Read *How to End the Sibling Wars* (30)

A. The parents were asked to read *How to End The Sibling Wars* (Bienick) and select from the reading several interventions to implement with their child.

B. The parents were assisted in implementing chosen techniques from the assigned book, and role play was utilized to help the parents increase their skills and confidence in the new techniques.

C. The parents' resistance to trying new techniques was addressed and the advantage of using new approaches was seeded with them.

31. Assess Dynamics of Underlying Conflicts (31)

A. The dynamics and alliances present in the family were assessed in a family session.

B. A structural intervention was implemented with the family to create new and healthier alliances between the members.

C. Key dynamics that create and promote sibling conflict were confronted.

32. Assign Family to Attend Experiential Camp (32)

A. The family was asked to make a verbal commitment to attend an experiential weekend camp to promote family trust, cooperation, and respect.

B. The experiential weekend camp experience was processed with family, and members identified key things they had gained from the weekend.

33. Develop a Sibling Alliance (33)

A. The siblings were assisted in identifying a common issue to negotiate with the parents.

B. The parents and siblings were taught basic negotiation skills and practiced them in role-play situations.

C. In a family session, siblings negotiated with the parents to expand their freedom and were able to convince the parents to expand their freedom under the condition that the siblings decrease their conflicts.

D. Despite coaching and encouragement, negotiations broke down when siblings started arguing again.

34. "Cloning the Perfect Sibling" Exercise (34)

A. The client was asked to complete the "Cloning the Perfect Sibling" exercise from *The Brief Adolescent Therapy Homework Planner* (Jongsma, Peterson, and McInnis).

B. The client processed the completed cloning exercise and identified key positive points about differences between siblings.

C. The client processed the completed cloning exercise but refused to see the positive points of individual differences.

35. Psychiatric/Psychological Evaluation Referral (35)

A. Options for a psychiatric or psychological evaluation were explained to the client and family.

B. The client was referred for a psychiatric evaluation.

C. The client was referred for a psychological evaluation.

D. The parents were asked to make a verbal commitment to follow through with the evaluation and report the results to the therapist.

36. Monitor Implementation of Assessment Recommendations (36)

A. The parents and the client were assisted in implementing the psychological/psychiatric evaluation's recommendations.

B. The importance of follow-through on the assessment recommendations for the client was emphasized with the parents.

C. The parents and the client were confronted for their inconsistent follow-through on the assessment recommendations.

D. The client and the parents reported following through on each of the recommendations of the evaluation and were given positive verbal affirmation for their efforts.

PHYSICAL/EMOTIONAL ABUSE VICTIM

CLIENT PRESENTATION

1. Confirmed Report of Physical Abuse by an Adult (1)*

A. The client's self-report of being assaulted by his/her parent has been confirmed by a children's protective services worker.

B. The client's parent reported that the other parent has physically assaulted the client on more than one occasion.

C. The client provided a detailed account of the assault by his/her parent and the resulting injuries.

D. The physical abuse reported by the client was reported to children's protective services as required by mandatory reporting statutes.

2. Evidence of Victimization (2)

A. Bruises were evident on the client's body.

B. The client worked to explain away the injuries on his/her body, refusing to blame an adult for inflicting the injuries.

C. Past records of bruises and wounds revealed the extent of the client's victimization.

D. Since coming into treatment, the client has not reported receiving any bruises or wounds from his/her caregivers.

3. Fearful/Withdrawn (3)

A. The client appeared very fearful and withdrawn from others and avoids all but necessary interpersonal contacts.

B. Fear seems to dominate the client's contacts with others.

C. The client verbalized fear of further physical abuse by the caregiver.

D. Since establishing trust in counseling, the client has started to be less fearful and withdrawn and a little more open about himself/herself.

4. Closed/Detached (3)

A. The client presented in a closed and detached manner, with little visible interest in others or things.

B. The client showed little interest in the counseling process and was careful not to reveal anything significant about himself/herself.

C. The client seemed very closed and made a conscious effort to keep others at a safe distance and in the dark about himself/herself.

D. Since establishing a relationship with the therapist, the client has started to be more open about himself/herself and less fearful.

---

* The numbers in parentheses correlate to the number of the Behavioral Definition statement in the companion chapter with same title in *The Adolescent Psychotherapy Treatment Planner* (Jongsma, Peterson, and McInnis) by John Wiley & Sons, 2000.

5. Mistrustful/Anxious (3)

A. There is a mistrustful, anxious manner to the client when he/she interacts with others.

B. The client's body language and facial expressions seemed to indicate a high level of mistrust of others, especially adults.

C. The client reported a history of not being able to trust adults in his/her family because they rarely did what they said they would and often harmed him/her.

D. The client has begun to verbalize some connections between childhood pain and present attitudes of detachment and fear of others.

6. Low Self-Esteem (3)

A. The client's self-image seemed to be very low, as he/she seldom made eye contact and frequently made self-disparaging remarks.

B. The client reported feeling worthless and unloved for as long as he/she can remember.

C. The client's experience in the accepting environment of counseling has started to boost his/her sense of self-esteem.

7. Angry/Aggressive (4)

A. The client has an angry, aggressive manner that is obvious to nearly everyone.

B. The client reported an increase in the frequency and severity of angry, aggressive behavior toward peers and adults.

C. The blame for aggressive behaviors was projected onto others.

D. The client described having a quick temper that has resulted in his/her destroying many of his/her own possessions.

E. There has been a sharp decrease in client's anger and aggressiveness since he/she started to disclose about his/her being physically and emotionally abused.

F. The client has begun to realize how his/her anger and aggression are the result of what he/she saw and experienced in the home as a child.

8. Recollections of the Abuse (5)

A. The client indicated he/she felt constantly haunted by the distressing memories of his/her past emotional and physical abuse.

B. The client reported that the memories of the abuse intrude on his/her consciousness under a variety of circumstances.

C. The client described a chaotic childhood in which he/she was the victim of ongoing emotional and physical abuse.

D. The incidences of intrusive thoughts of the abuse has significantly diminished.

E. The client has begun to verbalize some connections between childhood pain and present attitudes of detachment and fear of others.

9. Strong Feelings When around Perpetrator (6)

A. The client indicated he/she feels intense anger and rage whenever he/she comes into contact with the perpetrator.

B. The caregivers have reported that the client becomes tearful and fearful immediately when the perpetrator is near.

C. The client expressed that he/she experiences mixed feelings of fear, anger, and rage whenever he/she encounters the perpetrator.

D. The client indicated that since talking in therapy, his/her feelings are not as intense or scary when he/she comes into contact with the perpetrator.

10. Depressed/Irritable (7)

A. The client presented with a depressed mood and manner that contained an irritable edge.

B. Between the client's depression and accompanying irritability, he/she was not willing or able to disclose about himself/herself in counseling session.

C. The client reported a pattern of social withdrawal and detachment from feelings.

D. Since starting on antidepressant medication, the client's depression and irritability have decreased and he/she is beginning to self-disclose in counseling session.

11. Passive/Apathetic (7)

A. There was a strong passive, apathetic quality to the client that reflects little interest in what might happen to self or others.

B. Because of his/her apathetic, passive manner, the client showed little interest in the counseling process.

C. The client reported that as far back as he/she can remember he/she has not been concerned about what happens to him/her.

D. The client has exhibited less apathy and passivity since he/she has become more actively involved in therapy.

12. Regressive Behavior (8)

A. The client presented with numerous regressive behaviors such as baby talk and thumb sucking.

B. The client reported that he/she has begun to wet the bed since the abuse began.

C. Since beginning to share his/her physical and emotional abusive past, the client's regressive behaviors are reported to be decreasing.

13. Sleep Disturbance (9)

A. The client reported having difficulties falling asleep, waking up frequently, and feeling tired and unrested in the morning.

B. The client indicated he/she has been experiencing frequent night terrors and recurrent nightmares.

C. The client has started to talk about the abuse he/she experienced in childhood and is now reporting fewer night terrors and more restful sleep.

D. The client has begun making connections between his/her sleeping difficulties and the history of being abused.

14. Running Away (10)

A. The client reported running away from home on several occasions to escape from the physical abuse.

B. It seems the client has used running away as an attempt to draw attention to the abusiveness in his/her home.

C. There has not been an incident of running away since the abuse of the client has started to be addressed.

INTERVENTIONS IMPLEMENTED

1. Build Trust (1)*

A. A level of trust was built with client through use of unconditional positive regard.

B. Warm acceptance and active listening techniques were used to establish trust with the client that would enable him/her to express feelings and facts surrounding the abuse.

C. The client has formed a trust-based relationship, which has increased his/her ability to express facts and feelings about the abuse.

D. Despite the use of unconditional positive regard, warm acceptance, and active listening, the client remains hesitant to share feelings and facts about the abuse.

2. Explore Facts of the Abuse (2)

A. The client was assisted in clarifying and expressing the facts associated with the abuse.

B. Support and encouragement were given to the client to increase his/her level of disclosure of the facts about the abuse.

C. Even with support and encouragement being given to the client, he/she still had difficulty expressing and clarifying the facts about the abuse.

D. The client openly outlined the facts associated with the most recent incident of his/her being a victim of abuse.

3. "Take the First Step" Exercise (3)

A. The client was asked to complete the "Take the First Step" exercise from *The Brief Adolescent Therapy Homework Planner* (Jongsma, Peterson, McInnis) to assist him/her in disclosing the story of the abuse.

B. The disclosure exercise that the client had completed was processed with the client, and key benefits of disclosing the abuse were identified and reinforced.

C. The client's partially completed disclosure exercise was processed and he/she gently confronted about his/her fear of disclosing the abuse.

D. The client showed some relief at being given the opportunity to fully disclose the facts of the abuse that he/she has experienced.

E. The client has failed to complete the disclosure exercise and was again asked to do so.

4. Report Physical Abuse (4)

A. An assessment was conducted on the client to substantiate the nature and extent of the physical abuse.

B. The client was sent to a physician to confirm and document the physical abuse.

---

* The numbers in parentheses correlate to the number of the Therapeutic Intervention statement in the companion chapter with the same title in *The Adolescent Psychotherapy Treatment Planner* (Jongsma, Peterson, and McInnis) by John Wiley & Sons, 2000.

C. The physical abuse of the client was reported to the state child protection agency for further investigation.

D. The parents were notified about the client's revelation of physical abuse and that, as required by law, it was reported to the state child protection agency for investigation.

5. Assess Veracity of Charges (5)

A. The family, client's physician, and criminal justice officials were consulted to assess the truthfulness of client's allegations of physical abuse.

B. The truthfulness of the client's allegations regarding physical abuse was confirmed by family, physician, and child protective services worker.

C. Consultation with the family, physician, and child protective service worker resulted in divided opinions regarding the veracity of the client's allegations of abuse.

6. Assess for Removal from Home (6)

A. The family environment was assessed to determine if it was safe for the client.

B. The family environment was determined to be unsafe for the client and he/she was moved to a safe, temporary placement outside the home.

C. After the family environment was assessed, a recommendation was made that a temporary restraining order be sought for the perpetrator.

7. Make Home Safe for Children (7)

A. An agreement was made with the perpetrator to move out of the home and not visit until the parents and protective service worker give their approval.

B. It was recommended to the nonabusive parent to seek a restraining order against the perpetrator.

C. The nonabusive parent was assisted in obtaining a restraining order and implementing it on a consistent basis.

D. Parent was monitored and supported for consistent implementation of "no contact" agreement between the perpetrator and the victim.

E. The parent was confronted on his/her inconsistent enforcement of restraining order to keep the perpetrator from the presence of the client.

8. Explore Feelings about Abuse (8)

A. The client's feelings toward the perpetrator were identified and explored.

B. Encouragement and support were given to the client as he/she was assisted in expressing and clarifying his/her feelings associated with the abuse experiences.

C. Even with support and encouragement, the client had difficulty clarifying and expressing any feelings about the abuse experiences.

D. The client expressed pain, anger, and fright as he/she told the story of the abuse.

9. "My Thoughts and Feelings" Exercise (9)

A. The client was asked to complete and process the "My Thoughts and Feelings" exercise from *The Brief Adolescent Therapy Treatment Planner* (Jongsma, Peterson, and McInnis) to help him/her practice openness.

B. The client was reminded that openness leads to health, whereas secrecy leads to staying sick.

C. The client's barriers to being more open were explored, identified, and removed.

D. The client was open in his/her expression of thoughts and feelings.

E. The client remains emotionally shut down and unwilling to express feelings openly.

10. Reassure Client of Protection (10)

A. The client was repeatedly reassured of concern and care of others in keeping him/her safe from further abuse.

B. The client was reassured by the parents and others that they were looking out for his/her safety.

C. The client's anxiety level seems to be diminishing as he/she accepts reassurance of safety.

11. Confront Denial of Family and Perpetrator (11)

A. Family sessions were conducted in which the family's denial of the client's abuse was confronted and challenged.

B. The perpetrator was asked to list all his/her rationalizations for the abuse.

C. Confrontation was used to process the perpetrator's list of rationalizations for the abuse.

D. Confrontation was used with the perpetrator to break through his/her denial of abusing the client.

E. The use of confrontation and challenges has been effective in breaking through the perpetrator's denial, and he/she is now taking ownership and responsibility for the abuse.

F. The perpetrator remains in denial about abusing the client in spite of confrontation and challenge to his/her rationalizations.

12. Confront Excusing Perpetrator (12)

A. The client was asked to create and process a list of reasons he/she was abused by the perpetrator.

B. Each time the client made an excuse for the perpetrator's abuse, he/she was confronted and reminded that he/she did in no way deserve being abused.

C. The message was given to the client that even though he/she is not perfect, the abuse was not deserved.

D. The client continued to excuse the perpetrator for the abuse and engaged in self-blame.

E. The client has begun to place clear responsibility for the abuse on the perpetrator and has discontinued self-blame.

13. Reassure That Abuse Not Deserved (13)

A. The client was reassured that the physical abuse he/she received was in no way deserved no matter what he/she had done wrong, if anything.

B. The message of not deserving the abuse no matter what happened was consistently given to the client.

C. The client was educated regarding his/her deserving personal respect and controlled responses in punishment situations.

14. **Reinforce Holding Perpetrator Responsible (14)**

A. All statements by the client that hold the perpetrator responsible for the abuse were reinforced.

B. The client was asked to list all the reasons the perpetrator was responsible for the abuse.

C. The client was reminded that regardless of any misbehavior on his/her part it was still the perpetrator's fault for the abuse.

D. The client has consistently made statements putting responsibility for the abuse firmly on the perpetrator.

15. **Support Confrontation of Perpetrator (15)**

A. The client was prepared in order to build his/her confidence for confronting the perpetrator in a family session.

B. Role play was used with the client to provide him/her with experience in confronting the perpetrator.

C. Family sessions were conducted in which the parents and the client confronted the perpetrator with the abuse.

D. Confrontation of the perpetrator with the abuse was modeled by the parents in family sessions.

E. In the family session, the client read a letter that he/she wrote outlining why the perpetrator was responsible for the abuse.

16. **Process Perpetrator Apology (16)**

A. The client was assessed to determine his/her readiness to hear and accept an apology from the perpetrator.

B. The perpetrator's apology was processed for genuineness and level of honesty.

C. A family session was conducted in which the perpetrator apologized to the client and family for the abuse.

17. **Counsel Parents on Boundaries (17)**

A. The parents were counseled on what are and what are not appropriate discipline boundaries.

B. Past inappropriate disciplinary boundaries that allowed for abusive punishment were addressed and new appropriate boundaries established.

C. New appropriate boundaries for nonabusive, reasonable discipline were monitored for parents' honoring and enforcing them.

D. The parents reported that they have successfully implemented disciplinary measures that are nonabusive and reasonable.

18. **Monitor Perpetrator Group Participation (18)**

A. The perpetrator attended and participated in the required effective parenting and anger management groups.

B. The gains made by the perpetrator in group were monitored and reinforced.

C. The perpetrator was confronted on his/her noncompliance with attending required groups.

19. Facilitate Perpetrator Psychological Evaluation/Treatment Referral (19)

A. The perpetrator was referred for a psychological evaluation.

B. The perpetrator cooperated with all aspects of the evaluation.

C. All treatment recommendations of the evaluation were given and explained to the perpetrator.

D. The perpetrator was asked to make a commitment to follow through on each of the treatment recommendations of the evaluation.

20. List Appropriate Parental Disciplines (20)

A. The parents were asked to list all the acts of appropriate discipline they could envision.

B. The parents' list of appropriate disciplinary behavior was reviewed, with reasonable approaches being encouraged and reinforced.

C. The parents were monitored for their use of discipline techniques that reinforce reasonable, respectful actions and appropriate boundaries.

D. The parents were confronted and redirected when discipline was not reasonable and respectful.

21. Construct Genogram That Identifies Abuse (21)

A. A multigeneration family genogram was constructed with the family members.

B. The family members were assisted in identifying patterns of physical abuse from the multigenerational family genogram.

C. Ways to begin breaking the physically abusive family patterns were identified and implemented by family members.

D. The family members acknowledged that the pattern of multigenerational physical abuse is existent and vowed to stop this pattern within their own family.

22. Assess Family Stress Factors (22)

A. Family dynamics were assessed to identify stress factors and events that may have contributed to the abuse.

B. The family members were assisted in identifying effective ways to cope with stress in order to reduce the probability of abuse.

C. The family was directed to key community and professional resources that could assist them in effectively coping with family stressors.

D. The family members were assisted in identifying steps to take to reduce environmental stressors that may contribute to the precipitation of violence.

23. Evaluate Family for Substance Abuse (23)

A. Family sessions were conducted to assess issues of substance use and abuse within the family.

B. The parents were referred for a substance abuse assessment.

C. The parents cooperated and completed the requested substance abuse assessments.

D. Efforts to assess the issue of substance use and abuse within the family were met with denial and resistance.

24. Perpetrator Substance Abuse Treatment Referral (24)

A. The perpetrator was referred to a substance abuse program.

B. The perpetrator successfully completed a substance abuse program and is now involved in aftercare.

C. The perpetrator was referred but refused to follow through on completing a substance abuse program.

25. Assign Letter to Perpetrator (25)

A. The client was asked to write a letter expressing his/her feelings of hurt, fear, and anger to the perpetrator.

B. The completed letter to the perpetrator was processed, providing the client with assistance and support in expressing the feelings connected to the abuse.

C. The client's inability to complete the assigned letter was explored, with blocks being identified and processed.

D. The client was asked to write the letter expressing his/her feelings about the abuse to the perpetrator but refused to do so, saying he/she did not want to feel those feelings again.

26. Assign Forgiveness Letter (26)

A. The client was educated on the key aspects of forgiveness, with special emphasis being given to the power involved.

B. The client was asked to complete a forgiveness letter to the perpetrator while asserting the right to safety.

C. The client was given a forgiveness exercise to complete and to process in the next session.

D. The assigned letter of forgiveness was processed and the evident empowerment provided by the experience was reinforced.

27. Assign Letting-Go Exercise (27)

A. The potential benefits of the process of letting go of anger and hurt were explored with the client.

B. A letting-go exercise was assigned in which the client would bury an anger list about the perpetrator.

C. The letting-go exercise was processed with the client and feelings were identified and expressed.

D. The client struggles with letting go of feelings of hurt and anger and is not yet able to reach this objective.

E. The client reported that he/she has successfully let go of his/her feelings of hurt and anger regarding being an abuse survivor.

28. Interpret Anger Triggered by Perpetrator (28)

A. Expressions of anger and aggression by the client were interpreted as being triggered by feelings toward the perpetrator.

B. Displays of seemingly unrelated anger and aggression were reflected to the client as indications of how angry he/she must be toward the perpetrator.

C. The client's general displays of anger and aggression have diminished as he/she has developed insight into his/her feelings of anger focused on the perpetrator.

29. Promote Family Support and Nurturing (29)

A. Family members were taught the importance of emotional support and nurturing to the client and how each could provide it for him/her.

B. Positive reinforcement was given to family members for incidents of support and nurturing given to the client.

C. The family position that the client should forget the abuse now and move on was confronted and processed, with members being reminded of the client's need for ongoing support and nurturing in order to fully heal.

30. Identify a Basis for Self-Esteem (30)

A. The client's talents, importance to others, and spiritual value were reviewed with him/her to assist in identifying a basis for self-worth.

B. The client was asked to verbally affirm each of his/her positive strengths and attributes that were identified.

C. Positive self-talk was developed around the client's strengths and attributes that he/she could use on a daily basis to affirm himself/herself.

31. Formulate Future Plans (31)

A. The client was probed to determine what future plans he/she has developed.

B. The client was asked to complete the following sentences to assist and encourage the idea of future plans: "I imagine that ___," "I will ___," "I dream that someday ___."

C. The client was encouraged to include interaction with peers and family as part of his/her future plans.

D. The client struggled to envision any future plans despite assistance and encouragement to do so.

32. Reinforce Positive Self-Descriptive Statements (32)

A. Every positive self-descriptive statement made by the client was affirmed and reinforced.

B. The client's negative statements about himself/herself were confronted and reframed.

C. The client's pattern of making more positive than negative self-statements was recognized, reinforced, and encouraged to continue in that direction.

33. Reinforce Self-Worth (33)

A. Unconditional positive regard, genuine warmth, and active listening were used to reinforce the client's self-worth.

B. Large doses of praise for any accomplishment by client were used to reinforce his/her self-worth.

C. The client's pattern of making more positive than negative self-statements was recognized, reinforced, and encouraged to continue in that direction.

34. Encourage Participation in Activities (34)

A. The client was encouraged to actively participate in peer group interaction and extracurricular activities.

B. The client's excuses and barriers to increased social involvement were explored and removed.

C. Situations involving peer groups and extracurricular activities were role-played with the client to build his/her social skills and confidence level in social situations.

D. Despite encouragement and social skill building, the client remains resistant to peer group and extracurricular activity participation.

35. Promote Self-Protection (35)

A. Various actions for the client to take to protect himself/herself from future abuse were identified and reinforced.

B. Efforts were made to empower the client to take necessary steps to protect himself/herself if the situation warranted it.

C. The client was bombarded with statements of empowerment regarding protecting himself/herself.

36. "Letter of Empowerment" Exercise (36)

A. The client was asked to complete the "Letter of Empowerment" exercise from *The Brief Adolescent Therapy Homework Planner* (Jongsma, Peterson, McInnis) to assist him/her in expressing thoughts and feelings about abuse.

B. Unconditional positive regard and active listening were used to help the client express thoughts and feelings about the abuse.

C. Barriers and defenses of the client that prevent expression of thoughts and feelings about the abuse were identified, addressed, and removed.

D. Efforts to encourage the client to express thoughts and feelings about the abuse have not been effective, and the client remains closed regarding the abuse.

E. The client completed the "Letter of Empowerment" exercise and reported that it has helped him/her express thoughts and feelings about the abuse.

F. The client has failed to complete the empowerment exercise and was redirected to do so.

37. Explore Loss of Trust in Adults (37)

A. The client was encouraged to express his/her loss of trust in adults.

B. The client was assisted in connecting his/her loss of trust to the perpetrator's abuse and the failure of others to protect him/her.

C. The client rejected assistance in identifying and expressing loss of trust and stood firm that he/she still trusts adults.

38. Teach Discriminating Trust Judgments (38)

A. The client was educated in the process of making discriminating judgments about trusting people.

B. The client was assisted in identifying key factors that make some people trustworthy and others untrustworthy.

C. Various scenarios of individuals were presented to the client to practice his/her trust-discrimination skills.

39. Teach Share-Check Technique (39)

A. The share-check technique was taught to the client to increase skills in assessing an individual's trustworthiness.

B. Role-play situations were used with the client to build his/her skill and confidence in using the share-check technique.

C. The client was asked to make a commitment to use the share-check technique and report the results of the experience.

D. The client reported success at using the share-check method of gradually building trust in others.

40. Victim Support Group Referral (40)

A. The benefits of the client attending a support group were identified and discussed.

B. The client was referred to a support group for teens who have been abused to decrease his/her feelings of being the only one in this situation.

C. The client's experience of attending a support group with the others who are in the same situation was processed.

D. The client indicated he/she felt different from all the others in the support group.

E. The client reported feeling empowered and understood after having attended a support group of fellow survivors of abuse.

41. Assign Drawing Pictures of Self (41)

A. The client was asked to draw pictures that reflect how he/she feels about himself/herself.

B. The client drew detailed pictures about how he/she feels about self.

C. With encouragement, the client drew several vague, undetailed pictures of self.

D. The client willingly talked about each of the pictures he/she drew, identifying specific feelings about himself/herself.

E. The client refused to do such "stupid, childish things" as drawing pictures.

42. Assign Drawing Faces of Self (42)

A. The client was asked to draw pictures of his/her own face before, during, and after the abuse occurred.

B. The client drew three faces in detail and explained the feelings they represented.

C. The client attempted but could not draw the faces to reflect how he/she felt before, during, and after the abuse occurred.

43. Educate Regarding Adopting Aggressive Behaviors (43)

A. The client was assessed regarding adopting the aggressive behaviors that he/she had been exposed to in the home.

B. The client was informed that, unless treated, many victims of abuse go on to abuse others, most often those they love.

C. The client's aggressive behaviors were pointed out to him/her and addressed.

D. The client's aggressive behaviors have diminished, and he/she has stated a desire to not follow the example or repeat the cycle of aggressive violence.

44. Encourage Empathy for Others' Feelings (44)

A. Role-play and role-reversal techniques were used to sensitize the client to the target of his/her angry feelings.

B. The possible consequences of losing control over angry feelings were identified.

C. The client has verbalized empathy for the pain and fear that his/her aggression causes in others.

45. Conduct Substance Abuse Evaluation (45)

A. The client's pattern of substance use was evaluated.

B. The client was cooperative in all aspects of the substance abuse evaluation.

C. The client was resistive to the evaluation, provided only limited information, and denied any use.

D. The results of the substance abuse evaluation indicate that the client has a chemical-dependence problem.

E. The substance abuse evaluation did not provide evidence for a chemical-dependence problem on the part of the client.

46. Interpret Substance Use as Maladaptive Coping (46)

A. The client was given the interpretation that substance abuse has been a maladaptive coping behavior to avoid feelings connected to the abuse.

B. The interpretation of substance abuse as a maladaptive coping behavior was processed with the client, and healthier ways to express feelings were explored, identified, and encouraged.

C. The client agreed that he/she was using substance abuse as an escape from feelings of pain and rage.

D. The client denied that his/her substance abuse was in any way related to being a victim of abuse.

47. Substance Abuse Treatment Referral (47)

A. The client was referred to a substance abuse–specific treatment program.

B. The client was given a substance abuse treatment referral and made a commitment to follow through on it.

C. Substance abuse–specific treatment was started with the client to address his/her abuse issues.

D. The client was unwilling to make any commitment to follow through on the recommended referral for a substance abuse program.

48. Contract Termination of Substance Abuse (48)

A. A contract to terminate all substance use was developed with the client and signed by him/her.

B. The no-substance-use contract was monitored for the client's compliance and follow-through.

C. The client was confronted on his/her failure to keep the terms of the no-substance-use contract.

D. Positive feedback and encouragement were given to the client for keeping the terms of the no-substance-use contract.

E. Because the client has failed to terminate substance abuse, a referral was made for more intensive chemical dependence treatment.

POSTTRAUMATIC STRESS DISORDER

CLIENT PRESENTATION

1. Traumatic Event (1)*

A. The client described a traumatic experience that exposed him/her to actual or threatened death.

B. The client described a traumatic experience that resulted in serious injury to self and/or others.

C. The client described a history of being physically and/or sexually abused.

D. The client was open and talkative about the traumatic event(s).

E. The client was guarded and reluctant to talk about the traumatic event(s).

2. Intrusive, Distressing Thoughts (2)

A. The client reported that he/she has experienced frequent intrusive, distressing thoughts or images about the traumatic event.

B. The client was visibly upset when describing the distressing images of the traumatic event.

C. The frequency and intensity of the client's intrusive, distressing thoughts or images have started to decrease as he/she works through his/her thoughts and feelings about the traumatic event.

D. The client denied experiencing any intrusive, distressing thoughts or images about the traumatic event.

3. Disturbing Dreams (3)

A. The client reported experiencing frequent nightmares or distressing dreams since the traumatic event first occurred.

B. The client has continued to be troubled by disturbing dreams associated with the trauma.

C. The client has experienced a mild reduction in the frequency of the disturbing dreams.

D. The client has not experienced any disturbing dreams about the traumatic event since the last therapy session.

4. Flashbacks, Hallucinations, Illusions (4)

A. The client reported experiencing numerous flashbacks, hallucinations, or illusions that the traumatic event is recurring.

B. The client experienced a flashback or hallucination during today's therapy session when discussing the traumatic event.

C. The frequency of the client's flashbacks, hallucinations, or illusions have started to decrease as he/she makes productive use of therapy.

---

* The numbers in parentheses correlate to the number of the Behavioral Definition statement in the companion chapter with same title in *The Adolescent Psychotherapy Treatment Planner* (Jongsma, Peterson, and McInnis) by John Wiley & Sons, 2000.

D. The client denied experiencing any recent flashbacks, hallucinations, or illusions.

5. Intense Emotional Distress (5)

A. The client has experienced a significant amount of emotional distress and turmoil since the traumatic event first occurred.

B. The client was visibly distressed and upset when discussing the traumatic event.

C. The intensity of the client's emotional distress when discussing the traumatic event has started to diminish.

D. The client has been able to talk about the traumatic event without displaying a significant amount of emotional distress.

6. Strong Physiological Reaction (6)

A. The client reported that he/she often exhibits an intense physiological reaction (e.g., trembling and shaking, palpitations, dizziness, shortness of breath, sweating) when reminded of the traumatic event.

B. The client demonstrated a strong physiological reaction (e.g., trembling and shaking, shortness of breath, sweating) when discussing the traumatic event in today's therapy session.

C. The client's negative physiological reactions have started to decrease in intensity when talking about the traumatic event.

D. The client did not experience any negative, physiological reaction when discussing the traumatic event.

7. Avoidance of Talking about Trauma (7)

A. The client has avoided conversations about the trauma and also tries to avoid thinking about it.

B. In an attempt to avoid the feelings associated with the trauma, the client has avoided talking about it.

C. The client's general avoidance of the subject of the trauma has waned and he/she is willing to discuss it briefly.

D. The client is now able to think about, talk about, and experience feelings about the trauma without fear of being overwhelmed.

8. Avoidance of Activities Associated with Trauma (8)

A. The client has avoided engaging in activities, going places, or interacting with people associated with the traumatic event.

B. The client acknowledged that he/she avoids activities, places, or people that remind him/her of the traumatic event because of the fear of being overwhelmed by powerful emotions.

C. The client has started to tolerate exposure to activities, places, or people that remind him/her of the traumatic event without feeling overwhelmed.

D. The client has returned to a pretrauma level of functioning without avoiding people or places associated with the traumatic event.

9. Limited Recall (9)

A. The client reported that he/she is unable to recall some important aspects of the traumatic event.

B. The client's emotional distress has been so great that he/she is unable to recall many details of the traumatic event.

C. The client has started to recall some of the important details of the traumatic event.

D. The client recalled most of the important aspects of the traumatic event.

10. Lack of Interest (10)

A. The client has displayed little interest in activities that normally brought him/her pleasure before the traumatic event.

B. The client has significantly reduced his/her participation in social or extracurricular activities since the traumatic event.

C. The client verbalized little or no interest in socializing or participating in extracurricular activities.

D. The client has started to participate in more social or extracurricular activities.

E. The client has participated in social or extracurricular activities on a regular, consistent basis.

11. Social Detachment (11)

A. The client has become more withdrawn since the traumatic event first occurred.

B. The client appeared aloof and detached in today's therapy session.

C. The client has started to socialize with a wider circle of peers.

D. The client has become more outgoing and interacts with his/her peers on a regular, consistent basis.

12. Emotionally Constricted (12)

A. The client has generally appeared flat and constricted in his/her emotional presentation since the traumatic event.

B. The client's affect appeared flat and constricted when talking about the traumatic event.

C. The client acknowledged that he/she is reluctant to share his/her deeper emotions pertaining to the traumatic event because of the fear of losing control of his/her emotions.

D. The client has started to show a wider range of emotions about the traumatic event in the therapy sessions.

E. The client has been able to express his/her genuine emotions about the traumatic event without feeling overwhelmed.

13. Pessimistic Outlook (13)

A. The client has developed a pessimistic outlook on the future and often feels overwhelmed by feelings of helplessness and hopelessness.

B. The client verbalized feelings of helplessness and hopelessness during today's therapy session.

C. The client has gradually begun to develop a brighter outlook on the future.

D. The client expressed a renewed sense of hope for the future in today's therapy session.

E. The client's willingness to assert himself/herself and assume healthy risks reflected his/her renewed sense of hope and feelings of empowerment.

14. Sleep Disturbance (14)

A. The client has experienced significant disturbances in his/her sleep patterns since the traumatic event.

B. The client reported having problems falling asleep.

C. The client has experienced frequent early morning awakenings.

D. The client reported recent improvements in his/her sleep.

E. The client reported experiencing a return to his/her normal sleep patterns.

15. Irritability (15)

A. The client has displayed irritability and moodiness since the trauma occurred.

B. The client's irritability has resulted in many incidents of verbal outbursts of anger over small issues.

C. The client is becoming less irritable as the trauma is processed and underlying feelings are resolved.

16. Lack of Concentration (16)

A. The client has not been able to maintain concentration on schoolwork or other tasks.

B. The client states that his/her concentration is interrupted by flashbacks to the traumatic incident.

C. The client's concentration is becoming more focused as the feelings surrounding the trauma are resolved.

17. Hypervigilance/Mistrustfulness (17)

A. The client has developed a deep mistrust of others because of the traumatic event.

B. The client described himself/herself as being overly vigilant when he/she goes out into public places because of fear of possible harm or danger.

C. The client appeared guarded and mistrustful during today's therapy session.

D. The client has slowly begun to develop trust when in the presence of others and relaxed acceptance with several individuals.

E. The client's increased trust in others has helped to stabilize his/her mood and allowed him/her to work through many thoughts and feelings about the traumatic event.

18. Anxiety/Fearfulness (17)

A. The traumatic event has been a significant contributing factor to the client's high level of anxiety and fearfulness.

B. The client appeared visibly anxious and fearful when discussing the traumatic event.

C. The intensity of the client's anxiety and fearfulness has started to diminish when he/she talks about the traumatic event.

D. The client has demonstrated a marked decrease in the frequency and intensity of his/her anxious moods and fearfulness.

19. Exaggerated Startle Response (18)

A. The client has often displayed an exaggerated startle response when exposed to any sudden, unexpected stimuli.

B. The client displayed an exaggerated startle response in today's therapy session.

C. The client reported that he/she no longer startles as easily or dramatically when exposed to unexpected stimuli.

20. Symptoms for One Month (19)

A. The client has displayed a variety of symptoms associated with posttraumatic stress for over a month.

B. The client's symptom pattern has begun to decrease in intensity.

C. The client reported being free of all symptoms associated with the traumatic incident.

21. Guilt (20)

A. The client has been troubled by strong feelings of guilt since the traumatic event first occurred.

B. The client expressed feelings of guilt about surviving, causing, or not preventing the traumatic event.

C. The client has begun to work through and resolve his/her feelings of guilt about the traumatic event.

D. The client verbally denied experiencing any feelings of guilt about the traumatic event.

E. The client has successfully resolved his/her feelings of guilt about the traumatic event.

22. Depression (20)

A. The client reports experiencing a significant amount of depression and unhappiness since the traumatic event first occurred.

B. The client expressed strong feelings of sadness and hurt about the traumatic event.

C. The client's level of depression has begun to diminish as he/she works through many of his/her thoughts and feelings about the traumatic event.

D. The client did not appear sad or depressed when talking about the traumatic event.

E. The frequency and intensity of the client's depressed moods have decreased significantly.

23. Low Self-Esteem (20)

A. The client's self-esteem has decreased significantly since the traumatic event.

B. The client verbalized feelings of low self-esteem, inadequacy, and insecurity.

C. The client has begun to take steps to improve his/her self-esteem and develop a positive self-image.

D. The client verbalized positive self-descriptive statements during today's therapy session.

E. The client has worked through many of his/her feelings surrounding the traumatic event and has developed a healthy self-image.

24. Angry Outbursts/Aggression (21)

A. The client described a persistent pattern of exhibiting intense outbursts of rage or becoming physically aggressive.

B. The client expressed strong feelings of anger and rage about the traumatic event.

C. The client has recently struggled to control his/her hostile/aggressive impulses.

D. The client was able to talk about the traumatic event with much less anger and resentment.

E. The frequency and severity of the client's angry outbursts and aggressive behaviors have decreased significantly.

INTERVENTIONS IMPLEMENTED

1. Build Trust (1)*

A. The focus of today's therapy session was on building the level of trust with the client through consistent eye contact, active listening, unconditional positive regard, and warm acceptance.

B. The client received unconditional positive regard and warm acceptance to help increase his/her ability to identify and express feelings connected to the traumatic event.

C. The therapy session was helpful in building the level of trust with the client.

D. The therapy session did not prove to be helpful in building the level of trust with the client, as he/she remained guarded in talking about the traumatic event.

2. Explore Facts of Traumatic Event (2)

A. The client was gently encouraged to tell the entire story of the traumatic event.

B. The client was given the opportunity to share what he/she recalls about the traumatic event.

C. Today's therapy session explored the sequence of events before, during, and after the traumatic event.

3. Probe Emotional Reaction during Trauma (3)

A. Today's therapy session explored the client's emotional reaction at the time of the trauma.

B. The client was able to recall the fear that he/she experienced at the time of the traumatic incident.

C. The client was able to recall the feelings of hurt, anger, and sadness that he/she experienced during the traumatic incident.

D. The client was unable to recall the emotions that he/she experienced during the traumatic incident.

E. A client-centered therapy approach was used to explore the client's emotional reaction at the time of the traumatic incident.

4. Identify Negative Impact of Traumatic Event (4)

A. The client was asked how the traumatic event has negatively impacted his/her life.

---

* The numbers in parentheses correlate to the number of the Therapeutic Intervention statement in the companion chapter with the same title in *The Adolescent Psychotherapy Treatment Planner* (Jongsma, Peterson, and McInnis) by John Wiley & Sons, 2000.

B. The client's current level of functioning was compared to his/her pretrauma level of functioning.

C. The client identified various ways that the traumatic event has negatively impacted his/her life.

D. The client shared how the traumatic event has caused him/her to experience a considerable amount of emotional distress.

E. The client shared that the traumatic event has caused him/her to become more isolated and mistrustful of others.

5. Explore Effects of PTSD Symptoms (5)

A. Today's therapy session explored the effects that the PTSD symptoms have had on the client's personal relationships, functioning at school, and social/recreational life.

B. The client acknowledged that his/her erratic and unpredictable shifts in mood have placed a significant strain on his/her personal relationships.

C. The client identified how the traumatic event has had a negative impact on his/her school functioning.

D. The client verbally recognized how he/she has become more detached and engaged in significantly fewer social/recreational activities since the traumatic event.

6. Assess Anger Control (6)

A. A history of the client's anger control problems was taken in today's therapy session.

B. The client shared instances where his/her poor control of anger resulted in verbal threats of violence, actual harm or injury to others, or destruction of property.

C. The client identified events or situations that frequently trigger a loss of control of his/her anger.

D. The client was asked to identify the common targets of his/her anger to help gain greater insight into the factors contributing to his/her lack of control.

E. Today's therapy session helped the client realize how his/her anger control problems are often associated with underlying painful emotions about the traumatic event.

7. Teach Anger Management Techniques (7)

A. The client was taught mediational and self-control strategies to help improve his/her anger control.

B. The client was taught guided imagery and relaxation techniques to help improve his/her anger control.

C. Role-playing and modeling techniques were used to demonstrate effective ways to control anger.

D. The client was strongly encouraged to express his/her anger through controlled, respectful verbalizations and healthy physical outlets.

E. A reward system was designed to reinforce the client for demonstrating good anger control.

8. Teach Deep Muscle Relaxation (8)

A. The client was taught deep muscle relaxation methods along with deep breathing and positive imagery to induce relaxation and decrease his/her emotional distress.

B. The client reported a positive response to the use of deep muscle relaxation methods and positive imagery techniques to help feel more relaxed and less distressed.

C. The client appeared uncomfortable and unable to relax when being instructed in the use of deep muscle relaxation and guided imagery techniques.

9. Utilize EMG Biofeedback (9)

A. EMG biofeedback was utilized to help increase the depth of the client's relaxation.

B. The client reported a positive response to the use of EMG biofeedback to increase the depth of his/her relaxation and reduce intensity of his/her emotional distress.

C. The client reported little to no improvement in his/her ability to relax through the use of EMG biofeedback.

10. Teach Relaxation Techniques to Induce Sleep (10)

A. The client was instructed to utilize relaxation techniques to help induce calm before attempting to go to sleep.

B. The client was encouraged to utilize the *10 Minutes to Relax* audiotapes to induce calm before attempting to go to sleep.

C. The client reported that the relaxation tapes have been helpful in inducing calm and allowing him/her to fall asleep much sooner.

D. The client reported that he/she has continued to have trouble falling asleep even after using the relaxation techniques.

11. Implement Systematic Desensitization (11)

A. An imaginal, systematic desensitization program utilizing positive guided imagery was designed to help reduce the client's emotional reactivity to the traumatic event.

B. The client verbally agreed to follow through with the implementation of the imaginal systematic desensitization program during therapy sessions.

C. The client reported that the use of imaginal systematic desensitization and positive guided imagery has helped to significantly reduce his/her emotional reactivity to the traumatic event.

D. The client reported a minimal reduction in his/her emotional reactivity to the traumatic event after use of imaginal systematic desensitization.

E. The client has experienced a decrease in the reduction of his/her emotional reactivity to the traumatic event as a result of the imaginal systematic desensitization program.

12. Explore Feelings Surrounding Traumatic Event (12)

A. Today's therapy session explored the client's feelings before, during, and after the traumatic event.

B. The client was given support and affirmation when retelling the story of the traumatic event.

C. The retelling of the traumatic incident helped to reduce the client's emotional distress.

D. The client has continued to exhibit a significant amount of emotional distress when telling the story of the traumatic event.

13. Identify Negative Self-Talk (13)

A. Today's therapy session identified how the client's negative self-talk and pessimistic outlook are associated with the trauma.

B. Today's therapy session focused on how the client's pessimistic outlook and strong self-doubts interfere with his/her willingness to take healthy risks.

C. A cognitive-behavioral therapy approach was utilized to identify the client's self-defeating thoughts.

D. The client was helped to identify ways to cope with the trauma that are more adaptive than continuing to rely on unsuccessful coping strategies.

14. Replace Distorted, Negative, Self-Defeating Thoughts (14)

A. The client was helped to replace his/her distorted, negative self-defeating thoughts with positive, reality-based self-talk.

B. The client was encouraged to make positive self-statements to improve his/her self-esteem and decrease his/her emotional pain.

C. The client was given the homework assignment to make at least one positive self-statement daily around others.

D. The client's distorted, negative, self-defeating thoughts were challenged to help him/her overcome the pattern of catastrophizing events and/or expecting the worst to occur.

E. The client reported experiencing increased calm by being able to replace his/her distorted, cognitive, self-defeating thoughts with positive, reality-based self-talk.

15. Teach Gradual Approach to Avoided Stimuli (15)

A. The client was assisted in developing a plan to decrease his/her emotional reactivity by gradually approaching previously avoided stimuli that trigger thoughts and feelings associated with the trauma.

B. The client developed a hierarchy of steps that he/she can take to gradually approach the previously avoided stimuli that trigger thoughts and feelings associated with the trauma.

C. The client was trained in the use of relaxation, deep breathing, and positive self-talk prior to attempting to gradually approach the previously avoided stimuli.

D. The client reported that the use of relaxation, deep breathing, and positive self-talk has helped him/her gradually approach the previously avoided stimuli without experiencing a significant amount of distress.

E. The client failed to practice using the relaxation techniques and positive self-talk because of his/her fear of being overwhelmed by painful emotions.

16. Monitor Sleep Patterns (16)

A. The client was encouraged to keep a record of how much sleep he/she gets every night.

B. The client was trained in the use of relaxation techniques to help induce sleep.

C. The client was trained in the use of positive imagery to help induce sleep.

D. The client was referred for a medication evaluation to determine whether medication is needed to help him/her sleep.

17. Utilize Eye Movement Desensitization and Reprocessing (EMDR) (17)

A. The client was trained in the use of eye movement desensitization and reprocessing (EMDR) technique to reduce his/her emotional reactivity to the traumatic event.

B. The client reported that the EMDR technique has been helpful in reducing his/her emotional reactivity to the traumatic event.

C. The client reported partial success with the use of the EMDR technique to reduce emotional distress.

D. The client reported little or no improvement with the use of the EMDR technique to decrease his/her emotional reactivity to the traumatic event.

18. Group Therapy Referral (18)

A. The client was referred for group therapy to help him/her share and work through his/her feelings about the trauma with other individuals who have experienced traumatic incidents.

B. The client was given the directive to self-disclose about his/her traumatic experience at least once during the group therapy session.

C. The client's involvement in group therapy has helped him/her realize that he/she is not alone in experiencing painful emotions surrounding a traumatic event.

D. The client's active participation in group therapy has helped him/her share and work through many of his/her emotions pertaining to the traumatic event.

E. The client has not made productive use of the group therapy sessions and has been reluctant to share his/her feelings about the traumatic event.

19. Medication Evaluation Referral (19)

A. The client was referred for a medication evaluation to help stabilize his/her moods and decrease the intensity of his/her angry feelings.

B. The client and parent(s) agreed to follow through with the medication evaluation.

C. The client was strongly opposed to being placed on medication to help stabilize his/her moods and reduce emotional distress.

20. Monitor Effects of Medication (20)

A. The client's response to the medication was discussed in today's therapy session.

B. The client reported that the medication has helped to stabilize his/her moods and decrease the intensity of his/her angry feelings.

C. The client reports little or no improvement in his/her moods or anger control since being placed on the medication.

D. The client reports that he/she has consistently taken the medication as prescribed.

E. The client has failed to comply with taking the medication as prescribed.

21. Hold Family Session to Facilitate Offering of Support (21)

A. A family therapy session was held to allow the client to express his/her feelings about the traumatic event in the presence of his/her family members.

B. A family therapy session was held to give family members the opportunity to provide much-needed emotional support to the client.

C. The client responded favorably to the show of support from his/her family members.

D. Today's therapy session allowed all the family members to express their feelings about the traumatic event.

E. Today's family therapy session explored the factors that interfere with the family members' ability to provide emotional support and nurturance to the client.

22. Inform Family about the Traumatic Event (22)

A. The family members were informed how the traumatic event impacted the client and his/her subsequent adjustment.

B. The client was given the opportunity to share how the traumatic event has impacted his/her adjustment and ability to cope.

C. The family members' denial about the impact of the traumatic event was challenged and confronted in today's therapy session.

D. The family members were given the opportunity to express their thoughts and feelings about how the traumatic event impacted the survivors.

23. Assign Books on PTSD (23)

A. The client was given a list of books about PTSD and the recovery process and encouraged to select one to read.

B. The client was instructed to read *I Can't Get Over It* (Matsakis) to help him/her learn more about PTSD and the recovery process.

C. Processed the reading of *I Can't Get Over It* in today's therapy session.

D. The client followed through in reading *I Can't Get Over It* and found it helpful in identifying ways to recover from the traumatic event.

E. The client failed to start reading *I Can't Get Over It* and was encouraged to do so to help gain an understanding of the recovery process involved with PTSD.

PSYCHOTICISM

CLIENT PRESENTATION

1. Bizarre Thought Content (1)*

A. The client's thought content contains many bizarre elements.

B. Delusions of grandeur, persecution, and reference dominate the client's thought content.

C. The client reported feeling often under the influence and control of others and unable to do anything about it.

D. The client's bizarre thought content has slowly decreased and he/she is starting to think more clearly and rationally.

2. Illogical Speech (2)

A. The client presented with several speech oddities, which included perseverations, neologisms, and clanging.

B. There is a vague, abstract, and repetitive quality to the client's speech.

C. A looseness of associations dominates the client's speech.

D. The client's speech has begun to be more logical and coherent, free from neologisms and clanging.

3. Perception Disturbances (3)

A. The client's perceptions appeared disturbed by auditory hallucinations.

B. The client revealed a history of having periodic auditory and visual hallucinations.

C. The level or degree of the client's hallucinations has affected all areas of his/her functioning.

D. The client presented in a fearful, preoccupied manner related to his/her persistent auditory hallucinations.

E. Since beginning a medication regime, the client's hallucinations have become manageable and his/her level of daily functioning has markedly improved.

4. Disturbed Affect (4)

A. The client's affect had a blunt, flat quality, with no range being evident.

B. In most situations the client's affect is grossly inappropriate.

C. There is a dull, flat quality to the client's affect.

D. The client has recently started to show some appropriate spontaneity in his/her affect.

E. The client has started to regain his/her range of affect since taking medication regularly.

---

* The numbers in parentheses correlate to the number of the Behavioral Definition statement in the companion chapter with same title in *The Adolescent Psychotherapy Treatment Planner* (Jongsma, Peterson, and McInnis) by John Wiley & Sons, 2000.

5. Lost Sense of Self (5)

A. The client presented as being very lost and confused.

B. The client's boundaries and identity seem to be confused and diffused.

C. Often, the client reported feeling lost and confused as if in a fog.

D. Consistently, the client responds inappropriately to what others do or say to him/her.

E. The client has shown steady improvement in his/her sense of identity and is now able to identify the boundaries between himself/herself and others as well as give an accurate description of person, place, and time.

6. Diminished Volition (6)

A. The client presented exhibiting low energy and little interest in anything.

B. It is evident from talking to the client that he/she has persistent difficulty following a course of action through to its logical conclusion.

C. The client reported having no past or present goals and identified with living mostly for the present moment.

D. Ambivalence dominates the client's talk and actions.

E. The client is showing improved interest initiative and follow-through with activities.

7. Relationship Withdrawal (7)

A. The client presented as withdrawn and fearful.

B. In the recent past, the client has gradually withdrawn more and more from others and become focused on fearful thoughts and feelings.

C. The client gives a clear message of being fearful of others and wanting others at a distance from him/her.

D. The client's fear of social contact has diminished and he/she is responding appropriately to social overtures from others.

8. Tense/Frightened (7)

A. The client presented in a tense and frightened manner.

B. There is a hypervigilance to the client's reactions and interactions to others that reflect a level of tension and fear.

C. In the counseling session, the client appeared visibly tense and in a state of near fright.

D. Gradually the client has become less tense and frightened and able to relate more openly about himself/herself.

9. Closed/Guarded (7)

A. The client appeared closed and guarded.

B. The client works to keep others at a safe distance from himself/herself.

C. The client's manner in counseling sessions is closed and guarded, revealing very little about himself/herself.

D. The client's psychomotor abnormalities have terminated and no unusual facial or motor reactions to internal stimuli are apparent.

10. Aloof/Distant (8)

A. The manner of the client is aloof and distant.

B. The client's pattern of relationships with others reflects a distance and aloofness, avoiding any closeness.

C. The client reported a history of having no close friends and a preference for a few acquaintances.

D. The client showed no interest in the therapist or the counseling process.

E. Recently, the client is relating with a bit more warmth, spontaneity, and interest in others.

11. Poor Social Skills (8)

A. The client is socially awkward and has an inept manner.

B. In his/her contacts with others, the client makes sure to keep a good degree of emotional distance.

C. The client reported that in most social situations he/she feels awkward and threatened.

D. On a consistent basis the client seems to misinterpret the actions and motives of others.

E. After becoming involved in his/her counseling sessions, the client has started to initiate interactions and does not misinterpret the motives and actions of others to as great a degree.

12. Impulsive Thoughts/Feelings/Actions (9)

A. The client reported a history of sexual and aggressive impulsive acts that have most often been directed at friends and family.

B. The fantasies of the client are consistently sexual and aggressive.

C. The blame for his/her sexual and aggressive impulses and fantasies are often put on others.

D. Since starting on medications, a steady decrease in the client's impulsive and aggressive acts and fantasies has occurred.

13. Psychomotor Abnormalities (10)

A. The client's manner is marked by numerous unusual mannerisms and facial grimaces.

B. The client's interactions with his/her environment are very limited.

C. The client displays catatonic patterns that range from stupor to rigidity to excitement.

D. The client has become less guarded and more open in relationships with the therapist and others.

INTERVENTIONS IMPLEMENTED

1. Assess Thought Disorder (1)*

A. A clinical interview was conducted to assess the pervasiveness of the client's thought disorder.

B. The client was guarded yet cooperative throughout the clinical interview.

* The numbers in parentheses correlate to the number of the Therapeutic Intervention statement in the companion chapter with the same title in *The Adolescent Psychotherapy Treatment Planner* (Jongsma, Peterson, and McInnis) by John Wiley & Sons, 2000.

C. The pervasiveness of the client's thought disorder was established and appropriate interventions developed and implemented to address it.

2. Determine Nature of Psychosis (2)

A. A clinical interview was conducted with the client to determine whether the client's psychosis is brief and reactive or long term in nature.

B. The client was referred for a psychiatric evaluation to confirm the nature of the psychosis.

C. The nature of the psychosis was established and confirmed.

3. Provide Supportive Therapy (3)

A. Supportive therapy was used with the client to reduce his/her distrust, alleviate fears, and promote openness.

B. An approach of genuine warmth and understanding was used with the client to build trust and a sense of security.

C. The client's fears and mistrust have started to decrease and he/she is beginning to open up.

D. Despite a supportive approach, the client continues to be fearful, mistrustful, and closed.

4. Conduct Psychological Testing (4)

A. A psychological evaluation was conducted to determine the severity and type of the psychosis.

B. The client was referred for psychological evaluation to determine the severity and type of the psychosis.

C. A psychological evaluation could not be completed due to the client's inability to focus.

D. The client approached the evaluation in a straightforward manner and was cooperative with the examiner.

5. Gather Family Mental Illness History (5)

A. The client's family history was explored to identify incidents of mental illness, traumas, or stressors.

B. A positive history of family mental illness was established, and family coping strategies were identified.

C. An exploration of the client's family history revealed no evidence of serious mental illness within known members of the immediate and extended family.

6. Explain Psychotic Process (6)

A. The nature of the psychotic process was explained to the client and his/her family.

B. The biochemical component of psychosis and its confusing effect on rational thought was emphasized to the client and his/her parents.

C. The client's and parents' questions regarding psychotic process were solicited and answered.

D. The importance of family members showing understanding and support of the psychotic member was emphasized and reinforced.

E. Despite attempts to explain the psychotic process, the client and family members were confused by the illness, its causes, and its effects.

7. Medication Referral (7)

A. The client was referred for an evaluation for antipsychotic medications.

B. The client's and family's resistance to psychotropic medication was explored and resolved.

C. The client was asked to make a commitment to take medications as prescribed.

D. The client followed through with the referral to a physician for an evaluation, and antipsychotic medications have been prescribed.

8. Monitor Medication Compliance/Effectiveness (8)

A. The client was monitored for prescription compliance, side effects, and overall effectiveness.

B. The client was redirected, as he/she was inconsistent in taking the prescribed medications.

C. The client was verbally affirmed and reinforced for taking medications as prescribed.

D. The client reported that the antipsychotic medication is providing relief from the thought-disorder symptoms.

9. Arrange for Appropriate Level of Care (9)

A. The client was assessed for his/her needs in terms of level of supervised care.

B. Inpatient treatment was recommended and arranged for the client, as he/she is seriously disabled by the psychotic symptoms.

C. The client does not require inpatient or residential care presently but he/she will be monitored for his/her need in the future.

D. Family assistance and support were enlisted to secure inpatient treatment for the client.

10. Probe Stressors (10)

A. Internal and external stressors that may have precipitated the psychotic episode were probed.

B. The client was assisted in identifying recent internal and external stressors in his/her life.

C. An assessment of the client's current life situation revealed significant internal and external stressors in his/her daily life.

D. No significant internal or external stressors could be identified by the client as triggers for the most recent psychotic episode.

11. Explore Feelings Surrounding Stressors (11)

A. The client's feelings surrounding the stressors that triggered the psychotic episode were explored and validated.

B. The client's feelings were processed in a warm, supportive manner.

C. The client was unable to identify and clarify negative feelings associated with the stressors in his/her life.

12. Identify Threats and Develop Plan (12)

A. The client and family were assisted in identifying the environmental stressors that contributed to the psychotic break.

B. The client and family were helped to develop a plan to cope with or reduce environmental stressors.

C. The environmental stressors have been reduced due to the intervention of others on behalf of the client.

13. Explore History of Losses, Traumas (13)

A. The client's history of traumas, losses, and separations was explored.

B. The client was resistive to identifying or talking about losses, traumas, and separations in his/her history.

C. The client identified several traumatic events in his/her past that have contributed to fear, self-doubt, and emotional fragility.

14. Probe Underlying Needs and Feelings (14)

A. The underlying needs and feelings that contribute to the client's internal conflict and irrational beliefs were probed.

B. The client was assisted in connecting his/her feelings and needs with internal conflicts and irrational beliefs.

C. The client was encouraged to let go of unrealistic needs and accompanying feelings.

D. The client described a history of rejection, abandonment, and abuse that has permanently scarred his/her sense of empowerment.

15. Educate Family Regarding Illness (15)

A. In family sessions, the family members were educated on the client's illness, its causes, symptoms, treatment, and prognosis.

B. Questions raised by the family about the nature, treatment, and prognosis of the client's psychotic illness were answered.

C. Unfounded or unrealistic beliefs or attitudes held by family members were addressed and processed.

16. Encourage Here-and-Now Activities for the Client (16)

A. The value and importance of here-and-now activities in the client's recovery were stressed with the parents and other family members.

B. The parents were asked to identify some here-and-now activities and to encourage the client's involvement.

C. The parents and the client were given affirmation and reinforcement for the client's getting involved in here-and-now activities.

D. The client has been resistant to involving himself/herself in extracurricular social/recreational activities.

17. Teach Family about Double-Bind Messages (17)

A. The family was taught about double-bind messages that are inconsistent and contradictory and how they negatively impact family members.

B. The family was assisted in recognizing double-bind messages within the family that cause anxiety, confusion, and psychotic symptoms for the client.

C. The family was asked to make a commitment to stop using double-bind messages.

D. Family members were confronted when they used double-bind messages in family sessions.

E. The frequency of the instances of double-bind messages has decreased significantly, as reported by the client and observed within family therapy sessions.

18. Confront Indirect and Disjointed Communications (18)

A. In a family session, the parents were taught to make their communicating consistently clear and direct.

B. Role-play situations were used in a family session to give the parents an opportunity to practice clear and direct communications.

C. The parents were assisted in recognizing the negative impact that indirect and disjointed communication has on the client in terms of confusion and anxiety.

D. Confrontation was utilized with the parents when their communication became indirect and disjointed with the client, and the frequency of this dysfunctional style has diminished.

19. Reduce Family's Level of Criticism and Hostility (19)

A. Family sessions were held in which members were encouraged to express their feelings about the client and his/her illness.

B. Feelings of criticism and hostility toward the client were vented by members in family sessions.

C. The family members were supported and affirmed regarding the frustration and difficulty in living with the client and his/her illness.

D. The family members were helped to develop a genuine sense of understanding of the client and his/her illness.

E. The family members were encouraged to practice compassion toward the client and to be understanding of the lack of control the client has over his/her sometimes bizarre symptoms.

20. Assist Parents in Setting Limits on Inappropriate Behavior (20)

A. The parents were encouraged to express their thoughts and feelings about the client's inappropriate aggression and sexual behavior.

B. The parents were assisted in developing and setting firm limits (without hostility toward the client) on his/her inappropriate aggressive and sexual behavior.

C. Consistent support and encouragement were given to the parents for their efforts to set firm limits on the client.

D. The client has responded positively to the parents setting firm limits, and this has resulted in a reduction in inappropriate aggressive and sexual behavior.

21. Encourage Family to Express Feelings Regarding Illness (21)

A. Feelings of frustration, guilt, fear, and depression associated with the client's illness were normalized for family members.

B. Encouragement, support, and understanding were given to family members who shared their feelings about the client's illness and behavior patterns.

C. Family members were confronted and warned about the negative consequences of holding onto negative feelings about the client's illness.

22. Arrange Academic Opportunities (22)

A. Explore with the client and the parents the possibilities for ongoing academic training while the client is in treatment.

B. Arrange for the client to receive ongoing academic training and encourage his/her follow-through and skill development.

C. Although the client has shown a reduction in many of the psychotic symptoms, he/she is resistant to returning to the academic setting and dealing with the social and cognitive demands inherent in that setting.

23. Educate School Personnel on Client (23)

A. The parents were asked to sign a confidentiality release in order for the therapist and school officials to exchange information.

B. School officials were told what to expect from the client and encouraged to create a supportive, accepting environment for him/her.

C. School personnel have responded favorably to direction and have provided the client with the necessary structure and support in the academic setting.

D. School personnel have not responded favorably to direction and have not provided the client with the necessary structure and support in the academic setting.

24. Confront Illogical Speech (24)

A. The client was informed that his/her illogical speech would be gently confronted when they occur in order to refocus his/her thinking.

B. The client was confronted when his/her speech became illogical.

C. To each gentle confrontation the client has responded positively in a cooperative manner and worked to refocus his/her own thoughts.

D. Despite using gentle confrontation, the client still has found it frustrating and not effective in helping him/her refocus.

25. Encourage Focus on External Reality (25)

A. The client was reminded in clear terms of the difference between external reality and distorted fantasy.

B. The client was encouraged and directed to focus on the reality of the external world.

C. The client was directed to check things out with the therapist or others when he/she is confused or unsure of what is reality and what is fantasy.

D. The client has become more adept at differentiating between fantasy and reality and responding appropriately to external circumstances.

26. Help Differentiate Sources of Stimuli (26)

A. The client was assisted in developing skills to differentiate between sources of stimuli from self-generated messages and the reality of the external world.

B. Positive feedback and encouragement were given to the client for successfully differentiating stimuli.

C. The client struggles to differentiate between internal cognitive stimuli and reality-based stimuli.

D. The client was encouraged to consult others when he/she is unsure of the source of the stimuli.

E. The client is able to reliably differentiate between internal hallucinatory stimuli and external reality.

27. Restructure Irrational Beliefs (27)

A. The client's irrational beliefs were identified and restructured into reality-based phenomenon.

B. Each of the client's irrational beliefs was restructured using reality-based evidence.

C. Restructured beliefs were reinforced with the client and their daily use was encouraged.

D. The client's irrational beliefs have diminished and his/her thoughts are reality-based fairly consistently.

28. Interpret Inaccurate Perceptions and Bizarre Associations (28)

A. The client's inaccurate perceptions and bizarre associations were identified.

B. Each bizarre association and inaccurate perception was interpreted to the client as being reflective of unspoken fears of rejection or losing control.

C. The client was asked to use the new interpretations in his/her daily routine when the inaccurate perceptions and bizarre associations occur.

29. Set Limits on Aggressive/Sexual Behavior (29)

A. Firm limits were set for the client on his/her inappropriate aggressive and sexual behavior, along with specific consequences for violating each limit.

B. Appropriate anger and sexual behavior were identified for the client and reinforced.

C. The client was assisted in identifying triggers that precede inappropriate aggressive or sexual acts.

D. The client was taught several techniques to use in controlling his/her impulsiveness.

E. The client's inappropriate sexual and aggressive behavior has ceased as he/she has responded to the setting of firm limits on such behavior.

30. Monitor Daily Level of Functioning (30)

A. The client's daily level of functioning was monitored for reality orientation, personal hygiene, and affect appropriateness.

B. Feedback was given to the client on his/her progress in each area of activities of daily functioning.

C. The client was redirected when he/she was not doing as expected or progressing in each area of his/her daily functioning.

D. Positive progress in areas of daily function was reinforced and further development was encouraged.

E. The client's functioning within the activities of daily living continues to be problematic and shows a lack of progress.

31. Teach Alternative Social Interactions (31)

A. The client was taught new, positive social skills to be used with family and friends.

B. Role play and behavioral rehearsal were used to give the client the opportunity to practice each new social skill.

C. The client was asked to make a commitment to try the new social skills he/she has learned with either family or friends.

32. Demonstrate Acceptance (32)

A. Acceptance was demonstrated to the client through a calm, nurturing manner, eye contact, and active listening.

B. The acceptance demonstrated to the client through a calm, nurturing manner, eye contact, and active listening has reduced his/her fear and has allowed him/her to be more open.

C. Despite a calm, nurturing approach, eye contact, and active listening, the client still is fearful and closed in the counseling sessions.

D. The acceptance demonstrated to the client in counseling session has helped him/her relate more frequently and appropriately to family and others.

33. Reinforce Appropriate Responses to Others (33)

A. Appropriate social and emotional responses to others were identified with the client.

B. Role play and behavior rehearsal were used to give the client the opportunity to practice appropriate responses to others and to reinforce the responses.

C. The client's appropriate social and emotional responses to others were verbally encouraged and reinforced.

D. The client was gently confronted and redirected when his/her responses were not socially or emotionally appropriate to others.

34. Family Support Group Referral (34)

A. The options for a family support group were explored, and resistance to acknowledging the need for support was addressed.

B. The family was referred to a support group for family members who have a mentally ill loved one.

C. The positives of support groups were identified and the family was encouraged to attend at least one session.

D. The family members were confronted on their belief that they can "handle it on their own."

E. Despite encouragement, the family still is resistant to even trying a support group meeting.

RUNAWAY

CLIENT PRESENTATION

1. Running Away for More than a Day (1)*

A. The parents reported that the client has run away from home for more than one day on numerous occasions.

B. The client explained his/her running away was necessary for personal safety until things cooled off at home.

C. The client indicated that his/her running away is nothing to be concerned about.

D. The client has not run away from home since issues within the family have started to be addressed and resolved.

2. Running to Noncustodial Parent (2)

A. The client presented a pattern of running away to the noncustodial parent's home after he/she becomes upset with the custodial parent.

B. The client indicated reluctantly that running to the noncustodial parent's home when he/she is upset has enabled him/her to get his/her way.

C. The parents reported being unhappy with the client's pattern of running to the noncustodial parent, but felt helpless to do anything about it.

D. The client has stopped his/her runaway pattern as he/she has seen the custodial and noncustodial parent begin to work together in their parenting.

3. Running across State Lines (3)

A. The client reported running away from home and traveling to another state.

B. The client indicated that he/she has run away across state lines and has plans to do it again without getting caught.

C. The parents expressed fear that the client would run away again across state lines and never return.

D. The client made an agreement to not run away but to work instead on family issues in therapy sessions.

4. Running Away at Least Twice Overnight (4)

A. The client has run away from home overnight on two or more occasions.

B. The parents indicated the client has run away overnight on two occasions after he/she was confronted about his/her behavior.

C. The client has agreed to work on conflicts with parents in therapy sessions.

5. Running Away for More than 48 Hours (5)

A. The client has run away from home for 48 hours or more on a least one occasion.

---

* The numbers in parentheses correlate to the number of the Behavioral Definition statement in the companion chapter with same title in *The Adolescent Psychotherapy Treatment Planner* (Jongsma, Peterson, and McInnis) by John Wiley & Sons, 2000.

B. The client has run away for more than 48 hours and had to be returned home by the police.

C. The parents expressed fear that the client has definite plans to run away, as they have discovered him/her making arrangements.

D. The client has offered assurance that he/she does not plan to run away again.

6. Poor Self-Image (6)

A. The client presented with eyes downcast, low voice, and making numerous self-disparaging remarks.

B. The client reported he/she does not like himself/herself and feels ashamed of what he/she is.

C. There is a strong negative, dark, and shame-based quality to all comments the client makes regarding self and life in general.

D. The client has a quick, negative way of responding to any compliments or positive statements.

E. The client's sense of self-worth has increased as issues within the family have started to be addressed.

7. Home Environment (7)

A. The facade of a warm, trusting family has started to crumble as the client has begun telling of parents' neglect and emotional abuse.

B. The client expressed love toward the parents but said that the parents' fighting and drinking upset him/her.

C. The client has begun to express how he/she has never felt wanted or accepted by either parent.

D. The client described his/her home as chaotic, abusive, and sometimes violent.

E. Interviews with the family have brought the abuse and violence to a halt.

8. Conflict with Parents (8)

A. Anger and defiance are very evident in each of the client's responses to the parents' requests.

B. The client reported having numerous angry encounters with parents, teachers, and siblings.

C. The client stated he/she does not listen to what parents say or follow their "stupid rules."

D. The client's level of conflict with parents has begun to decrease as he/she has taken an active part in the family therapy sessions.

9. Victim of Abuse (9)

A. The client described incidents in which severe abusive punishments were used to address his/her misbehavior.

B. The client's claims of abuse have been reported to the protective services as mandated by law.

C. The client related a long history of parental emotional abuse that included being blamed for siblings' actions, called negative, hurtful names, and being shamed in front of others.

D. The client identified a pattern of both parents leaving the home for hours or days when conflict occurred.

E. The client has begun to verbalize insight into how his/her history of being abused has played a major role in his/her running away.

10. Trust (9)

A. The client presented in a cautious, mistrustful manner.

B. The client reported he/she does not trust anyone outside of his/her immediate family, and the immediate family is trusted only on a limited basis.

C. The client sees no one as being worthy of his/her trust and that is why he/she has to watch out for number one.

D. The client stated he/she has started to trust the therapist a little and that this is an uncomfortable feeling.

INTERVENTIONS IMPLEMENTED

1. Build Trust (1)*

A. Initial level of trust was established with the client through the use of unconditional positive regard.

B. Warm acceptance and active listening techniques were utilized to establish the basis for a trusting relationship with the client.

C. The client has formed a trust-based relationship and has started to share his/her feelings with the therapist.

D. Despite the use of active listening, warm acceptance, and unconditional positive regard, the client remains hesitant to trust and share.

2. Explore Causes of Pain (2)

A. The client was educated regarding the many aspects of emotional pain and how it exhibits itself.

B. The client was asked to list the situations that cause him/her to experience emotional and physical pain sufficient to motivate running away.

C. The client was asked to identify his/her pain threshold on a scale of 1 to 10 and at what point he/she begins to express the pain and how he/she does it.

D. The client revealed a history of abuse, neglect, and abandonment that has motivated his/her running away.

E. The client described an ongoing conflict of authority and control that motivated the running away.

3. Identify Positive Ways to Resolve Conflict (3)

A. The client was asked to list all the positive, constructive ways he/she could think of to resolve conflictual situations.

* The numbers in parentheses correlate to the number of the Therapeutic Intervention statement in the companion chapter with the same title in *The Adolescent Psychotherapy Treatment Planner* (Jongsma, Peterson, and McInnis) by John Wiley & Sons, 2000.

B. The client was assisted in choosing from his/her conflict-resolution list several constructive ways that conflictual situations could be addressed.

C. In monitoring the client's implementation of new conflict-resolution methods, he/she appears to be making an effort to put them into practice when a conflict presents itself.

D. The client is resistive to adopting constructive ways to resolve conflict and continues to project blame for all conflict onto others.

4. Teach Conflict-Resolution Methods (4)

A. The client was taught various methods of conflict resolution.

B. The client was assisted in selecting two to three resolution techniques to begin implementing into his/her daily life.

C. The client has successfully implemented effective conflict-resolution methods that have led to a more peaceful, respectful interaction within the family.

D. The client is resistive to adopting constructive ways to resolve conflict and continues to project blame for all conflict onto others.

5. Promote Healthy Family Communication (5)

A. Family therapy sessions were conducted to determine the patterns of communication within the family.

B. The parents were instructed in healthy, respectful communication behavior and asked to begin using it immediately.

C. In family sessions, healthy communication styles were modeled for family, and members were encouraged to implement them.

D. Unhealthy, disrespectful communication patterns were blocked and pointed out in family session, and new, healthy ones were substituted and tried.

E. Family members have begun to speak to each other with more respect, caring, and understanding instead of the inflammatory, critical, disrespectful style that was used previously.

6. Problem-Solving Group Referral (6)

A. The client was asked to attend a problem-solving group to improve his/her skills.

B. The client's attendance, participation, and progress were monitored, and verbal affirmation was given the client on progress made.

C. The client has refused to attend the problem-solving group.

7. Teach Acceptance of Responsibility (7)

A. The family and client were asked to assign a percentage to their part in causing conflict.

B. The family was assisted in sorting out the question of who is responsible for the problems until a general agreement was reached.

C. The client and parents were asked to use "I" statements to indicate acceptance of their part of the problem(s).

D. All family members have difficulty accepting their role in causing conflict, readily projecting the blame for conflict onto others.

8. Explore Child Abuse Evidence (8)

A. The client described instances from his/her own childhood of emotional, verbal, and physical abuse.

B. A genogram was constructed with the family that revealed a multigenerational pattern of child abuse that included the client.

C. A strong pattern of maternal physical and emotional neglect during the client's early years was uncovered while completing the biopsychosocial assessment with family.

D. The family has a multiyear history of involvement with protective services.

E. Past incidents of physical abuse were minimized by family members.

F. Family members would not directly answer questions related to physical or sexual abuse.

9. Procure Respite Care for Client (9)

A. Options for respite placement were presented to the client and family for their consideration and reaction.

B. Conditions for the placement of the client outside of the home were worked out with the family (i.e., visitation, criteria for returning home).

C. A schedule for individual and family sessions was established with the goal of working on the specific issues that need to be resolved before the client can return safely to the home.

D. The client has been removed from the home and placed in an alternative, protective setting while resolution of family issues is sought.

10. Assess Parental Substance Abuse (10)

A. The parents were referred to a local substance abuse agency for a full substance abuse assessment.

B. A substance abuse assessment was conducted on both parents.

C. It was recommended that the parents submit to a substance abuse assessment, which they declined as they saw no need for it.

D. It is evident that the parents have serious substance abuse problems, and a referral for treatment has been made.

11. Create Genogram (11)

A. The family was assisted in developing a multigenerational genogram that had a special focus on relationships between members and continuing unresolved conflicts.

B. The family was assisted in identifying relationship patterns and family conflicts that are still unresolved.

C. The parents were resistive to acknowledging long-standing conflict between extended family members and themselves and also resisted taking any responsibility for these conflicts.

D. The parents acknowledged long-standing conflicts with extended family members and indicated sincere interest in attempting to resolve these conflicts.

12. Resolve Extended Family Conflicts (12)

A. The parents were assisted in focusing on unresolved conflicts between themselves and their parents, and they were encouraged to take the necessary steps now to begin resolving those long-standing conflicts.

B. The parents were given several options, rituals, and acts of restoration that could resolve issues with their now-deceased parents.

C. The parents have taken constructive steps toward beginning a healing of broken relationships between themselves and other extended family members.

D. The parents have continued their feuding attitude toward extended family members and refused to take steps toward conflict resolution.

13. Identify Parental Rejection (13)

A. The parents were helped to look closely at their parenting style and techniques to identify any interaction, techniques, or messages that convey rejection to the client.

B. New approaches, techniques, and messages were explored to replace the negative ones that were identified as conveying rejection to the client.

C. The parents have acknowledged that they are conveying messages of rejection and have begun to attempt to convey affirmation and acceptance to the client.

D. The parents are resistive to any suggestion that they have harmed the client by messages of rejection.

14. Parenting Class Referral (14)

A. The parents were strongly encouraged to attend a parenting class, and resistance to the idea was resolved.

B. The parents' gains from attending parenting classes were affirmed and supported.

C. The parents have rejected the idea of attending classes to learn more effective parenting skills.

15. Assign Books on Parenting (15)

A. The parents were encouraged to read *Between Parent and Teenager* (Ginott) or *P.E.T.* (Gordon) or *Raising Responsible Children in a Permissive Society* (Glenn and Neilsen) to further their knowledge and understanding of adolescents.

B. The parents have followed through on reading about parenting techniques, and key ideas that they have learned from the reading were processed.

C. The parents have not followed through on reading about effective parenting and were redirected to do so.

D. The parents have begun to implement some of the new ideas learned from reading about effective parenting.

16. Help Parents Affirm and Value Client (16)

A. The parents were guided in looking at the things parents can do to make children feel affirmed, valued, and part of the family.

B. The parents were asked to list five affirming things they could begin to do as part of relating to and parenting the client.

C. A commitment was requested from the parents to implement and use consistently these affirming techniques.

D. The parents have made significant progress in implementing actions that affirm the client's value.

17. Identify and Communicate Unmet Needs (17)

A. The client was asked to make a complete list of all of his/her needs that he/she feels are not being met within the family system.

B. The client had difficulty identifying significant social, emotional, or physical needs.

C. The client listed many serious physical and emotional needs that have not been met within the family system.

D. The client read his/her list of unmet needs to the parents in family session, with the parents being instructed to just listen and affirm what they heard.

18. Teach Meeting Own Needs (18)

A. The client was assisted in looking at his/her unmet needs and deciding which of them the client could meet himself/herself.

B. The client was taught the value of meeting one's own needs whenever possible.

C. The client has taken healthy, constructive steps toward meeting some of his/her own emotional needs.

D. The client remains focused on blaming the parents for not meeting his/her needs and refuses to take constructive steps to meet his/her own needs.

19. Feelings about Home Exercise (19)

A. The client was asked to complete the "Home by Another Name" or "Undercover Assignment" exercise from *The Brief Adolescent Therapy Homework Planner* (Jongsma, Peterson, McInnis) to assist in externalizing issues that have been kept covert.

B. Verbal support and encouragement were given to the client to aid him/her in taking the risks to look at long-hidden, difficult, family conflict issues.

C. The client was firmly but respectfully confronted on his/her pattern of keeping secrets and shown how doing this has a negative impact on him/her and the family.

D. The client has revealed family conflict issues that have been denied and covered for a long time.

20. "Airing Your Grievances" Exercise (20)

A. The client was asked to complete the "Airing Your Grievances" exercise from *The Brief Adolescent Therapy Homework Planner* (Jongsma, Peterson, McInnis) to help him/her become capable of verbalizing and addressing important personal issues.

B. The parents were confronted about unrealistic developmental expectations or unrealistic solutions to adolescent issues.

C. Completing the "Airing Your Grievances" exercise has helped the client clarify and verbalize important personal issues.

D. The client has not completed the "Airing Your Grievances" exercise and was redirected to do so.

21. Encourage Respectful Verbalization of Feelings (21)

A. The client's angry and negative feelings were normalized as part of the education about feelings.

B. The client's expression of negative feelings and anger was encouraged, with an emphasis on being respectful and using "I" statements.

C. Fears and barriers to the client taking risks and sharing negative feelings were explored, and solutions that would allow him/her to express these angry feelings were suggested.

D. The client has begun to express feelings of anger and hurt that had been previously suppressed.

E. The client has found it very difficult to express his/her negative emotions and continues to suppress feelings like anger, hurt, frustration, and disappointment.

22. Teach Communication with Parents (22)

A. Ways to increase constructive, respectful communication between the client and the parents were identified, and a commitment from him/her was elicited to implement and consistently follow through on this style of communicating.

B. The client's implementation and follow-through were monitored, and the client was confronted regarding his/her inconsistent use of the new communication techniques.

23. Explore Fears of Independence (23)

A. The client's fears of independence were explored and challenged.

B. A list was created with the client to put in black and white the advantages and disadvantages of independence and dependence.

C. The client acknowledged having a lack of confidence in his/her ability to live independent of parents.

D. The client now seems to want to emancipate from the home responsibly.

24. Help Parents Promote Independence and Maturity (24)

A. The parents were asked to list all the specific ways they could help the client toward becoming more mature and independent.

B. The parents were assisted in selecting and implementing the best ways to foster independence and maturity with the client.

C. The parents are supporting, encouraging, and reinforcing the client in becoming more independent and mature.

25. Assist in Feelings Identification (25)

A. A printed list of feeling adjectives was used to increase the client's ability to identify and label his/her own feelings and those of others.

B. Various situations were created and presented to the client for him/her to identify how the individuals in those situations might be feeling.

C. The client was asked to keep a daily feelings journal and share it weekly with the therapist.

D. Although it is difficult for the client, he/she has begun to identify and express his/her feelings with some clarity and openness.

26. Develop/Promote Role Awareness (26)

A. The client was asked to describe his/her role in the family and how that role impacts his/her parents.

B. The client's awareness of how his/her role affects the parents was expanded by the therapist's perception and feedback.

C. The client was confronted with specific ways his/her role has a negative impact on the parents and their relationship.

D. The client was requested to take a leave of absence from his/her role of "assistant parent."

27. Identify Covert Family Conflicts (27)

A. In family sessions, the family was supported and assisted in identifying unresolved conflicts within the family that have not yet been addressed.

B. The family members were asked what were they willing to do to change things within the family and then asked if they were ready to free the client from being the symptom bearer of the family problem.

C. The client was prepared for letting go of the role of symptom bearer and coached about how that role could be replaced with a responsible, adjusted teenager.

28. Make Structural Changes within Family (28)

A. During a family session, the structure of the family was assessed to determine whether structural changes could increase healthy family interaction.

B. A structured intervention was developed from the assessment and implemented by the family.

C. The structured intervention that was implemented was reported to be working well.

29. Develop/Implement Strategic Change (29)

A. The family was assessed during family session to determine the strategic intervention that would best address family issues and increase their degree of healthy functioning.

B. A strategic intervention was developed with the family, who agreed to fully and consistently implement the intervention.

C. The strategic intervention was monitored and adjusted to maximize positive results.

D. All family members reported a positive impact from the newly implemented strategic intervention.

30. Arrange or Conduct Psychological Evaluation (30)

A. The client was referred for a complete psychological evaluation to establish or rule out affective disorder, psychotic process, ADHD, or substance abuse.

B. The parents were asked to sign a release for exchange of information and recommendations with the evaluation partner.

C. Significant emotional and behavioral problems were revealed through the psychological/psychiatric evaluation of the client.

D. It was confirmed that the client has serious substance abuse problems that need to be addressed in chemical dependence treatment.

E. The client was diagnosed with a serious mental illness that needs to be addressed through treatment.

F. The client was diagnosed with an attention-deficit disorder that contributes to his/her current behavioral problems.

31. Monitor Evaluation Follow-Through (31)

A. The family reported following through on each of the evaluation's recommendations.

B. The parents' failure to follow through on the psychological evaluation recommendations was addressed.

C. The parents' resistance and concerns about the client taking psychotropic medication were addressed, and the issue was resolved when the parents committed to a medication trial.

32. Contract for a Neutral Placement (32)

A. The parents and the client were assisted in developing a contract for the client's placement in a neutral setting as a temporary living arrangement.

B. Basic guidelines were established regarding the client living outside of the family, which included specification of the frequency of contact with parents and the nature of this contact.

C. A schedule for regular, consistent family sessions was established to continue to actively work on family conflicts while the client is living outside the family.

SEXUAL ABUSE PERPETRATOR

CLIENT PRESENTATION

1. Arrest and Conviction for a Sexual Offense (1)*

A. The client has been charged with and convicted of a sexual offense and ordered into treatment.

B. The client is currently on probation for a sexually related offense.

C. The client reported a history of repeated sexually related offenses.

D. The client has not been charged with or investigated for any sexual offense since he/she began treatment.

2. Sexual Abuse of Younger Victim (2)

A. The client has been arrested and convicted for sexually abusing a younger sibling.

B. The client has been charged with sexually abusing a younger child in his/her community.

C. The client is suspected of sexually abusing his/her younger siblings and other younger children in the community.

D. There have been no further accusations or charges of abuse brought against the client since he/she started treatment.

3. Language with Sexual Content (3)

A. The client presented as being unusally open with talk that was very sexually explicit.

B. It is reported by teachers and other adults that the client's talk frequently contains sexual innuendos and references.

C. The client confirmed that he/she likes to talk about sexual things.

D. The client's sexual references have diminished significantly.

4. Sexualized Relationships (4)

A. The client's relationships have a definite and consistent sexual context to them.

B. The client seemed to quickly sexualize most if not all relationships.

C. The client acknowledged having sexual feelings toward most people with whom he/she relates.

D. The client has started to consciously work at forming genuine, respectful relationships.

5. Sexually Preoccupied (5)

A. The client seemed to be sexually preoccupied a majority of his/her free time.

B. The client reported having frequent thoughts, dreams, and fantasies about sexual things.

C. The client indicated that whenever his/her mind wanders it always goes to sexual things.

* The numbers in parentheses correlate to the number of the Behavioral Definition statement in the companion chapter with same title in *The Adolescent Psychotherapy Treatment Planner* (Jongsma, Peterson, and McInnis) by John Wiley & Sons, 2000.

D. The client has engaged in the use of pornographic magazines, videos, and Internet sites.

E. The client has recently reported a decrease in his/her sexual preoccupation and now will think of other things.

6. Sexual Self-Interest (5)

A. The client reported a history of numerous sexual encounters with partners with whom he/she had little or no emotional attachment.

B. The described sexual behaviors are focused on self-gratification only and with no interest in the needs or concerns of the other partner.

C. The client indicated he/she sees sexual satisfaction as his/her right.

D. The client has begun working at changing his/her thinking regarding the issue of sexual self-interest.

7. Family History of Incest (6)

A. The client and parents reported a multigenerational pattern of sexual abuse within the family.

B. The parents indicated that several family members have been convicted of sexually related offenses that include incest.

C. The parents denied any history of incest, despite legal documents that indicate otherwise.

D. The client revealed several family secrets that involved incestuous relationships between family members.

8. Childhood Sex Abuse (7)

A. The client is very guarded and closed about his/her childhood sex abuse.

B. The client provided specific examples from his/her childhood of instances in which he/she was sexually abused.

C. The client has begun to verbalize some insight and understanding into how previous instances of childhood pain are connected to his/her acts of sexual perpetration and a sense of detachment from others.

9. Use of Pornographic Materials (8)

A. The client admitted having in his/her possession a significant amount of sexually explicit videos and magazines.

B. The client acknowledged being caught by parents visiting adult Internet sites and calling 900 numbers.

C. The client admitted spending a large portion of his/her free time with a variety of pornographic materials.

D. The client reported he/she has disposed of all his/her pornographic materials but experienced some difficulty in doing so.

INTERVENTIONS IMPLEMENTED

1. Build Trust (1)*

A. Initial trust level was established with the client through the use of unconditional positive regard.

B. Warm acceptance and active listening techniques were utilized to establish the base for a trusting relationship where thoughts and feelings could be openly shared.

C. The client has formed a trust-based relationship and has started to share openly his/her thoughts and feelings.

D. Despite the use of active listening, warm acceptance, and unconditional positive regard, the client remains guarded, mistrustful, and willing to disclose only on a superficial level.

2. Initiate Self-Disclosure (2)

A. A celebrity interview format was utilized to start the client talking about nonthreatening topics.

B. The client's self-disclosures were affirmed, encouraged, and reinforced.

C. Despite the use of nonthreatening approaches, the client remained guarded and willing to disclose only superficial information.

3. Develop a No-Sexual-Contact Agreement (3)

A. The client and family were assisted in developing a no-sexual-contact agreement between the client and any others.

B. The parents agreed to implement and enforce the no-sexual-contact contract.

C. The client was asked to and did sign the no-sexual-contact agreement.

4. Monitor No-Sexual-Contact Agreement (4)

A. The no-sexual-contact agreement was monitored for the parents' and the client's follow-through.

B. The parents were confronted on their inconsistency of follow-through on enforcing the no-sexual-contact agreement.

C. The parents were given positive feedback on enforcing and monitoring the no-sexual-contact agreement.

D. The client was given positive verbal feedback on his/her compliance in abiding by the no-sexual-contact agreement.

E. The client was confronted on his/her pushing the limits of the no-sexual-contact agreement.

5. Restrictive Setting Referral (5)

A. Since the client failed to keep the no-sexual-contact agreement, a more restrictive, supervised, treatment setting was sought for him/her.

B. The client was referred to a 24-hour residential treatment program specifically designed for adolescent sexual offenders.

* The numbers in parentheses correlate to the number of the Therapeutic Intervention statement in the companion chapter with the same title in *The Adolescent Psychotherapy Treatment Planner* (Jongsma, Peterson, and McInnis) by John Wiley & Sons, 2000.

C. The client completed an admission interview and was accepted for placement in a residential treatment program for adolescent sexual offenders.

6. Explore Incidents of Sexual Misconduct (6)

A. The client was asked to describe in detail each incident of sexual misconduct he/she committed.

B. The client's history of incidents of sexual misconduct was processed and examined for incompleteness and lack of honesty.

C. The client expressed ownership for his/her sexual misconduct.

D. Denial and rationalizations were offered by the client for his/her sexual misconduct.

7. "Getting Started" Exercise (7)

A. The client was asked to complete and process the "Getting Started" exercise from *The Brief Adolescent Therapy Homework Planner* (Jongsma, Peterson, McInnis) to familiarize him/her with treatment-specific terminology.

B. The client was assisted in gaining a working knowledge of key treatment concepts.

C. The client was encouraged to ask questions about any aspects of or concepts related to his/her treatment.

8. Educate about Inappropriate Sexual Behavior and Offender Cycle (8)

A. The client was educated about inappropriate sexual behavior and the offender cycle.

B. All questions of the client about the offender cycle were answered.

C. Key points of the necessity of maintaining appropriate sexual boundaries were clarified and reinforced with the client.

9. Increase Awareness and Respect of Boundaries (9)

A. The client was assisted in building his/her awareness of and respect for personal boundaries.

B. The client's barriers to being aware of personal boundaries were identified and addressed.

C. The client was encouraged to ask questions when he/she was in doubt about personal boundaries.

D. Key points of the necessity of maintaining appropriate boundaries were clarified and reinforced with the client.

10. Conduct Role Plays to Teach Boundaries (10)

A. Role plays were used with the client to practice maintaining appropriate boundaries in social situations.

B. The client was given feedback regarding his/her actions in the role plays, and appropriate behaviors were modeled for him/her.

C. The client was given positive feedback for honoring and respecting appropriate personal boundaries.

11. Confront Sexual References in Speech/Behavior (11)

A. Sexual references in the client's speech and behavior were pointed out to him/her.

B. The client was assisted in increasing his/her awareness of sexual references in his/her speech and behaviors.

C. The client's feelings and thoughts that underlie the sexual references were explored and processed.

D. The client was resistive to sexual references being pointed out in his/her speech and behavior.

12. Assign Gathering of Feedback about Sexualized Speech (12)

A. The client was asked to gather feedback from others regarding sexual references they note in the client's speech and behavior.

B. Feedback that was gathered by the client from others was processed and language options were explored.

C. The client was encouraged to identify and implement alternative behavior and language patterns.

13. Gather Sexual History (13)

A. A thorough sexual history was collected from the client and the parents.

B. The client and family were confronted on the vagueness of the information given regarding their sexual histories.

C. The client and family provided complete and honest information regarding the client's sexual history.

14. Explore for Sexual Abuse (14)

A. The client's childhood history was gently explored for sexual abuse.

B. The client was asked specifically how others respected or violated his/her physical boundaries as a child.

C. The client was presented with data on the percent of perpetrators who are themselves abused, and the data was processed for his/her response.

D. The possibility of the client being a victim of sexual abuse was explored with his/her parents.

E. The client and the parents acknowledged that the client has been a victim of sexual abuse.

15. Identify Consequences of Sexual Abuse (15)

A. The client was asked to list the consequences of being a victim of sexual abuse.

B. The list of consequences resulting from being a victim of sexual abuse was processed with the client.

C. The client was assisted in making the connection between his/her own victimization and the development of his/her current attitudes and patterns of sexual abuse perpetration.

D. The client was unable to identify any concrete consequences of being a victim of sexual abuse and stated that the abuse had no impact on his/her current behavior.

16. **Play Games to Initiate Disclosure (16)**

A. The UnGame (The UnGame Company) and the Talking, Feeling, and Doing Game (Creative Therapeutics) were played with the client to give him/her opportunities to share things about himself/herself and to increase self-awareness.

B. The client was assisted in identifying his/her likes and dislikes to help expand self-awareness.

C. Positive affirmation and reinforcement were given to the client's self-disclosures while playing The UnGame.

17. **Teach Feelings Identification (17)**

A. The client was taught key aspects of identifying feelings.

B. Feelings' charts and other aids were used to give the client experience in identifying and expressing feelings.

C. The client was reinforced for identifying, labeling, and expressing himself/herself in counseling sessions.

D. Despite education, charts, and assistance, the client still seemed to ignore and avoid his/her feelings.

18. **Reinforce Feeling Recognition (18)**

A. The client was reminded of the positive benefits of identifying, labeling, and expressing his/her own feelings and of being sensitive to the feelings of others.

B. The client was given feedback on each occasion where he/she failed to show an awareness of the feelings of others.

C. Positive reinforcement was given to the client on each occasion where he/she showed recognition of the feelings of others without outside direction.

19. **Support Client in Describing Sexual Victimization (19)**

A. Barriers and defenses that prevented the client's openness regarding his/her being sexually abused were addressed and removed.

B. The client's fears about disclosing the details of his/her own sexual abuse were processed and resolved.

C. The client was encouraged and supported in telling the story of his/her own sexual victimization.

D. Even with support and encouragement, the client was unable to tell any of the details related to his/her own sexual abuse.

20. **Support Client Telling Parents of Victimization (20)**

A. The client's fears about revealing his/her sexual victimization to his/her parents were identified, processed, and resolved.

B. The worse-case-scenario approach was used in preparing the client to tell parents about his/her sexual victimization.

C. The client was assisted and supported in telling the story of his/her own sexual abuse to the parents.

D. The client's experience of telling the story of abuse to the parents was processed.

E. Even with preparation, assistance, and support, the client refused to tell parents the story of his/her sexual abuse experience and again started denying any such experience.

21. Survivors' Support Group Referral (21)

A. The benefits of attending a support group for survivors of sexual abuse was identified and reinforced.

B. The client was referred to a support group for survivors of sexual abuse and encouraged to attend.

C. Resistance on the client's part to attending a support group for survivors of sexual abuse was explored and addressed.

D. The client's positive response to attending a group for survivors of sexual abuse was reinforced, and further attendance was encouraged.

22. Gather History of Emotional/Physical Abuse (22)

A. The client's history was explored for evidence of him/her being a victim of physical or emotional abuse.

B. The client was open to giving a detailed history in all areas except parental methods of discipline.

C. The client was resistive to his/her history being explored, providing only superficial information and some tangential anecdotes.

23. Perpetrator Group Treatment Referral (23)

A. The need for group treatment for sexual perpetrators was explained to the client.

B. The client was referred to a group treatment program specifically developed for sex offenders.

C. The client's acceptance of group treatment was affirmed and reinforced.

D. The client was very resistive to the referral to a group therapy treatment program for sex offenders.

24. Identify Exploitive Beliefs (24)

A. The client was assisted in identifying and processing his/her thoughts and beliefs that gave him/her justification for being sexually abusive.

B. The client was assisted in identifying socially acceptable thoughts that are respectful and not exploitive of others.

C. New respectful, nonexploitive thoughts were affirmed and reinforced with the client as he/she used them in daily interactions.

D. The client's justification for holding to old beliefs and resistance to new respectful, nonexploitive ones was confronted and addressed.

25. Connect Thinking Errors to Offending Behaviors (25)

A. The client was educated on how thinking errors can have a significant impact on sexual offending behavior.

B. The client was assisted in identifying his/her own thinking errors and connecting them with his/her sexual offending behaviors.

C. Various ways to correct thinking errors were explored with the client.

D. The client struggled to make connections between his/her thinking errors and offending behaviors, and only with assistance did he/she make a weak connection.

26. Conduct Psychological Testing (26)

A. Psychological testing was arranged for the client to confirm or rule out severe emotional issues or psychopathology.

B. The client was cooperative with all aspects of the psychological evaluation.

C. The client was uncooperative with the psychological testing to the point that it could not be completed.

D. The psychological testing results indicated that the client has severe emotional issues that underlie his/her perpetration of sexual abuse.

E. No significant or severe emotional issues were discovered by the psychological testing.

27. Present Psychological Evaluation Feedback (27)

A. The results of the psychological testing were presented and interpreted to the client, and his/her questions were answered.

B. The recommendations of the testing for ongoing treatment were emphasized with the client.

C. The client was asked to make a commitment to follow through in completing all the recommendations of the psychological testing.

D. The client was disinterested in the psychological evaluation recommendations and would not make a commitment to follow through on them.

28. Medication Referral (28)

A. The client was referred for a physician evaluation for psychotropic medications.

B. The client followed the recommendations and completed the physician evaluation for possible medications.

C. Psychotropic medications have been ordered for the client and he/she has agreed to take them consistently.

29. Monitor Medications (29)

A. The client's psychotropic medication was monitored for effectiveness and for the client's compliance in taking them as prescribed.

B. The client and parents were directed and encouraged to report any side effects of the psychotropic medication to the prescribing physician.

C. The client was confronted on his/her failure to take the medications as prescribed.

D. The client's compliance and the overall effectiveness of the psychotropic medication were reported to the prescribing physician.

30. "Anger Control" Exercise (30)

A. The client was asked to complete the "Anger Control" exercise from *The Brief Adolescent Therapy Homework Planner* (Jongsma, Peterson, McInnis) to increase anger recognition and ways to effectively control it.

B. The client was asked to complete an exercise from the *Anger Workbook* (Blodeau) to increase anger recognition and ways to effectively control it.

C. The "Anger Control" exercise was processed, and gains in ways to control anger were identified and affirmed.

D. The client has learned new strategies to control his/her anger and has reported that these have been effective in helping him/her manage anger more effectively.

31. Anger Management/Assertiveness Group Referral (31)

A. The client was referred to an assertiveness training group to build skills in effectively controlling angry feelings.

B. The client was referred to an anger management group to build skills in effectively controlling angry feelings.

C. The benefits and gains from attending an assertiveness/anger management group were explored and identified.

D. The client followed through on the referral to anger management/assertiveness group and reported positive gains.

32. Encourage Increased Peer Involvement (32)

A. The client was helped to identify specific ways he/she could increase positive social involvement with peers.

B. Barriers that have held the client back from involvement with peers were explored, processed, and removed.

C. The client was asked to identify two ways to increase socialization that he/she would like to try and then to plan how he/she would go about implementing them.

D. Assistance and encouragement did not seem to reduce the client's resistance to increasing peer involvement.

E. The client has successfully increased his/her positive social involvement with peers.

33. Role-Play Peer Interaction (33)

A. Role plays of peer social situations were used to give the client the opportunity to build confidence and comfort with peer interactions.

B. The experience of the social situation role plays was processed to reinforce gains.

C. The client reported that he/she is feeling more confident and comfortable with peer interactions.

34. Promote New Social Activity (34)

A. A list of possible new social activities was developed with the client, and he/she was asked to choose one to implement each week.

B. The client was monitored for his/her compliance of trying one new social activity each week.

C. The client processed the experience of the new social activity and identified the specific gains he/she obtained from the experience.

D. The client's failure to attempt a new social activity was explored and addressed.

35. Assign Initiating Peer Conversation (35)

A. The client's fears and inhibitions associated with conversations with peers were explored and processed.

B. The client was asked to engage a peer in conversation once daily.

C. The client's experience of engaging a peer in daily conversation was processed and gains were identified and reinforced.

D. The client's lack of follow-through on engaging a peer in daily conversation was explored and addressed.

36. Experiential Camp Referral (36)

A. The benefits of an experiential camp were explored and identified with the client.

B. The client was referred to an experiential camp to assist in building his/her interpersonal skills and self-confidence.

C. The camp experience was processed with the client, and gains were identified and reinforced.

D. The client reported that the experiential camp was of little positive benefit to him/her.

E. The client has refused to follow through with the referral to the experiential camp.

37. Assign Books on Dating (37)

A. The client was asked to read *Dating for Dummies* (Browne) or *The Complete Idiot's Guide to Dating* (Kurinsky) to help his/her awareness of appropriate and inappropriate behavior with the opposite sex.

B. All questions raised by the client's reading of dating books were answered and processed.

C. Role play was used to further build the client's relationship skills and awareness of appropriate behavior with the opposite sex.

D. The client politely declined to read dating books that were recommended.

38. Teach SAFE Formula for Relationships (38)

A. The SAFE formula for relationships (avoid relationships that are Secret, Abusive, used to avoid Feelings, or Empty of caring and commitment) was taught to the client.

B. All the client's questions about the SAFE formula were addressed and answered.

C. The client was given various scenarios of relationships and asked how they did or did not fit the SAFE formula.

D. The client was assisted in identifying how to implement the SAFE formula into his/her daily life.

E. The client was monitored and redirected in his/her use of the SAFE formula.

F. Positive feedback and reinforcement were given to the client for consistently putting the SAFE formula into daily practice.

39. Explore Family Patterns of Sexual Abuse (39)

A. A genogram was developed with the family that depicted the extended family's boundary-breaking patterns of interaction and identified members' inappropriate sexual behavior.

B. Boundary-breaking patterns of interaction and sexual abuse behavior identified by the genogram were processed and addressed with the family.

C. Ways to begin breaking unhealthy patterns of interaction and sexual behavior were explored with the family.

40. Explore Family Sexual Patterns, Beliefs, Behaviors (40)

A. Family sessions were conducted in which the family members' sexual patterns, beliefs, and behaviors were explored and identified.

B. The family was assisted in identifying which sexual patterns, beliefs, and behaviors need to be changed and coached on how they might begin to go about doing it.

C. The family was encouraged to implement their planned changes of identified inappropriate sexual patterns, beliefs, and behaviors.

D. The family members were confronted on their resistance to moving beyond identification and changing the identified unhealthy sexual patterns, beliefs, and behaviors.

41. Develop/Implement Structural Intervention (41)

A. Family sessions were conducted in which structural interventions were developed, specific plans for implementation made, and a verbal commitment elicited for follow-through.

B. Structural interventions were monitored for their effectiveness and adjusted as needed.

C. The family was monitored and encouraged regarding their follow-through on the structural interventions that they developed.

D. The family's lack of follow-through on structural interventions was confronted, addressed, and resolved.

42. Assign Increased Involvement of Detached Parent (42)

A. A family session was conducted to implement the strategic intervention of directing the detached parent to take charge of the client's sexual education and behavior.

B. Guidance and encouragement were provided to the detached parent in following through on becoming active in the client's supervision and sex education.

C. The detached parent's follow-through was monitored, and all aspects of positive implementation were affirmed and reinforced.

D. The inconsistent follow-through of the detached parent on the strategic intervention was addressed with him/her.

43. Parents' Support Group Referral (43)

A. The positive benefits of attending a support group for the parents of perpetrators were identified with the parents.

B. The parents' were made aware of times and locations of support group meetings and encouraged to attend.

C. The parents' resistance and barriers to attending a support group for the parents of perpetrators were addressed and resolved.

44. Parenting Education Group Referral (44)

A. The parents strengths and weaknesses in parenting were explored.

B. Concerns of the parents about parenting teens were explored and processed.

C. The parents were referred to an education group on parenting teenagers.

D. The parents accepted the referral to an education group on parenting techniques and have begun to attend the meetings.

E. The parents have refused to accept a referral to a parenting education group.

45. Assign Books on Parenting (45)

A. It was suggested that the parents read books such as *Between Parent and Teenager* (Ginott) to expand their understanding of teens and to build their parenting skills.

B. Knowledge gained by the parents from reading books on parenting techniques was processed and key concepts were reinforced.

C. The parents read small portions of the books that were suggested and processed what information they had gained.

D. The parents have not followed through on the recommendation to read any of the material recommended on effective parenting techniques.

46. Develop New Family Rituals (46)

A. The members were educated on the meaning, use, and benefits of establishing rituals for the family.

B. The family was assisted in identifying and developing family rituals of transition, healing, belonging, and identity that would increase family structure, connection, and meaning.

C. Ways to implement the new family rituals were explored and agreed to.

D. Continued work to establish the family rituals was encouraged and reinforced.

47. Feelings' Awareness Exercises (47)

A. The client was asked to complete the exercise "Your Feelings and Beyond" or "Surface Behavior/Inner Feelings" from *The Brief Adolescent Therapy Homework Planner* (Jongsma, Peterson, McInnis) to expand his/her awareness of feelings.

B. A variety of scenarios were given to the client to help him/her identify how he/she would feel and how he/she thought others might feel in a given situation.

C. The client was gently confronted and helped to recognize situations where he/she was showing a lack of awareness of others' feelings.

D. The client has demonstrated an increased ability to recognize and express his/her own feelings as well as to recognize the feelings of others.

48. Assign Fantasy Journal (48)

A. The client was asked to keep a daily journal of his/her sexual fantasies.

B. The client's sexual fantasy journal was reviewed for patterns of appropriate and inappropriate fantasies in order to provide feedback, redirection, and reinforcement.

C. The client was worked with to make his/her journal entries less vague and more specific.

D. The client was confronted on his/her journal entries that lacked openness and honesty.

E. The client's sexual fantasy journal material shows evidence of a preoccupation with inappropriate sexual urges.

F. The client's sexual fantasy journal material shows evidence of only appropriate and expected sexual thoughts.

49. Teach Masturbatory Satiation Technique (49)

A. Instruction was given to the client regarding implementing a masturbatory satiation technique.

B. The client was asked to make a commitment to implementing and following through with the masturbatory satiation technique.

C. The client's tapes were reviewed and confirmed compliance with the masturbatory satiation technique.

D. The client's failure to follow through with the masturbatory satiation technique was confronted and processed.

50. Define Appropriate/Inappropriate Sexual Fantasies (50)

A. The client was asked to a make a list of the major themes of each of his/her sexual fantasies.

B. Education and guidance were given to the client concerning what constitutes an appropriate and inappropriate sexual fantasy.

C. The client was assisted in creating appropriate sexual fantasies.

D. Feelings of other parties that were a part of the client's sexual fantasies were reflected to the client to increase his/her sensitivity to others.

E. The client was given feedback that rejected fantasies involving pain and exploitation as inappropriate.

51. Assess Sincerity of Remorse (51)

A. The client was asked to talk about his/her feelings regarding the victim(s) and his/her acts of perpetration.

B. The sincerity of the client's remorse was assessed to determine his/her ability to make a genuine apology for the abuse.

C. The sincerity of the client's remorse for his/her sexual abuse was questionable.

D. The client seemed sincere in his/her remorse and regret for his/her acts of sexual abuse.

52. "Opening the Door to Forgiveness" Exercise (52)

A. The client was asked to complete the "Opening the Door to Forgiveness" exercise from *The Brief Adolescent Therapy Homework Planner* (Jongsma, Peterson, and McInnis) to prepare him/her to apologize to the victim and to forgive himself/herself.

B. The client's barriers to making a genuine apology were addressed and processed to their resolution.

C. The client still does not appear to be ready to apologize for his/her acts of sexual abuse.

D. The client does appear to be ready to make a genuine apology for his/her acts of sexual abuse.

53. Letter of Apology (53)

A. The purpose and benefit of writing a letter of apology to the victims of his/her sexual abuse were explored and processed with the client.

B. The client was asked to write a letter of apology to his/her victim that is genuine.

C. The client's written letter of apology was presented and processed, and feedback was given on his/her letter of apology regarding its sincerity and genuineness.

D. The client was given direct feedback on the lack of sincerity and genuineness in his/her letter of apology.

54. Role-Play Verbal Apology (54)

A. Role play was used with the client to assess his/her readiness to verbally apologize to the victim and to evaluate what further work needs to be done.

B. Role plays revealed that the client is ready to make an apology to the victim, and that process was set in motion.

C. Role plays clearly identified the issues that the client still needs to work on in order for him/her to be at the point of making an apology.

D. Role reversal was used with the client to further his/her sensitivity to the feelings and reactions of the victim.

55. Support Apology to Victim and Family (55)

A. A family session was conducted in which the client, in the presence of his/her family, apologized to the victim and victim's family.

B. The apology session was processed with the client, and his/her feelings were identified and expressed.

C. The client's follow-through on giving a sincere, genuine apology was affirmed and reinforced.

56. Identify Relapse Triggers (56)

A. Education was provided to the client regarding identifying, recognizing, and handling triggers that could cause a relapse into perpetrating sexual abuse.

B. The client was assisted in specifically identifying his/her sexual abuse relapse triggers.

C. The importance of maintaining awareness of sexual abuse relapse triggers was emphasized with the client.

57. Teach Coping Strategies for Relapse Triggers (57)

A. The need for behavioral and cognitive coping strategies for sexual abuse relapse triggers were presented and explained to the client.

B. Specific behavioral and cognitive strategies were developed for each of the client's identified sexual abuse relapse triggers.

C. Role play and behavioral rehearsal were used for the client to practice implementing the behavioral and cognitive coping strategies developed for his/her relapse triggers.

D. The client was reminded of the importance of maintaining an awareness of relapse triggers and timely use of the cognitive and behavioral strategies.

58. Develop and Process an Aftercare Plan (58)

A. The client was educated on the components of an effective aftercare plan to prevent future sexual abuse perpetration.

B. The client was asked to develop a written aftercare plan.

C. The aftercare plan developed by the client was processed in a family session, and family input and feedback was incorporated into a revised aftercare plan.

D. A copy of the finalized aftercare plan was given to each family member.

E. The client was assisted in implementing his/her aftercare plan.

F. The client was monitored and redirected for implementation and follow-through on his/her aftercare plan.

59. Suggest Periodic Checkups (59)

A. The value of periodic behavioral/emotional/cognitive checkups was presented to the client and his/her family as part of the aftercare plan.

B. The client and family were requested and encouraged to make a commitment to a system of periodic checkups as part of the aftercare plan.

C. Periodic checkups were made part of the client's aftercare plan, and follow-through was monitored.

D. The client and family were confronted on their failure to follow through on their commitment to periodic follow-up appointments.

60. Hold Checkups and Give Feedback (60)

A. Regular checkup sessions were held in which the client's aftercare plan was reviewed for its effectiveness and his/her follow-through with its components.

B. After review, the client was given feedback on the aftercare plan and necessary adjustments were suggested.

C. The client's failure to follow through with the aftercare plan was identified, addressed, and resolved.

61. Sex Offender Risk Assessment Referral (61)

A. The client was referred to complete a sex offender risk assessment.

B. The client followed through on the referral and completed a specific sex offender assessment.

C. Despite encouragement, the client refused to follow through with the recommended sexual offender risk assessment referral.

62. Report Revealed Sexual Offenses (62)

A. The client was informed of the therapist's legal requirement to report any sexual offenses that are revealed to him/her.

B. Sexual offenses revealed by the client were reported to the appropriate authorities.

63. Process Sexual Abuse Investigation (63)

A. The client reported the outcome of the investigation and the results were processed.

B. Issues of responsibility for behavior and respecting personal boundaries were processed in regard to the incident of sexual abuse perpetration.

C. The client was firmly confronted on his/her failure to take responsibility for the incidents of sexual abuse perpetration.

SEXUAL ABUSE VICTIM

CLIENT PRESENTATION

1. Self-Report of Sexual Abuse (1)*

A. The client reported that he/she has been sexually abused.

B. The client was guarded and evasive when being questioned about whether he/she has ever been sexually abused.

C. The client has previously reported to being sexually abused, but has since recanted these earlier statements.

D. The client has verbally denied being sexually abused, although there is other evidence to suggest that he/she has been abused.

2. Physical Signs of Sexual Abuse (2)

A. The medical examination revealed physical signs of sexual abuse.

B. The medical examination did not reveal any physical signs of sexual abuse.

3. Vague Memories of Sexual Abuse (3)

A. The client reported that he/she has vague memories of inappropriate childhood sexual contact.

B. The client's vague memories of inappropriate childhood sexual contact have been corroborated by significant others.

C. The client's vague memories of inappropriate childhood sexual contact have not been corroborated by significant others.

4. Strong Interest in Sexuality Issues (4)

A. The client has displayed a strong interest in or curiosity about issues related to sexuality since his/her sexual victimization.

B. The client exhibited a strong interest in or curiosity about issues related to sexuality in the therapy session.

C. The client's strong interest in or curiosity about issues related to sexuality has masked deeper feelings of sadness, hurt, and helplessness about his/her own sexual victimization.

D. The client has demonstrated less preoccupation with issues related to sexuality since addressing his/her own sexual abuse issues.

5. Sexual Promiscuity/Sexualization of Relationships (5)

A. The client has become sexually promiscuous since being sexually abused.

B. The client has demonstrated a pattern of sexualizing many of his/her interactions with others.

---

* The numbers in parentheses correlate to the number of the Behavioral Definition statement in the companion chapter with same title in *The Adolescent Psychotherapy Treatment Planner* (Jongsma, Peterson, and McInnis) by John Wiley & Sons, 2000.

C. The client's sexual promiscuity and sexualization of relationships has arisen out of his/her underlying feelings of sadness, anger, hurt, and vulnerability about the past sexual abuse.

D. The client acknowledged that he/she engages in frequent seductive or sexually promiscuous behavior to meet his/her unmet dependency needs.

E. The client has successfully worked through his/her thoughts and feelings about the past sexual abuse and eliminated his/her pattern of engaging in overly seductive or sexually promiscuous behavior.

6. Recurrent and Intrusive Recollections of Sexual Abuse (6)

A. The client has experienced recurrent, intrusive, and distressing recollections of the past sexual abuse.

B. The client has reexperienced intrusive and distressing recollections of the past sexual abuse after coming into contact with the perpetrator and/or having exposure to sexual topics.

C. The client denied being troubled any longer by intrusive recollections of the sexual abuse.

7. Recurrent Nightmares (6)

A. The client has experienced recurrent nightmares of the past sexual abuse.

B. The client reported that he/she continues to be troubled by recurrent nightmares of the past sexual abuse.

C. The client has reexperienced nightmares of the sexual abuse since coming into contact with the perpetrator and/or being exposed to sexual topics.

D. The client stated that he/she is no longer troubled by nightmares of the past sexual abuse.

8. Dissociative Flashbacks, Delusions, or Hallucinations (7)

A. The client reported experiencing dissociative flashbacks of the past sexual abuse.

B. The client reported experiencing delusions and hallucinations related to the past sexual abuse.

C. The client reported reexperiencing dissociative flashbacks, delusions, or hallucinations since coming into contact with the perpetrator and/or being exposed to sexual topics.

D. The client stated that dissociative flashbacks, delusions, or hallucinations have ceased.

9. Anger and Rage (8)

A. The client expressed strong feelings of anger and rage about the past sexual abuse.

B. The client has exhibited frequent angry outbursts and episodes of rage since the onset of the sexual abuse.

C. The frequency and intensity of the client's angry outbursts have decreased since he/she has felt more secure and started to work through his/her feelings about the sexual abuse.

D. The intensity of the client's anger has decreased whenever he/she talks about the past sexual abuse.

E. The client has demonstrated a reduction in the frequency and intensity of his/her angry outbursts and episodes of rage.

10. Disturbance of Mood and Affect (9)

A. The client has experienced frequent and prolonged periods of depression, anxiety, and irritability since the sexual abuse occurred.

B. The client appeared visibly depressed when talking about the sexual abuse.

C. The client appeared anxious when talking about the sexual abuse.

D. The client's moods have gradually started to stabilize as he/she works through his/her feelings of sadness, anxiety, insecurity, and anger about the past sexual abuse.

E. The client's moods have stabilized and he/she reports no longer being troubled by frequent or prolonged periods of depression, anxiety, or irritability.

11. Fearfulness/Distrust (10)

A. The client stated that he/she has felt strong feelings of fearfulness and a marked distrust of others since being sexually abused.

B. The client's fearfulness has slowly started to diminish and he/she is beginning to establish trust with significant others.

C. The strong support from family and individuals outside the family has helped to decrease the client's fearfulness and distrust.

D. The client has successfully worked through many of his/her feelings surrounding the sexual abuse and has established close, trusting relationships with significant others.

12. Social Withdrawal (10)

A. The client has become significantly more withdrawn from others since the onset of the sexual abuse.

B. The client appeared detached and withdrawn in today's therapy session when the topic of the sexual abuse was being discussed.

C. The client acknowledged that he/she has become more withdrawn because of his/her feelings of low self-esteem and distrust of others.

D. The client has started to become more assertive and outgoing in interactions with family members, significant adults, and peers.

13. Family Denial (10)

A. The family members present in today's therapy session stated that they do not believe that the client was sexually abused.

B. The client's family members are currently divided about whether to believe the client's report that he/she has been sexually abused.

C. The client's family members acknowledged that the sexual abuse occurred, but have minimized the importance of the issue or the impact that it has had on the client.

D. The denial in the family system about the sexual abuse has ceased.

14. Family Secrecy (10)

A. The client and family members have been secretive about the sexual abuse and until recently have not disclosed it to any individuals or agencies outside of the family.

B. Today's therapy session revealed that key family member(s) remain unaware of the sexual abuse.

C. Therapy has helped to eliminate the secrecy within the family about the sexual abuse.

15. Inappropriate Parent-Child Boundaries (10)

A. The inappropriate parent-child boundaries within the family system have been one of the significant contributing factors to the emergence of the sexual abuse.

B. The parents have established very weak and inappropriate parent-child boundaries.

C. The parent(s) have started to take active steps to establish appropriate parent-child boundaries.

D. Therapy has helped to establish appropriate parent-child boundaries and generational lines in the family to greatly minimize the risk of sexual abuse occurring in the future.

16. Substance Abuse (11)

A. The client reported engaging in a significant amount of substance abuse since the sexual abuse began.

B. The client has often used alcohol or drugs as a maladaptive coping mechanism to ward off any painful emotions associated with the sexual abuse.

C. The client has begun to use positive coping mechanisms to deal with his/her painful emotions surrounding the sexual abuse instead of turning to drug or alcohol abuse.

D. The client has ceased using alcohol or drug abuse as a way to ward off any painful emotions associated with the sexual abuse.

17. Feelings of Guilt and Shame (12)

A. The client expressed strong feelings of guilt and shame about the past sexual abuse.

B. The client has continued to experience strong feelings of guilt and shame about the past sexual abuse, despite being given reassurance that he/she is not responsible for the sexual abuse.

C. The client's feelings of guilt and shame have started to decrease as he/she now recognizes that the perpetrator is responsible for the sexual abuse.

D. The client has successfully worked through and resolved his/her feelings of guilt and shame about the past sexual abuse.

18. Low Self-Esteem (12)

A. The client expressed strong feelings of low self-esteem and insecurity about the past sexual abuse.

B. The client's self-esteem has started to improve as he/she works through his/her feelings about the past sexual abuse.

C. Strong family support has helped to increase the client's self-esteem.

D. The client verbalized several positive self-descriptive statements during today's therapy session.

19. Inappropriate Sexual Behavior (13)

A. The client has a history of engaging in inappropriate sexual behavior with younger children.

B. The client acknowledged that his/her sexual behavior with younger children is inappropriate.

C. The client's unresolved feelings about his/her past sexual victimization has contributed to the emergence of his/her inappropriate sexual behavior with younger children.

D. The client reported that he/she has not recently engaged in any inappropriate sexual behavior.

E. The client's risk for engaging in inappropriate sexual behavior toward younger children appears to be greatly reduced because of the successful resolution of issues related to his/her past sexual victimization.

INTERVENTIONS IMPLEMENTED

1. Build Trust (1)*

A. Today's therapy session focused on building the level of trust with the client through consistent eye contact, active listening, unconditional positive regard, and warm acceptance.

B. The therapy session was helpful in building the level of trust with the client.

C. The therapy session did not prove to be helpful in building the level of trust with the client, as he/she remained guarded in talking about the sexual abuse.

2. Encourage Expression of Feelings (2)

A. The client was given encouragement and support to tell the entire story of the sexual abuse and to express feelings that he/she experienced during and after the abuse.

B. The client described the sequence of events before, during, and after the sexual abuse incidents, but did not show or talk of any feelings.

C. Client-centered principals were used to encourage and support the client in expressing his/her feelings about the past sexual abuse.

D. The parent(s) were encouraged to allow the client opportunities at home to express his/her thoughts and feelings about the sexual abuse.

3. Report Sexual Abuse (3)

A. The sexual abuse was reported to the appropriate child protection agency.

B. Criminal justice officials have been informed of the sexual abuse.

C. The client has been referred for a medical examination to determine whether there are any physical signs of the sexual abuse and/or to evaluate any health problems that may have resulted from the sexual abuse.

D. The client and family members were supportive of the sexual abuse being reported to the appropriate child protection agency or criminal justice officials.

E. The client and family members objected to the sexual abuse being reported to the appropriate child protection agency or criminal justice officials.

4. Assess Veracity of Sexual Abuse Charges (4)

A. Consulted with child protection case manager and criminal justice officials to assess the veracity of the client's sexual abuse charges.

B. Consulted with the physician who examined the client to assess the veracity of the sexual abuse charges.

* The numbers in parentheses correlate to the number of the Therapeutic Intervention statement in the companion chapter with the same title in *The Adolescent Psychotherapy Treatment Planner* (Jongsma, Peterson, and McInnis) by John Wiley & Sons, 2000.

C. Consultation with the child protection case managers, criminal justice officials, and physician has provided strong support for the client's reports that he/she has been sexually abused.

D. Consultation with the child protection case managers, criminal justice officials, and physician has provided inconclusive evidence about whether the client has been sexually abused.

E. Consultation with the child protection case managers, criminal justice officials, and physician has provided little or no support for the client's reports that he/she has been sexually abused.

5. Consultation to Develop Appropriate Treatment Interventions (5)

A. Consulted with the criminal justice officials and child protection case managers about developing appropriate treatment interventions.

B. Consulted with the client's physicians about developing appropriate treatment interventions.

C. After consulting with the child protection case managers, criminal justice officials, and physician, the recommendation was made that the client should receive individual therapy to address sexual abuse issues.

D. The consultation meeting with the child protection and criminal justice officials produced the recommendation that family therapy be mandatory.

E. After consulting with the child protection case managers and criminal justice officials, it was determined that the perpetrator be required to participate in his/her own therapy.

6. Reveal Sexual Abuse to Family (6)

A. A conjoint therapy session was held to reveal the sexual abuse to key family member(s) or caregiver(s).

B. A family therapy session was held to eliminate the secrecy about the client's sexual abuse.

C. A conjoint therapy session was held to reveal the nature, frequency, and duration of the sexual abuse to key family member(s) and/or caregiver(s).

7. Remove Perpetrator from Home (7)

A. Consulted with criminal justice officials and child protection case managers to determine whether the perpetrator should be removed from the home.

B. Recommendation was made that the perpetrator be removed from the home in order to protect the client and siblings from future occurrences of sexual abuse.

C. The perpetrator was court-ordered to leave the home and was forbidden to have any contact with the client and/or family member(s).

D. The perpetrator was required to leave the home, but will be allowed supervised visitation with the client and/or family member(s).

E. Recommendation was made that the perpetrator be allowed to remain in the home under the conditions that he/she agrees to and follows through with treatment.

8. Protect Client and Other Children (8)

A. Consulted with criminal justice officials and child protection case managers about implementing the necessary steps to protect the client and other children in the home from future sexual abuse.

B. A family therapy session was held to discuss and identify the appropriate steps that need to be taken to protect the client and other children in the home from future sexual abuse.

C. An individual therapy session was held to provide the client with the opportunity to identify what steps he/she feels need to occur in order to feel safe.

9. Consult about Placement of Client (9)

A. Consulted with criminal justice officials and child protection case managers to assess whether the client is safe to remain in the home or should be removed.

B. The decision was made that the client be allowed to remain in the home, and the perpetrator was required to leave.

C. The decision was made to allow the client to continue living in the home because it was felt that the nonabusive parent would take the necessary steps to protect him/her from further sexual abuse.

D. Recommendation was made that the client be placed in a foster home to ensure his/her protection from further sexual abuse.

E. Recommendation was made that the client be placed in a residential treatment program to ensure his/her protection from further sexual abuse and provide treatment for his/her emotional/behavioral problems.

10. Confront Denial within Family System (10)

A. The family members' denial about the impact of the sexual abuse was confronted and challenged so that they can begin to provide the support the client needs in order to make a healthy adjustment.

B. The family members' denial of the sexual abuse was strongly challenged and responsibility for the sexual abuse was placed on the perpetrator.

C. The therapy session was helpful in working through the family members' denial surrounding the sexual abuse, and they agreed to follow through with the necessary treatment and support.

D. The therapy session was not successful in working through the family members' denial about the sexual abuse.

11. Empower Client Self-Protection (11)

A. Today's therapy session sought to empower the client by reinforcing the steps necessary to protect himself/herself.

B. Today's therapy session sought to empower the client by praising and reinforcing his/her decision to report the sexual abuse to the appropriate individuals or agencies.

C. The client was strongly encouraged to contact a child protection hot line, police, or the therapist if he/she is ever sexually abused in the future.

D. The client was helped to identify a list of safe places to go when he/she feels at risk of sexual abuse.

E. The client was taught effective assertiveness and communication skills to help him/her stand up for himself/herself and feel safe.

12. Establish Boundaries within Family System (12)

A. The family members were counseled about establishing appropriate parent-child boundaries to ensure the protection of the client and other children in the home from further sexual abuse.

B. The family members were counseled about establishing appropriate adult-child boundaries regarding privacy, physical contact, and verbal content.

C. An assessment of the family system revealed weak and blurred parent-child boundaries.

D. Today's therapy session sought to strengthen the roles and responsibilities of the nonabusive parent in enforcing appropriate privacy, physical contact, verbal content, and adult-child boundaries.

13. Elicit Support from Family Members (13)

A. The family members were encouraged to provide emotional support and nurturance for the client to help him/her cope with the sexual abuse.

B. Today's therapy session was successful in eliciting support and nurturance for the client from the other family members.

C. An individual therapy session was held with the nonabusive parent to explore the factors contributing to his/her resistance to providing emotional support and nurturance for the client.

D. A family therapy session was held with the siblings to explore their reluctance to provide emotional support and nurturance for the client.

E. The parent(s) were instructed to provide frequent praise and positive reinforcement to the client to help him/her build self-esteem and feel accepted in the family system.

14. Assign Increased Time Spent with Nonabusive Parent (14)

A. The disengaged, nonabusive parent was directed to spend more time with the client in leisure, school, or household activities.

B. The client and disengaged, nonabusive parent were assisted in identifying a list of activities that they would like to do together.

C. The client verbalized his/her need to spend greater time with the disengaged, nonabusive parent in leisure, school, or household activities.

D. The disengaged, nonabusive parent verbalized a commitment to spend increased time with the client.

E. Today's therapy session explored the factors contributing to the distant relationship between the client and the nonabusive parent.

15. Identify Stress Factors or Precipitating Events (15)

A. Today's therapy session explored the stress factors or precipitating events that contributed to the emergence of the sexual abuse.

B. Today's therapy session explored the family dynamics that have contributed to the emergence of the sexual abuse.

C. Today's therapy session was helpful in identifying the stress factors or precipitating events that contributed to the emergence of the sexual abuse.

D. Today's therapy session identified several family dynamics that have contributed to the emergence of the sexual abuse.

E. The family members were taught positive coping strategies and effective problem-solving approaches to help them manage stress and overcome the identified problems.

16. Gather Details about Where Abuse Occurred in Home (16)

A. The client was given an assignment to draw a diagram of the house where the sexual abuse occurred, indicating where everyone slept, to help gain greater insight into the factors or precipitating events that led up to the sexual abuse.

B. The client recounted the story of the sexual abuse as he/she shared the diagram of the house where the sexual abuse occurred.

C. The client's drawing of the diagram where the sexual abuse occurred was helpful in identifying the precipitating events leading up to the sexual abuse.

D. The client shared a diagram of the house where the sexual abuse occurred, but was guarded in talking about the details or the precipitating events that led up to the sexual abuse.

E. The client refused to complete the assignment of drawing a diagram showing where the sexual abuse occurred.

17. Assign Family Kinetic Drawing (17)

A. The client was instructed to produce a family kinetic drawing to help in assessing the dynamics that possibly contributed to the emergence of the sexual abuse.

B. The client's family kinetic drawing provided insight into the family dynamics that have contributed to the emergence of the sexual abuse.

C. The client's family kinetic drawing produced little or no insight into the factors contributing to the emergence of the sexual abuse.

D. The client's completion of the family kinetic drawing led to a productive discussion about his/her family relationships.

18. Construct Family Sex Abuse Genogram (18)

A. The client and family members constructed a multigenerational family genogram that identified the history of sexual abuse within the family.

B. The construction of the multigenerational family genogram helped the client to realize that other family members have been sexually abused and that he/she is not alone.

C. The construction of the multigenerational family genogram helped the perpetrator recognize the cycle of repeated boundary violations within the extended family.

D. The construction of a multigenerational family genogram helped the family members voice their commitment to taking the necessary steps to end the cycle of sexual abuse within their family.

19. Assign Letter to Perpetrator (19)

A. The client was given a homework assignment to write a letter to the perpetrator and bring it to the following therapy session for processing.

B. The client expressed strong feelings of sadness, hurt, and disappointment in his/her letter to the perpetrator.

C. The client expressed strong feelings of anger about the sexual abuse in his/her letter to the perpetrator.

D. The client expressed a willingness to share the letter directly with the perpetrator.

E. After processing the letter, the client reported that he/she is not ready to share his/her thoughts and feelings about the sexual abuse directly with the perpetrator.

20. Utilize Empty-Chair Technique (20)

A. The empty-chair technique was utilized to help the client express his/her feelings about the sexual abuse to the perpetrator.

B. The empty-chair technique was utilized to help the client express and work through his/her feelings toward the nonabusive parent.

C. The client made productive use of the empty-chair technique to express strong feelings of sadness, hurt, and anger about the sexual abuse to the perpetrator.

D. The client made productive use of the empty-chair technique to express strong feelings of sadness, hurt, and anger toward the nonabusive parent for failing to protect him/her from the sexual abuse.

E. The client appeared uncomfortable with the empty-chair technique and had difficulty expressing his/her thoughts and feelings about the sexual abuse.

21. Assign Feelings Journal (21)

A. The client was instructed to keep a journal in which he/she records experiences or situations that evoke strong emotions pertaining to the sexual abuse.

B. The client shared several entries from his/her journal that reflected his/her strong emotions about the sexual abuse.

C. The client reported that the journal has helped him/her work through many of his/her thoughts and feelings about the past sexual abuse.

D. Today's therapy session explored why the client has failed to keep a journal.

22. "You Are Not Alone" Exercise (22)

A. The client was given the "You Are Not Alone" exercise from *The Brief Adolescent Therapy Homework Planner* (Jongsma, Peterson, and McInnis) to help him/her express feelings connected to the sexual abuse and decrease feelings of guilt and shame.

B. The client reported that he/she found the "You Are Not Alone" exercise helpful in reducing his/her feelings of guilt, shame, anger, and fear.

C. The client did not follow through with completing the "You Are Not Alone" exercise and the assignment was given again.

23. Teach Guided Fantasy and Imagery Techniques (23)

A. Guided fantasy and imagery techniques were used to help the client identify and express his/her thoughts and feelings associated with the sexual abuse.

B. The client reported a positive response to the use of guided fantasy and imagery techniques to help him/her identify his/her thoughts, feelings, and unmet needs associated with the sexual abuse.

C. Guided fantasy and imagery techniques were used, but the client still had difficulty identifying and expressing his/her thoughts, feelings, and unmet needs associated with the sexual abuse.

24. **Utilize Art Therapy to Express Feelings toward Perpetrator (24)**

A. Art therapy techniques (e.g., drawing, painting, sculpting) were employed to help the client identify and express his/her feelings toward the perpetrator.

B. The client made productive use of the therapy session and was able to express strong feelings of anger toward the perpetrator in his/her artwork.

C. The client's artwork reflected feelings of sadness, anger, hurt, and disappointment that he/she experiences in regard to his/her relationship with the perpetrator.

D. The client appeared uncomfortable and had difficulty expressing his/her feelings toward the perpetrator through art.

25. **Employ Art Therapy to Express Impact on Life (25)**

A. The client was instructed to create a drawing or sculpture that reflected how the sexual abuse has impacted his/her life and feelings about himself/herself.

B. The client made productive use of the art therapy session and was able to vividly express how the sexual abuse has impacted his/her life and feelings about self.

C. The client's artwork reflected how the sexual abuse has caused the client to feel small, helpless, and vulnerable.

D. The client's artwork reflected feelings of guilt and shame about the sexual abuse.

E. The client appeared uncomfortable and had difficulty expressing through his/her artwork how the sexual abuse has impacted his/her life or feelings about self.

26. **Confront Perpetrator (26)**

A. The perpetrator's denial of the sexual abuse was confronted.

B. The client was helped to prepare to confront the perpetrator about the sexual abuse.

C. The client confronted the perpetrator about how the sexual abuse has negatively impacted his/her life and feelings about self.

D. The perpetrator was confronted about minimizing the significance of the sexual abuse.

E. The perpetrator was confronted with the facts of the sexual abuse, but continued to deny sexually abusing the client.

27. **Facilitate Perpetrator Apology (27)**

A. The perpetrator was helped to prepare to apologize to the client and other family members about the sexual abuse.

B. The perpetrator apologized to the client and family members for the sexual abuse.

C. The perpetrator listened appropriately to the client and family members' expression of anger, hurt, and disappointment about the sexual abuse and then offered a sincere apology.

D. A decision was made to postpone the apology session because the perpetrator does not appear ready to offer a sincere or genuine apology to the client and family members.

28. **Sexual Offender's Group Referral (28)**

A. The perpetrator was referred to a sexual offender's group to address his/her inappropriate sexual behaviors.

B. The perpetrator was required by the legal system to attend a sexual offender's group.

C. The perpetrator has consistently attended the sexual offender's group.

D. The perpetrator has failed to consistently attend the sexual offender's group.

E. The perpetrator has been an active participant in the sexual offender's group and stated that it has helped him/her identify the factors contributing to his/her inappropriate sexual behaviors.

29. Assign *Allies in Healing* (29)

A. The client's parents and significant others were assigned to read *Allies in Healing* (Davis) to assist them in understanding how they can help the client recover from the sexual abuse.

B. The client's parents followed through in reading *Allies in Healing* and found it helpful in identifying ways that they can help the client recover from the sexual abuse.

C. The parents have failed to start reading *Allies in Healing* and were encouraged to do so to help them understand how they can help the client recover from the sexual abuse.

30. Assign *Out of the Shadows* (30)

A. The client's family was assigned to read *Out of the Shadows* (Carnes) to expand their knowledge of sexually addictive behaviors.

B. The client's family read *Out of the Shadows* and found it helpful in expanding their knowledge about sexually addictive behaviors.

C. The client's family failed to read *Out of the Shadows* and were encouraged to do so to expand their knowledge of sexually addictive behaviors.

31. Assign Forgiveness Letter (31)

A. The client was given a homework assignment to write a forgiveness letter to the perpetrator and bring it back to the following session for processing.

B. The client's letter reflected his/her readiness to offer forgiveness to the perpetrator and/or significant family member(s).

C. The client verbalized his/her forgiveness to the perpetrator and/or significant family member(s) in today's therapy session.

D. After processing the client's letter, it was evident that the client is not ready to offer forgiveness to the perpetrator and/or significant family member(s).

32. Facilitate Symbolically Letting Go (32)

A. The client was directed to bring an object to the next therapy session that symbolizes the significance of the sexual abuse in his/her life.

B. The client brought in an object to today's therapy session that symbolized the significance of the sexual abuse in his/her life.

C. Processed with the client what he/she would like to do with the symbol of the sexual abuse.

D. The client identified ways to dispose of the symbol of the sexual abuse to signify his/her readiness to move on with his/her life.

33. Differentiate Victim versus Survivor (33)

A. The client was helped to differentiate between being a victim and being a survivor.

B. The client identified both the positive and negative consequences of being a victim and being a survivor.

C. The client verbalized that his/her increased confidence and positive feelings about self have allowed himself/herself to feel more like a survivor of sexual abuse than a victim.

D. The client reported that he/she continues to harbor unresolved feelings about the sexual abuse and is not ready to label himself/herself as being a survivor of sexual abuse.

34. Reinforce Ability to Survive Sexual Abuse (34)

A. The idea that the client can survive sexual abuse was introduced by asking, "What will you be doing in the future that shows you are happy and have moved on with your life?"

B. The client identified several positive behaviors or tasks that he/she would be performing in the future that would show he/she is happy and has moved on with his/her life.

C. The client was reinforced for taking positive steps to work through the issues related to his/her sexual victimization.

D. The client was reinforced for taking active steps to achieve personal happiness and move on with his/her life.

E. The client explored the factors contributing to his/her reluctance or resistance to taking positive steps to move on with his/her life.

35. Assign Self-Portrait (35)

A. The client was instructed to draw a self-portrait to assess his/her self-esteem.

B. The client's self-portrait during the beginning stage of treatment reflected his/her feelings of low self-esteem, helplessness, and worthlessness.

C. The client's self-portrait during the middle stage of therapy reflected increased feelings of self-worth and esteem.

D. The client's self-portrait during the end stage of therapy reflects significant improvements in his/her self-esteem.

36. Survivor Group Referral (36)

A. The client was referred to a survivor group with other adolescents to assist him/her in realizing that he/she is not alone in having experienced sexual abuse.

B. The client was given the directive to self-disclose at least once during the group therapy session.

C. The client's participation in the survivor group with other adolescents has helped him/her realize that he/she is not alone in experiencing sexual abuse.

D. The client has actively participated in the survivor group therapy sessions and verbalized many of his/her feelings about the past sexual abuse.

E. The client has offered support to other members of the survivor group when they have shared their thoughts and feelings about their own sexual abuse experiences.

37. Teach Share-Check Method of Building Trust (37)

A. The client was taught the share-check method of building trust to help him/her realize that the amount of information he/she shares with others is related to a proven level of trustworthiness.

B. The client reported that learning the share-check method has helped him/her decide how much information he/she can share with certain individuals.

C. The client identified a list of individuals whom he/she feels are trustworthy.

D. The client has continued to struggle with issues of trust and has difficulty sharing his/her thoughts and feelings with even trustworthy individuals.

38. Encourage Participation in Peer Group Activities (38)

A. The client was encouraged to participate in positive peer group or extracurricular activities to improve his/her self-esteem and gain a sense of acceptance.

B. The client developed a list of positive peer group or extracurricular activities that will provide him/her with the opportunity to establish friendships and improve self-esteem.

C. The client reported that his/her participation in positive peer group or extracurricular activities has helped him/her improve self-esteem and gain a sense of acceptance.

D. The client acknowledged that his/her feelings of low self-esteem and shame have contributed to his/her reluctance to become involved in positive peer group or extracurricular activities in the past.

39. List Supportive People (39)

A. The client was asked to develop a list of resource people outside of the family to whom he/she can turn for support, guidance, and affirmation.

B. The client was given a homework assignment to seek support or guidance from at least one individual outside of his/her family before the next therapy session.

C. The client reported that he/she has benefited from receiving support, guidance, and affirmation from individuals outside of his/her family.

D. The support that the client has received from resource people outside of the family has helped him/her cope with the trauma of the sexual abuse.

E. The client has been hesitant to turn to the resource people outside of the family for support, guidance, or affirmation because of his/her mistrust.

40. Teach Appropriate/Inappropriate Touching (40)

A. The client was helped to identify both appropriate and inappropriate forms of touching and affection.

B. The client was encouraged to accept and initiate appropriate forms of touching with trusted individuals.

C. The client reported that allowing himself/herself to give and receive affection has helped him/her cope with the pain of the sexual abuse.

D. The client's mistrust of others has remained high, and as a result, he/she has much difficulty accepting and initiating appropriate forms of touching, even with trusted individuals.

41. Connect Painful Emotions to Promiscuous Behavior (41)

A. The therapy session was helpful in identifying how underlying, painful emotions (e.g., fear, hurt, sadness, anxiety) are related to the emergence of the client's sexually promiscuous or seductive behavior.

B. The client acknowledged that his/her sexually promiscuous or seductive behavior has been associated with underlying, painful emotions arising from the sexual abuse.

C. A client-centered therapy approach was utilized to help the client make a connection between his/her underlying, painful emotions and his/her sexually promiscuous or seductive behavior.

D. Role-playing and modeling techniques were used to demonstrate appropriate ways for the client to express his/her underlying painful emotions.

E. The client was helped to identify more appropriate ways to express his/her painful emotions and meet his/her needs instead of through sexually promiscuous or seductive behavior.

42. Provide Sex Education (42)

A. The client was provided with sex education in an attempt to eliminate his/her pattern of engaging in sexually promiscuous or seductive behavior.

B. The client was helped to identify the risks involved with his/her sexually promiscuous or seductive behavior.

C. The client explored the factors contributing to his/her sexually promiscuous or seductive behavior.

43. Arrange for Substance Abuse Evaluation (43)

A. The client was referred for a substance abuse evaluation to assess the extent of his/her drug or alcohol usage and to determine the need for treatment.

B. The findings from the substance abuse evaluation revealed the presence of a substance abuse problem and the need for treatment.

C. The evaluation findings did not reveal the presence of a substance abuse problem or the need for treatment in this area.

D. The client was supportive of the recommendation to receive substance abuse treatment.

E. The client voiced his/her objection to receiving substance abuse treatment.

44. Arrange for Psychological Testing (44)

A. The client was referred for psychological testing to rule out the presence of a severe psychological disorder.

B. The findings from the psychological testing reveal the presence of serious emotional problems and the need for a medication evaluation.

C. The findings from the psychological testing do not support the presence of any severe psychological disorder.

D. The client approached the psychological testing in an honest, straightforward manner and was cooperative with any request directed toward him/her.

E. The client was uncooperative and resistant to engage during the evaluation process.

45. Medication Evaluation Referral (45)

A. The client was referred for a medication evaluation to help stabilize his/her mood.

B. The client and parents agreed to follow through with a medication evaluation by a physician.

C. The client verbalized strong opposition to being placed on medication to help stabilize his/her mood.

D. The client reported that the psychotropic medication has helped to stabilize his/her mood.

E. The client reported little or no improvement on the medication.

46. Assess Parents' Psychiatric and/or Substance Abuse Problem (46)

A. The client's parent(s) were assessed for the possibility of having a psychiatric disorder and/or a substance abuse problem.

B. The client's parent(s) agreed to seek substance abuse treatment.

C. The client's parent(s), because of their denial, have refused to seek substance abuse treatment.

D. The parent(s) were referred for a psychiatric evaluation and therapy to address their psychiatric disorder.

E. The parent(s) refused to comply with the recommendation to seek a psychiatric evaluation and/or therapy.

SEXUAL ACTING OUT

CLIENT PRESENTATION

1. Sexual Self-Interest (1)*

A. The client reported a history of multiple sexual encounters with casual partners where there was little if any emotional attachment.

B. The lone interest in any encounter for the client is his/her own sexual self-gratification.

C. The client talks readily and freely about his/her sexual adventures in graphic detail.

D. Since becoming engaged in the counseling process, there has been a decrease in the client's sexual behaviors and sexualized talk.

2. Sexually Active without Birth Control (2)

A. The client reported being sexually active for more than a year without using any birth control.

B. The client has had an abortion in the past year.

C. The client showed little if any concern about becoming pregnant, despite being very sexually active.

D. Recently the client has expressed concern over becoming pregnant and made an appointment at a family planning agency.

3. Sexually Active with No Commitment (3)

A. The client indicated he/she is involved in a sexual relationship but does not see it lasting.

B. The client reported being sexually active with one partner but that both are free to "date others."

C. The client verbalized being sexually active with one partner but did not want this to tie him/her down.

D. The client has expressed a desire to have a relationship in which there is mutual commitment.

4. Ignores Safe Sex (4)

A. The client verbalized that safe sex is not an important concern for him/her.

B. The client reported he/she does not bother with safe sex practices as it spoils being "free and spontaneous."

C. The client presents in a manner that reflects little regard for himself/herself.

D. The client expressed an increasing commitment to practicing safer sex.

---

* The numbers in parentheses correlate to the number of the Behavioral Definition statement in the companion chapter with same title in *The Adolescent Psychotherapy Treatment Planner* (Jongsma, Peterson, and McInnis) by John Wiley & Sons, 2000.

5. Sexually Provocative Dress and Behavior (5)

A. The client's dress and behavior are sexually provocative.

B. The client indicated that his/her dress and behavior have been labeled by others as highly sexual.

C. The client denied being aware that his/her behavior and dress are sexually provocative.

D. The client has begun to dress and act in a less sexually provocative manner.

6. Talks Freely of Sexual Activity (6)

A. If not stopped, the client would have filled the session with his/her sexual exploits.

B. The client talked freely and without any sense of shame about his/her sexual experiences.

C. The client indicated that talking about his/her sexual experiences has turned off others.

D. The amount of bragging about his/her sexual exploits has decreased as the client has become engaged in therapy and started to share more about his/her personal self.

7. Substance Abuse (7)

A. The client reported a pattern of using alcohol and drugs previous to and during his/her sexual activity.

B. The client does not see any connection between his/her substance abuse and his/her sexual activity.

C. The client refuses to see anything wrong with his/her substance use.

D. The client showed an attitude of liking to party because that's what everyone is doing.

E. The client acknowledged that his/her substance abuse is an escape and has terminated it.

8. Low Self-Esteem (8)

A. A sense of low self-esteem predominates the client's manner, and he/she rarely makes eye contact or has a positive thing to say.

B. The client frequently makes self-disparaging remarks and is negative about future.

C. The client indicated he/she has always felt inferior to and less than others.

D. The client expressed that his/her feelings are not worth the therapist's time.

E. As the client has begun to talk in counseling, there has been a decrease in self-disparaging remarks and a more positive view of the future.

F. The client made a connection between his/her low self-esteem and his/her sexual promiscuity.

9. Depressed/Irritable (9)

A. The client presented in a manner that is both depressed and irritable.

B. The client's touchiness and irritability seem to be a shield and mask for his/her underlying depression.

C. The client's irritability makes it difficult for him/her to invest in the counseling process.

D. As the client's irritability has lessened, he/she has started to talk about the termination of sexual acting out.

10. Sad/Quiet (9)

A. The client presented in a sad, quiet manner.

B. The client prefers doing to talking and seems to view talking as a waste of time.

C. There is a deep sense of sadness to the client that he/she finds difficult to identify or put into words.

D. The client has started to emerge from his/her quietness and start talking more about himself/herself.

11. Hypomania (10)

A. The client presented as very impulsive and energetic, with an inability to focus and pressured speech.

B. The client's impulsiveness and energy has caused him/her difficulties in school, at home, and in the community.

C. The client's inability to focus has made it difficult to establish a relationship in therapy with him/her.

D. The client has started to become engaged in therapy and is able to focus and disclose some about himself/herself.

12. Friendly/Outgoing (10)

A. The client presents a friendly and outgoing manner to nearly everyone.

B. There seems to be little shame or social anxiety present with this client.

C. The client quickly became overfamiliar with the therapist.

D. The client seems to use his/her friendly, outgoing manner to keep others from getting too close or knowing him/her more than superficially.

13. Oppositional (11)

A. The client displayed an attitude of opposition to all authority figures.

B. The client described a pattern of not following social mores, ignoring parental rules, and not respecting authorities.

C. There is present within the client the belief that "I don't have to" or "I am not going to listen to anyone."

D. The client reported openly about his/her sexual activity without regard for social mores.

14. Angry/Rebellious (11)

A. The client's manner is dominated by anger and rebellion.

B. The client's anger and rebellion have made it difficult for him/her to form positive, supportive relationships with others.

C. The client's anger and rebellion have diminished, and he/she is now starting to talk more openly and honestly about self.

15. Childhood (12)

A. The client described his/her childhood as being very unstable, with constant family conflict.

B. The client provided numerous examples from his/her childhood of parents blaming him/her for their problems and misbehavior.

C. The client was aware of the details of parental history of sexual relationships with numerous partners.

D. The client has begun to verbalize some insight into how childhood experiences are connected to his/her present sexual behaviors.

INTERVENTIONS IMPLEMENTED

1. Build Trust (1)*

A. An initial trust level was established with the client through use of unconditional positive regard to facilitate the expression of intimate facts and feelings.

B. Warm acceptance and active listening techniques were used to establish the basis for a trusting relationship.

C. The client has formed a trust-based relationship and has started to identify and express some intimate facts and feelings.

D. Despite the use of active listening, warm acceptance, and unconditional positive regard, the client remains closed to sharing and identifying intimate facts and feelings.

2. Gather Sexual History (2)

A. The client's history of sexual activity, education, and practices was gathered.

B. The client's history of sexual partners was explored to assess the degree of emotional attachment he/she had with each.

C. Only a partial history was gathered due to client's refusal to provide information in some areas.

3. Explore Feelings about Sexual Activity (3)

A. Client thoughts and feelings about his/her sexual history and current practices were explored.

B. Positive verbal reinforcement was given to the client for identifying thoughts and feelings.

C. Client's lack of feelings connected to sexual behavior was pointed out.

4. List Reasons for Sexual Activity (4)

A. The client was asked to list the reasons for his/her sexual activity.

B. The client was confronted with the negative consequences of engaging in sexual activity at such an early age.

C. The client's reasons for his/her sexual activity were probed and faulty logic was addressed and restructured.

5. Process the Reasons for Sexual Activity (5)

A. The client's completed list of reasons for sexual activity was processed, with the pros and cons of each being identified.

---

* The numbers in parentheses correlate to the number of the Therapeutic Intervention statement in the companion chapter with the same title in *The Adolescent Psychotherapy Treatment Planner* (Jongsma, Peterson, and McInnis) by John Wiley & Sons, 2000.

B. After considering the pros and cons of the reasons for sexual activity, the client was asked to identify any changes he/she would now make in his/her sexual activity.

6. **Explore History for Sexual Abuse (6)**

A. Client's history was explored to determine whether he/she had been a victim of sexual abuse.

B. Parents were asked whether the client had been a victim of sexual abuse.

C. It was confirmed that the client has been a victim of sexual abuse and that this experience has had a significant impact on his/her sexual attitudes and behavior.

D. Neither the parents nor the client provided any evidence that the client has been a victim of sexual abuse.

7. **Connect Sexual Abuse and Current Sexual Activity (7)**

A. The client was assisted in looking at the connection between being treated as a sexual object and treating others as such.

B. Verbal support and encouragement was given to the client as he/she shared how sexual abuse has affected him/her.

C. The client has developed insight into the impact of his/her being a sexual abuse victim on his/her current sexual acting out.

D. The client denied any connection between his/her sexual abuse experience and his/her current sexual activity.

8. **Explore Feelings of Low Self-Esteem (8)**

A. The client was asked to make a list of his/her positive and negative characteristics.

B. Client's feelings of low self-esteem were explored in terms of awareness, depth of feeling, and means of expression.

C. Positive characteristics identified by the client about himself/herself were affirmed and reinforced.

D. Despite a warm, supportive approach, the client still talked negatively about himself/herself.

E. The client's low self-esteem was evident in his/her lack of ability to identify positive characteristics about himself/herself and in frequent self-disparaging remarks.

9. **Identify Sources of Low Self-Esteem (9)**

A. The client was assisted in identifying the negative messages he/she received and where each came from.

B. The client was shown the connection between the negative messages he/she has received and his/her low self-esteem.

C. With support, the client was able to identify and express his/her feelings of hurt and shame about his/her rejection and abuse experiences.

D. The client identified negative messages he/she has received, but insisted these messages had no effect on him/her.

10. Connect Past Rejection with Current Fear (10)

A. The client was helped to become aware of his/her fear of rejection and its connection to his/her past life experiences of abuse, abandonment, and rejection.

B. Past experiences of rejection and abandonment were explored with client to build his/her awareness of their current impact on sexual acting out in search of acceptance and affirmation.

C. The client remains in denial about the impact of the past experiences of rejection and abandonment.

D. The client has acknowledged the connection between his/her history of rejection and abuse and his/her current sexual promiscuity.

11. Connect Underlying Feelings with Current Sexual Activity (11)

A. The client was assisted in making connections between his/her low self-esteem, fear of rejection, and current sexual promiscuity.

B. Despite assistance, the client still found it difficult to connect his/her low self-esteem, fear of rejection, and current sexual promiscuity.

C. The idea of building self-esteem by saying no to sexual activity was seeded with client.

D. The client has acknowledged the connection between his/her history of rejection and abuse and his/her current sexual promiscuity.

12. Identify Constructive Ways to Build Self-Esteem (12)

A. The client's use of sexual activity as a vehicle to build his/her self-esteem was confronted as self-defeating behavior.

B. The negative consequences of using sex to build self-esteem were reviewed with the client.

C. Positive ways to build self-esteem were explored with the client.

D. A plan was developed with the client to build his/her self-esteem in positive ways, and he/she was asked to make a commitment to implement the plan.

E. The client's plan to build self-esteem was monitored for implementation, with gains being recognized and reinforced.

13. "Three Ways to Change Yourself" Exercise (13)

A. Using the "Three Ways to Change Yourself" exercise from *The Brief Adolescent Therapy Homework Planner* (Jongsma, Peterson, McInnis), the client was asked to draw three pictures of changes he/she desires.

B. The completed exercise on changes for self was processed, and the details of the desired changes were affirmed and reinforced with the client.

C. The client completed the exercise, but details were very sketchy and the client would not be pinned down.

D. A plan for implementation to achieve the changes desired by the client was made and a commitment solicited about when and how this plan would begin.

14. Explore Family Rejection Affirmation (14)

A. The family-of-origin dynamics of rejection versus affirmation were explored with the client.

B. The family messages of rejection that were identified were challenged and alternative interpretations were offered to the client.

C. Even with assistance, the client struggled to identify affirming or rejecting messages in his/her family of origin.

D. The client is beginning to connect negative/rejecting family messages with his/her current sexual behavior.

15. Assist Family in Expressing Their Feelings (15)

A. Family sessions were held that focused on members' feelings toward each other and the ways in which they interact.

B. Family members revealing feelings toward each other cleared the air and allowed new ways of interaction to be implemented.

C. In family sessions, the family members remained superficial in their expression of feelings and socially polite in their interactions, thus keeping and ensuring the status quo of distance.

16. Interpret Sexual Activity (16)

A. The client's sexual activity was interpreted to him/her as a maladaptive way of seeking attention and affirmation that was missing in the family.

B. On a scale of 1 to 10 (10 being absolute truth), the client rated the truth of the interpretation that he/she was searching for affirmation as a ____, and this rating was processed.

C. The interpretation of the client's sexual activity as a search for affirmation was presented to the family in a session for each member's reaction and feedback.

D. The client rejected the interpretation that his/her sexual activity is a search for affirmation on the grounds that no one controls his/her behavior.

17. Teach Value of True Sexual Intimacy (17)

A. The client was taught the value of reserving sexual intimacy for a committed, mutually respectful relationship with longevity.

B. The client was assisted in developing a list of relationship characteristics that would indicate the potential for true sexual intimacy.

18. Teach the Rewards of Respectful Sexual Activity (18)

A. The client was taught the benefits of sexual activities that are respectful and mutual versus the negatives of using sex as a way of getting someone to love you or merely obtaining pleasure.

B. The client was assisted in identifying the pros and cons of sexual activity based on mature love versus self-centered motivations.

C. The client indicates that he/she has a hard time understanding any reason for sex other than self-based pleasure.

19. Assess Depression (19)

A. The client was assessed for level of depression and the possibility of a referral for medication.

B. The client was cooperative in his/her assessment for depression.

C. The concept and feeling of depression was explored with the client to find out his/her perception of what depression is and what it is like when he/she is depressed.

20. Arrange for Psychological Testing (20)

A. A psychological evaluation was conducted with the client to assess for emotional or personality factors that may contribute to sexual acting out.

B. With encouragement, the client followed through in a cooperative way with the psychological evaluation.

C. A psychological evaluation could not be completed due to the client's uncooperative, oppositional behavior.

D. The psychological assessment found evidence of emotional and personality factors that contribute to the client's sexual acting out.

E. No underlying emotional or personality factors were identified through the psychological assessment.

21. Interpret Sexual Activity as Coping Strategy for Depression (21)

A. The interpretation of sexual activity as a coping strategy for depression was given to the client.

B. On a scale of 1 to 10 (with 10 being absolute truth), the client rated the truth of the interpretation that his/her sexual activity was an antidote for depression as a ____, and the rating was processed.

C. The client rejected the interpretation of sex as the only sure good feeling he/she knows.

22. Teach Birth Control/Safe Sex (22)

A. The value of using birth control and practicing safe sex, as well as the risks associated with promiscuity, was taught to the client.

B. The client was referred to Planned Parenthood for its birth control resources and educational programs regarding the risks attached to sexual promiscuity.

C. The issue of birth control and safer sex was the focus of a family session.

D. Although the client has indicated he/she will continue to be active sexually, he/she did give a commitment to obtaining birth control and practicing safer sex.

23. Explore Underlying Causes for Reckless Sexual Practices (23)

A. The possible underlying wishes of the client for pregnancy or death as a motivation for reckless sexual practices were explored.

B. In the exploration, the client acknowledged that he/she did not care what happened as a result of the sexual activity.

C. The client remained in denial and oblivious to any underlying wishes attached to reckless sexual behavior.

24. Explore Substance Abuse (24)

A. The client's pattern and extent of substance abuse was explored and evaluated.

B. The client was not open to talking about his/her substance use.

C. The client denied any use of experimentation with substances.

D. In exploring the client's substance use, he/she revealed a pattern of substance use before, during, or after sexual activity.

25. Identify Role of Substance Abuse (25)

A. The client was assisted in identifying the role substance abuse played in numbing, escaping, or avoiding feelings of fear, guilt, and shame associated with sexual promiscuity.

B. It was difficult for the client to connect his/her substance use with escaping or numbing feelings.

C. The client acknowledged that feelings of guilt and shame surround his/her sexual promiscuity and agreed that he/she used substance abuse to cope with these feelings.

26. Solicit a Commitment to Terminate Substance Abuse (26)

A. The client was asked to make a commitment to terminate all substance use immediately.

B. The client's verbal commitment to terminate substance use was monitored for follow-through and to give encouragement, reinforcement, and guidance.

C. The client refused to commit to terminate all substance abuse.

27. Assess Impulsiveness (27)

A. The level of the client's impulsiveness was assessed to rule out or confirm ADHD or mania as contributing factors to his/her sexual activity.

B. The client was cooperative and helpful in the assessment process.

C. A referral was made for a psychiatric evaluation to confirm a diagnosis of bipolar disorder.

D. The client refused to cooperate with the assessment, saying that everything is fine with him/her.

28. Assess Need for Medications (28)

A. The client was assessed for his/her need for or possible benefit from psychotropic medication.

B. Parents and client were consulted about their feelings regarding psychotropic medication.

C. The parents' and the client's resistance to psychotropic medication was addressed and resolved.

29. Psychotropic Medication Referral (29)

A. The client was referred for a medication evaluation by a physician.

B. The client followed through and completed a medication evaluation.

C. The parents and the client filled the prescription, and the client has started to take the prescribed medication.

30. Monitor/Assess Medication Effectiveness (30)

A. The client was monitored for medication compliance.

B. The effectiveness of the client's medication was assessed and possible side effects were monitored.

C. The effectiveness of the client's medication was communicated to the prescribing physician.

D. The client was confronted with his/her own inconsistency in taking prescribed medications.

E. The client was asked to report all side effects to either parents, therapist, or physician.

F. The client reported that the medication has had a positive impact in reducing the targeted symptoms.

SEXUAL IDENTITY CONFUSION

CLIENT PRESENTATION

1. Confused/Uncertain (1)*

A. The client showed a good deal of uncertainty about his/her basic sexual orientation.

B. The client exhibited a high level of anxiety regarding the issue of his/her sexual orientation.

C. The client has gradually begun to be more comfortable and less anxious about his/her sexual orientation.

2. Sexual Fantasies/Desires Surrounding Same-Sex Partners (2)

A. The client expressed distress about his/her fantasies and desires for same-sex partner.

B. The client tried hard to convince himself/herself that the desire for a same-sex partner did not upset him/her.

C. The client reported a long history of fantasies and desires for same-sex partners that went back to late childhood.

D. The client reported feelings of conflict and distress around sexual fantasies and desires with same-sex partners.

E. The client has begun to process his/her desires and fantasies involving same-sex partners and is no longer feeling overwhelmed.

3. Guilt/Shame (3)

A. A strong sense of guilt and shame dominate the client's mood and manner.

B. The client reported a pattern of guilt and shame surrounding the homosexual feelings, desires, and fantasies he/she was experiencing.

C. The client described being unable to feel comfortable with others due to guilt and shame he/she constantly feels.

D. The client's feelings of guilt and shame have decreased since he/she has started to accept his/her sexual orientation.

4. Feelings of Worthlessness (3)

A. The client's presentation reflected a low sense of self-esteem, and he/she avoided any eye contact and made consistent self-disparaging remarks.

B. The client described himself/herself as being totally worthless.

C. Due to his/her homosexual feelings, the client did not see any way for him/her to feel okay about self.

D. As the client has acknowledged his/her homosexual orientation, he/she has started to entertain the possibility of feeling okay about self.

* The numbers in parentheses correlate to the number of the Behavioral Definition statement in the companion chapter with same title in *The Adolescent Psychotherapy Treatment Planner* (Jongsma, Peterson, and McInnis) by John Wiley & Sons, 2000.

5. Depressed/Withdrawn (4)

A. The client presented in a depressed, withdrawn manner with low energy and a lack of interest in things.

B. The client reported a pattern of depression that has led him/her to withdraw from others and from life's activities.

C. The client described a history of being depressed that he/she can trace back to early teens and his/her questions about his/her homosexual orientation.

D. Since stating his/her sexual orientation, the client appeared less depressed and has started to interact with others.

6. Concealing Sexual Identity from Parents (5)

A. The client admitted he/she has always worked hard to keep his/her homosexual urges hidden from parents.

B. The client reported avoiding any sexual questions parents have raised concerning him/her.

C. The client has started to be more open with parents regarding his/her struggle with sexual identity.

7. Sexual Experimentation (6)

A. The client reported recent homosexual experimentation that has raised questions about his/her sexual orientation.

B. The client has involved himself/herself in impulsive, reckless sexual experimentation.

C. The client's homosexual experimentation has strengthened his/her conviction that he/she is not heterosexual.

D. The client indicated curtailing most of his/her sexual experimentation because he/she feels more certain of his/her sexual orientation.

8. Parents' Concern over Client's Possible Homosexuality (7)

A. The parents showed distress and concern about the issue of their child being homosexual.

B. The parents raised numerous questions about the issue of their child's possible homosexuality.

C. The parents verbalized feelings of anger and rejection toward the client as the client talked of his/her homosexual orientation.

D. The level of the parents' distress and concern has decreased since openly discussing the issue of the client's homosexuality.

9. Disclosure of Homosexuality to Parents (8)

A. The client reported that he/she recently disclosed his/her homosexuality to parents.

B. The client indicated that his/her parents are struggling with his/her disclosure of homosexuality.

C. The client was crushed by the parental rejection he/she received on disclosing his/her homosexuality.

D. The client was surprised and shocked by the acceptance he/she received from parents after disclosing his/her homosexuality.

10. Parents' Feelings of Failure (9)

A. The client reported that his/her parents are feeling responsible and to blame for his/her homosexuality.

B. The parents expressed feelings of failure in regard to their child's homosexuality.

C. The parents denied any feeling of responsibility or failure due to the client's homosexuality.

D. The parents have begun to work through their feelings of failure in regard to the client's homosexuality.

INTERVENTIONS IMPLEMENTED

1. Build Trust (1)*

A. Trust was actively built with the client through the use of unconditional positive regard and active listening.

B. Warm acceptance and active listening techniques were utilized to build trust with the client.

C. An initial level of trust was established with the client, and he/she is now being encouraged to express his/her feelings concerning own sexual identity.

D. The client is now being encouraged to express the fear, anxiety, and distress he/she is feeling about the issue of his/her sexual identity confusion.

E. Despite trust and encouragement, the client struggled to express even a few feelings around his/her identity confusion.

2. Conduct Suicide Assessment (2)

A. A suicide assessment was conducted with the client, who was open and honest about his/her feelings.

B. Inpatient care was recommended and arranged for the client since a serious suicide risk was assessed.

C. The client was uncooperative throughout the suicide assessment.

D. The results and recommendations of the suicide assessment, which did not find serious risk to exist, were communicated to the client and the parents.

E. Although the client denied any suicide plan or ideation, his/her level of anxiety and depression related to the sexual identity struggle suggests that ongoing monitoring of suicide potential is necessary.

3. Sign No-Self-Harm Contract (3)

A. A no-self-harm contract was developed and the client encouraged to sign it.

B. The client was encouraged to verbalize a commitment to and to sign a no-self-harm contract.

C. The no-self-harm contract was monitored for follow-through, and the need for a more supervised level of care was determined to be necessary.

* The numbers in parentheses correlate to the number of the Therapeutic Intervention statement in the companion chapter with the same title in *The Adolescent Psychotherapy Treatment Planner* (Jongsma, Peterson, and McInnis) by John Wiley & Sons, 2000.

4. Gather Sexual History (4)

A. A history of sexual desires, experiences, and fantasies was gathered.

B. The client's current level of sexual functioning could not be fully assessed due to his/her resistance to revealing information on sexual experiences, desires, and fantasies.

5. Explore Questions about Sexual Identity (5)

A. The reasons the client began to question his/her sexuality were explored.

B. The client identified the questions he/she has about his/her sexuality and the experiences that have triggered the questions.

6. Teach Commonality of Same-Sex Experiences (6)

A. The client was taught the commonality of same-sex experiences in youth and informed that these do not necessarily indicate homosexuality.

B. Questions and concerns regarding same-sex experiences were processed and answered.

C. The client was reminded that same-sex experiences in youth do not necessarily indicate homosexuality but are a common part of sexual exploration.

7. Assign Rating of Sexual Attraction (7)

A. The client was asked to rate on a scale of 1 to 10 his/her sexual attraction to both males and females.

B. The ratings of the client were processed and assessed.

C. The client gave a high rating to his/her sexual attraction to same-sex peers and a low rating to opposite-sex peers.

D. The client gave a high rating to attraction to opposite-sex peers and a relatively low rating to same-sex peers.

E. The client gave sexual attraction ratings of approximate equal value to both same-sex and opposite-sex peers.

8. Assign Writing of Future Biography (8)

A. The client was asked to write two biographies, projected 20 years into the future, one of life as a homosexual and the other of life as a heterosexual.

B. The client's two future biographies were read and processed.

C. The question, "Which life was more satisfying, and which had more regret?" was asked and processed.

D. The client's projected future showed a strong identification of self as a homosexual.

E. The client's projected future showed a clear identification of self as a heterosexual.

9. Allow Self-Evaluation of Identity Evidence (9)

A. A nonjudgmental atmosphere was created to allow the client to evaluate the evidence and to resolve his/her confusion regarding sexual identity.

B. After reviewing his/her sexual experiences, thoughts, and feelings, the client has identified himself/herself as homosexual.

C. After reviewing his/her sexual experiences, thoughts, and feelings, the client has identified himself/herself as heterosexual.

10. **List of Deciding Factors (10)**

A. The client was asked to make a list of all the factors that influenced his/her decision on sexual identity.

B. The completed list was processed and key factors were confirmed.

C. The client's list could be processed only in a limited way due to its being incomplete and vague.

D. The client listed a preponderance of factors that supported the homosexual identity.

E. The client listed a preponderance of factors that supported a heterosexual identity.

11. **Explore Feelings about Self as Homosexual (11)**

A. The client's feelings regarding seeing self as homosexual were explored.

B. The client was assisted in identifying and expressing feelings about accepting self as a homosexual.

C. Feelings that were identified by the client as egosyntonic were affirmed and reinforced.

D. The client seemed relieved to finally accept himself/herself as homosexual.

E. The client expressed strong feelings of anxiety and fear of the future regarding accepting self as a homosexual.

12. **Explore Negative Emotions about Hiding Sexual Identity (12)**

A. The client's negative emotions related to hiding and denying his/her sexuality were explored.

B. Specific reasons for the client hiding or denying his/her sexuality were identified.

C. Specific reasons for the client hiding or denying his/her sexual identity were probed and challenged.

D. A warm, accepting, nonjudgmental approach was used to encourage the client to take risks and be more open about his/her sexual identity.

13. **Explore Religious Conflicts with Sexual Identity (13)**

A. The client's religious convictions were explored for ways they may cause conflict with his/her sexual identity.

B. The shame and guilt surrounding religious convictions and sexual identity were assessed and processed.

14. **Compassionate Clergy Referral (14)**

A. The client was referred to a compassionate clergy member who will listen to his/her struggles on sexual identity.

B. The client's experience with clergy was processed and positive aspects of the experience were affirmed and reinforced.

15. **Teach Safer Sex (15)**

A. Details of safer sex guidelines were taught to the client.

B. The client's questions related to the details of safer sex practices were answered.

C. The client was asked to make a commitment to consistently follow safer sex guidelines.

D. The client's adherence to a safer sex commitment was monitored, and he/she was confronted when not following that commitment.

16. Identify Myths and Replace with Positive Beliefs (16)

A. The client was assigned to identify 10 myths about homosexuals and, on a scale of 1 to 5, rate how firmly he/she believes in each.

B. The identified myths and their ratings were processed, then the client was assisted in replacing each with more realistic positive beliefs.

C. The client was reminded of the positive beliefs about homosexuality to reinforce his/her sexual identity.

D. Myths and negative statements about homosexuality by the client were confronted.

17. List Advantages/Disadvantages of Disclosing Sexual Identity (17)

A. The client was asked to make a list of advantages and disadvantages of disclosing sexual orientation to family and significant others.

B. The client processed his/her list of advantages and disadvantages of disclosing sexual orientation to the family and significant others.

C. The client's inability to list advantages of disclosing sexual identity were explored and addressed.

18. Explore Homophobic Peer Experiences (18)

A. The client's peer relationships were explored.

B. Assistance was provided to the client in describing homophobic experiences in peer relationships.

C. Ways to respond to homophobic and rejection experiences in peer relationships were identified.

19. Support Group Referral (19)

A. The client was assisted in identifying the benefits of attending a support group for lesbian and gay adolescents.

B. The client was referred to a lesbian/gay adolescent support group.

C. The client's experience in attending support group was processed, and positive aspects were affirmed and reinforced.

D. The client's resistance to attending a support group was explored and resolved.

E. The client made a commitment to attend a support group for gay and lesbian adolescents.

20. Identify Gay/Lesbian Peers (20)

A. The client was encouraged to identify other lesbian and gay adolescents from school and support groups as possible companions in social activities.

B. The client's fears regarding initiating social contact were addressed and resolved.

C. The client was asked to commit to making one attempt each week to initiate a social activity.

21. Develop Plan of Sexual Identity Disclosure (21)

A. The client was asked to develop a detailed plan for disclosing his/her sexual orientation.

B. The client's plan for disclosing his/her sexual identity was probed, and possible questions and reactions from others were identified and addressed.

C. The client's inability to develop a plan for disclosing his/her sexual identity was explored.

D. The client appeared ready to go forward with the plan for disclosing his/her sexual identity.

22. Role-Play Sexual-Orientation Disclosure (22)

A. Role play was utilized to prepare the client for disclosing sexual orientation to significant others.

B. Issues that were identified from role plays were addressed and resolved.

C. Feelings that emerged from role plays were recognized, expressed, and processed.

23. Support and Guide Sexual Identity Disclosure Plan (23)

A. The plan developed by the client for disclosure of sexual identity was reviewed and he/she encouraged to enact the plan.

B. The client was given support, encouragement, and guidance as he/she implemented his/her sexual orientation disclosure plan.

C. The client's hesitancy and fear to go forward with his/her plan was explored and addressed.

24. Process Reactions to Sexual Orientation Disclosure (24)

A. The client was probed about the reactions of significant others to his/her disclosure.

B. Significant others' reactions were role-played to provide opportunities to process their reactions.

C. Encouragement and positive feedback were given to the client for disclosing his/her sexual orientation.

D. The client reported that family members were shocked, angry, disappointed, and worried when he/she announced his/her sexual orientation.

E. The client reported that family members were accepting and supportive when he/she disclosed his/her sexual orientation.

25. Solicit Parents' Cooperation with Family Sessions (25)

A. Conjoint sessions were arranged with the parents to process the client's disclosure of his/her homosexual orientation.

B. The parents were encouraged to attend and participate in family therapy sessions.

C. The parents' resistance to attending family sessions about their child's sexual orientation was addressed.

26. Process Parents' Reactions to Client's Identity Disclosure (26)

A. The parents' reactions to the client's disclosure of homosexual identity were explored.

B. Emotional support and understanding was provided to the parents in regard to their reaction to the client's disclosure.

C. The parents were encouraged to express their thoughts and feelings about the disclosure.

D. The client's parents were very resistive to supporting the client's sexual identity.

E. The client's parents were supportive of the client's homosexual identity, but expressed fears regarding future adjustment.

27. Educate Parents about Homosexuality (27)

A. The parents were given an education about homosexuality, its possible causes, reversibility, lifestyle choices, and so forth.

B. The parents' questions regarding aspects of homosexuality were elicited and answered.

C. The parents were specifically reminded that homosexuality is not caused by faulty parenting or mental illness.

D. The benefits to the parents and the client of accepting the client's sexual orientation were explored and identified.

28. Assign Parents Books on Homosexuality (28)

A. The parents were directed to books and other resources on homosexuality and the homosexual individual.

B. Questions from the parents' readings were answered.

C. The parents were encouraged to seek opportunities to increase their knowledge and understanding of homosexuality.

D. The parents have refused to follow through on reading information regarding homosexuality.

29. Parent Support Group Referral (29)

A. Options for the parents to attend a support group for parents and friends of lesbians and gays (PFLAG) were explored and barriers identified.

B. The possible benefits of attending a support group were identified and processed.

C. The parents were referred and encouraged to attend a support group for parents and friends of lesbians and gays.

D. Barriers to attending a support group were resolved and the parents were encouraged to attend.

E. The parents' support group experience was processed and positive benefits were identified and reinforced.

30. Process Parents' Religious Beliefs about Homosexuality (30)

A. The parents were asked to list their religious beliefs regarding homosexuality.

B. The parents' religious beliefs were processed, and beliefs that were problematic to acceptance of homosexuality were identified.

C. Empathy was conveyed to the parents in regard to coming to some peace with their religious beliefs and the client's homosexuality.

D. The parents' religious beliefs were firmly opposed to acceptance of homosexual relationships and behavior.

E. Although the parents have held religious beliefs that are condemnatory of homosexual practice, they are open to reexamining these beliefs.

31. Parent Clergy Referral (31)

A. The parents were referred to a gay/lesbian-positive clergy to assist them in coming to terms with their beliefs regarding the Bible's condemnation of the client's homosexuality.

B. Gay- and lesbian-positive books were suggested for the client and parents to read and discuss.

32. Assign Parents Books on Religion and Homosexuality (32)

A. The parents were asked to read Chapter 4 in *Beyond Acceptance* (Griffen, Wirth, and Wirth) and to process key ideas with the client.

B. The parents were asked to read the chapter entitled "The Bible and Homosexuality: The Last Prejudice" from *The Good Book* by Gomes and to process key concepts and reactions with the client.

C. Assigned readings were processed with the parents and opportunities to increase their level of acceptance were explored and encouraged.

SOCIAL PHOBIA/SHYNESS

CLIENT PRESENTATION

1. Lack of Eye Contact (1)*

A. The parents and teachers reported that the client displays very little eye contact during his/her social interactions with others.

B. The client displayed poor eye contact during today's therapy session.

C. The client demonstrates satisfactory-to-good eye contact with individuals around whom he/she feels comfortable, but exhibits poor eye contact with unfamiliar people.

D. The client maintained good eye contact during today's therapy session.

E. The parents and teachers reported that the client consistently maintains good eye contact.

2. Quiet and Reserved (1)

A. The client reported a history of being quiet and reserved in the majority of his/her social interactions.

B. The client was very quiet in today's therapy session and initiated few conversations.

C. The client often does not respond to overtures from other people.

D. The client has started to appear more at ease in the therapy sessions, evidenced by the increased number of conversations that he/she initiates.

E. The client was much more open and talkative in today's therapy session.

3. Shyness/Social Anxiety (2)

A. The client described himself/herself as being shy and anxious in many social situations.

B. The client appeared anxious (e.g., hand tremors, lack of eye contact, fidgeting, restless, stammering) and inhibited during today's therapy session.

C. The client's social anxiety has gradually started to diminish, and he/she reported feeling more at ease in his/her conversations with others.

D. The client reported feeling confident and relaxed in the majority of his/her recent social interactions.

E. The client has interacted socially with his/her peers on a regular, consistent basis without excessive fear or anxiety.

4. Avoidance of Unfamiliar People (2)

A. The client has consistently avoided contact with unfamiliar people.

B. The client expressed feelings of anxiety about interacting with unfamiliar people.

C. The client has started to initiate more conversations with unfamiliar people.

D. The client has initiated social contacts with unfamiliar people on a consistent basis.

---

* The numbers in parentheses correlate to the number of the Behavioral Definition statement in the companion chapter with same title in *The Adolescent Psychotherapy Treatment Planner* (Jongsma, Peterson, and McInnis) by John Wiley & Sons, 2000.

5. Withdrawal in New Social Situations (2)

A. The parents and teachers reported that the client usually withdraws from others in social situations.

B. The client verbalized feelings of anxiety about interacting with others when placed in new social settings.

C. The client has recently started to assert himself/herself in new social settings.

D. The client has interacted with others in new social situations on a regular, consistent basis.

6. Social Isolation/Withdrawal (3)

A. The client described a persistent pattern of withdrawing or isolating himself/herself from most social situations.

B. The client acknowledged that his/her social withdrawal interferes with his/her ability to establish and maintain friendships.

C. The client has gradually started to socialize with a wider circle of peers.

D. The client has become more outgoing and interacted with his/her peers on a regular, consistent basis.

7. Excessive Isolated Activities (3)

A. The client has spent an excessive or inordinate amount of time involved in isolated activities instead of socializing with peers.

B. The client verbalized an understanding of how his/her excessive involvement in isolated activities interferes with his/her chances of establishing friendships.

C. The client reported spending less time in isolated activities and has started to seek out interactions with his/her peers.

D. The client has achieved a healthy balance between time spent in isolated activities and social interactions with others.

8. No Close Friendships (4)

A. The client described a history of having few or no close friendships.

B. The client does not have any close friends at the present time.

C. The client expressed feelings of sadness and loneliness about not having any close friends.

D. The client has begun to take steps (e.g., greeting others, complimenting others, making positive self-statements) to try to establish close friendships.

E. The client has now established close friendships at school and/or in the community.

9. Enmeshed Family Relationships (4)

A. The client has established an enmeshed relationship with his/her parents that interferes with his/her opportunities to socialize with peers.

B. The parents verbally recognized how they reinforce the client's excessive dependency at the expense of his/her peer friendships.

C. The parents have encouraged the client to become more independent.

D. The parents have reinforced the client's positive social behavior and set limits on overly dependent behavior.

E. The client has achieved a healthy balance between socializing with his/her peers and spending time with family members.

10. Overly Rigid Parents (4)

A. The parents' rigid and strict enforcement of rules and boundaries has decreased the opportunities that the client has to socialize with his/her peers.

B. The client expressed frustration about the parents being overly rigid and not allowing many opportunities for him/her to socialize with others.

C. The client effectively asserted himself/herself with parents and requested that he/she be given the opportunity to socialize more with peers.

D. The parents verbally recognized the need to loosen the rules and boundaries to allow for increased opportunities for the client to socialize with his/her peers.

E. The parents have established appropriate and fair boundaries that allow the client to spend time with peers and fulfill his/her responsibilities at home and school.

11. Hypersensitivity to Criticism/Rejection (5)

A. The client has been very hesitant to become involved with others for fear of being met by criticism, disapproval, or perceived signs of rejection.

B. The client described a history of experiencing excessive or undue criticism, disapproval, and rejection from parental figures.

C. The client acknowledged that he/she tends to overreact to the slightest sign of criticism, rebuff, or rejection and subsequently withdraws from other people.

D. The client has begun to tolerate criticism or rebuff from others more effectively.

E. The client has continued to interact with others even in the face of criticism, disapproval, or perceived slights from others.

12. Excessive Need for Reassurance (6)

A. The client has been very reluctant to become involved with others unless he/she receives strong signs of assurance that he/she is liked or accepted.

B. The client has often sought reassurance from others in order to feel positive about himself/herself.

C. The client has started to reassure himself/herself with positive self-talk instead of turning excessively to others for approval and affirmation.

D. The client has achieved a healthy balance between affirming self and seeking affirmation from others.

13. Reluctance to Take Risks (7)

A. The client has been reluctant to engage in new activities or take personal risks because of the potential for embarrassment or humiliation.

B. The client verbalized a desire to engage in new activities or take healthy risks to help improve his/her self-esteem and develop friendships.

C. The client has started to take healthy risks in order to find enjoyment, build self-esteem, and establish friendships.

D. The client has engaged in new activities and assumed healthy risks without excessive fear of embarrassment or humiliation.

14. Negative Self-Image (8)

A. The client's negative self-image and lack of confidence has interfered with his/her ability to establish friendships.

B. The client verbalized several self-derogatory remarks and compared self unfavorably to others.

C. The client shared his/her viewpoint of self as being socially unattractive.

D. The client's increased confidence in self has helped him/her be more outgoing.

E. The client has consistently verbalized positive statements about himself/herself in the presence of others.

15. Poor Social Skills (8)

A. The client has established poor social skills and presents as socially immature.

B. The client has lacked awareness and sensitivity to the social cues and interpersonal nuances that are necessary to build positive peer friendships.

C. The client has started to develop an awareness of the social skills needed to build meaningful friendships.

D. The client has displayed good social skills in his/her recent interactions with peers and adults.

E. The client has developed a number of essential social skills that have enhanced the quality of his/her interpersonal relationships.

16. Lack of Assertiveness (9)

A. The client historically has much difficulty asserting himself/herself in social situations where it is indicated.

B. The client has generally avoided any social situations that involve the potential for conflict.

C. The client has started to assert himself/herself more often instead of withdrawing from interpersonal problems or conflicts.

D. The client has recently asserted himself/herself in an effective manner during conflict with others.

17. Family History of Excessive Criticism (9)

A. The client reported a history of receiving undue or excessive criticism from his/her family members.

B. The client appeared sad, anxious, and upset when describing the criticism he/she has received from family members in the past.

C. The parents acknowledged that their overly harsh or critical remarks have contributed to the client's social anxiety, timidity, and low self-esteem.

D. The client asserted himself/herself with parents about their overly critical remarks and asked them to cease making derogatory remarks in the future.

E. The parents have increased the frequency of their positive statements toward the client and refrained from making any overly critical or hostile remarks about the client.

18. Physiological Distress (10)

A. The client's social anxiety has been manifested in his/her heightened physiological distress (e.g., increased heart rate, profuse sweating, dry mouth, muscular tension, and trembling).

B. The client was visibly anxious (e.g., trembling, shaking, sweating, appearing tense and rigid) when talking about his/her social relationships.

C. The client reported that he/she has recently experienced less physiological distress when interacting with others.

D. The client has been able to consistently interact with other people in a variety of social settings without experiencing physiological distress.

INTERVENTIONS IMPLEMENTED

1. Arrange for Psychological Testing (1)*

A. A psychological evaluation was conducted to assess the severity of the client's anxiety and help provide greater insight into the dynamics contributing to the emergence of his/her shyness and social anxiety.

B. The client was cooperative during the psychological testing and provided insight into the factors contributing to his/her social anxiety or shyness.

2. Arrange for Psychoeducational Evaluation (2)

A. The client received a psychoeducational evaluation to rule out the presence of a learning disability that may be contributing to his/her social withdrawal in the school setting.

B. The client was cooperative during the psychoeducational evaluation and appeared to put forth his/her best effort.

C. The client's low self-esteem and feelings of insecurity appeared to interfere with his/her performance during the psychoeducational evaluation.

3. Speech/Language Evaluation Referral (3)

A. The client was referred for a comprehensive speech/language evaluation to rule out any impairment that may contribute to his/her social withdrawal.

B. The client was accepting of the need for a comprehensive speech/language evaluation.

C. The comprehensive speech/language evaluation revealed the presence of a speech/language impairment that contributes to the client's social withdrawal.

D. The comprehensive speech/language evaluation did not reveal the presence of a speech/language impairment that would contribute to the client's social withdrawal.

4. Provide Evaluation Feedback (4)

A. The client and his/her parents were given feedback on the findings from the psychological evaluation.

B. The psychological testing results confirmed the presence of an anxiety disorder that contributes to the client's shyness and social withdrawal.

* The numbers in parentheses correlate to the number of the Therapeutic Intervention statement in the companion chapter with the same title in *The Adolescent Psychotherapy Treatment Planner* (Jongsma, Peterson, and McInnis) by John Wiley & Sons, 2000.

C. The psychological testing results indicated that the client is experiencing a significant amount of depression that is contributing to his/her social withdrawal.

D. The psychoeducational evaluation results revealed the presence of a learning disability that contributes to the client's lack of confidence and social withdrawal in the school setting.

E. The psychoeducational evaluation results did not reveal the presence of a learning disability that may contribute to the client's social withdrawal.

5. Build Trust (5)

A. Today's therapy session focused on building the level of trust with the client through consistent eye contact, active listening, unconditional positive regard, and warm acceptance.

B. Unconditional positive regard and warm acceptance helped the client increase his/her ability to identify and express feelings.

C. The therapy session was helpful in building the level of trust with the client, and he/she became more open and relaxed.

D. The session was not helpful in building the level of trust with the client, who remained quiet and reserved in his/her interactions.

6. Utilize *In Vivo* Systematic Desensitization (6)

A. A systematic desensitization program was designed to help decrease the client's social anxiety and increase the frequency and duration of social contacts.

B. The client and parents verbally agreed to follow through with the implementation of the systematic desensitization program.

C. The client and parents followed through with the implementation of the systematic desensitization program and reported a reduction in social anxiety.

D. The client and parents partially followed through with the systematic desensitization program and reported a minimal reduction in social anxiety.

E. The client and parents failed to follow through with the implementation of the systematic desensitization program, and as a result, the client did not experience a decrease in the reduction of his/her social anxiety.

7. Develop Reward System/Contingency Contract (7)

A. A list of rewards was developed to reinforce the client for initiating social contacts and/or engaging in leisure/recreational activities with peers.

B. A reward system was designed to reinforce the client for initiating social contacts and/or engaging in leisure/recreational activities with peers.

C. The client signed a contingency contract specifying the rewards for increasing his/her social contacts and/or specifying negative consequences for failing to initiate the agreed-upon number of social contacts.

D. The client has recently increased his/her social contacts and successfully met the goals of the reward system.

E. The client failed to follow through with the conditions outlined in the contingency contract and did not increase his/her social contacts.

8. Teach Guided Imagery/Relaxation (8)

A. The client was taught guided imagery and deep muscle relaxation techniques to help decrease his/her social anxiety.

B. The client consistently practiced the guided imagery and deep muscle relaxation techniques at home between the therapy sessions.

C. The client reported a positive response to the use of guided imagery or deep muscle relaxation techniques to help decrease his/her social anxiety.

D. The client reported that the guided imagery and deep muscle relaxation techniques have not been helpful in reducing his/her social anxiety.

9. Reinforce Positive Self-Talk (9)

A. The client was encouraged to utilize positive self-talk as a means of managing his/her social anxiety or fears.

B. Role-playing and modeling techniques were used to teach the client positive self-talk to reduce social anxiety or fears.

C. The client reported that the use of positive self-talk between the therapy sessions helped to reduce his/her social anxiety.

D. The client reported that he/she tried to use positive self-talk, but still felt overwhelmed by his/her social anxiety.

E. The client failed to follow through with utilizing positive self-talk as a means to reduce his/her social anxiety or fears.

10. Assign Initiating Social Contact (10)

A. The client was given the directive to initiate one social contact per day.

B. The client followed through with the directive to initiate at least one social contact per day.

C. The client partially followed through with the directive to initiate one social contact per day.

D. The client failed to follow through with the directive to initiate one social contact per day.

E. Role-playing and modeling techniques were utilized to teach effective ways to initiate social contacts.

11. Assign Initiating Phone Calls (11)

A. The client was given a homework assignment to initiate three phone calls per week to different individuals.

B. Role-playing and modeling techniques were utilized to teach appropriate ways to initiate conversations during phone calls.

C. The client complied with the homework assignment and called three different individuals per week since the last therapy session.

D. The client partially followed through with the homework assignment to make phone calls to three different individuals per week.

E. The client failed to follow through with the homework assignment to make three phone calls per week to different individuals.

12. Use Role Playing to Teach Social Skills (12)

A. Behavior rehearsal, modeling, and role-playing techniques were used to teach positive social skills and appropriate ways to initiate conversations with others.

B. The client was able to identify several positive social skills after engaging in the behavior rehearsal and role-playing exercises.

C. After role-playing in the therapy session, the client expressed a willingness to practice the newly learned social skills in his/her everyday situations.

D. The client reported that he/she recently practiced the social skills that were taught through role playing.

E. The client did not follow through with practicing many of the social skills that were modeled in the previous therapy session.

13. Reinforce Social Behavior (13)

A. The parents were strongly encouraged to praise and reinforce any emerging positive social behavior.

B. The client's positive social behavior was praised during today's therapy session.

C. The client was asked to list some positive social behavior that he/she exhibited.

14. "Greeting Peers" Exercise (14)

A. The client was given the "Greeting Peers" exercise from *The Brief Adolescent Therapy Homework Planner* (Jongsma, Peterson, and McInnis) to reduce social isolation and help him/her begin to take steps toward establishing peer friendships.

B. The client successfully completed the "Greeting Peers" exercise and was reinforced for initiating social contacts.

C. The client partially completed the "Greeting Peers" exercise, initiating contact with some peers socially, but it was an anxiety-producing experience for the client.

D. The client did not follow through in completing the "Greeting Peers" exercise and the assignment was given again.

15. Encourage Participation in Peer Group Activities (15)

A. The client was strongly encouraged to participate in extracurricular or positive peer group activities to provide opportunities to establish meaningful friendships.

B. The client was assisted in developing a list of positive peer group activities that will provide him/her with the opportunity to establish meaningful friendships.

C. The client verbalized an understanding of how his/her feelings of insecurity and inadequacy contribute to his/her reluctance to become involved in positive peer group activities.

D. The client reported to recently participating in positive peer group activities.

E. The client denied participating in any recent extracurricular or positive peer group activities.

16. Assign Overnight Visit with Friend (16)

A. The client was given the homework assignment to either invite a friend for an overnight visit and/or set up an overnight visit at the friend's home.

B. The client was given the opportunity to express and work through his/her fears and anxiety about inviting a friend for an overnight visit or setting up an overnight visit at the friend's home.

C. The client complied with the directive to have an overnight visit with a friend, which resulted in some anxiety but also in pride of accomplishment.

D. The client failed to set up an overnight visit with a friend.

17. List Similarities with Peers (17)

A. The client was assisted in developing a list of similarities between himself/herself and his/her peers.

B. The client was assisted in developing a list of activities that he/she could engage in with peers.

C. The client was encouraged to share his/her interests with peers who have similar interests.

18. Identify Positive Role Models (18)

A. The client identified his/her role models and listed several reasons that he/she admired each role model.

B. The client was strongly encouraged to engage in behavior or activities that help him/her identify with role models and connect with his/her peers at the same time.

C. The client reported that he/she was able to connect with peers by engaging in behavior or activities similar to those of his/her role models.

19. "Show Your Strengths" Exercise (19)

A. The client was assigned the "Show Your Strengths" exercise from *The Brief Adolescent Therapy Homework Planner* (Jongsma, Peterson, and McInnis) to help the client identify his/her strengths or interests that could be used to initiate social contacts and establish friendships.

B. The client successfully completed the "Show Your Strengths" exercise and felt good about sharing the results with peers, as they were receptive.

C. The client did not follow through with completing the "Show Your Strengths" exercise and was asked again to work on it.

20. Assign Social Experiences Journal (20)

A. The client was asked to keep a journal of his/her positive and negative social experiences between therapy sessions.

B. Processed the client's positive and negative social experiences that were listed in his/her journal.

C. The client failed to develop a list or keep a journal of his/her positive and negative social experiences.

21. Provide Feedback on Negative Social Behavior (21)

A. The client was given feedback on his/her negative social behaviors that interfere with his/her ability to establish and maintain friendships.

B. The client appeared defensive when given feedback on his/her negative social behaviors.

C. The client responded favorably to constructive criticism about his/her negative social behaviors and identified more appropriate social behaviors that will help him/her establish and maintain friendships.

22. Contact School Officials about Socialization (22)

A. School officials were contacted about ways to increase the client's socialization (e.g., writing for school newspaper, tutoring a more popular peer, pairing the client with another popular peer on classroom assignment).

B. The school officials agreed to assign tasks or activities that will enable the client to socialize with peers.

C. The consultation with school officials was helpful in increasing the client's socialization with his/her peers.

23. Instruct Parents/Teachers to Reinforce Social Behavior (23)

A. The parents and teachers were instructed to observe and record positive behaviors by the client in between therapy sessions.

B. The parents and teachers were encouraged to reinforce the client for engaging in positive social behaviors.

C. The client was strongly encouraged to continue to engage in the positive social behaviors to help him/her establish lasting friendships.

24. Identify Past Coping Mechanisms to Reduce Social Anxiety (24)

A. The client was assisted in identifying positive coping mechanisms that he/she used in the past to reduce his/her anxiety in social settings.

B. The client was strongly encouraged to utilize successful coping strategies from the past that helped to reduce his/her social anxiety.

C. The client reported successfully reducing his/her social anxiety by employing coping strategies that were successful in the past.

25. Teach Assertiveness Skills (25)

A. The client was taught effective assertiveness skills to help communicate his/her thoughts, feelings, and needs more openly and directly.

B. Role-playing techniques were used to teach effective assertiveness skills.

C. The client reported that newly acquired assertiveness skills helped him/her feel more confident in social situations.

D. The client failed to use assertiveness skills that were recently taught.

26. Employ *Skillstreaming: The Adolescent Kit* (26)

A. *Skillstreaming: The Adolescent Kit* was employed to help teach the client positive social skills.

B. The client was able to identify several positive social skills through the use of *Skillstreaming: The Adolescent Kit.*

C. The client was given a homework assignment of implementing three positive social skills that were learned through the use of *Skillstreaming: The Adolescent Kit.*

27. Employ The Helping, Sharing, and Caring Game (27)

A. The Helping, Sharing, and Caring Game was employed to help establish rapport with the client.

B. After playing The Helping, Sharing, and Caring Game, the client was able to identify several positive social skills that will help him/her establish and maintain friendships.

C. The client was given the homework assignment of exercising three positive skills that were discussed while playing The Helping, Sharing, and Caring Game.

28. Explore History of Traumas (28)

A. The client's background was explored for a history of rejection experiences, harsh criticism, abandonment, or trauma that may have contributed to the client's low self-esteem and social anxiety.

B. The client developed a time line where he/she identified significant historical events, both positive and negative, that have occurred in his/her background.

C. The client identified a history of abandonment and/or traumatic experiences that coincided with the onset of his/her feelings of low self-esteem and social anxiety.

D. Exploration of the client's background did not reveal any significant rejection or traumatic experiences that contributed to the onset of his/her social anxiety.

29. Explore Feelings Associated with Traumas (29)

A. The client was given the opportunity to express his/her feelings about past rejection experiences, harsh criticism, abandonment, or trauma.

B. The client was instructed to use a journal to record his/her thoughts and feelings about past rejection experiences, harsh criticism, abandonment, or trauma.

C. The empty-chair technique was employed to facilitate expression of feelings surrounding past rejection experiences, harsh criticism, abandonment, or trauma.

D. The client was instructed to draw pictures that reflect his/her feelings about past rejection experiences, harsh criticism, abandonment, or trauma.

30. Assign Letter to Critical Individual(s) (30)

A. The client was given the directive to write a letter to individual(s) to whom he/she perceives as having subjected himself/herself to unfair criticism, rejection, or harassment.

B. After reviewing the client's letter, his/her feelings about the unfair criticism, ridicule, or harassment were processed.

31. Explore Family Dynamics/Stressors (31)

A. A family therapy session was held to explore the dynamics within the family system that contribute to the client's feelings of anxiety and insecurity.

B. The client and family members were asked to list the stressors that have had a negative impact on the family and have contributed to the client's feelings of anxiety and insecurity.

C. The client and family members were asked to identify the things that they would like to change within the family.

D. The therapy session was helpful in identifying the family dynamics that have contributed to the client's feelings of anxiety and insecurity.

E. The therapy session did not reveal any significant stressors within the family system that have contributed to the client's feelings of anxiety and insecurity.

32. Assign Family Kinetic Drawing (32)

A. The client was asked to produce a family kinetic drawing to provide insight into the dynamics that may contribute to his/her social phobia.

B. The client's family kinetic drawing was helpful in providing insight into the factors contributing to his/her social phobia.

C. The client's family kinetic drawing did not shed any insight into the factors contributing to his/her social phobia.

33. Reinforce Parents' Limits on Dependent Behavior (33)

A. The parents were strongly encouraged to reinforce the client's steps toward greater independence.

B. The parents were challenged to set limits on the client's overly dependent behaviors (e.g., immature whining and complaining, shadowing parents in social settings).

C. The client was encouraged to engage in independent activities outside the home and/or away from parents.

D. The client followed through with the recommendation to engage in independent activities outside the home.

E. The client failed to follow through with the recommendation to engage in independent activities outside the home.

34. Teach Parents to Ignore Mild Oppositional Behavior (34)

A. The parents were instructed to ignore occasional and mild oppositional or aggressive behaviors by the client (unless they become too intense or frequent) during the initial stages of treatment so as not to extinguish emerging assertive behaviors.

B. The parents were helped to identify times when it is best to ignore mild oppositional or aggressive behavior versus times when it is appropriate to set limits for more intense oppositional or aggressive behavior.

35. Explore Parental Reinforcement of Dependency (35)

A. The therapy session explored how the overly enmeshed parents reinforce the client's dependency and social anxiety while impeding his/her chances to socialize with peers.

B. The parents were encouraged to engage in social activities (e.g., going out on date together) independent of the client.

C. The parents followed through with the recommendation to engage in social activities independent of the client.

D. The parents failed to follow through with the recommendation to socialize with others independent of the client.

36. Teach Power of Secondary Gain (36)

A. A family therapy session was held to explore whether the client achieves any secondary gain from his/her social anxiety and withdrawal.

B. The client and parents were assisted in identifying the secondary gain(s) that are achieved from his/her social anxiety and withdrawal.

C. The therapy session was helpful in showing how the client's social withdrawal reduces his/her social anxiety in the short run and maintains a close relationship with his/her parents.

D. The client verbally recognized how his/her social withdrawal and unwillingness to take healthy risks prevents him/her from experiencing rejection, but also interferes with chances to establish friendships.

E. The family therapy session failed to identify any secondary gain that is achieved from the client's social anxiety and withdrawal.

37. Assess Parents for Being Overly Strict (37)

A. A family therapy session was held to explore whether the parents are overly rigid or strict in the establishment of rules and boundaries to the point where client has little opportunity to socialize with peers.

B. The client was instructed to draw a house and then describe what it is like to live in that house.

C. The client was taught effective assertiveness and communication skills to help him/her assert self with parents about them being overly rigid or strict in their enforcement of rules and boundaries.

D. The client was asked to identify which rules he/she would like to change in the family.

38. Encourage Parents to Loosen Rules (38)

A. The parents were encouraged and challenged to loosen their rules and boundaries to allow the shy, timid client increased opportunities to socialize with peers.

B. The parents agreed to loosen some of the rules and boundaries to allow the client an increased opportunity to socialize with his/her peers.

C. The parents were resistant to the idea of loosening their rules and boundaries.

D. The client and parents identified an appropriate curfew and a list of social activities that the client can engage in with his/her peers.

39. Utilize Empty-Chair Technique (39)

A. The empty-chair technique was utilized to provide the client with the opportunity to express his/her feelings toward the overly critical, rejecting, or absent parent.

B. The client made constructive use of the empty-chair technique to express feelings of anger, hurt, and sadness toward the overly critical, rejecting, or absent parent.

C. The client had difficulty expressing his/her feelings toward the overly critical, rejecting, or absent parent through the use of the empty-chair technique.

40. Employ Art Therapy Techniques (40)

A. The client was instructed to draw a picture in the therapy session reflecting his/her fears of what will possibly happen if he/she asserts self with others or engages in social activities with unfamiliar people.

B. After finishing his/her drawing the client was able to verbally identify his/her fears of what may happen if he/she asserts self with others or engages in social activities with unfamiliar people.

C. The client's drawing reflected his/her fears about embarrassing or humiliating self in front of others.

D. The client produced a drawing that reflected his/her fears about being ignored or rejected by others.

41. Employ Music Therapy Techniques (41)

A. The client shared a song that reflected his/her insecurities and social anxiety.

B. The client shared a song that afterward led to a discussion of how the song reflects his/her insecurities and what he/she can do to overcome the insecurities or social anxiety.

C. The client was encouraged to share his/her interest in music with peers to help establish friendships.

42. Group Therapy Referral (42)

A. The client was referred for group therapy to improve his/her social skills.

B. The client was supportive of the recommendation to participate in group therapy to help improve his/her social skills.

C. The client voiced his/her objection to being referred for group therapy to improve his/her social anxiety.

43. Instruct Client to Self-Disclose in Group Sessions (43)

A. The client was given the directive to self-disclose at least two times in each group therapy session.

B. The client complied with the directive to self-disclose twice in today's group therapy session.

C. The client failed to follow through with the directive to self-disclose at least twice in today's therapy session.

D. The client was encouraged to make positive self-statements or share positive life experiences in the group therapy sessions.

44. Art Therapy Group Referral (44)

A. The client was referred to an art therapy group to help him/her express feelings and reveal aspects of self to others through his/her artwork.

B. The client was given the directive to share and talk about his/her artwork with other members of the art therapy group.

C. The client was resistant to share or talk about his/her artwork with the other members of the art therapy group.

45. Medication Evaluation Referral (45)

A. The client was referred to a physician for a medication evaluation with an eye to decreasing his/her anxiety or emotional distress.

B. The client and parents agreed to follow through with the recommendation to receive a medication evaluation from a physician.

C. The client was strongly opposed to being placed on medication to help decrease his/her social anxiety or emotional distress.

46. Monitor Medication Effects (46)

A. The client reported that the medication has helped to decrease his/her anxiety and stabilize moods.

B. The client reports little or no improvement while on the medication.

C. The client has not complied with taking his/her medication on a regular basis.

D. The client reported experiencing side effects from the prescribed medication.

SPECIFIC PHOBIA

CLIENT PRESENTATION

1. Persistent and Unreasonable Fear (1)*

A. An immediate anxiety response has been exhibited by the client each time he/she encounters the phobic stimulus.

B. The client reported that the strength of his/her phobic response has been increasing in the past several months.

C. The client described the level of fear he/she experiences in response to the phobic stimulus as paralyzing.

D. The client indicated that although the phobia is of recent origin, it has quickly become very persistent and unreasonable.

E. As the client has become engaged in therapy, there has been a decrease in the intensity and frequency of the phobic response.

2. Avoidance and Endurance of Phobia (2)

A. The client reported that his/her avoidance of the phobic stimulus has caused major interference in his/her normal daily routines.

B. The client indicated that the intensity of his/her anxiety in response to the phobic stimulus has resulted in marked personal distress.

C. The client questioned whether he/she would ever be able to resolve the phobia.

D. The client has progressed to the point where the phobic stimulus does not create interference in his/her normal daily routines or cause him/her marked distress.

3. Sleep Disturbance (3)

A. The client reported that his/her sleep has been disturbed by frequent dreams of the feared stimulus.

B. The client indicated his/her disturbed sleep pattern has started to affect his/her daily functioning.

C. The client's sleep has improved as he/she has worked toward resolving the feared stimulus.

4. Dramatic Fear Reaction (4)

A. At the slightest mention of the phobic stimulus, the client indicated he/she has a dramatic fear reaction.

B. The client's reaction to the phobic stimulus is so dramatic and overpowering that it is difficult to calm him/her down.

C. The client reported his/her reaction to the phobic stimulus is rapidly becoming more and more dramatic.

---

* The numbers in parentheses correlate to the number of the Behavioral Definition statement in the companion chapter with same title in *The Adolescent Psychotherapy Treatment Planner* (Jongsma, Peterson, and McInnis) by John Wiley & Sons, 2000.

D. There has been a marked decrease in the client's dramatic fear reaction to the phobic stimulus since he/she has started to work in therapy sessions.

5. Parental Reinforcement (5)

A. The parents have catered to the client's fear and have thus reinforced and increased it.

B. The parents' own fears seemed to be projected onto and acted out by the client.

C. The parents have worked to curb their reaction to the client's fears, which has resulted in a marked decrease in the client's level of fear.

INTERVENTIONS IMPLEMENTED

1. Build Trust (1)*

A. Initial trust level established with the client through the use of unconditional positive regard.

B. Warm acceptance and active listening techniques were utilized to establish the basis for a trusting relationship.

C. The client has formed a trust-based relationship and has begun to express his/her fearful thoughts and feelings.

D. Despite the use of active listening, warm acceptance, and unconditional positive regard, the client remains hesitant to trust and to share his/her thoughts and feelings.

2. Assess Client's Fear (2)

A. The history of the development of the client's phobic fear was gathered.

B. The range of stimuli for the client's fear was discussed in depth and assessed.

C. Times and instances when the client was free from the fear while in the presence of the phobic stimulus were explored.

D. It was clear from the assessment of the client's phobic fear that he/she becomes overwhelmed and virtually paralyzed when in the presence of the phobic stimulus.

3. Construct Anxiety Hierarchy (3)

A. The client was directed and assisted in constructing a hierarchy of anxiety-producing situations.

B. The client was successful in identifying a range of stimulus situations that produced increasingly greater amounts of anxiety.

4. Teach Progressive Relaxation (4)

A. The client was taught progressive relaxation methods.

B. Behavioral rehearsal was utilized to increase the client's mastery of the relaxation methods.

C. The client was successful in developing relaxation techniques using the deep muscle and guided imagery methods.

---

* The numbers in parentheses correlate to the number of the Therapeutic Intervention statement in the companion chapter with the same title in *The Adolescent Psychotherapy Treatment Planner* (Jongsma, Peterson, and McInnis) by John Wiley & Sons, 2000.

D. The client was instructed to continue to practice the deep muscle relaxation methods as a homework assignment.

5. Use EMG Biofeedback (5)

A. EMG biofeedback techniques were utilized to facilitate the client's relaxation skills.

B. The client achieved deeper levels of relaxation from the EMG biofeedback experience.

6. Teach Guided Imagery (6)

A. Guided imagery techniques were taught to the client to enhance relaxation.

B. The when and where of putting guided imagery to use was discussed with the client.

C. A plan for implementation was developed and the client was asked to make a commitment to utilizing the techniques in the identified circumstances.

7. Implement Systematic Desensitization (7)

A. A systematic desensitization procedure was utilized to reduce the client's phobic response.

B. The desensitization procedure was observed to produce a marked decrease in the client's phobic response.

C. The client reported that his/her level of anxiety has been reduced significantly since the implementation of the systematic desensitization procedures.

8. Assign *In Vivo* Desensitization (8)

A. An *in vivo* desensitization experience was assigned to the client in which he/she had graduated contact with his/her phobic stimulus.

B. The "Gradually Facing a Phobic Fear" exercise from *The Brief Adolescent Therapy Homework Planner* (Jongsma, Peterson, McInnis) was assigned to the client to help prepare him/her to directly face the phobic fear.

C. The client's successful *in vivo* encounter with the phobic stimulus was processed, and the client was asked to repeat the encounter.

9. Employ Stimulus Desensitization Interventions (9)

A. A session was conducted with the client in which he/she was surrounded with pleasant pictures, readings, and storytelling related to the phobic stimulus situation.

B. The client remained calm and relaxed while the phobic stimulus situation was depicted in pictures, informational material, and storytelling.

C. The client's ability to face the phobic fear was affirmed and his/her ability to cope was reinforced.

10. Interject Use of Humor (10)

A. Situational humor, jokes, riddles, and stories about the phobic stimulus were used to decrease the client's tension and seriousness regarding the fear.

B. The client was asked to start each day by telling the parents a joke, riddle, or silly story about the phobic stimulus.

C. A humorous side was pointed out for each issue/fear the client raised.

11. Assign and Process *Phobia Workbook* Exercise (11)

A. The client was asked to complete an exercise on coping skills from the *Phobia Workbook* (Bourne).

B. The completed *Phobia Workbook* exercise was processed and new possibilities for handling phobic fear were identified.

C. A plan was developed for implementing the new coping strategies from the *Phobia Workbook,* and the client was asked to make a commitment to follow through and use each strategy.

D. New coping strategies from the *Phobia Workbook* have been successful in reducing the client's fear response.

12. Role-Play Coping Strategies (12)

A. A role play was conducted with the client in regard to one of his/her phobic fears.

B. The role play was processed and a strategy to address the client's fear was identified.

C. The role play was repeated with the client using the new coping strategy.

D. The client committed to using the new coping strategy in everyday situations when the fear occurs.

E. The client reported that the new coping strategy developed from the role play has been successful in reducing his/her level of phobic fear.

13. Read "The Green Dragon" (13)

A. The story "The Green Dragon" (*Stories for the Third Ear* by L. Wallas) was read with the client, and ways of handling fears that appeared in the story were explored.

B. The client was asked to choose one of the coping strategies from "The Green Dragon" and implement it when the phobic fear arises.

C. The client reported that the coping strategy identified from "The Green Dragon" has been helpful in reducing the phobic fear.

14. Teach Use of Therapist as Coping Strategy (14)

A. The client was introduced to the strategy "The Therapist on the Inside" (Grigoryev, in *101 Favorite Play Therapy Techniques*), and the details of implementation were gone over carefully.

B. The client was asked to commit to implementing the internalized therapist strategy in face of the phobic fear in everyday life, then to report the results.

C. The internalized therapist strategy was monitored, with adjustments being made and with the client's positive implementations being reinforced.

15. Utilize "Finding What Works" Strategy (15)

A. The "Finding What Works" approach (*Guide to Possibility Land* by O'Hanlon and Beadle) was explored with the client to find times in the past when he/she responded effectively to the phobic stimulus situation.

B. A solution was identified in which the client had effectively coped with his/her phobic stimulus in the past, and the client was asked to use this solution whenever confronted by the fear in the future.

C. The fear-reduction solution was monitored for the client's follow-through, and positive feedback was given each time the client used the solution with success.

16. Trance to Cope with Fear (16)

A. The client was induced into a light trance and asked to visualize a movie in which he/she confronts and successfully responds to the phobic stimulus situation.

B. After the client came out of the trance, the evident attitude of coping with the phobic stimulus was reinforced.

C. The client reported that he/she was able to encounter the phobic stimulus situation with reduced fear and increased confidence since the trance technique was used.

17. Play Game Close to Phobic Object (17)

A. A game of the client's choice was played with him/her in the presence of the feared object.

B. The experience of being close to the feared object was processed, and positive reinforcement was given to the client for his/her accomplishment.

18. Implement Strategic Intervention of Symptom Enactment (18)

A. The client was given the prescription of acting out his/her symptom daily at a specific time and in specific ways.

B. The client was asked to make a commitment to following through as prescribed.

C. The client's follow-through was monitored, and effective utilization was affirmed and reinforced.

D. The client reported that the symptom enactment procedure has helped him/her reduce his/her phobic fear.

19. Enlist Family Support (19)

A. In family session, the parents were taught various ways to give support to the client when he/she experienced his/her phobic fear and were coached not to give support when the client panicked or failed to face fear.

B. The parents' implementation of the support intervention strategy was monitored, and they received support, encouragement, and, as necessary, redirection.

C. The client has been more successful in overcoming the phobic stimulus situation since the parents have reinforced the client's encounters.

20. Identify Parental Reinforcement of Phobia (20)

A. The parents were assisted in identifying the ways in which they reinforce the client's phobia.

B. The family was assisted in identifying ways each member could reinforce the client's success in overcoming the phobia.

C. The parents were confronted when they were observed reinforcing the client's fear.

21. Assess Family Members Modeling Fear (21)

A. Family members were assessed for their own phobic fear responses that teach the client to be afraid.

B. Family members were confronted on their own phobic fear responses that reinforce the client's phobic fear.

C. Family members were taught new ways of responding to their phobic stimulus situations that would not reinforce the phobic fear.

D. The family members who continue to experience phobic fear of their own were referred for individual counseling to treat this condition.

22. Explore Symbolic Meanings of Phobic Situation (22)

A. The possible symbolic meaning of the client's phobic stimulus was probed and discussed.

B. Selected interpretations of the phobic stimulus were offered to the client, and each was processed with him/her.

23. Clarify and Differentiate Present Fears from Past Pains (23)

A. The client was asked to list his/her present fears and also past emotionally painful experiences that may be related to the current fear.

B. The client was assisted in clarifying and separating his/her present irrational fears from past emotionally painful experiences.

C. Since the client was successful in separating past emotionally painful experiences from the present, he/she has reduced his/her level of phobic fear.

24. Encourage the Expression of Feelings (24)

A. The positive value of expressing feelings was emphasized with the client.

B. Using active listening and unconditional positive regard techniques, the client was encouraged to express his/her feelings regarding the past painful experiences.

C. Gentle questioning was used with the client to help him/her start sharing feelings from the past.

D. Feelings that were shared regarding past painful experiences were affirmed and supported.

25. Link Past Pain with Present Anxiety (25)

A. The connection the client was making between his/her past emotional pain and present anxiety was pointed out.

B. When talking about his/her present fear the client was reminded of how he/she connected it to his/her past emotional pain.

C. Since the client was successful in separating past emotionally painful experiences from the present, he/she has reduced his/her level of phobic fear.

26. Distinguish Real from Imagined Fear (26)

A. The client was asked to make a list of all his/her fears, then put an asterisk beside the ones that he/she believed were, without question, rational and reasonable.

B. The client was helped to differentiate and make clear distinctions between real and imagined fear-producing situations.

C. The client was confronted when he/she was observed in session talking as if an irrational fear were reasonable and acceptable.

27. Identify Disturbed Schemas and Automatic Thoughts (27)

A. The client was asked to list all thoughts and ideas he/she has before a panic attack.

B. Using client's list of anxiety-producing thoughts, he/she was assisted in identifying all distorted schemas and automatic thoughts that precede and contribute to his/her anxiety response.

28. Revise Core Schemas and Replace Negative Talk (28)

A. Cognitive restructuring was used to teach the client how to revise his/her core schemas.

B. The client was assisted in developing positive, realistic self-talk to replace negative, distorted messages.

C. Role play and behavioral rehearsal were used to give the client an opportunity to implement positive, realistic self-talk in coping with his/her fear.

D. The client was confronted when parts of old schemas or distorted, negative messages appeared in his/her thought processing.

E. The cognitive restructuring has been successful in reducing the client's phobic fear response.

29. Assign "How to Conquer Anxiety, Fears, and Phobias" (29)

A. The client was asked to read "How to Conquer Anxiety, Fears, and Phobia" from *The Feeling Good Handbook* (Burns) and identify five key ideas from the reading.

B. The reading regarding conquering phobias was processed with the client, and key ideas and strategies were identified and reinforced.

30. Assign "Cost-Benefit Analysis" (30)

A. The client was asked to complete "Cost-Benefit Analysis" from *Ten Days to Self-Esteem* (Burns) to help identify the pros and cons of his/her fears and phobias.

B. The cost-benefit analysis exercise was processed with the client, and special emphasis was placed on identifying the benefits that the client receives from maintaining the fear.

C. The idea of letting go of the phobic fear/anxiety was explored with the client, with emphasis placed on the positive, freeing aspects of doing so.

31. "Panic Attack Rating Form" Exercise (31)

A. The client was asked to use "Panic Attack Rating Form" from *The Brief Adolescent Therapy Homework Planner* (Jongsma, Peterson, McInnis) to assist in journaling his/her anxiety experiences.

B. Journal entries were reviewed, and patterns of anxiety antecedents and consequences were identified.

32. Verbally Reinforce Progress (32)

A. The client's progress in overcoming the phobic fear was reviewed and verbally reinforced.

B. The client was asked to list all circumstances in which he/she was successful in overcoming the phobic stimulus situation, and the success was reinforced.

33. Medication Referral (33)

A. The client was referred for a physician evaluation for possible psychotropic medications.

B. The client was asked to commit to following through on all recommendations of the physician evaluation.

C. Communication was established with the physician pre- and postevaluation.

34. Monitor Medication Compliance and Effectiveness (34)

A. The client was informed about major side effects of the medication and asked to report any that he/she experiences.

B. The client was monitored for compliance with the prescription, and the effectiveness was also noted.

C. The client was confronted when he/she reported not taking the medication consistently, and positive aspects of medication were reinforced with the client.

SUICIDAL IDEATION/ATTEMPT

CLIENT PRESENTATION

1. Recurrent Thoughts of or Preoccupation with Death (1)*

A. The parents reported that the client exhibits a strong preoccupation with the subject of death and talks about this topic frequently.

B. The client spoke about death at length in today's therapy session.

C. The client's music preferences, artwork, poetry, written notes, and/or letters have often reflected themes of death.

D. The client did not talk about death in today's therapy session.

E. The client denied experiencing any recent thoughts of death.

2. Suicidal Ideation without a Plan (2)

A. The client reported experiencing suicidal thoughts, but has not developed a specific plan to carry out those thoughts.

B. The client acknowledged expressing suicidal thoughts as a "cry for help," but denied having a specific plan to harm himself/herself.

C. The client denied experiencing any recent suicidal thoughts.

D. The client has taken positive steps to overcome his/her depression or manage stress and has not experienced any further suicidal thoughts.

3. Passive Death Wishes (2)

A. The parents reported that the client has expressed wishes that he/she were dead.

B. The client reported a passive wish to die, but has not developed any specific suicidal thoughts or plans.

C. The client denied experiencing any recent passive death wishes.

D. The client has developed a renewed interest in life and has not experienced any further passive death wishes.

4. Suicidal Ideation with a Plan (3)

A. The client expressed suicidal thoughts in today's therapy session and admitted that he/she has developed a specific plan to take his/her life.

B. The client's suicide risk is high because of his/her recurrent suicidal thoughts, development of a specific plan, and the means to carry out the plan.

C. The client acknowledged that he/she has recently contemplated suicide briefly, but has not experienced a desire or urge to follow through on a specific plan.

D. The client verbally denied experiencing any recent suicidal thoughts or having a plan to harm himself/herself.

---

* The numbers in parentheses correlate to the number of the Behavioral Definition statement in the companion chapter with same title in *The Adolescent Psychotherapy Treatment Planner* (Jongsma, Peterson, and McInnis) by John Wiley & Sons, 2000.

E. The client's suicide risk has decreased substantially since the onset of therapy, and he/she no longer experiences suicidal thoughts.

5. Recent Suicide Attempt (4)

A. The client and parents reported that the client has made a recent suicide attempt.
B. Received a phone call that the client has made a serious suicide attempt.
C. The client reported that he/she has recently made a slight or superficial suicidal gesture.
D. The client denied making any recent suicide attempts.
E. The client's suicide risk has decreased significantly since the onset of therapy and he/she has not made any further suicide attempts.

6. History of Suicide Attempt (5)

A. The client's current suicidal risk needs to be closely monitored because he/she has made suicide attempts in the past.
B. The client reported making a serious suicide attempt in the past.
C. The client denied ever making any suicide attempts.

7. Family History of Depression (6)

A. The client and parents reported a strong history of depression in the family background.
B. The client and parents reported a history of suicide in the family background.
C. The client expressed strong feelings of sadness about the death of a family member who committed suicide.
D. The client has experienced recurrent suicidal thoughts and compared himself/herself to another family member who has committed suicide.

8. Depression (6)

A. The client reported a history of depression that has been present for several months.
B. The client reported a history of mood swings from elation to depression that occur within a day.
C. The client appeared visibly depressed during today's therapy session and expressed a desire to die.
D. The client reported feeling somewhat less depressed recently.
E. The client's depression has lifted and he/she is showing renewed interest in life and the future.

9. Helplessness/Hopelessness (7)

A. The client is troubled by strong feelings of helplessness and hopelessness and questions whether life is worthwhile.
B. The client has developed a bleak, pessimistic outlook on life and doubts whether his/her life will ever improve.
C. The client sees little hope that he/she will be able to overcome his/her current life stressors or problems.
D. The client's feelings of helplessness and hopelessness have decreased and he/she is beginning to develop a new sense of hope for the future.

E. The client has experienced a renewed sense of hope and empowerment and no longer questions his/her ability to cope with life's stressors.

10. **Painful Life Events (8)**
   A. The client has experienced suicidal thoughts since his/her parents separated or obtained a divorce.
   B. The client has experienced suicidal thoughts since experiencing the death of a family member or close friend.
   C. The client experienced suicidal thoughts after experiencing a traumatic event.
   D. The client experienced suicidal thoughts after a recent failure experience.
   E. The client experienced suicidal thoughts after feeling humiliated around his/her peers or family members.

11. **Rejection Experiences/Broken Relationships (8)**
   A. The client reported feeling rejected by his/her family members.
   B. The client reported experiencing suicidal thoughts after feeling rejected by his/her peers.
   C. The client contemplated suicide after experiencing a broken relationship.
   D. The client experienced suicidal thoughts after having a serious falling out with a close friend.

12. **Social Withdrawal (9)**
   A. The emergence of the client's suicidal thoughts have coincided with his/her social withdrawal from others.
   B. The client has become more withdrawn and questions whether other people truly care about him/her.
   C. The client has begun to seek out support, affirmation, or acceptance from others.
   D. The client has taken active steps to socialize with others.

13. **Feelings of Alienation (9)**
   A. The client reports to feeling alienated and misunderstood by others.
   B. The client has taken active steps to overcome his/her feelings of alienation.
   C. The client has begun to establish a positive network of supportive individuals.

14. **Lethargy and Apathy (9)**
   A. The client appeared lethargic, listless, and apathetic during today's therapy session.
   B. The client expressed apathy about his/her life and finds little joy or reward in living.
   C. The client reported recently experiencing some pleasure or reward in his/her life.
   D. The client reports regaining a sense of direction in life and feeling motivated to achieve personal goals.

15. **Self-Destructive Behavior (10)**
   A. The parents described a history of the client engaging in self-destructive behavior (e.g., cutting or harming self) when he/she is emotionally upset or stressed.

B. The client acknowledged that he/she has engaged in self-destructive behavior, but denied experiencing any intent to take his/her life.

C. The client reported engaging in self-destructive or harmful behavior as a way to block out his/her emotional pain.

D. The client has not engaged in any recent self-destructive or harmful behavior.

16. Potentially Dangerous Behavior (10)

A. The client described a pattern of engaging in reckless or potentially dangerous behavior and showing little regard for his/her personal safety.

B. The client acknowledged that he/she has engaged in reckless or potentially dangerous behavior as a way to seek thrills and excitement and also escape from his/her emotional pain.

C. The client reported that he/she has recently engaged in reckless, potentially dangerous behavior.

D. The client denied engaging in any recent reckless, potentially dangerous behavior.

E. The client's behavior and moods have stabilized since the onset of therapy and he/she has not engaged in any reckless or potentially dangerous behavior.

17. Dangerous Drug or Alcohol Abuse (10)

A. The client reported a history of engaging in dangerous drug or alcohol abuse as a way to escape from his/her emotional distress.

B. The client reported a history of engaging in dangerous drug or alcohol abuse that demonstrated little regard for his/her personal safety.

C. The client has continued to abuse drugs and alcohol as a maladaptive coping mechanism for emotional distress.

D. The client has not engaged in any recent drug or alcohol abuse.

E. The client has ceased his/her pattern of engaging in dangerous drug or alcohol abuse and has found more adaptive ways to deal with his/her emotional pain.

INTERVENTIONS IMPLEMENTED

1. Assess Suicidal Risk (1)*

A. The client's suicide risk was assessed by evaluating the extent and/or severity of his/her suicidal thoughts.

B. The client's suicide risk was assessed by exploring for the presence of primary and backup suicide plans.

C. The client's past was explored for any previous suicide attempts.

D. The client's family history was assessed for previous suicide attempts.

2. Monitor Suicide Potential (2)

A. The client's suicide potential has continued to be closely monitored in the therapy sessions.

* The numbers in parentheses correlate to the number of the Therapeutic Intervention statement in the companion chapter with the same title in *The Adolescent Psychotherapy Treatment Planner* (Jongsma, Peterson, and McInnis) by John Wiley & Sons, 2000.

B. Consulted with the client's parents and significant others to assess the client's suicide potential.

3. Notify Family/Significant Others (3)

A. The client's family and significant others were notified after the client expressed suicidal ideation.

B. The client's family and significant others were instructed to form a 24-hour suicide watch until the crisis subsides.

4. Arrange for Psychological Assessment (4)

A. The client was referred for a psychological evaluation to assess the severity of his/her depression and risk for suicide.

B. The results from the psychological assessment showed that the client is experiencing strong feelings of depression and is at high risk for suicide.

C. The results from the psychological testing indicated that the client is experiencing a moderate amount of depression and is at risk for suicide.

D. The results from the psychological testing indicated that the client is experiencing a mild amount of depression, and is a low risk for suicide.

E. The results from the psychological testing did not reveal the presence of a depressive disorder, even though the client has expressed suicidal thoughts in the past.

5. Evaluate Need for Hospitalization (5)

A. The client was assessed for the need for inpatient hospitalization after expressing suicidal thoughts.

B. The client was admitted to an inpatient psychiatric unit because of his/her suicide risk.

C. The decision was made to place the client in a partial hospitalization program because of his/her suicide risk and depth of depression.

D. The evaluation did not reveal the need for inpatient hospitalization, but the client's suicide potential will continue to be closely monitored on an outpatient basis.

E. The client was involuntarily placed in an inpatient psychiatric unit after expressing suicidal thoughts and refusing to be evaluated for admission into a hospital setting.

6. Solicit Promise to Contact Therapist or Help Line (6)

A. The client agreed to contact an emergency help line, parents, significant others, or therapist if he/she experiences a strong urge to harm himself/herself in the future.

B. The client refused to promise to contact an emergency help line, parents, significant others, or therapist if he/she experiences a strong urge to harm himself/herself in the future; therefore, arrangements were made to admit the client to an inpatient psychiatric unit.

C. The client's parents agreed to contact an emergency help line, significant others, or therapist if they perceive the client as being at risk for suicide in the future.

D. The client's parents were instructed to bring the client to the emergency room in the future if he/she makes a serious suicide threat or attempt.

7. Provide Emergency Help Line (7)

A. The client was given the telephone number of a 24-hour-a-day emergency help line in the event that he/she experiences a strong wish to die in the future.

B. The client refused to agree to contact an emergency help line in the future if he/she becomes suicidal; therefore, arrangements were made to admit the client to an inpatient psychiatric unit.

C. The client reported that he/she recently contacted an emergency help line after experiencing suicidal thoughts and found the consultation helpful in lifting his/her mood and ceasing his/her suicidal thoughts.

8. Establish Suicide Contract (8)

A. A suicide contract was formulated, with the client identifying what he/she will and won't do when experiencing suicidal thoughts or impulses in the future.

B. The client signed a suicide contract agreeing to contact an emergency help line, family members, significant others, or therapist if he/she experiences strong suicidal thoughts or impulses in the future.

C. The client refused to sign a suicide contract; therefore, arrangements were made to admit the client to an inpatient psychiatric unit.

9. Inform about Telephone Availability of Therapist (9)

A. The client was informed of the therapist's availability through telephone contact if a life-threatening urge develops.

B. The client was encouraged to contact the emergency service or the answering service if he/she develops a life-threatening urge after normal work hours.

10. "No-Self-Harm Contract" Exercise (10)

A. The client signed the "No-Self-Harm Contract" from *The Brief Adolescent Therapy Homework Planner* (Jongsma, Peterson, and McInnis) that stipulated his/her promise not to harm himself/herself.

B. By signing the "No-Self-Harm Contract," the client realized that there is a supportive network of individuals or agencies to whom he/she can turn when experiencing suicidal thoughts or urges.

C. The client was instructed to place the "No-Self-Harm Contract" in a private, but easily accessible place where important telephone numbers could be quickly obtained if needed.

D. After experiencing suicidal thoughts in between therapy sessions, the client complied with the terms of the "No-Self-Harm Contract" and contacted one of the individuals or agencies listed.

11. Remove Lethal Weapons (11)

A. The parents were instructed to remove any firearms or other potentially lethal weapons from the client's easy access in the event that he/she experiences suicidal thoughts in the future.

B. The parents complied with the recommendation to remove firearms or other lethal weapons from the client's easy access.

C. The parents were confronted about their failure to remove firearms or other lethal weapons from the client's easy access.

12. Assess Parents' Understanding of Client's Distress (12)

A. A therapy session was held with the parents to assess their understanding of the causes for the client's emotional distress and suicidal thoughts.

B. The therapy session with the parents proved to be helpful in identifying the significant contributing factors or causes of the client's emotional distress or suicidal urges.

C. The parents expressed confusion and uncertainty about the causes of the client's emotional distress and suicidal urges.

D. The client's perspective of the causes for his/her emotional distress was shared with the parents.

E. The parents were encouraged to provide support and empathy for the client's perspective of what is contributing to his/her emotional distress.

13. Explore Despair Related to Family Relationships (13)

A. Today's therapy session explored the client's feelings of despair related to his/her family relationships.

B. Today's therapy session revealed that the client is experiencing a significant amount of distress in regard to his/her family relationships.

C. The client denied that his/her emotional despair is related to his/her family relationships.

D. The client agreed to meet with his/her family members in an upcoming therapy session to share his/her feelings of anger, hurt, and sadness about family relationships.

E. The client reported that he/she does not feel ready to meet with family members to share his/her feelings of anger, hurt, and sadness about family issues.

14. Promote Communication in Family Therapy (14)

A. A family therapy session was held to promote the communication of the client's feelings of hurt, sadness, and anger.

B. The family members demonstrated empathy, support, and understanding for the client's feelings of sadness, hurt, and anger.

C. Family members appeared to become defensive when the client began to share his/her feelings of sadness, hurt, and anger.

D. The client and parents were given the homework assignment to meet for 10 to 15 minutes each day to allow the client the opportunity to share his/her significant thoughts and feelings about any important issues.

15. Antidepressant Medication Referral (15)

A. The client was referred for a psychiatric evaluation to help determine whether an antidepressant would help to reduce his/her feelings of depression and risk for suicide.

B. The client and parents agreed to follow through with a psychiatric evaluation.

C. The client verbalized his/her strong opposition to being placed on medication to help reduce his/her feelings of depression.

16. Monitor Medication Effectiveness (16)

A. The client reported that the antidepressant medication has helped to decrease his/her feelings of depression.

B. The client reported little or no improvement in his/her moods since being placed on the antidepressant medication.

C. The client reported that he/she has consistently taken the antidepressant medication as prescribed.

D. The client has failed to consistently take the antidepressant medication as prescribed.

17. Monitor Appetite and Sleep Patterns (17)

A. The client was encouraged to return to his/her normal patterns of eating and sleeping to help reduce his/her depression.

B. The client was instructed to monitor his/her patterns of eating and sleeping between therapy sessions.

C. The client reported that the monitoring of his/her food intake helped him/her realize the need to return to normal eating patterns.

D. The client was referred for a medication evaluation to determine whether medication would help reduce feelings of depression and help induce sleep.

E. The client was taught relaxation techniques to use at night to help induce calm and readiness for sleep.

18. Explore Sources of Emotional Pain (18)

A. Today's therapy session explored the sources of the client's emotional pain that underlie his/her suicidal ideation and feelings of hopelessness.

B. The exploration of the client's emotional pain revealed that he/she is experiencing a lot of unresolved feelings about a past traumatic incident.

C. The exploration of the client's emotional pain revealed that the client is experiencing a lot of unresolved feelings about a past broken relationship.

D. Today's therapy session explored periods of time when the client felt empowered in order to identify positive coping mechanisms that he/she used in the past to resolve conflict or deal with stress.

19. Identify Hopelessness and Helplessness (19)

A. The client's sadness and depression was interpreted as an expression of his/her feelings of hopelessness and helplessness.

B. The client's suicidal thoughts or wishes for death were interpreted as a cry for help.

C. The client's dangerous acts of rebellion were interpreted as reflecting underlying feelings of hopelessness and a cry for help.

D. The client was helped to identify more effective ways to meet his/her needs so that he/she will not remain depressed or suicidal.

E. The client was helped to identify more effective ways to meet his/her needs instead of acting out in a dangerous or rebellious manner.

20. Explore Causes for Suicidal Behavior (20)

A. The client was encouraged to express his/her feelings related to suicidal behavior to gain insight into the causes and motives for this behavior.

B. The client was able to gain insight into the causes and motives for his/her suicidal actions after he/she identified the feelings he/she was experiencing before the suicidal behavior.

C. The client appeared guarded and was reluctant to share his/her feelings pertaining to the recent suicidal behavior.

D. A client-centered therapy approach was utilized to help the client get in touch with his/her feelings related to the recent suicidal behavior.

E. A psychoanalytic therapy approach was utilized to explore the etiology of the client's suicidal behavior.

21. "Renewed Hope" Exercise (21)

A. The client was instructed to read the short story "Renewed Hope" from *The Brief Adolescent Therapy Homework Planner* (Jongsma, Peterson, and McInnis) to show him/her the benefit of sharing emotional pain instead of internalizing it.

B. The client shared that "Renewed Hope" helped him/her identify the causes and/or sources of his/her emotional pain and suicidal thoughts.

C. The client reported that he/she was able to share his/her painful emotions with significant others after reading "Renewed Hope."

D. The client reported that he/she read "Renewed Hope," but did not gain insight into the factors contributing to his/her emotional pain.

E. The client failed to read "Renewed Hope" and was again asked to read it.

22. Identify Positive Things in Life (22)

A. The client was helped to identify positive things in his/her present life situation to help reduce his/her feelings of depression and provide a sense of hope.

B. In today's therapy session, the client was first asked to identify his/her strengths and interests, then was encouraged to share these strengths or interests with his/her family members and peers in the upcoming week.

C. The client was instructed to record one positive self-descriptive statement in a journal each day.

D. The client was given the homework assignment to verbally share three positive things about his/her day with family members at dinner or before going to bed.

E. The client was encouraged to look for or verbally recognize the positives in other people to help him/her relate to others and gain acceptance.

23. "Symbols of Self-Worth" Assignment (23)

A. The client was given the "Symbols of Self-Worth" assignment from *The Brief Adolescent Therapy Homework Planner* (Jongsma, Peterson, and McInnis) to increase his/her feelings of self-worth and provide a renewed sense of hope.

B. The client completed the "Symbols of Self-Worth" assignment and brought in several objects reflecting past achievements and personal meaning.

C. The client brought in several objects symbolizing his/her strengths or interests and was encouraged to share these strengths or interests with peers in the upcoming week.

D. The client reported that after completing the "Symbols of Self-Worth" assignment, he/she regained an interest in and enthusiasm for previously enjoyed social or extracurricular activities.

E. The client failed to complete the "Symbols of Self-Worth" assignment, but was again asked to read it and bring in his/her symbols of self-worth to the next therapy session.

24. Teach Coping Strategies (24)

A. The client was helped to identify various coping strategies that he/she can use to minimize the risk of him/her becoming suicidal in the future.

B. The client was strongly encouraged to express his/her thoughts and feelings directly to others instead of internalizing them and becoming suicidal.

C. The client was given the homework assignment to initiate three social contacts each day to help him/her become less internally focused.

D. The client was encouraged to engage in regular physical exercise or activity to help reduce stress and eliminate a pattern of brooding about life's problems.

25. Utilize Past Successful Problem-Solving Approaches (25)

A. The client was first asked to review problem-solving approaches that were successful in the past, then encouraged to utilize these same approaches to solve the problems in his/her current life situation.

B. The client was helped to realize how his/her reliance on previous problem-solving techniques no longer seems to be helpful, and he/she was encouraged to find new, alternative ways to solve current life problems.

C. The client was taught effective assertiveness skills to help him/her manage stress and overcome current life problems.

D. The client was encouraged to seek compromises as a way to resolve or end conflict with significant others.

E. The client was encouraged to brainstorm with a friend or consult with a mentor to identify ways to overcome current life problems.

26. Explore Feelings of Grief (26)

A. The client was given the opportunity to share his/her feelings of grief about broken, close relationships.

B. The client was provided with support and empathy in expressing his/her feelings of grief and sadness about past losses or separations.

C. The client was given empathy and support in expressing his/her feelings of sadness about past rejection experiences.

D. The client was instructed to utilize a journal to record his/her thoughts and feelings about the broken, close relationship.

27. Encourage Participation in Social Activities (27)

A. The client was strongly encouraged to reach out to friends and participate in enriching social or school activities.

B. The client was given the homework assignment to engage in at least one social activity per week with his/her peers.

C. The client reported that he/she has complied with the therapeutic recommendation to initiate at least one social contact per week and that this has helped to renew his/her interest and enthusiasm for life.

D. Today's therapy session processed the client's experiences in various social activities and reinforced his/her socialization initiatives.

E. The client was instructed to perform acts of altruism or kindness with friends and peers to help improve his/her self-esteem and gain acceptance.

28. Role-Play Social Skills (28)

A. Behavior rehearsal, modeling, and role-play techniques were used to teach the client positive social skills and how to relate to peers more efficiently.

B. The client was able to identify several positive social skills after engaging in the behavior rehearsal and role-playing exercises.

C. After role playing, the client expressed a willingness to practice the newly learned social skills in his/her everyday situations.

D. The client reported that the newly learned social skills have helped him/her relate to peers and gain acceptance.

E. The client reported that he/she did not follow through with practicing many of the social skills that were modeled in the previous therapy sessions.

29. Encourage Broadening Social Network (29)

A. The client was encouraged to broaden his/her social network by initiating one new social contact per week instead of excessively clinging to one or two friends.

B. The client complied with the directive to initiate one social contact per week and reported that it has helped to increase his/her confidence in conversing with others.

C. The client failed to follow through with the directive to initiate one social contact per week because of his/her feelings of insecurity and inadequacy.

D. Role-playing techniques were utilized to model effective ways to initiate conversations with social contacts.

E. The client was given the homework assignment to initiate three phone calls per week to different individuals.

30. Identify Negative Cognitive Messages (30)

A. Today's therapy session helped the client develop an awareness of how his/her negative self-talk reinforces feelings of hopelessness and helplessness.

B. The client was encouraged to replace his/her negative cognitive messages with more positive ways of thinking to overcome feelings of hopelessness and helplessness.

C. The client was given the homework assignment to verbalize three positive statements each day in the presence of others to overcome feelings of helplessness and hopelessness.

D. The client reported that the use of positive self-talk between therapy sessions helped to reduce his/her feelings of helplessness and hopelessness.

E. The client failed to follow through with utilizing self-talk and, as a result, has continued to be troubled by feelings of helplessness and hopelessness.

31. Replace Catastrophizing, Fortune-Telling, and Mind Reading (31)

A. The therapy session identified how the client's tendency to overcatastrophize painful life events proves to be self-defeating, as it reinforces his/her feelings of hopelessness and helplessness.

B. The client was taught how to use realistic self-talk to learn more effective ways to cope with painful life events.

C. The client was taught effective communication and assertiveness skills to help him/her resolve conflict and communicate feelings more directly, instead of falling back on previous patterns of catastrophizing, fortune-telling, and mind reading.

D. The therapy session helped the client become aware of how catastrophizing, fortune-telling, and mind reading only reinforce his/her sense of hopelessness and helplessness.

32. Employ Penitence Ritual (32)

A. The client was given empathy and support in expressing his/her feelings of grief, guilt, and helplessness about surviving an incident fatal to others.

B. The client was helped to develop a penitence ritual to help overcome his/her feelings of guilt about the fatal incident.

C. Processed with the client when, where, and how to implement the penitence ritual.

D. In today's follow-up therapy session, the client shared his/her thoughts and feelings about implementing the penitence ritual.

E. The client reported that the penitence ritual was helpful in decreasing his/her feelings of guilt about the fatal incident.

33. Reinforce Statements of Hope (33)

A. The client was reinforced for expressing statements that reflected hope and a desire to live.

B. The parents were encouraged to reinforce any positive statements by the client that reflect hope and an interest in living.

C. The client was helped to identify the positive steps that he/she took to overcome feelings of helplessness and cease having suicidal urges.

D. The client was encouraged to continue to engage in healthy or adaptive behavior that has provided him/her with a renewed sense of hope and contributed to resolution of suicidal urges.

E. The client identified the support from significant others as being helpful in providing him/her with a renewed sense of hope and eliminating suicidal urges.